TRANSDISCIPLINARY VOCATIONAL ASSESSMENT: ISSUES IN SCHOOL-BASED PROGRAMS

Library of Congress Cataloging-in-Publication Data

Levinson, Edward M., 1952-
    Transdisciplinary vocational assessment : issues in school-based
  programs / Edward M. Levinson.
        p.   cm.
    Includes bibliographical references (p.) and index.
    ISBN 0-88422-118-0 (pbk.) : $42.50
    1. Vocational evaluation--United States. 2. Handicapped youth-
-Vocational education--United States. 3. Counseling in vocational
education--United States. 4. Occupational aptitude tests.
I. Title.
LC1048.V63L48   1993
371.4'25--dc20   92-53226
                                                 CIP

 4 Conant Square
Brandon, Vermont 05733

Cover design: Sue Thomas

Printed in the United States of America.

TRANSDISCIPLINARY VOCATIONAL ASSESSMENT: ISSUES IN SCHOOL-BASED PROGRAMS

EDWARD M. LEVINSON
Indiana University of Pennsylvania

Clinical Psychology Publishing Co., Inc.
4 Conant Square
Brandon, Vermont 05733

TABLE OF CONTENTS

FOREWORD

Recent years have witnessed an increased interest in the vocational assessment and programming of youth with disabilities. Historically, vocational/career education has been a major goal of education; preparing students for the world of work continues to be a major focus of new educational reforms and a major objective accepted by school administrators. Federal support for this educational objective is clearly documented by the vast array of educational, vocational, and rehabilitation legislation designed to mandate the development and implementation of school-based vocational services. Legislation such as the Vocational Rehabilitation Act, The Vocational Education Amendments Act, The Career Incentive Act, and the CETA Amendments all provided federal support for the establishment of school-based vocational programming services. Much of this legislation was targeted to combat the high unemployment and underemployment rates among individuals with disabilities.

The pursuit of postsecondary education is often an unrealistic goal for many individuals with disabilities. For these students, postschool employment becomes the major objective of their educational program, particularly at the secondary school level. Despite attempts to provide disabled individuals with the skills they need in order to obtain and maintain satisfying employment following the completion of school, the unemployment and underemployment rates among this population greatly exceed those that exist for the nondisabled population. Legislators and educators alike believe that vocational assessment can assist in designing educational and vocational programs for students that will increase the likelihood of employment following the completion of school.

Recently, the Carl D. Perkins Vocational Education Act of 1984 (P.L. 98-524) was reauthorized, requiring that schools provide an "assessment of student needs in relation to vocational education and jobs" (Sec 302 (b) (6)) and that this include an "assessment of the interests, abilities and special needs of such students with respect to completing sucessfully the vocational education program" (Sec 204 (c) (1)). This legislation also requires that the vocational planning emanating from such an assessment be coordinated among representatives from a variety of professional fields including vocational and special education. In October, 1990, P.L. 94-142 (The Education for All Handicapped Children Act) was amended and renamed the Individuals With Disabilities Education Act (IDEA). In addition to reauthorizing and expanding many of the provisions of P.L. 94-142, several new discretionary programs were added including special programs on transition. The law now includes transition services and assistive technology services as new definitions of special education services that must be addressed in a student's IEP. Under the law, plans for a student's transition from school to work and community living must be included in the IEP by the time the student reaches age 16. Rehabilitation counseling and social work services are also included as related services under this law. As the full effects of IDEA and the Perkins Act are realized, it is likely that school-based vocational assessment services will be increasingly available to students with disabilities.

Traditionally, vocational assessment has been confined to vocational rehabilitation facilities and has largely been the responsibility of vocational evaluators and rehabilitation counselors. However, the Perkins Act has shifted the responsibility for providing vocational assessment services from vocational rehabilitation personnel to school personnel. For the most part, school counselors; school psychologists; regular, special, and vocational education teachers; and school administrators have little background and training in this area. Unfortunately, the majority of reference materials pertaining to vocational assessment have been written for and by vocational rehabilitation personnel and are based upon rehabilitation models of assessment. For these reasons, available references have limited usefulness for educators who are confronted with the responsibility of establishing and implementing vocational assessment programs in schools.

In reviewing these references, I sensed a need for a volume on vocational assessment written from an educational and psychological perspective, designed primarily for educational personnel, and which included a description of program models appropriate for implementation within school settings. Consistent with current trends in the field and with current legislative mandates, I believed that such a text should focus upon cooperation among a variety of school-based professionals including teachers (special, vocational, and regular), counselors, psychologists, and administrators; should incorporate the roles of community-based professionals and parents; and should offer practical, time- and cost-effective methods for establishing and implementing vocational assessment programs within school-based settings. This book is designed to satisfy these objectives and is targeted for school-based professionals such as school administrators; vocational, regular, and special education teachers; school counselors; school psychologists; and vocational/transition specialists who may be involved in the establishment or implementation of vocational assessment programs. Because I believe that vocational assessment should involve a school–community partnership, the book advocates a "transdisciplinary" model, which includes professionals in mental health, vocational rehabilitation, and social service agencies. As such, it is hoped that the book will be of value to professionals in these fields as well.

To some degree, we are all a product of our experiences and training. This book is an outgrowth of my 14 years of training and experience as a practicing school psychologist, my 3-year involvement in developing and implementing a school-based vocational assessment program, and my 8 years of experience in university teaching and in the training of school psychologists. I hope that whatever "unique" perspective or slant the reader may detect regarding issues discussed in this book is interpreted in light of this background.

The book would not have been possible had it not been for the emotional, technical, and clerical support received by the author. Thanks go first to my wife, Kathy, and daughter, Breann Curtis, for their love and for their understanding and acceptance of the long hours I spent away from them while researching and writing this book. For their review of chapter drafts and insightful and helpful feedback, thanks go to Bill Barker, Fred Capps, Sue McFadden, Michele Orf, and "anonymous" reviewers. Thanks also go to Fred Capps, Randy Elston, Lisa Folino, Tom Hohenshil, Lynne McKee, Terry Morris, Michael Peterson, Dorothy Spitzer, Ted Timko, and Nancy Yauger, with whom I have coauthored the numerous articles and chapters that formed the foundation for this book. Thanks also go to Gayle Fleming and Julie King for their clerical assistance and support. Special thanks go to Tom Hohenshil, who, unbeknownst to him, taught me to believe that I was actually capable of writing a book like this. Last, but most important, I want to thank my parents, George and Alice Levinson, and my aunt, Lillian Craig, whose love led me to develop the skills and characteristics necessary to write a book like this. This book is dedicated to them.

1 INTRODUCTION TO TRANSDISCIPLINARY SCHOOL-BASED VOCATIONAL ASSESSMENT

It is work which gives flavor to life.

—Amiel

Work is an integral aspect of American life. During a typical day, one spends approximately 8 hours sleeping, 8 hours working, and 8 hours engaged in other activities. Fully one half of one's waking hours are spent working. Anderson (1982) estimated that during the course of one's life, an individual spends approximately 94,000 hours working. The vast amount of time and energy one devotes to work has prompted many writers and researchers to suggest that work may influence social and personal development and may ultimately have an impact upon the quality of life an individual experiences. In his book *Working*, Studs Terkel (1974) writes:

> It is about a search, too, for daily meaning as well as daily bread, for recognition as well as cash, for astonishment as well as torpor; in short, for a sort of life rather than a Monday through Friday sort of dying. (pp. xiii)

In *Work in America*, the Special Task Force to the Secretary of Health, Education and Welfare (1973) writes:

> . . . clearly work is central to our lives. . . . According to Freud, work provides us with a sense of reality; to Elton Mayo, work is a bind to the community; to Marx, its function is primarily economic. . . . [W]ork . . . plays a pervasive and powerful role in the psychological, social and economic aspects of our lives. . . . [I]t influences, and is influenced by, other basic institutions—family,

community . . . and schools. . . . [T]he type of work performed has always conferred a social status on the worker and the worker's family . . . which in turn has determined the family's class standing, where they lived, where the children went to school, and with whom the family members associated—in short, the life style and life chances of all family members. (pp. 1–4)

Does work really have an impact upon the meaning and value an individual attaches to his or her life? Does it really influence one's overall life adjustment? Research suggests that self-concept is intimately related to work performance and work satisfaction and that adjustment to work is associated with overall life satisfaction. Super (1974) viewed work as an implementation of one's self-concept, and believed that job satisfaction and self-concept were intimately related. Dore and Meachum (1983) tested this proposition and found empirical support for it. Greenhaus (1971), Kalanidi and Deivasenapathy (1980), and Snyder and Ferguson (1976), among others, have found a positive relationship between self-concept or self-esteem and job satisfaction. Such a relationship has face validity as well, for as Coles (1978) notes, people find it almost impossible to talk about themselves without reference to the kind of work they do. The sheer frequency with which statements such as "I am a(n) . . . (occupation)" are made offers experiential validity for the notion that our views about ourselves are at least partially influenced by the kind of work we do.

In addition to suggesting a link between work and feelings of worth, research has also indicated that an individual's general life adjustment is associated with adjustment to work. Adjustment to work can be conceptualized as consisting of two components: job satisfaction and job performance. Both job satisfaction and job performance appear to be associated with the kind of adjustment people make to life in general. Compared to satisfied workers, dissatisfied workers tend to experience a greater frequency of both physical and mental health problems (Kornhauser, 1965; O'Toole, 1973; Portigal, 1976) and display lower levels of overall life satisfaction (Bedeian & Marbert, 1979; Haavio-Manilla, 1971; Iris & Barrett, 1972; Orphen, 1978; Schmitt & Mellon, 1980). Whereas dissatisfied workers tend to quit jobs more frequently than satisfied workers, poor-performing workers tend to be terminated from their jobs more frequently than satisfactorily performing workers. The end result of either of these scenarios is often unemployment. The economic cost of supporting unemployed workers (who either quit or are terminated from their jobs) via welfare, unemployment, and other dependency programs should be readily apparent to the reader.

The individual cost of unemployment and turnover is evident in a study conducted by Sanborn, Sanborn, and Cimbolic (1974), who found that individuals who are unemployed or frustrated in their work, or who have experienced a major change in occupational status in the previous 12 months, are increasingly more likely to commit suicide than are individuals in more rewarding occupational situations. Thus, research indicates that the adequacy of one's occupational choice, and the degree to which one adequately adjusts to work, has a tremendous impact upon one's overall happiness and quality of life.

EDUCATION AND UNEMPLOYMENT: THE PLIGHT OF INDIVIDUALS WITH DISABILITIES

The school experience assumes a critical role in determining the extent to which individuals acquire the skills necessary to make a positive adjustment to work. Whereas in the mid-1960s school administrators did not believe that schools should provide specific job training or vocational assistance to students, that belief reversed itself in the late 1970s (McCleary & Thompson, 1979). Over the last 10 years, educators have come to accept vocational/career development as a major goal of public education (Goodlad, 1979).

Are schools doing an adequate job in providing students with the skills they need to secure and maintain satisfying and productive employment? Do students perceive the vocational/career-related services they receive during the school years to be adequate? Data suggest that the answer to both of these questions is no. Chapman and Katz (1983) found that most of the students they surveyed believed that their high school vocational planning assistance was inadequate. Similarly, Johnson, Baughman, and O'Malley (1982) found that two thirds of the high school seniors surveyed reported that they wanted more vocational planning assistance than had been provided. Similar attitudes have been expressed by parents. A 1976 Gallup poll (Gallup, 1976) found that 80% of adults surveyed believed that high schools should place greater emphasis on vocational planning, and 52% of those surveyed believed that more vocational/career assistance should be provided to students in elementary school.

Among the school-age population, students with disabilities are at particularly high risk in securing and maintaining satisfying and productive employment following the completion of school. Historically, individuals with disabilities have been overrepresented among this country's unemployment and underemployment rates (Bell & Bergdorf, 1983; Bowe, 1980). Stark, Baker, Menousek, and McGee (1982) cite U.S. Department of Labor statistics indicating that 87% of the approximately 6 million mentally retarded individuals in this country have the potential to be employed in the competitive job market, and that 10% are capable of working in a sheltered workshop environment. However, the percentage of mentally retarded individuals who are actually employed is considerably lower. It has been estimated that 21% of all students with disabilities would be fully employed or enrolled in college following the completion of school, that 40% would be underemployed and at the poverty level, and that 26% would be unemployed and on welfare (3% were estimated to be totally dependent and institutionalized, whereas 8% were estimated to be in their home community and idle much of the time). Levitan and Taggart (1977) noted that 40% of all adults with disabilities are employed compared to 74% of the nondisabled population.

More recent studies offer similar statistics. Batsche (1982) estimated that only two fifths of adults with mental and physical disabilities are employed during a typical year as compared to three fourths of persons without disabilities and that out of every 100 individuals with disabilities, only 25 are fully employed, 40 are unemployed, 25 are on welfare, and 10 are institutionalized or are idle. Poplin (1982) noted that out of the 30 million people with disabilities in this country, only 4.1 million are employed, and that 85% of employed disabled individuals earn less than $7,000 per year, and 52% of this same population earn less than $2,000 per year. Crites, Smull, and Sachs (1984) surveyed 1,469 mentally retarded persons living in locations other than community group homes or state institutions and found a 77% unemployment rate. The President's Committee on the Employment of the Handicapped reports that only 21% of handicapped persons will become fully employed, 40% will be underemployed and at the poverty level,and 26% will be on welfare (Pennsylvania Department of Education & Labor and Industry, 1986). Rusch and Phelps (1987) have reported that 67% of Americans with disabilities between the ages of 16 and 64 are not working. Of those persons with disabilities who are working, 75% are employed on a part-time basis, and of those who are not employed, 67% indicated that they would like to be employed.

Numerous statewide surveys have also been undertaken to assess the employment status of young people with disabilities who are no longer in school. Studies in Florida (Fardig et al., 1985), Washington (Edgar, 1987), Colorado (Mithaug, Horiuchi, & Fanning, 1985), Vermont (Hasazi, Gordon, & Roe, 1985), and Nebraska (Schalock & Lilley, 1986) have indicated that the employment rate for individuals with disabilities is generally higher for females than for males and ranges between 45% and 70% depending upon the severity of the disability and geographical location. There is also evidence that a large number of those disabled individuals who are employed are employed on a part-time basis, and some studies indicate that many of those employed are earning minimum wage or less. Similarly, Brodsky (1983) reported that of the students with disabilities she surveyed, 56% had never received any community-based vocational training during their school years and that only 6% were involved in community employment (57% were employed in work activity centers), 60% reported earning less than $1,000 per year, and 16% reported earning no income. It is estimated that almost two thirds of Americans with disabilities between the ages of 16 and 24 are not working (Harris & Associates, 1986).

In addition to the high unemployment and underemployment rates that characterize individuals with disabilities, these individuals also demonstrate an elevated high school attrition rate. Edgar (1987) reports that 42% of students with learning and behavioral disabilities leave school before graduating and that 18% of mentally retarded students do the same. Rusch and Phelps (1987) cite a survey done by Owing and Stocking in 1985 in which 30,000 sophomores and 28,000 seniors including those self-identified as disabled were studied on a longitudinal basis. The findings indicated that those students with mild disabilities fared poorly regardless of whether they were receiving regular or special education services. They reported that 22% of the 1980 sophomores had dropped out of school between their sophomore and senior years as compared with 12% of students without disabilities. More recently, the *Twelfth Annual Report to Congress on the Implementation of the Education of the Handicapped Act* (U.S. Department of Education, Office of Special Education and Rehabilitative Services, 1990) indicated that 47% of all students with disabilities do not graduate from high school with either a diploma or certificate of completion. These data are corroborated by data gathered by Wagner and Shaver (1989), who found that 44% of students with disabilities failed to graduate from high school and 36% of the students with disabilities dropped out of school.

Contrary to popular belief, the unemployment and underemployment rates among individuals with disabilities do not appear to be the result of a lack of available job opportunities. A review of occupational trends and predictions between now and the year 2000 indicates that in the future jobs will be available for individuals who do not possess high-level skills, including individuals with cognitive disabilities who have been appropriately and adequately trained. Projections include a significant increase in the number of jobs for health service workers, cleaning and building service workers, food preparation workers, food service workers, and personal service workers (Silvestri & Lukasiewicz, 1987). Thus, with appropriate special and vocational education services, many individuals with cognitive disabilities should be able to enter and maintain employment successfully in these and other fields.

What are the costs associated with the high underemployment and unemployment rates among the disabled population? Poplin (1982) estimated the cost of supporting unemployed and disabled individuals to be approximately $114 billion per year and suggested that this figure is increasing annually. Batsche (1982) offered similar statistics and estimated that the cost of maintaining an unemployed individual with a disability in an institution in Illinois exceeded the cost of educating a person at Harvard! In 1984, the U.S. Department of Education, Office of Special Education and Rehabilitative Services (1990) reported that of the 16 million noninstitutionalized persons of working age with disabilities, as many as 15 million are potentially employable at an approximate cost savings of $144 billion per year.

The social, physical, and emotional benefits to be derived by individuals with disabilities from successful adjustment to work are not to be slighted by the economic benefits to be derived by society. Just as successful adjustment to work is likely to be accompanied by increased feelings of self-worth, greater overall life satisfaction, and a higher quality of life among the non-disabled population, so too are these benefits likely to be derived by individuals with disabilities. In fact, Bolton (1982) has summarized several studies which suggested that individuals with disabilities may place *greater* value on work than do individuals without disabilities and, given similar work-related situations, may experience a higher level of overall job satisfaction.

LEGISLATIVE INITIATIVES

Given (a) the high unemployment and underemployment rates that exist among persons with disabilities in this country, (b) the high percentages of individuals with disabilities who continue to live at home while being supported by dependency programs operated by state and federal governments, and (c) the elevated high school dropout rates that exist among this population, it appears clear that schools have not adequately prepared individuals with disabilities for successful integration into society. In an attempt to reverse this trend, considerable government legislation has been passed over the last 15–20 years. Legislation designed to assist individuals with disabilities in securing and maintaining productive employment can be found in the fields of special education, vocational education, and vocational rehabilitation. This legislation has generally focused on providing these individuals with adequate vocational assessment, training, counseling, and placement services, in addition to whatever related social service or community agency support these students might need in order to maintain and secure satisfying and productive employment. Table 1-1 summarizes some of this legislation. Some of the more significant legislative initiatives are briefly summarized below.

The Education for All Handicapped Children Act (P.L. 94-142)

A landmark piece of special education legislation that has had an impact on the vocational opportunities afforded handicapped schoolchildren is

Table 1-1.
Legislation Addressing Vocational Education and Transition for Individuals with Disabilities

Year	Law	Title	Content
1973	P.L. 93-112	The Rehabilitation Act	Mandatory civil rights statutes for disabled individuals
1973	P.L. 93-568 Sec. 503, 504	The Rehabilitation Act	Addresses discrimination against individuals in programs receiving federal funds
1973	P.L. 93-380	Education of the Handi-capped Act	Fundamental rights for disabled children to a free, appropriate public education (revised in P.L. 94-142)
1975	P.L. 94-142	Education of All Handi-capped Children Act	Fundamental right of all handicapped children to a free, appropriate public education established as a national policy
1976	P.L. 94-486	Vocational Education Amendments	Defines the terminology of the disabled population in vocational education
1978	P.L. 95-602	Rehabilitation Compre-hensive Services and Developmental Disabilities amendments	Protects the right of individuals receiving service under P.L. 94-142; also provides money to states for providing specific services for developmentally disabled children
1982	P.L. 97-300	The Job Training Partnership Act	Authorizes job training and place-ment service for low-income and displaced workers, covering adults and youth
1983	P.L. 98-199	The Education of the Handicapped Act amendments	Addresses the right to quality educa-tion and transitional services for the disabled, with emphasis on special education (based on P.L. 94-142)
1984	P.L. 98-524	The Carl D. Perkins Vocational Education Act	Determines vocational education as a related service (to P.L. 94-142) and as an integral component of a student's preparation for independence. Requires vocational assessment for students placed in vocational education
1986	P.L. 99-496	The Job Training Part-nership Act amendments	Calls for appropriate assessment of youth prior to training; includes the disabled as eligible participants in JTPA programs
1990	P.L. 101-476	Individuals with Disabilities Education Act	Requires that transition plans be developed for handicapped students

the Education for All Handicapped Children Act of 1975 (P.L. 94-142). This bill mandated that a free, appropriate public education be provided to all handicapped children between the ages of 3 and 22 and called for

". . . organized educational programs which are directly related to the preparation of individuals for paid or unpaid employment, or for additional preparation for a career requiring other than a baccalaureate or advanced degree." In 1983, P.L. 94-142 was amended by P.L. 98-199, which increased the vocational opportunities afforded handicapped students by initiating state demonstration grants designed to improve secondary education programs, create incentives for employers to hire the handicapped, increase educational opportunities for the handicapped at the secondary school level, increase supported work opportunities, and make better use of job placement services for the disabled.

Individuals With Disabilities Education Act (P.L. 101-476)

In October, 1990, P.L. 94-142 (The Education for All Handicapped Children Act) was amended and renamed the Individuals With Disabilities Education Act (IDEA). In addition to reauthorizing and expanding many of the provisions of P.L. 94-142, several new discretionary programs were added including special programs on transition, a new program to improve services for children and youth with severe emotional disturbance, and a research and information dissemination program on attention deficit hyperactivity disorder (ADHD). Additionally, the law now includes transition services and assistive technology services as new definitions of special education services that must be addressed in a student's IEP. Under the law, plans for a student's transition from school to work and community living must be included in the student's IEP by the time the student reaches age 16. Rehabilitation counseling and social work services will also be included as related services under this law. Last, the services and rights under this law are more fully expanded to include children with autism and traumatic brain injury.

The Rehabilitation Act

The Rehabilitation Act of 1973 was a notable piece of vocational rehabilitation legislation that provided federal support for the training of individuals with both physical and mental disabilities. This piece of legislation authorized the awarding of grants to vocational rehabilitation agencies for counseling, training, and other vocationally related services and required that priority be given to those individuals who were the most severely disabled. This law required that a counselor, the disabled individual, and the disabled individual's parent or guardian participate in developing an Individualized Written Rehabilitation Plan (IWRP), which incorporated a description of the services to be provided to the disabled individual and a description of what agency or agencies would be responsible for providing each of the services identified. This legislation was amended in 1978 by P.L. 95-602, which encouraged the development of joint cooperative relationships among the fields of special education, vocational education, and vocational rehabilitation and emphasized the provision of independent living arrangements for individuals with disabilities.

Section 504 of the Rehabilitation Act of 1973 is frequently referred to as the bill of rights for individuals with disabilities because it prohibits discrimination on the basis of disability in any program that receives federal monies. The Rehabilitation Act also calls for servicing individuals with disabilities in the least restrictive environment and requires that vocational counseling, guidance, and placement services be provided to students with disabilities on a nondiscriminatory basis.

The Vocational Education Act

In the field of vocational education, the Vocational Education Act of 1963 (P.L. 88-210) provided federal grants to states in an effort to improve and maintain quality vocational education programs. This legislation was also designed to facilitate the development of new vocational education programs and to provide part-time employment to individuals while they received vocational training. The legislation also allowed (but did not mandate) funds to be used for the vocational training of individuals with disabilities. P.L. 88-210 was amended in 1968 (P.L. 90-576) and again in 1976 (P.L. 94-486) to provide federal support for persons with disabilities who had not been given access to publically supported vocational education programs. These pieces of legislation called upon states to develop plans that interfaced and integrated special and vocational education, insured that secondary school students with disabilities received the vocational services they needed, and facilitated the mainstreaming of students with disabilities into classes with their nondisabled peers.

The Carl D. Perkins Vocational Education Act

In 1984, the Carl D. Perkins Vocational Education Act (P.L. 98-524) amended the Vocational Education Act of 1963. This far-reaching piece of legislation mandated increased services for both disabled and disadvantaged individuals. The Act requires that information about vocational education opportunities be provided to parents and students no later than the beginning of the 9th grade or at least 1 year before the student enters the grade in which vocational education is offered. The Act also requires that information about eligibility requirements for enrolling in vocational education programs be provided to parents and students, and that once enrolled in vocational education, students receive the following: an assessment of interests, abilities, and special needs; special services including adaptation of curriculum, instruction, equipment, and facilities; guidance, counseling, and career development activities conducted by a professionally trained counselor; and special counseling services designed to facilitate transition from school to postschool employment or training. Major provisions of the Perkins Act are summarized in Table 1-2.

Table 1-2.
Major Purposes of P.L. 98-524, The Carl D. Perkins Act

—To improve quality of vocational education programs

—To make vocational education accessible to all people including the handicapped and disadvantaged

—To improve the academic foundations of vocational education students

—To assist economically depressed areas in raising the vocational competencies of students

—To provide training and retraining in new skills for which there is a demand

—To aid in the application of new technologies (including computers) in terms of employment or occupational goals

—To promote cooperation between the private sector and public agencies

From a vocational assessment standpoint, the Perkins Act is clearly a landmark piece of legislation. Although many school systems throughout the country had initiated vocational assessment services for disabled and disadvantaged students prior to the passage of this legislation, many school systems had not. The Perkins Act is likely to provide the impetus necessary to motivate school personnel to develop and implement school-based vocational assessment services for these students. Although states may offer different directions to local school districts regarding the development of vocational assessment programs (and, as a consequence, these programs will be structured differently), it is apparent that all programs will be developed to meet the minimum criteria stated in the Act and summarized above. However, in several instances, states may offer more detailed guidelines, and mandate more comprehensive assessment services than are specified in the Perkins Act. As an example, the following guidelines were developed by the Pennsylvania Department of Education, Bureau of Vocational and Adult Education, to assist local educational agencies in implementing the requirements of P.L. 98-524. This excerpt is included to provide the reader with a sense of the type of vocational assessment service likely to be encouraged by the Perkins Act.

All disadvantaged and handicapped students *enrolled* in vocational education shall receive assessment of their interests, abilities, and special needs to enhance their successfully completing their vocational education training program.

Vocational assessment for the handicapped and disadvantaged may be supported with federal funds after the students have been enrolled in a vocational education program. Enrollment is defined as the time when the student has been selected for placement into a vocational education program. Vocational assessment may be done any time after the student has been selected. The local education agency must develop a process to do periodic vocational assessment of all disadvantaged and handicapped students while enrolled in vocational education programs.

1. The purpose of vocational assessment for students enrolled in vocational education is to:
   a. validate the proper vocational education placement
   b. provide an understanding of the student's needs and abilities to assist his/her opportunity to successfully complete her/his vocational education training program
   c. identify appropriate teaching techniques and needed supplemental support services
   d. identify realistic vocational obtainable skills
   e. provide the student with vocational information and feedback concerning abilities so a proper transitional plan is implemented
   f. suggest appropriate job placement

Disadvantaged and handicapped students not enrolled in vocational education are not eligible for vocational assessment services funded with disadvantaged and handicapped allocations.

2. Vocational assessment may include, but not be limited to the following activities:
   a. interests, documented through career counseling activities
   b. records of counseling sessions
   c. standardized test scores where math and reading grade levels are indicated
   d. results of vocational aptitude testing
   e. teacher made and administered tests
   f. an analysis of how the student can best learn certain work tasks
   g. an analysis of the curriculum, equipment and facility adaptation
   h. commercially or locally prepared assessment instruments. (pp. 14-15)

A multidisciplinary team is recommended to implement the vocational assessment of disadvantaged and handicapped students enrolled in vocational education. The MDT (multidisciplinary team) and IEP for the handicapped, if vocational education is a component of the IEP, may be used to meet this requirement of the Carl Perkins Act.

3. Vocational Assessment should include all of the following components:

a. interest survey

b. assessment of abilities
   (1) Academic level
   (2) Vocational aptitudes (hands-on dexterity, coordination, form perception, and spatial relations)

c. assessment of learning styles

d. special needs
   (1) Curriculum adaptation
   (2) Equipment and facility adaptation
   (3) Remedial vocational skill instruction
   (4) Special counseling
   (5) Additional and/or individualized instruction. (pp. 14-15)

Optimism concerning the potential effect of the Perkins Act on the increased provision of vocational assessment services for disabled and disadvantaged students must be tempered with caution. A recent report by the National Assessment of Vocational Education, United States Department of Education (1989), specifically designed to assess the effects of the Perkins Act, suggested that:

1. Most school districts received financial rewards that were too small to mount new initiatives of any size. Expenditures under the set-asides for special populations tended to support ancillary services or remedial academic instruction for individual students rather than upgrading access of students to high-quality vocational education programs.

2. Districts that received funds under the disadvantaged set-aside were more likely than those that did not receive such funds to indicate that they provided vocational assessments to academically disadvantaged students. However, such assessments appeared to do little to determine or upgrade the vocational programs in which students were enrolled. Districts receiving such funds were no more likely than districts not receiving such funds to provide academic remediation, summer jobs, alternative schools, curricular modifications, or other related services.

3. Vocational assessments that were conducted had little relationship to decisions made about placement of students in vocational programs. The report stated:

> Although an assessment could be an important first step in finding the most challenging program, in many schools it is an isolated event of little consequence to vocational placement. . . . [A]ssessment does not play much role in placing a student in a particular vocational program. . . . Counselors and teachers were sometimes unsure about what to do with the results of vocational interest or ability tests [and] the district's offerings or the local job possibilities were quite limited, so there was no way students could enroll in programs of their choice. (pp. 14-15)

4. School districts with higher per pupil grants under the handicapped set-aside were more likely to modify facilities for disabled students and were slightly (but not significantly) more likely to provide vocational assessments than were districts without funding.

Although this evaluation of the effects of the Perkins Act offers some reason for optimism, it also clearly identifies limitations and difficulties with the legislation. A major problem with the legislation, as perceived by this writer (and as documented in the report just discussed), is its suggestion that vocational assessment should be conducted *after* placement in a vocational program has been made (i.e., to validate placement as appropriate). This is evident in the Pennsylvania guidelines summarized above. It is this author's opinion that the major benefit of vocational assessment (particularly for students with disabilities) is to provide data that can be used to identify *appropriate* vocational placements for students (and thus should be conducted *prior* to placement in a vocational training program). Also, by encouraging that vocational assessments be conducted following placement in a vocational class, the legislation infers that such assessments should be conducted no earlier than the 9th or 10th grade. As will be discussed, the transdisciplinary vocational assessment model advocated by this writer suggests that vocational assessments be initiated as early as the 6th grade. This is to allow time (prior to placement in a vocational program) for implementation of the academic and prevocational training that a disabled or disadvantaged student may need in order to succeed in a vocational training program. Unfortunately, the legislation may also inadvertently discourage service delivery to disabled and disadvantaged students *not* enrolled in vocational education programs, and to students who are not identified as handicapped or disadvantaged (as evident in the Pennsylvania guidelines).

EFFICACY OF VOCATIONAL TRAINING

Contrary to popular opinion, the high unemployment and underemployment rates that exist among individuals with disabilities do not appear to be due to a lack of access to vocational education. Disabled and disadvantaged students enrolled in public high schools take *more* vocational classes than do other students (National Assessment of Vocational Education, 1989). Based upon data collected from the 1987 High School Transcript Study (HSTS; which analyzed the enrollment patterns of 11th-graders during the 1985–1986 academic year), students with disabilities earned an average of 5.20 credits of vocational education compared to 4.02 credits for students without disabilities over 4 years of high school. These credits amounted to 27% of all the credits earned by students with disabilities (as compared with 18.3% of all the credits earned by students without disabilities). Similarly, disadvantaged students earned an average of 4.39 credits in vocational education during high school (23.6% of their total credits) compared to 3.01 credits in vocational education earned by advantaged students (12.1% of their total credits).

Students with disabilities have also had greater access to work-based (cooperative education, paid work experience, and work study programs) courses than have their nondisabled peers. Almost 17% of the total vocational credits earned by students with disabilities were in work-based courses (compared with 10% for students without disabilities). Disadvantaged students earned approximately 10% of their total vocational credits in work-based courses (compared to 7.2% for advantaged students).

Also contrary to popular belief, disabled and disadvantaged students spend little time training for jobs in low-level occupations in the service industry (food service, cosmetology, building maintenance, household services). The HSTS indicated that only 12.6 % of disabled students' total vocational credits (13.6% of disadvantaged students' total vocational credits) were earned in these fields.

Given these data, it appears that lack of access to vocational training is not a major factor contributing to the high unemployment and underemployment rates among persons with disabilities. Is it that vocational training programs are largely ineffective in providing students who have disabilities with the skills necessary to secure and maintain employment? Flynn (1982a, b) conducted a comprehensive review of the literature investigating the effectiveness of vocational education for individuals with and without disabilities. Although he found few well-controlled and empirically sound studies, Flynn (1982b) concluded that vocational education appeared to be more effective for disabled and disadvantaged youth than it was for nondisabled students. His literature review suggested that at the secondary school level, work-study programs enhanced the development of broad vocationally relevant skills and might be an effective means of improving the chances for vocational success among mildly mentally retarded youth. Flynn (1982b) also concluded that highly structured and intensive vocationally oriented programs appeared capable of increasing the opportunities for adults with more severe disabilities to retain competitive employment. He concluded that such programs might enhance the educational and career prospects of socioeconomically disadvantaged youth as well. Flynn (1982a) found that vocational education was no more effective than the general education curriculum in enhancing the career preparation of men with disabilities, but that it did appear to confer labor market advantages (higher wages, lower unemployment, greater educational attainment) to women with disabilities. Flynn (1982a) concluded that for the nondisabled population, secondary school vocational education should provide broad literacy training and teach work habits like punctuality and dependability (because these are more saleable to employers), rather than provide specific skill training. He recommended that specific skill training be left to postsecondary vocational education.

If students with disabilities are being afforded adequate access to vocational education (especially work-related programs that appear to be most closely related to vocational success), and there are some data indicating that these programs are effective, why are students with disabilities disproportionately represented among this nation's unemployed? One explanation for the high unemployment and underemployment rates among individuals with disabilities in this country may be the *inappropriate* placements of students with disabilities in vocational programs. That is, students with disabilities have historically been placed into programs in which they are disinterested, unprepared, and ill suited. It is natural to assume that these inappropriate placements have occurred largely because placement decisions were based on inadequate or inappropriate information. For example, this author knows of a school district (during the early to mid-1980s) in which students with disabilities were "mainstreamed" into regular vocational education programs based upon two factors: (1) which class period the student had free, once he or she had been scheduled for all academic classes, and (2) which vocational classes had openings during the student's "free" period. Certainly, decisions made in such a manner are unlikely to result in appropriate placements and are, for most students, doomed to fail. Although students with disabilities may have adequate access to vocational education programs, and although these programs, in and of themselves, may be largely effective in facilitating acquisition of the skills necessary for successful adjustment to work and community living, a mismatch between the student's "work personality" (e.g., abilities, interests, temperament, work habits) and the requirements and demands of the training program will likely result in inadequate preparation. Thus, a major use of vocational assessment data should be to identify realistic and appropriate vocational placments for students. Assessments should be conducted prior to placement and as early in a student's educational career as is appropriate given developmental and practical considerations.

As Maddy-Bernstein (1990) has suggested, biases, inappropriate assessment, lack of assessment, and insufficient information are just a few of the issues that have traditionally hampered vocational decision making for special populations. She cites a study conducted by Stodden, Meecham, Bisconer, and Hodell (1989) as an illustration of such inappropriate and ineffective use of assessment data. These authors reviewed the educational records of 127 secondary school students in nine high schools and four special schools to determine how vocational assessment data were being used. They found that, in many instances, vocational goals were being written into a student's Individual Education Plan (IEP) without using the vocational assessment results. They also learned that assessment data were often unavailable to teachers at the time IEPs were being developed. These IEPs contained only a few, vaguely stated vocational goals. Additionally, it was found that many different students had the same vaguely worded vocational goals listed on their IEPs! Relatedly, Cobb and Phelps (1983) reviewed IEPs in Illinois to determine if vocational evaluation data were present on IEPs. They concluded that use of vocational assessment data was limited. Although readers are cautioned not to overgeneralize the results of these studies, the studies do illustrate some of the potential problems confronting school personnel relative to the use of vocational assessment data with disabled students.

Historically, inappropriate placements of students with disabilities into vocational training programs can be traced to a lack of available vocational assessment services and to the lack of a professional group trained to provide quality vocational services to this population. Special educators, traditionally charged with the responsibility of providing services to students with disabilities in the public schools, have previously lacked knowledge and skill in vocational/career education. Until recently, special educators emphasized the academic, rather than the vocational, preparation of students with disabilities. Vocational educators, although knowledgeable about vocational programming, historically have lacked an understanding of the special learning needs of students with disabilities. Hohenshil and Warden (1978) noted that in almost every reference regarding vocational education for students with disabilities, vocational educators cited an urgent need for diagnostic services to assist them in identifying, planning, and evaluating instructional programs for these students. Although school counselors have traditionally been responsible for vocational/career assessment and planning at the secondary school level, their lack of training and experience with disabled students have discouraged them from delivering appropriate services to this population. In contrast, school psychologists, who are largely responsible for assessing and diagnosing students with disabilities, have historically received little training in vocational assessment or vocational planning. Thus, no one professional group was adequately trained to facilitate appropriate and successful placements of students with disabilities into vocational programs.

In recent years, school counselors, school psychologists, special education teachers, vocational education teachers, and other school personnel have received additional training designed to improve their ability to provide quality vocational services to students with disabilities. With better trained personnel, and with an increase in the development of school-based vocational assessment services, schools are in a better position than they ever have been in terms of ensuring appropriate and successful vocational placements for these students. As Parker (1974) indicated, the availability and use of vocational assessment data have been found to be critical factors in the establishment and development of vocational programs for students with disabilities. Similarly, Peterson (1981) surveyed vocational assessment personnel in Texas and found overwhelming agreement that vocational assessment is crucial to developing an appropriate educational program for secondary students with disabilities.

It is interesting to note that relatively few studies have been conducted on the efficacy of vocational assessment services. Menz (1978) evaluated the results of a high-risk youth group program in Wisconsin and found that involvement in a vocational evaluation program resulted in reported improvements in attitude and behavior of students. More recently, Neubert (1986) studied the use of vocational evaluation results in three school districts and concluded that vocational evaluators played a major role in assisting students with disabilities in gaining access to vocational programs; lack of coordination between special education and vocational education was problematic; support services in vocational education were critical in facilitating access to and success in vocational education; lack of appropriate curriculum adaptation in vocational education hindered access to vocational education; vocational evaluation reports did not appear to be used for planning IEPs nor were vocational objectives included as significant components of IEPs; and recommendations from vocational evaluation were utilized when there were administrative directions or support for this to occur.

ORIGIN, DEFINITION, AND PURPOSES
OF VOCATIONAL ASSESSMENT

The process of vocational assessment (also termed vocational evaluation) originated within the field of vocational rehabilitation and was originally designed to determine who was eligible for services provided by state and federal vocational rehabilitation agencies and to assist rehabilitation workers in developing a treatment plan for those individuals determined to be eligible for services (McCray, 1982). The overall objective of the evaluation was to determine what services were needed in order for an individual to be placed in competitive employment.

Partially as a result of legislation, and partially as a result of a national trend toward the inclusion of vocational and career education as an integral part of secondary education, educational personnel have slowly imported vocational evaluation procedures into the schools. This importation of rehabilitation evaluation procedures began in the mid- to late 1970s and continues (albeit with more sophistication) today. As Sitlington and Wimmer (1978) stated:

> Vocational assessment has been the responsibility of rehabilitation centers in the past. If career education is to be a viable framework for American education, and realistically prepare students to function as well-adjusted adults, vocational assessment must become the responsibility of the public schools. Handicapped students, in particular, need the systematic feedback from these procedures to aid in occupational decision-making from the elementary through the secondary school years. (p. 85)

However, as schools began to import rehabilitation-based assessment concepts, problems developed. As the New Jersey State Department of Education (1978) stated:

> A void existed in the literature pertaining to vocational evaluation of students within the field of education. The present state of the art concerned itself with vocational rehabilitation, and as a result, the concepts and strategies do not lend themselves readily to public education. (p. ii)

Although there is clearly an overlap between the general goals of rehabilitation-based and school-based vocational assessment procedures (both have successful adjustment to work and community living as goals), differences in the age and nature of the populations served by the assessments, differences in training and background of personnel charged with the responsibility of conducting the assessments, and practical and logistical variables associated with the setting (school vs. rehabilitation center) in which the assessment was to be conducted all contributed to difficulty in importing rehabilitation-based methodology into the school setting. Whereas rehabilitation centers serviced adults, schools serviced children and adolescents. Whereas rehabilitation centers serviced many individuals with physical disabilities, schools largely serviced individuals with mental or behavioral disabilities. Whereas rehabilitation personnel were trained in use of work sampling procedures and other work-intensive assessment procedures (i.e., situational assessment, simulated work experiences), educational personnel had no training or experience in use of these assessment procedures. Hence, schools were forced to modify and adapt traditional rehabilitation-based assessment procedures to meet the characteristics and needs present in schools. School-based vocational assessment procedures have evolved over the last 10–15 years as a result of this recurring adaptation and modification.

Today, school-based vocational assessment programs utilize the skills and expertise of a wide variety of school-based professionals, target students with mild and moderate disabilities and disadvantaged students for services, and begin assessment as early as the 6th grade. The National Association of Vocational Education Special Needs Personnel Committee on Vocational Assessment (1981) suggested that disabled and disadvantaged students should have priority in receiving vocational assessment services and that assessment should be conducted at least 1 year prior to placement in vocational education. However, the Committee suggested that it would be desirable to initiate assessments as early as age 12 or 13. Similarly, Peterson (1981) suggested that vocational assessment should be made available to all students during their school career, but that disabled and disadvantaged students should be given priority in terms of receiving these services. He suggested that vocational assessment should be initiated in grades 7–8 and continue throughout secondary school. However, the New Jersey State Department of Education (1978) suggested that vocational assessment should be an integral component of a student's total career development beginning in preschool and continuing through secondary school. Given the life-to-death concept of career development proposed by many career development theorists, and the need to link assessment procedures to developmental theory (see Chapter 2), this idea may not be as farfetched as it may initially appear!

For the purposes of this book (and for simplicity), the terms *vocational assessment, career assessment, work evaluation,* and *vocational evaluation* will be considered to be synonymous, although some distinctions have been made among them in the literature. Whereas vocational assessment and career assessment refer to the types of procedures that most closely resemble those that occur in school settings, vocational evaluation and work evaluation refer to the types of procedures most closely associated with rehabilitation facilities. Elements of all of these can be found in school-based vocational assessment programs.

Work evaluation has been defined as a process of identifying an individual's physical, mental, and emotional abilities, limitations, and tolerances in order to predict his or her current and future employment potential and adjustment (Virginia Commonwealth University, 1966) and as a process whereby an individual's attitudes, aptitudes, interests, capabilities, physical capabilities, and tolerances are evaluated by use of standardized tests, job sampling, job trait, and other specialized techniques and procedures (Stout State University, 1965). Cobb (1981) defines three fundamental domains of vocational assessment as vocational interest, vocational achievement, and vocational aptitude. Neff (1970) defines four major approaches to work evaluation, including mental testing, job analysis, work sampling, and situational assessment.

The literature is replete with articles detailing the purposes of work evaluation. Sankovsky (1970) identifies the assessment of intellectual potential, present work skills, expected work skills, physical capacity, work behavior, and learning problems as the goals of work evaluation. Peterson (1981) states that vocational assessment can (a) determine whether students have adequate prerequisite skills for various types of vocational education programs, (b) suggest effective teaching techniques and instructional modifications for special students, (c) suggest needed support services, (d) provide the vocational teacher with improved information about the student, and (e) bridge the gap between special educators and vocational educators. Pruitt and Longfellow (1970) see work evaluation as assessing developmental problems, attitudinal problems, readiness problems, and role problems. Hoffman (1973) views work evaluation as the assessment of two factors: general employability factors, including social development, grooming, hygiene, work personality, physical tolerance, and performance rate; and specific employability factors, including skills, aptitudes, dexterities, achievement, interests, intelligence, and personality. Perhaps Roberts (1970) defined the purpose of vocational assessment in its simplest form. He suggested that the goal of assessment was to answer the following four questions:

1. Is the student ready to decide on a job training area?
2. If so, what?
3. If not, why not?
4. What is the treatment plan to bring about student or environmental change so that the student can make the decision?

Perhaps the two definitions that most closely resemble the philosophical perspective embodied in this text are the definitions of vocational assessment offered by the Vocational Evaluation and Work Adjustment Association (VEWAA, 1975) and by Dahl et al. (1980). VEWAA (1975) defines vocational assessment as:

A comprehensive process that utilizes work, real or simulated, as the focal point of assessment and vocational exploration, the purpose of which is to assist individuals in vocational development. Vocational evaluation incorporates medical, psychological, social, vocational, and economic data in the attainment of the goals of the evaluation process. (VEWAA, 1975; p. 86)

Dahl et al. (1980) define vocational assessment as:

. . . a comprehensive process conducted over a period of time, involving a multi-disciplinary team . . . with the purpose of identifying individual characteristics, education, training, and placement needs, which provides educators the basis for planning an individual's program, and which provides the individual with insight into his or her vocational potential. (Dahl et al., 1980; p. 1)

Although these definitions infer that vocational assessment must be a multidisciplinary process conducted by a variety of personnel (what one professional could provide psychological, vocational, *and* medical information as part of his or her assessment?), they unfortunately omit inclusion of some information (academic and educational data, for example) that should be a part of every school-based vocational assessment. These definitions also do not clearly depict the need to involve community-based professionals in the vocational assessment and planning process.

TRANSDISCIPLINARY SCHOOL-BASED ASSESSMENT

Transdisciplinary school-based vocational assessment (TVA) is defined as follows:

A comprehensive assessment conducted within a school setting whose purpose is to facilitate educational and vocational planning in order to allow a student to make a successful adjustment to work and community living. The assessment is conducted by educational, community agency, and state agency personnel, in cooperation and consultation with the student's parents, and incorporates an assessment of the student's psychological, social, educational/academic, physical/medical, and vocational functioning.

The term *transdisciplinary* is used instead of *multidisciplinary* in order to depict the need to involve professionals "across disciplines" in the vocational assessment process. Traditionally, the term *multidisciplinary* has been used in education to depict the need to involve educators from different fields *within* education in a particular process. For example, "multidisciplinary teams" responsible for identifying students with disabilities are composed of school psychologists, teachers, guidance counselors, school nurses, and school administrators, all of whom are educational personnel based in schools. These multidisciplinary teams do not typically include professionals from outside of the schools (they include professionals from multiple disciplines *within* schools).

Figure 1-1 depicts the transdisciplinary school-based vocational assessment program model. The model is one that involves both school and community-based professionals in the planning and development of school-based assessment programs, and in the gathering and use of assessment data. Four phases are included in the TVA model. Phase 1 involves planning, organizing and implementing the assessment program. Both community agency and school personnel are involved in this planning.

Phase 2 involves conducting an initial level 1 vocational assessment. This assessment yields data that are used to establish educational and vocational objectives to be included in a student's Individual Education Plan and Individual Transition Plan. These data are used for tentative identification of viable vocational training options for students, options that can form the basis for further vocational exploration. Data are also used to identify residential living options for the student, curricula modifications that might be necessary in order for the student to achieve success in vocational training, school-based support services the student may require, and community agency services the student may currently or eventually need in order to make a successful transition from school to work and community living.

Phase 3 consists of specific vocational training (which may occur in a variety of settings). Should additional problems or questions arise about the appropriateness of this training, a level 2 vocational assessment may be conducted. Following this assessment, a revised educational/vocational plan can be developed for the student, and modifications in training can be initiated. Phase 4 follows this training, and involves placement in a job, a postsecondary institution, and/or a residential living facility. To facilitate successful transition from school to work and community living, follow-up and ongoing support (if necessary) are provided as part of this phase.

Clearly, the extent to which all of the school and community-based professionals listed in Figure 1-1 will actually be involved in the TVA process will depend upon local resources. Thus, the reader should recognize that Figure 1-1 depicts the range of professionals who might actually be involved in the TVA process under ideal conditions. In reality, the implementation of this transdisciplinary model in various locales will differ both in terms of the actual professionals involved and in terms of the roles and responsibilities of these professionals (because of practical and logistical issues; see Chapter 6). Table 1-3 depicts the type of information

Figure 1-1.
Transdisciplinary School-Based Vocational Assessment Model

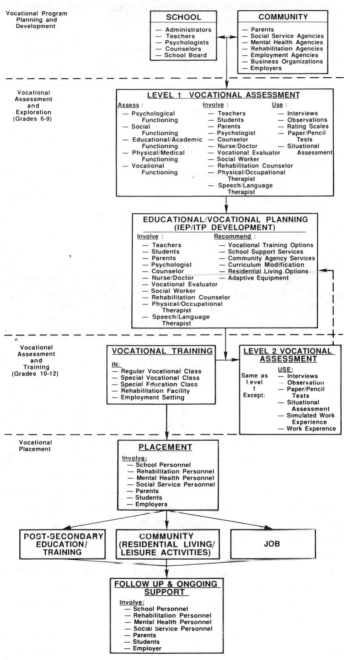

that should be included in the TVA under ideal conditions. Again, practical and logistical issues may influence the extent to which all of this information can be gathered and used by the transdisciplinary assessment team.

Table 1-3.
Type of Information in Vocational Assessment

Psychological Functioning	Social Functioning	Educational/ Academic Functioning
— Emotional Stability	— Adaptive Behavior	— Receptive/Expressive
— Needs	— Social/Interpersonal Skills	Language (Oral, Written)
— Temperament	— Independent Living Skills	— Reading Skills
— Values	— Hygiene	— Mathematics Skills
— Intelligence		— Range of Knowledge
— Behavioral Tendencies		(General Information)
Physical/Medical Functioning		Vocational Functioning
— Vision		— Vocational Interests
— Hearing		— Vocational Aptitudes
— Health		— Work Habits/Attitudes
— Strength		— Vocational/Career
— Dexterity/Motor Skills		Maturity
— Endurance		

SUMMARY

Work is an integral aspect of American life. The extent to which an individual makes a successful adjustment to work (performs his or her job satisfactorily and experiences satisfaction with the job) may influence that individual's physical and psychological well-being and overall quality of life. Hence, it is important to ensure that individuals develop the skills they need in order to secure and maintain satisfying and productive work.

As a result of nearly two decades of federal and state legislation, schools have come to assume a major responsibility for preparing individuals for the world of work. Research indicates that both parents and students perceive the vocational and career preparation that students receive in school to be inadequate. Moreover, statistics indicate that individuals with disabilities are at particularly high risk in securing and maintaining satisfying and productive work once they leave school. Individuals with disabilities are overrepresented among this country's underemployed and unemployed. The economic cost to society, and the personal cost to the individual, of providing support for these unemployed persons is tremendous. Despite being provided with adequate access to vocational training, and despite evidence that vocational training is effective in improving a disabled student's chances of vocational success, the high unemployment and underemployment rates among this population persist.

Transdisciplinary school-based vocational assessment is designed to provide the information needed by school personnel to facilitate students' educational and vocational planning, the goal of which is to allow students ultimately to acquire the skills they need to make a successful transition to work and community life. This assessment involves a variety of school, community agency, and state agency personnel, and includes an assessment of the student's psychological, educational/academic, physical/medical, vocational, and social functioning.

REFERENCES

Anderson, W. T. (1982). *Job satisfaction among school psychologists.* Unpublished doctoral dissertation, Virginia Polytechnic Institute and State University, Blacksburg.

Batsche, C. (1982). *Handbook for vocational school psychology.* Des Moines, IA: Iowa Department of Education.

Bedeian, A. G., & Marbert, L. D. (1979). Individual differences in self perception and the job-life satisfaction relationship. *Journal of Social Psychology*, *109*, 111-118.

Bell, C., & Bergdorf, L. (1983). *Accommodating the spectrum of individual abilities.* Washington, DC: U.S. Commission on Civil Rights Clearinghouse.

Bolton, B. (1982). *Vocational adjustment of disabled persons.* Austin, TX: Pro-Ed.

Bowe, F. (1980). *Rehabilitating America toward independence for disabled and elderly people.* New York: Harper & Row.

Brodsky, M. M. (1983). *A five year statewide follow-up of the graduates of school programs for trainable mentally retarded students in Oregon.* Unpublished doctoral dissertation, University of Oregon, Eugene.

Chapman, W., & Katz, M. R. (1983, March). Career information systems in secondary schools: A survey and assessment. *Vocational Guidance Quarterly*, 165-177.

Cobb, R. B. (1981). Vocational assessment of the special needs learner: The utility of commercial work sampling systems. *Journal of Vocational Special Needs Education, 3*(3), 30-32.

Cobb, R. B., & Phelps, L. A. (1983). Analyzing individualized education programs for vocational components: An exploratory study. *Exceptional Children*, *50*(1), 62-64.

Coles, R. (1978). Work and self-respect. In E. H. Erikson (Ed.), *Adulthood*. New York: Norton.

Crites, L. S., Small, M. W., & Sachs, M. L. (1984). *Demographic and functional characteristics of respondents to the mentally retarded community needs survey: Persons living at home with family.* Unpublished manuscript, University of Maryland, School of Medicine, Baltimore.

Dahl, P., et al. (1980). Mainstreaming guidebook for vocational educators teaching the handicapped. In Occupational Curriculum Laboratory, *An implementation manual for vocational assessment of students with special needs.* Denton, TX: East Texas State University.

Dore, R., & Meachum, M. (1983). Self-concept and interests related to job satisfaction of managers. *Personnel Psychology, 26,* 49-59.

Edgar, E. (1987). Secondary programs in special education: Are they justifiable? *Exceptional Children, 53*(6), 555-561.

Fardig, D. B., Algozzine, R. F., Schwartz, S. E., Hensel, J. E., & Westling, D. L. (1985). Postsecondary vocational adjustment of rural, mildly handicapped students. *Exceptional Children, 52*(2), 115-121.

Flynn, R. J. (1982a). National studies of the effectiveness of conventional vocational education: A research review. In K. P. Lynch, W. E. Kiernan, & R. Dybwad (Eds.), *Prevocational and vocational education for special needs youth: A blueprint for the 1980s.* Baltimore, MD: Paul H. Brookes.

Flynn, R. J. (1982b). Effectiveness of conventional and alternative vocational education with handicapped and disadvantaged youth: A research review. In K. P. Lynch, W. E. Kiernan, & R. Dybwad (Eds.), *Prevocational and vocational education for special needs youth: A blueprint for the 1980s.* Baltimore, MD: Paul H. Brookes.

Gallup, G. H. (1976, November 7). Eighth annual Gallup poll of the public's attitude toward public schools. *New York Teacher Magazine,* pp. 13-15.

Goodlad, J. I. (1979). *What are schools for?* Los Angeles, CA: University of California.

Greenhaus, J. H. (1971). Self-esteem as an influence on occupational choice and occupational satisfaction. *Journal of Vocational Behavior, 1,* 75-83.

Haavio-Manilla, E. (1971). Satisfaction with family, work, leisure, and life among men and women. *Human Relations, 24*(6), 585-601.

Harris, L., & Associates. (1986). *ICD survey of disabled Americans: Bringing disabled Americans into the mainstream: A nationwide survey of 1,000 disabled people.* New York: International Center for the Disabled (ICD).

Hasazi, S. B., Gordon, L. R., & Roe, C. A. (1985). Factors associated with the employment status of handicapped youth exiting high school from 1979 to 1983. *Exceptional Children, 51*(6), 455-469.

Hoffman, P. R. (1973). Work evaluation: An overview. In R. E. Hardy & J. G. Cull (Eds.), *Vocational evaluation for rehabilitation services.* Springfield, IL: Charles C. Thomas.

Hohenshil, T. H., & Warden, P. (1978). The emerging vocational school psychologist: Implications for special needs students. *The School Psychology Digest, 1,* 5-17.

Iris, B., & Barrett, G. V. (1972). Some relations between job and life satisfaction and job importance. *Journal of Applied Psychology, 56*(4), 301-307.

Johnson, L. D. , Baughman, G. G., & O'Malley, P. M. (1982). *Monitoring the future.* Ann Arbor, MI: University of Michigan Institute for Social Research, Survey Research Center.

Kalanidi, M. S., & Deivasenapathy, P. (1980). Self-concept and job satisfaction among the self-employed. *Psychological Studies, 25*(1), 39-41.

Kornhauser, A. W. (1965). *Mental health of the industrial worker*. New York: Wiley.

Levitan, S. A., & Taggart, R. (1977). *Jobs for the disabled*. Washington, DC: George Washington University Center for Manpower Policy Studies.

Maddy-Bernstein, C. (1990). Special considerations regarding career assessment for special groups. *Career Planning and Adult Development Journal*, 6(4), 37-40.

McCleary, L. E., & Thompson, S. D. (1979). *The senior high school principalship, Vol. 3, The summary report*. Reston, VA: National Association of Secondary School Principals.

McCray, P. (1982). *Vocational evaluation and assessment in school settings*. Menomonie, WI: Research and Training Center, Stout Vocational Rehabilitation Institute, University of Wisconsin - Stout.

Menz, F. E. (1978). *Vocational evaluation with adolescents: Description and evaluation of a program with reluctant learners*. Menomonie, WI: Research and Training Center, University of Wisconsin - Stout.

Mithaug, D. E., Horiuchi, C. N., & Fanning, P. N. (1985). A report on the Colorado statewide follow-up survey of special education students. *Exceptional Children*, 51(5), 397-404.

National Assessment of Vocational Education, United States Department of Education. (1989). *Final Report, Volume 1: Summary of findings and recommendations*. Washington, DC: Author.

National Association of Vocational Education Special Needs Personnel. (1981). Working paper on vocational assessment: Feedback wanted. *Newsnotes*, 6(1).

Neff, W. S. (1970). Vocational assessment: Theories and models. *Journal of Rehabilitation*, 36, 27-29.

Neubert, D. A. (1986). Use of vocational evaluation recommendations in selected public school settings. *Career Development for Exceptional Individuals*, 9(2), 98-105.

New Jersey State Department of Education. (1978). *Guidelines for establishing a vocational assessment system for the special needs student*. New Brunswick, NJ: Division of Vocational Education, Bureau of Special Programs.

Orphen, C. (1978). Work and non-work satisfaction: A causal correlational analysis. *Journal of Applied Psychology*, 63(4), 530-532.

O'Toole, J. (Ed.). (1973). *Work in America: Report of a special task force to the Secretary of Health, Education, and Welfare*. Cambridge, MA: MIT Press.

Parker, S. (1974). *Programs for the handicapped*. Washington, DC: Government Printing Office.

Pennsylvania Department of Education & Labor and Industry. (1986). *Pennsylvania transition from school to the workplace*. Harrisburg, PA: Author.

Peterson, M. (1981). Vocational special needs and vocational evaluation: The needed marriage of two fields. *Journal of Vocational Special Needs Education, 3*(3), 15-32.

Poplin, P. D. (1982). The development and execution of the vocational IEP: Who does what, when, to whom. In T. H. Hohenshil & W. T. Anderson (Eds.), *School psychological services in secondary vocational education: Roles in*

programs for handicapped students. Blacksburg, VA: Virginia Polytechnic
Institute and State University. (ERIC Document Reproduction Service No.
215245)

Portigal, A. H. (1976). *Towards the measurement of work satisfaction.* Paris:
Organization for Economic Cooperation and Development.

Pruitt, W. A., & Longfellow, R. E. (1970). Work evaluation: The medium and
the message. *Journal of Rehabilitation, 36,* 8-9.

Roberts, C. L. (1970). Definition, objectives, and goals in work evaluation. *Journal
of Rehabilitation, 36,* 13-15.

Rusch, F. R., & Phelps, L. A. (1987). Secondary special education and transition
from school to work: A national priority. *Exceptional Children, 53*(6),
487-492.

Sanborn, D. E., Sanborn, C. J., & Cimbolic, P. (1974). Occupation and suicide:
A study of two counties in New Hampshire. *Diseases of the Nervous System,
35,* 7-12.

Sankovsky, R. (1970). Toward a common understanding of vocational evaluation. *Journal of Rehabilitation, 36,* 10-12.

Schalock, R. L., & Lilley, M. A. (1986). Placement from community-based mental
retardation programs: How well do clients do after 8 to 10 years? *American
Journal of Mental Deficiency, 90*(6), 669-676.

Schmitt, N., & Mellon, P. M. (1980). Life and job satisfaction: Is the job central?
Journal of Vocational Behavior, 16(1), 51-58.

Silvestri, G. T., & Lukasiewicz, J. M. (1987). A look at occupational employment trends to the year 2000. *Monthly Labor Review, 110,* 46-63.

Sitlington, P.L., & Wimmer, D. (1978). Vocational assessment techniques for the
handicapped adolescent. *Career Development for Exceptional Individuals,
1,* 74-87.

Snyder, C. D., & Ferguson, L. W. (1976). Self-concept and job satisfaction.
Psychological Reports, 38(2), 603-610.

Special Task Force to the Secretary of Health, Education, and Welfare. (1973).
Work in America. Cambridge, MA: The MIT Press.

Stark, J. A., Baker, D. H., Menousek, P. E., & McGee, J. J. (1982). Behavioral
programming for severely mentally retarded/behaviorally impaired youth.
In K. P. Lynch, W. E. Kiernan, & J. A. Stark (Eds.), *Prevocational and
vocational education for special needs youth: A blueprint for the 1980s.*
Baltimore, MD: Paul H. Brookes.

Stodden, R. A., Meecham, K. A., Bisconer, S. W., & Hodell, S. L. (1989). The
impact of vocational assessment information on the individualized education planning process: Supporting curriculum-based assessment. *Journal for
Vocational Special Needs Education, 12*(1), 31-36.

Stout State University. (1965). *Vocational evaluation curriculum development
workshop.* Menomonie, WI: Author.

Super, D. E. (1957). *The psychology of careers.* New York: Harper & Row.

Terkel, S. (1974). *Working.* New York: Ballantine.

U.S. Department of Education, Office of Special Education and Rehabilitative
Services. (1990). *Twelfth annual report to Congress on the implementation*

of the Education of the Handicapped Act. Washington, DC: Government Printing Office.

Virginia Commonwealth University. (1966). *Proceedings of a training institute in work evaluation.* Richmond, VA: Author.

Vocational Evaluation and Work Adjustment Association. (1975). Vocational evaluation project final report [Special Edition]. *Vocational Evaluation and Work Adjustment Bulletin, 8.*

Wagner, M., & Shaver, D. M. (1989). *The transition experiences of youth with disabilities: A report from the National Longitudinal Transitional Study.* Menlo Park, CA: SRI International.

2 THEORIES OF VOCATIONAL DEVELOPMENT: THE FOUNDATION OF ASSESSMENT

As a parent of a newborn infant, you would never attempt to teach your new "bundle of joy" how to walk, how to skip, how to run, or how to drive a car. You understand that, developmentally, your child is not "ready" to perform such complex and difficult tasks at this point in his or her young life. Similarly, you would probably dismiss any pediatrician who, based upon an assessment of your infant's ability to run, recommended that you enroll your child in remedial track and field classes!

Although the above example may seem a bit extreme, it clearly illustrates the developmental theory that underlies and guides the appropriateness of any assessment or educational intervention, allowing users of assessment results to interpret and use assessment results more validly in planning educational programs. Consider, for example, the assessment of the perceptual-motor skills that underlie a child's ability to write letters of the alphabet. Although we would not be concerned about a 6-year-old child who evidenced letter reversals (writing *b* for *d,* for example), we would be concerned about a 10-year-old child who evidenced these same reversals. Our interpretation of these data is based upon our understanding of what is developmentally appropriate or normal from a perceptual-motor perspective for a particular aged child. Similarly, our use of these data is also based upon a developmental interpretation. That is, we might not prescribe any educational intervention for the 6-year-old; however, we might consider special programming of some nature for the 10-year-old. And, although we would probably not recommend vocational counseling for a 10-year-old who evidenced career indecision, we might consider such counseling for an undecided 17-year-old.

One can not develop or implement a valid vocational assessment program without an understanding of what is developmentally appropriate vocational behavior to expect of an individual at any given point in time. To design and implement a school-based vocational assessment program, one must understand vocational development theory and use such knowledge in deciding what traits will be assessed in a particular individual at any given grade or age level. Similarly, vocational development theory will allow assessment results to be placed in perspective and will allow users of the assessment data to generate developmentally appropriate recommendations for the student who has been assessed.

Career development has been defined as "the total constellation of psychological, sociological, educational, physical, economic, and chance factors that combine to shape the career of any individual over the lifespan" (Sears, 1982). The basic tenets of career development can be traced back to the early work of Frank Parsons, who in the 1909 classic book entitled *Choosing a Vocation*, proposed the following:

1. It is better to choose a vocation than merely to "hunt a job."
2. No one should choose a vocation without careful self-analysis that is thorough, honest, and made under guidance.
3. The youth should have a large survey of the field of vocations and not simply drop into the convenient or accidental position.
4. Expert advice, or the advice of men who have made a careful study of men and of vocations and of the conditions of success, must be better and safer for a young man than the absence of it. (pp. xiii-xiv)

Since the time of Parsons, numerous theorists have made a careful study "of vocations and of the conditions of success" and have proposed different developmental and theoretical perspectives based upon their study. However, it should be stated at the outset that even the most useful of these theoretical perspectives may be either incomplete, not well substantiated by research, or still in the process of being developed. As Isaacson (1986) has said, many of these so-called theories may be prematurely labeled as theories, and may be better thought of as position papers. It is important to understand that there is no one "correct" or "best" theory of career development.

The purpose of this chapter is to provide an overview of some of the more popular, well-accepted, and frequently used theories of career development, so as to provide readers with a framework that can be used when developing and implementing school-based vocational assessment programs. There is no agreed-upon classification system for organizing and categorizing the many different theoretical perpectives present in the literature. A useful dichotomy for categorizing career development theories, however, is the structural vs. process approach offered by Weinrach (1979). Structural approaches are those that provide an explicit link between people and the world of work. These approaches suggest that it is the interaction between people and the work environment that influences vocational behavior. Structural theories provide some means of organizing information about people and the world of work in a way that facilitates appropriate matching of people with jobs. As Weinrach (1979) has suggested, structural approaches have been criticized for being too simplistic and for "describing" vocational behavior rather than "explaining" it. Although it is true that structural approaches deemphasize a description of the process by which vocational decisions are made, their simplicity and practicality are strengths. In contrast, process theories provide no specific link between people and the world of work and, instead, attempt to identify the variables and processes that influence vocational development over time.

Arguably, John Holland's Theory of Vocational Personalities and Work Environments, a structural theory, and Donald Super's Vocational Development Theory, a process theory, are the two most frequently cited and useful theoretical approaches in the literature. Hence, they will be given extensive coverage in the remaining portion of this chapter. Two other structural approaches will be discussed: Roe's psychodynamic-oriented Theory of Career Choice; and Dawis, England, and Lofquist's Theory of Work Adjustment. Process theories given less extensive coverage in this chapter include the theories of career choice proposed by Gelatt, by Krumboltz, and by Harren. The chapter will conclude with a discussion of general theoretical principles, synthesized from the various perspectives reviewed, and will briefly discuss the application of developmental theory to students with disabilities.

STRUCTURAL APPROACHES

Theories that have often been referred to as "trait-factor" theories are examples of structural approaches. This section begins with a description of one of the most popular and well-known trait-factor theories, Holland's Theory of Vocational Personalities and Work Environments.

Trait-Factor Theory: Emphasis on the Work of John Holland

Trait-factor theories of career development focus upon factors that influence the choice of a career at any given point in time, and deemphasize a discussion of cumulative factors that may have occurred during one's lifetime that have an impact on career choice. As summarized in Seligman (1980), Katz (1963) offers the following tenets of the trait-factor perspective:

1. Each person is "keyed" to one or several "correct" occupations.

2. If left alone, people have a natural tendency to gravitate toward the "right" occupational choices.

3. Vocational counseling can make the process of occupational choice more efficient and effective.

4. The "key" can and should be learned during early adolescence.

5. The right occupational choice has a great impact on educational decisions.

6. The final occupational goal should be known early and should determine decisions related to and leading toward that goal. (p. 18)

John Holland's Theory of Vocational Personalities and Work Environments (Holland, 1966, 1973, 1985) incorporates many of these principles and is the most widely accepted and applied trait-factor theory in use today. Many high school and college vocational guidance centers/programs are based upon and organized according to Holland's theory. Although classified as a trait-factor theory, Holland's theory (as its title would suggest) might also be considered to be a personality theory that has widespread vocational applications. It is based upon some commonsense and frequently applied vocational stereotypes that have been validated by research. These vocational stereotypes are what allow us to form impressions of people and to ascribe characteristics to people when we know nothing about them except the kind of work they do.

Have you ever noticed that one of the first questions you ask someone you have just recently met is "What kind of work do you do?" The reason that we frequently ask this question of people is because the reply provides a wealth of information about the kind of person they are. Consider what impression you would form if your son or daughter came home and told you that s/he had just met the "love of their life" and was going to marry this "love" tomorrow. Although you have never met this person, what kind of an impression would you form if your son or daughter told you that this new "love" is a punk rock musician? Wouldn't you ascribe very different characteristics to this person if your son or daughter told you that this new love is an accountant? In fact, in thinking about this scenario, wouldn't you agree that if the "love" was an accountant, the couple (based upon the accountant's influence) would probably be less likely to rush impulsively into marriage on intense but short-lived emotion alone? These are examples of vocational stereotypes at work.

Holland suggests that the choice of a vocation is simply the expression of one's personality, and that people choose occupations that are consistent with their personalities. People with similar personalities select similar occupations. According to Holland, the extent to which individuals experience satisfaction with their jobs, perform their jobs well, and remain in their jobs for long periods of time depends upon the extent to which their personalities (their interests, abilities, values, temperaments, work habits, etc.) match the requirements and demands of the occupations they select. For example, a person who possesses artistic skills and interests; values freedom, autonomy, and flexibility; and abhors structure and conformity is probably better suited to be a punk rock musician than an accountant. The reverse is probably true for a person who possesses skills and interests in clerical and bookeeping tasks; is highly conforming, organized, and perfectionistic; and prefers orderly, structured, and predictable tasks. Would *you* feel confident in having your taxes prepared by an individual with long, purple and green hair wearing faded, patched blue jeans with holes, and a safety pin through one ear? On the other hand, how many rock musicians wear three-piece business suits to the recording studio and adhere to a strict 9-to-5 work schedule? The point is that the personality traits responsible for the punk rocker's appearance are the same traits likely to facilitate successful adjustment to a career as a musician, and unsuccessful adjustment to a career as an accountant.

Four basic assumptions constitute the heart of Holland's theory:

ASSUMPTION #1 — In our culture, most persons can be categorized as possessing one of six major personality orientations: realistic, investigative, artistic, social, enterprising, or conventional.

Holland believes that each personality orientation is a theoretical or ideal "type," consisting of relatively well-defined and distinct characteristics, that can be used as a model against which we can measure people. Holland does not believe that any one personality orientation alone can adequately describe any one person. Rather, he believes that each of our personalities can be adequately described by some combination of these six orientations. However, he does believe that most people resemble one type more so than they do other types. Although Holland does not spend much time describing the means by which these personality orientations develop, he does suggest that they are a product of heredity and environment. That is, people may be born with a biological predisposition to develop certain interests or skills, and may also develop such traits via interaction with peers and family members or as a result of other experiences they have as they develop. Once developed, these interests and skills create a particular disposition that leads individuals to think, perceive, and act in certain ways. In short, each personality type has a characteristic set of attitudes, beliefs, and values that lead to coping in predictable ways with given environmental problems. Lest the reader think that a theory of personality consisting of only six types is too simplistic to account for the variability that exists among people in the world today, recognize that multiple ordering of these six orientations allows for the creation of 720 different personality profiles!

The following provides a brief description of each of the six personality types:

Realistic—The realistic type demonstrates a preference for activities that require the use of tools and machines to solve problems and generally possesses manual, mechanical, manipulative, and technical skills. In contrast, these people tend not to engage in educational or therapeutic activities and tend not to possess strong verbal or interpersonal skills. Realistic types tend to be opinionated and to value concrete things. These characteristics generally lead them into agricultural, mechanical, and technical occupations and into jobs like carpenter, auto mechanic, farmer, electrician, etc.

Investigative—The investigative type demonstrates a preference for activities requiring the systematic and creative investigation of physical, biological, and cultural phenomena, which lead in turn to the acquisition of scientific and mathematical skills. Investigative types tend to be intelligent, scholarly, analytical, independent, curious, introspective, critical, and rational. They tend to be lacking in both leadership and interpersonal skills. Their traits lead them into science and math occupations, and into jobs like mathematician, biologist, botanist, chemist, physicist, etc.

Artistic—Artistic types demonstrate a preference for unstructured, independent, and unsystematized activities that require the manipulation of physical, verbal, or human materials to create art forms or products. They value originality, creativity, autonomy, and nonconformity and evidence an aversion to systematic, routine, and highly organized activities. These preferences lead to the acquisition of skills in art, music, dance, drama, and writing and to deficits in clerical and office-related skills. Artistic types tend to be expressive, idealistic, impulsive, emotional, creative, original, sensitive, and nonconformist. They tend to migrate into artistic occupations like musician, actress, choreographer, dancer, sculptor, etc.

Social—Social types demonstrate a preference for interacting with others for the purposes of helping, training, curing, or enlightening. They demonstrate an aversion to activities requiring the use of tools and machines. These traits lead them to develop strong verbal and interpersonal skills, and to acquire deficits in manual and technical competencies. Social types tend to be cooperative, patient, sociable, generous, helpful, empathic, idealistic, warm, kind, and understanding. Social types migrate into service-related and helping professions and into such jobs as teacher, counselor, social worker, etc.

Enterprising—Enterprising types demonstrate a preference for activities that entail the manipulation of others for the purpose of satisfying organizational goals or acquiring economic gain. They tend to demonstrate an aversion to observational, symbolic, and scientific activities. These preferences lead to the development of leadership, interpersonal, and persuasive competencies and to deficits in scientific competencies. Enterprising types tend to be assertive, aggressive, self-confident, ambitious, talkative, domineering, and energetic, and tend to value power, wealth, and status. These traits lead them into politics and business-related occupations, and into jobs like car salesman, politician, evangelist, etc.

Conventional—Conventional types have a preference for highly organized and structured activities that require the systematic manipulation of data. They prefer office-related and clerical types of activities such as record keeping, filing, organizing, and business machine operation. They demonstrate an aversion to unstructured, ambiguous, exploratory types of activities and prefer conformity to leadership. These traits lead to the development of clerical, computational, and business-system competencies and to deficits in artistic competencies. Conventional types tend to be careful, orderly, meticulous, precise, efficient, methodical, obedient, persistent, practical, unimaginative, inhibited, and inflexible. They tend to migrate into positions where they can follow rather than lead others and tend to populate clerical and office-related occupations.

ASSUMPTION #2—There are six model work environments that correspond to each of the six personality types: realistic, investigative, artistic, social, enterprising, and conventional.

Holland believes that each of these work environments presents specific requirements and demands and is typically populated by individuals of similar personality orientations. That is, realistic work environments are populated by realistic types, investigative work environments are dominated by investigative types, etc. Similarly, each of these work environments reinforces certain basic traits in people, while witholding reinforcement (and sometimes punishing) other traits. For example, realistic work environments, like a machine shop or a coal mine, require and reinforce physical skills/strength and manual, practical, mechanical, and manipulative problem-solving skills. These work environments also frown upon idealism; overt displays of compassion and warmth; and symbolic, abstract, higher level language. Social work environments are just the opposite. Holland believes, in a sense, that "birds of a feather flock together," and that people tend to surround themselves with people who possess similar interests, competencies, and values. By doing so, people then ensure themselves of some degree of acceptance and reinforcement of their own traits.

The following are brief descriptions of each of the six work environments:

Realistic—These work environments present concrete, physical tasks that require manual, mechanical, and manipulative skills often requiring physical exertion and the use of tools and machines. Typical settings include a farm, a construction site, and a machine shop.

Investigative—These work environments require use of creative, higher level, abstract thought to solve problems related to symbolic, scientific, and mathematical phenomena. This work environment values and reinforces scholarship, intelligence, and scientific accomplishments. A typical setting is a university research laboratory.

Artistic—These work environments present demands and requirements of an unstructured nature, usually involving the creative and imaginative use or production of art forms. This work environment values and reinforces creativity, originality, independence, autonomy, and freedom. Typical settings include a recording studio, a dance studio, a concert hall, and a theater.

Social—These work environments present demands that require extensive social and interpersonal contact, usually for the purpose of helping and teaching. This work environment values and reinforces compassion, concern, understanding, empathy, and cooperation. Typical settings include churches, schools, mental health centers, and social service agencies.

Enterprising—These work environments present demands that require the manipulation of others to attain self-interest or organizational-related goals. This work environment values and reinforces aggressiveness, ambition, influence, and persuasiveness and typically reinforces individuals with power, wealth, and/or status. Typical settings include a real estate office, a car dealership, and political offices.

Conventional—These work environments present tasks which require the explicit, systematic organization and ordering of verbal and mathematical data. Tasks usually are repetitive and routine and require little interpersonal contact. This work environment values and reinforces persistence, conscientiousness, efficiency, orderliness, and compliance. Typical settings include a business office, an accounting firm, and a post office.

Just as there are no "pure" personality types (all people possess characteristics from several types), there are no "pure" work environments. All work environments house jobs that require somewhat different skills and abilities. Whereas a school is a social work environment that mainly employs teachers (who are predominantly social types), secretaries (conventional types) and maintenance/janitorial workers (realistic types) are also employed in this work setting.

ASSUMPTION #3 — People search for environments that will let them exercise their skills and abilities, express their attitudes and values, and take on agreeable problems and roles.

This is Holland's "birds of a feather . . ." principle. People who have similar interests, skills, and values all search for the same kind of work environment, one that will allow them to become involved in activities and tasks in which they are both interested and skilled, and in which their values and attitudes are reinforced and shared by others. Hence, realistic types search for (and generally end up in) realistic work environments, social types search for (and generally end up in) social work environments, etc. Realistic work environments tend to be dominated by realistic types, social work environments tend to be dominated by social types, and so on.

ASSUMPTION #4 — Behavior is determined by an interaction between personality and work environment.

This is perhaps Holland's most important principle, and the one principle upon which the practical application of his theory is based. Holland believes that vocational outcomes, like job satisfaction, job performance, and length of service, can be predicted for any individual by simply comparing that individual's personality with the type of work environment he or she is entering. For example, an individual whose personality is dominated by a realistic orientation (practical, opinionated, mechanically oriented, less socially skilled) would appear to be well suited to function in a realistic work environment (such as a machine shop or an automobile repair shop), but not well suited to function in a social work environment (such as a mental health center or social service agency). Hence, if that realistic person were to enter a realistic work environment, one would predict that the individual would be reasonably satisfied with his or her job (because he or she would be required to perform tasks he or she enjoys), would perform the job reasonably well (because he or she possesses the skills and competencies necessary to perform the job), and would tend to remain in the job for a reasonable length of time (because he or she is satisfied, performing well, and surrounded by people who share similar attitudes, values, and beliefs). If that realistic individual entered a social work environment, however, one would predict a high level of job dissatisfaction (because he or she would be required to perform tasks he or she did not enjoy, such as comforting, helping, and teaching, and had no opportunity to perform tasks he or she did enjoy, such as using tools to build and fix things), a relatively low level of job performance (because his or her skills and competencies did not match the demands and requirements of the job), and would remain on the job for a relatively short period of time (because he or she would be dissatisfied and quit or be fired for performing inadequately).

Holland uses the term *congruence* to explain the relationship between one's personality and any given work environment. Congruence refers to situations in which realistic types work in a realistic environment, social types work in a social environment, etc. Incongruence occurs when a type works in an environment that provides demands, opportunities, and reinforcers incompatible with the person's preferences, skills, and values (e.g., a realistic type working in a social environment). The degree of congruence that exists between an individual's personality and work environment is used to make predictions about job satisfaction, job performance, and job stability.

Holland believes that some pairs of types are more similar and more closely related to one another than are other pairs of types. For example, social and enterprising types both tend to be outgoing, sociable, and interpersonally skilled (although their motives and values may differ greatly) and, hence, tend to be more similar to one another than are social and realistic types (who tend to be virtual opposites). Similarly, both artistic and investigative types tend to be creative, original, and interested in problems of an abstract nature (although the former type channels these traits into work in the arts, whereas the latter type channels these traits into work in the sciences and mathematics). Hence, they tend to be more similar to one another than are artistic types and conventional types (who tend to be virtual opposites). Holland uses the hexagonal model in Figure 2-1 to illustrate the psychological resemblances among types.

So far, this discussion has used pure types in its explanation of Holland's concepts. However, most people can be described accurately as some combination of the six types (although they may be more likely to resemble one type than another). Therefore, a person may be more accurately described as a Social-Enterprising-Artistic type, for example, than simply a Social type. Such an individual has a personality that is dominated by characteristics associated with the social type, but to a lesser extent possesses characteristics associated with the enterprising type, and to even a lesser extent possesses characteristics associated with the artistic type. Similarly, most occupations and jobs can be described accurately by some combination of work environments (although the job may resemble one work environment more so than it does any other work environment). For example, the requirements and demands inherent in the work environment of an elementary school teacher may be better depicted as a

Figure 2-1.
Holland's Hexagonal Model

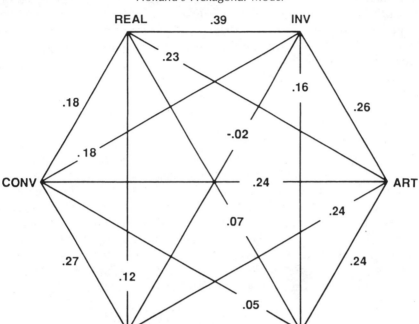

Note. From *The Self-Directed Search Professional Manual* (p. 39) by J. L. Holland, 1985. Odessa, FL: Psychological Assessment Resources. Copyright 1985 by Psychological Assessment Resources. Reproduced by permission.

combination of Social-Artistic-Enterprising (these teachers must be helpful, creative, and in control in order to function most effectively), rather than just Social (helpful). In contrast, a university faculty position may be better depicted as Social-Investigative-Artistic [although teaching (Social) is still a primary responsibility at this level, research involvement (Investigative) is also often required; there is not the same need to maintain control (Enterprising) over students as there is at the elementary school level]. Similarly, different fields of psychology often pose different responsibilities; hence slightly different types of people migrate into counseling psychology (helping emphasis; social types), for example, than migrate into experimental psychology (research emphasis; investigative types).

Within the hexagonal model in Figure 2-1, Holland uses the term *consistency* to describe the degree of relatedness among the types that depict one's personality or describe any given work environment. For example, a Social-Enterprising-Artistic personality is more consistent (because the types are more closely related) than is a Realistic-Social-Conventional personality (because this combination of types reflects the presence of inconsistent and often conflicting traits).

Finally, some persons may closely resemble a single type and show little resemblance to other types. Similarly, certain occupations and jobs may closely resemble one type of work environment and show little resemblance to other types of work environments. Holland uses the term *differentiation* to describe the degree to which an individual's personality or a particular work environment more closely resembles a single type, rather than multiple types. Personalities comprising a relatively equal number of characteristics from several types are considered to be less differentiated than are personalities dominated by characteristics from one type.

Although the degree of congruence that exists between one's personality and one's work environment is the primary basis for predicting potential work adjustment (job satisfaction, job performance, and job stability), consistency and differentiation allow one to assess the degree of confidence that can be placed in the prediction. Holland believes that consistent and highly differentiated personality profiles allow for more confident prediction than do less differentiated and inconsistent personality profiles.

From a vocational assessment perspective, use of Holland's theory would involve the following steps:

1. Assess an individual student's personality, and determine the degree to which characteristics of his or her personality match each of the six personality orientations (i.e categorize the student according to the six personality types; SIE, SAC, REC, etc.)

2. Assess the degree of consistency and differentiation inherent in the student's profile.

3. Identify work environments (occupations and jobs) or training programs related to those work environments that are congruent with the student's personality and recommend that the student explore these further. Temper prediction of adjustment to these work environments according to the degree of consistency and differentiation identified.

In order to help professionals use his theory in both assessment and counseling, Holland has developed an assessment tool designed to assist in identifying an individual's personality. This instrument, the Self-Directed Search (Holland, 1985), is discussed in chapter 5. Likewise, Holland has developed the *Dictionary of Holland Occupational Titles* (Gottfredson, Holland, & Ogawa, 1982), which categorizes most occupations and jobs available in the United States by Holland type. This volume has two listings of these jobs and their associated code. One listing is alphabetical by occupational title, whereas the other lists all jobs with the same code type together. Using these, a student can be assessed with an instrument that yields a Holland code representative of his or her personality, and can then utilize the *Dictionary* to identify occupations congruent with that personality.

A great deal of research has been conducted that validates Holland's work. Research investigating Holland's concept of congruence, in particular, has offered considerable support for the theory. Although a detailed description of the research investigating Holland's theory is beyond the scope of this section, suffice it to say that research investigating the concept of congruence with high school students (Cole, 1975; Werner, 1974; Wiggins & Westlander, 1977), college students (Elton, 1971; Holland, 1968; Morrow, 1971; Nafziger, Holland, & Gottfredson, 1975; Walsh & Lewis, 1972), and employed adults (Gottfredson, 1977, 1981; Hener & Meir, 1981; Meir & Erez, 1981; Mount & Muchinsky, 1978; Wiggins, 1976) has offered considerable support for the concept. Holland's theory in general, and the concept of congruence in particular, is so well regarded and accepted in the area of vocational psychology that it has become the basis for career counseling approaches and the organization of occupational information in high school and college counseling centers. Readers who are interested in additional research on Holland's theory are referred to Holland (1985). As Isaacson (1986) has noted, Holland's work has had a tremendous influence on the vocational/career assessment and counseling fields, and hardly a journal issue or book in these fields is published without reference to his work.

Minnesota Theory of Work Adjustment

The Theory of Work Adjustment (Dawis, England, & Lofquist, 1964; Dawis, Lofquist, & Weiss, 1968; Lofquist & Dawis, 1984) was developed at the University of Minnesota's Industrial Relations Center and was not specifically intended to be a theory of career development. Instead, it was intended to provide a system in which employment-related counseling could be developed and evaluated (Vandergoot, 1987). The theory suggests that adjustment to work is composed of two constructs: job satisfaction and job satisfactoriness (performance). Simply put, the theory suggests that if an individual is satisfied with his or her job and performing well on the job, he or she has demonstrated satisfactory adjustment to work.

The theory suggests that job satisfaction is influenced by the correspondence between one's needs and the reinforcer system present in the work environment. The degree to which one's relatively unique set of individual needs is satisfied within the work environment is the extent to

which that individual will experience satisfaction within that work environment. Research has indicated that at least 20 different work-related needs
can be identified and ultimately have an impact upon job satisfaction.
These needs are:

1. Ability utilization — The need to make use of abilities.
2. Achievement — The need to feel accomplishment.
3. Activity — The need to stay busy.
4. Advancement — The need to be able to advance on the job.
5. Authority — The need to tell others what to do.
6. Company policies and practices — The way company policies are put into practice.
7. Compensation — The need to feel as if one is being fairly compensated for work performed.
8. Co-workers — The need to get along well with co-workers.
9. Creativity — The need to try out one's own ideas.
10. Independence — The need to work alone.
11. Moral values — The need to perform work that does not go against one's conscience.
12. Recognition — The need to be recognized by others for having performed well.
13. Responsibility — The need to be free to use one's own judgment.
14. Security — The need to feel secure with one's job.
15. Social service — The need to feel as if one's work is being of service to others.
16. Social status — The need to feel respect from others.
17. Supervision-Human relations — The need to get along well with one's supervisor.
18. Supervision-Technical — The need to receive quality technical supervision.
19. Variety — The need to do different things.
20. Working conditions — The need to feel comfortable with the conditions under which one works.

The types of needs each individual possesses and the strength of these
needs vary from one individual to another. Similarly, different work
environments provide rewards that satisfy different needs. Whereas one
work environment may provide hefty salaries but no opportunity for
advancement, another may provide tremendous advancement potential,

but relatively low salaries. Under such circumstances, an individual who is just finishing school and entering the job market, and who has a family to support and loans to repay, may initially experience greater satisfaction in the former work environment. However, the needs an individual possesses (and the strength of these needs) are likely to change over the lifespan. So, as this individual establishes him- or herself in a career, repays loans, invests money, and has children grow into self-sufficiency, the need for compensation may decrease, and needs for recognition and advancement may increase. Under these circumstances, the Minnesota theory would predict that this individual would experience a decrease in job satisfaction in the former work environment and may search for a new job in a work environment more similar to the latter. If this individual's needs for recognition, status, and advancement were particularly strong, and he or she just happened to have inherited a large sum of money from a rich aunt, he or she would probably be willing even to take a hefty cut in pay in order to acquire a higher level position in another organization.

The Minnesota theory suggests that the degree of satisfaction one experiences in a work environment influences *tenure* or likelihood of remaining in that work environment for a reasonable length of time. The more satisfied one is with a job, the more likely it is that an individual will remain in that job. However, the less satisfied one is, the more likely it is that he or she will quit the job and attempt to find a different job that more adequately meets his or her needs.

However, job performance is also likely to influence one's tenure or job stability. Certainly, if one is performing the job inadequately, it is likely that he or she will either be fired or will be transferred to a different job within the same organization. According to the Minnesota theory, job satisfactoriness (performance) is influenced by a correspondence between one's abilities and the ability requirements inherent in the job. Hence, jobs like carpenter, plumber, or electrician will be performed adequately by those individuals who possess mechanical abilities, whereas jobs like teacher, writer, and lecturer will be performed adequately by those individuals who possess verbal/language abilities. This component of the theory clearly explains why the author of this book, a most mechanically inept but verbose individual, was, as a teen and young adult, fired from numerous part-time summer factory jobs and is now, instead, a tenured university faculty member teaching and writing articles and books like this! The theory also helps to explain why this author gives circular saws and electric screwdrivers to his wife for her birthday rather than receiving them from her instead!

Several instruments exist that can be used to assess an individual's needs and level of satisfaction with different aspects of the work environment. The *Minnesota Importance Questionnaire* (Gay, Weiss, Hendel, Dawis,

& Lofquist, 1971) can be used to assess the needs perceived to be most important by an individual, while the *Minnesota Satisfaction Questionnaire* (Weiss, Dawis, England, & Lofquist, 1967) can be used to assess an individual's overall job satisfaction and specific satisfaction with 20 aspects of a job. Although some research has been conducted to determine the types of rewards provided by different jobs (Borgen, Weiss, Tinsley, Dawis, & Lofquist, 1972), only a small pool of occupations have been analyzed for their reward systems (Vandergoot, 1987). This is a major disadvantage underlying the practical application of the theory. However, the theory clearly suggests the need to incorporate measures of interests, abilities, and needs into any comprehensive vocational assessment.

Ann Roe's Theory of Career Choice

Roe's (1956) theory of career choice is a psychodynamically oriented theory based partially upon Maslow's (1954) need-based theory of motivation. Maslow posits the existence of eight needs which are arranged in heirarchical order. These needs are:

Physiological needs—The need for food, water, sleep, etc.

Safety needs—The need to remain free from physical or psychological harm

Belongingness needs—The need for love, belongingness, and acceptance

Esteem needs—The need to master one's environment

Need for information

Need for understanding

Need for beauty

Self-actualization needs—The need to channel one's creative potential

Lower order needs (physiological) are of higher strength than are higher order needs (self-actualization) and will take precedence in motivating behavior. Hence, physiological needs will motivate behavior unless satisfied. If physiological needs are satisfied, then safety needs will motivate behavior. If both physiological and safety needs are satisfied, then belongingness needs will motivate behavior, etc.

Roe's theory grew out of research she conducted on factors related to career choice among artists and scientists (Roe, 1949, 1950, 1951, 1952). Although originally published in 1957, the theory was restated in 1964 (Roe & Siegelman, 1964). Roe was convinced that artists and scientists were very different kinds of people who interacted with others and with the world in very different ways. Her theory was an attempt to explain how unconscious needs, genetic influences, and early childhood experiences (rooted in parenting style) influenced personality development and career choice. The following statements outline her position:

1. Genetic factors set limits on the development of all traits; however, the degree of control exerted by genetics varies from one trait to another.

2. Environmental factors, particularly cultural background and socioeconomic status of the family, influence the types and degrees of developed traits.

3. Development of traits like interests, attitudes, and other traits that are not greatly influenced by genetics will be determined by experiences through which (unconscious) involuntary attention is directed.

4. (Unconscious) involuntary attention will be directed toward activities that satisfy needs.

5. Needs develop as a result of the patterning of early satisfactions and frustrations, which in turn is influenced by the strength of the needs.

6. Needs that are routinely satisfied as they appear will not become strong unconscious motivators.

7. Needs that are rarely satisfied, or for which satisfaction is delayed, will become unconscious motivators.

8. Interests are a reflection of attempts to satisfy needs.

Roe suggested that the emotional climate in the home and parent–child interactions influence eventual career choice. As depicted in Figure 2-2, Roe posits three types of emotional climates, each of which is characterized by a particular focus upon the child. This leads to the definition of six types of parent–child interactions:

1. Emotional concentration on the child: Overprotective — This parenting style is characterized by a tendency to foster dependency and to limit exploration and risk taking. Overprotective parents provide considerable attention, indulge their children, but also shelter and protect them. They routinely satisfy lower order needs, but require dependency and compliance in return for the satisfaction of higher level needs.

2. Emotional concentration on the child: Overdemanding — This parenting style is characterized by a tendency to set high goals for children and to foster achievement of these goals. Overdemanding parents provide considerable attention, but much of this attention is contingent upon the child's meeting certain predefined standards set by the parent. Love received by the child is contingent upon satisfaction of conditions imposed upon the child by the parent (usually conditions of conformity and achievement). Roe believes this child-rearing pattern is typical of upper-class families, and emphasizes the development of conceptual rather than motor skills.

Figure 2-2.
Roe's Emotional Climate Type

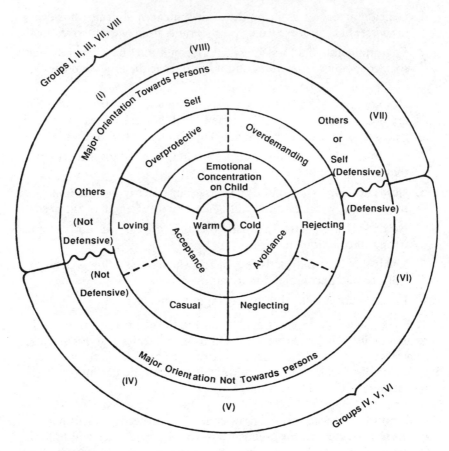

Groups

I.   Service
II.   Business Contact
III.   Organizations
IV.   Technology
V.   Outdoor
VI.   Science
VII. General Culture
VIII. Arts & Entertainment

Levels

1. Professional & managerial 1
2. Professional & managerial 2
3. Semiprofessional, small business
4. Skilled
5. Semiskilled
6. Unskilled

Note. Reprinted from "Early Determinants of Vocational Choice" by A. Roe, 1957, *Journal of Counseling Psychology, 4,* 212-217. Reprinted by permission of the American Psychological Association.

3. Acceptance: Loving—This parenting style is characterized by displays of love, warmth, and affection. Loving parents encourage independence, provide praise when warranted, and assist the child in solving his or her own problems without becoming overly intrusive. This parenting style is characterized by reasonable satisfaction of all needs.

4. Acceptance: Casual—This parenting style is characterized by mild affection and acceptance. Casually accepting parents are easygoing, and espouse a laissez-faire child-rearing philosophy. Rules may be set, but will not be strictly enforced. Attention is selectively provided to the child. Generally, most of the child's needs are satisfied.

5. Avoidance: Neglecting—This parenting style is characterized by lack of affection. Physical needs of the child are minimally satisfied, but emotional needs may go unmet. Neglecting parents ignore their children but do not necessarily express overt hostility and aggression. The child is often left alone to take care of him- or herself.

6. Avoidance: Rejecting—This parenting style is characterized by expressions of overt hostility. The child is degraded, physically and emotionally abused, and subjected to outright rejection. Physiological and safety needs may be satisfied, but love and esteem needs are not satisfied. Rejecting parents often deliberately withhold love.

Depending upon the type of home environment a child is exposed to, the child will develop a certain orientation toward people (categorized as toward/not toward people; toward self or others, if toward people; and defensive/not defensive). These orientations then lead individuals to migrate into certain occupations which are consistent with the orientation developed. Roe identifies eight occupational groups:

1. Service—These occupations are primarily concerned with serving and attending to the needs of others. Included are occupations in psychology, social work, and protective services.

2. Business Contact—These occupations are primarily concerned with face-to-face sales which involve some degree of persuasion and influence. Included are occupations like real estate and public relations.

3. Organization—These occupations are primarily concerned with the administration and efficient operation of businesses, industries, or governments.

4. Technology—These occupations are primarily concerned with production, maintenance, and transportation of commodities and utilities. Included are occupations in engineering, crafts, machine trades, transportation, and communication.

5. Outdoor—These occupations are primarily concerned with the cultivation and preservation of natural resources. Included are occupations in agriculture, forestry, and mining.

6. Science—These occupations are primarily concerned with scientific theory and its application under circumstances other than technology.

7. General Culture—These occupations are primarily concerned with the preservation and transmission of cultural heritage. Included are occupations in education, journalism, religion, and jurisprudence.

8. Arts and Entertainment—These occupations include those primarily concerned with the use of special skills in creative arts and entertainment.

Roe suggests that children from overprotective or overdemanding climates migrate into people-oriented occupations (like service and the arts), while children from rejecting or neglecting climates migrate into non-people-oriented occupations (like science and technology). Children exposed to loving-acceptance tend to migrate into people-oriented occupations, while those exposed to loving-casual climates do not.

Roe also suggests that within each occupational area, occupations can be categorized by levels. Six occupational levels are proposed:

1. Professional and Managerial 1—These occupations consist of important, high-level responsibilities and, if formal education is a prerequisite for entry, often require a doctoral degree or its equivalent.

2. Professional and Managerial 2—These occupations consist of medium-level responsibilities and often require education at or above the bachelor's degree, but below the doctoral degree.

3. Semiprofessional and Small Business—These occupations entail low-level responsibilities and require education at the high school or technical school level.

4. Skilled—These occupations require apprenticeships or other specialized training experiences.

5. Semiskilled—These occupations require some training and experience, but less formal and less specialized than those of skilled occupations.

6. Unskilled—These occupations require no special training or education and generally do not require much ability above that necessary to follow directions and to engage in rote, repetitive tasks.

Roe believes that although home atmosphere influences the type of occupation chosen, genetics and the involuntary pattern of expenditure of psychic energy influence the level achieved within this occupation. That is, an intelligent child from an accepting, high socioeconomic status home, who expends considerable energy in the pursuit of higher education, and who possesses high vocational aspirations, may migrate into a service-related occupation like psychologist, counselor, or social worker (professional and managerial; level 1 and 2 occupations). In contrast, a child from an accepting, low socioeconomic status home, who expends considerably less energy in the pursuit of higher education, and who possesses considerably lower vocational aspirations, may migrate into a service-related occupation like taxi driver, waiter, or bellman (semiskilled or unskilled; level 5 and 6 occupations). Figure 2-3 provides an example of Roe's occupational classification system.

Research investigating the validity of Roe's theory has provided only limited support for the theory. Several factors seem to be responsible for this, including the ambiguity of the theoretical concepts proposed (which makes it difficult to operationalize these concepts for empirical study), the difficulty inherent in defining and categorizing parenting styles and home climates, the omission of outside-the-home factors as an explanatory construct, the use of rather broad occupational classifications as a measure of one's orientation toward people, and the logistical and practical difficulties inherent in conducting longitudinal research necessary to investigate the validity of the theory (Issacson, 1986; Norris, Hatch, Engelkes, & Winborn, 1979). In contrast, Roe's theory was one of the first theories to address the role of personality in vocational decision making, is relatively comprehensive, highlights the role of parenting in vocational development (an often overlooked and ignored factor), and provides a relatively useful system by which occupations can be classified. The theory also clearly identifies the role unconscious needs may assume in the vocational decision-making process and suggests the importance of encouraging students to recognize and consider their needs when making vocational choices.

PROCESS APPROACHES

As previously mentioned, process approaches focus upon the processes that influence vocational development over a period of time and tend not to provide any explicit link between the individual and the world of work. Theories labeled by some as developmental or decision-making theories fall under the umbrella of process approaches.

Developmental Theories: Emphasis on the Work of Donald Super

Developmental theories assume that vocational/career development is an ongoing process that begins at birth and ends at death. Hence, these

Figure 2-3.
An Example of Roe's Classification System

LEVEL	SERVICE	BUSINESS CONTACT	ORGAN-IZATION	TECH-NOLOGY	OUTDOOR	SCIENCE	GENERAL CULTURAL	ARTS & EN-TERTAINMENT
I	Psychiatrist, Psychologist					Anthropologist oceanographer	Economist, lawyer	Architect
II	Social workers, counselors	Public relations worker	Hospital administrator, C.P.A.	Airplane pilot, engineer	Surveyor, landscape architect	Nurses, R.N., pharmacists	Clergymen, teachers high school and elementary	Actor, actress, designer
III	Police chief, recreation worker	Sales, auto, insurance	Hotel manager, stenographer	Draftsman, flight engineer	Forest ranger, county agent	Dental hygienist, x-ray technician	Radio announcer, TV announcer	Interior decorator, photographer
IV	Policeman, practical nurses	Driver salesman	Bookkeeper, salesclerk	Electrician, jeweler	Forestry technician, miner	Lab technician, optician		Letterer, paste-up man
V	Taxi driver, waiter		Typists, cashiers	Truck driver, plasterer	Chainman, rodman			
VI	Orderly, bellman		Mail machine operator, sorting machine operator	Bulldozer operator, cement mason	Roustabout, lumberjack			Pinboy

Note. Reprinted from "Early Determinants of Vocational Choice" by A. Roe, 1957, Journal of Counseling Psychology, 4, 212-217. Reprinted by permission of the American Psychological Association.

theories attempt to identify and explain the pattern of processes and factors that ultimately impacts on vocational decision making throughout the lifespan. In contrast, trait-factor theories, like Holland's, assume that vocational decision making is an event that occurs at a specific time and are primarily concerned with only those factors that influence vocational choice at this point. As such, developmental theories are truly "theories of vocational development," whereas trait-factor theories might be better thought of as "theories of vocational choice."

Developmental theories assume that the choice of a career is an orderly and rather predictable process consisting of a series of well-defined and hierarchical stages. These stages identify the issues, roles, and conflicts that most individuals confront at given points in their lives and provide a birth-to-death perspective of vocational maturation. As with other aspects of development, the age and rate at which individuals progress through each of these vocational stages will vary. Although vocational development theorists provide age ranges associated with each of these stages, one must interpret these age ranges cautiously and not rigidly. Just as some children begin to walk at 10 months and others at 13 months, there is normal variability inherent in the age ranges associated with these stages. The ages associated with the stages, however, do provide some guidelines that can be used to assess whether a student is progressing at an average rate in his or her vocational development. Although we would not be concerned about a child who began walking at 10 or 13 months, we might suspect deviation from what is considered to be developmentally normal if the child did not begin to walk until 24 months. The stages inherent in vocational development theory can be used in a similar fashion and can assist in identifying students who may be in need of some form of vocational intervention.

As Isaacson (1986) has suggested, probably no one has written as much about or had as much influence on the field of vocational development as has Donald Super. Super has devoted almost 50 years to the study of vocational development (Super, 1942) and is one of the most widely known and respected career development theorists in the world. His theory was first proposed in a relatively complete form in 1953 and has been continually modified ever since. Several other developmental experts have proposed theories similar to Super's. Most notable among these are Ginzberg, Ginsburg, Axelrod, and Herma (1951), and Tiedeman and O'Hara (1963). Readers who are interested in slightly different developmental perspectives are referred to these theorists.

Like Ginzberg et al.'s, Super's work was influenced by the life-stages concept proposed by Buehler (1933). Super proposed the existence of five major stages: Growth, Exploration, Establishment, Maintenance, and Decline. Each of these major stages is composed of several substages, and each is associated with several developmental tasks. Figure 2-4 summarizes these stages, substages, and developmental tasks. Although only two major stages generally occur during the traditional school years (Growth and Exploration), all stages are listed and summarized in keeping with the birth-to-death perspective inherent in developmental theory.

The following ten propositions underlie Super's theory:

1. People differ in abilities, interests, and personality.

2. Individuals are each qualified, by virtue of these characteristics, for a number of occupations.

3. Each of these occupations requires a characteristic pattern of abilities, interests, and personality traits—with tolerances wide enough, however, to allow for both some variety in occupations for each individual and some variety of individuals in each occupation.

4. Vocational preferences and competencies—the situations in which people live and work, and hence their self-concepts—change with time and experience, making choice and adjustment a continuous process.

5. This process (item 4 of this list) may be summed up in a series of life stages characterized as those of growth, exploration, establishment, maintenance, and decline. These stages can be subdivided into (a) the fantasy, tentative, and realistic phases of the exploratory stage and (b) the trial and stable phases of the establishment stage.

6. The nature of the career pattern is determined by the individual's parental socioeconomic level, mental ability, and personality characteristics and by the opportunities to which he or she is exposed.

7. Development through the life stages can be guided, partly by facilitating the process of maturation of abilities and interests and partly by aiding in reality testing and in development of the self-concept.

8. The process of vocational development is essentially that of developing and implementing a self-concept; it is a compromise process in which the self-concept is a product of the interaction of inherited aptitudes, neural and endocrine makeup, opportunity to play various roles, and evaluations of the extent to which the results of the role playing meet with the approval of superiors and fellows.

9. The process of compromise between individual and social factors, between self-concept and reality, is one of role playing, whether the role is played in fantasy; in the counseling interview; or in real-life activities such as school classes, clubs, part-time work, and entry-level jobs.

Figure 2-4.
Stages in Vocational Development

STAGE	GROWTH			EXPLORATION			ESTABLISHMENT		MAINTENANCE	DECLINE	
Substage	Fantasy	Interest	Capacity	Tentative	Transition	Trial	Commitment & Stabilization	Advancement		Deceleration	
Age Range	0-10	11-12	13-14	15-17	18-21	22-24	25-30	31-44	45-64	65-70	71 & on
Primary Task(s)	Increase Self Awareness and Awareness of the World of Work			Explore various vocational Options and Implement A Vocational Choice			Settle and Advance Within Chosen Occupation		Preserve Vocational Status and Gains	Cope With Declining Vocational Abilities and Begin to Adjust to Retirement	

10. Work satisfactions and life satisfactions depend on the extent to which the individual finds adequate outlets for his or her abilities, interests, personality traits, and values; they depend on his or her establishment in a type of work, a work situation, and a way of life in which he or she can play the kind of role that growth and exploratory experiences have led him or her to consider congenial and appropriate.

Simply put, Super believes that each of us has a relatively unique set of personality characteristics (interests, abilities, values, attitudes, etc.) that qualify us for a vast array of occupations. Although all occupations require a given set of abilities, interests, and personality traits, there is enough variability (tolerance) inherent in each characteristic set of traits to accommodate a variety of different kinds of people (providing the variability inherent in the traits possessed by these individuals is within the occupation's tolerance range). Super believes, as do most vocational theorists, that *there is no one right occupation for anyone.* There are *many* right occupations for everyone.

The traits that characterize one's personality and thereby qualify an individual for certain jobs develop as a result of one's progression through the five stages detailed in Figure 2-4 and are influenced by environmental factors such as socioeconomic status, parents, family, friends, and schooling. Super believes that the choice of a career is the process of implementing one's self-concept. Although the inextricable link between self-concept/self-esteem and career choice is undeniable and has been verified in numerous empirical studies (Dore & Meachum, 1973; Greenhaus, 1971; Kalanidi & Deivasenapathy, 1980; Snyder & Ferguson, 1976), no definitive cause–effect relationships have been uncovered between these variables. However, it seems logical to assume that each influences the other. That is, the initial choice of a career is influenced by one's self-perceptions, which then change as a function of the experiences one has in one's career. Because Super believes that the degree of satisfaction one attains from his or her work is proportional to the degree to which he or she has been able to implement a self-concept, and that as a result of one's career experiences self-concept may change, one may then find it necessary to modify or change careers in order to implement more fully a changed self-concept (and experience optimal satisfaction). Thus, vocational/career development becomes a continuous process of adjustment, change, and readjustment in both self-concept and in choice of work throughout the lifespan.

Super's idea of self-concept and its relationship to work is particularly important. In a sense it reflects the old adage "We are what we do." Super believes, as do many other theorists, that the kind of occupation we choose as life's work has a tremendous impact on how we perceive ourselves, and how others perceive us. Experiential validity for the notion that self-concept is heavily influenced by career choice is found in the sheer frequency with which statements like "I am a(n) . . . (occupation)" are made. This powerful statement implies that our whole being is defined by the kind of work we do. As Coles (1978) notes, people find it almost impossible to talk about themselves without reference to their occupation. This concept underscores the importance of assisting youth with both an understanding of themselves and their choice of a career. As Super and others believe, this choice will be a reflection of how the youth perceives him- or herself and, perhaps more important, may influence how the youth (and others) continues to see him- or herself in the future.

Super believes that the early years of life are a time of growth during which people develop the interests, skills, values, and attitudes (including attitudes about work) that become part of their personality. This is also the time during which one begins to learn about oneself, and to develop a self-concept. In adolescence, teens explore and "test out" their self-concepts via school, leisure, and part-time work experiences. Self-concept is further refined as a result of these experiences, and eventually a career is chosen in which one believes one can fully implement these self-concepts and experience satisfaction. Because the primary developmental task during adolescence is exploration and self-concept refinement, Super does not advocate career choice and preparation during these years. The fact that many adolescents finish high school and go on to college undecided about a major (and hence a career) may reflect the need to continue to explore careers and to test out self-concepts.

Once having selected and entered a career, there is an initial "settling in" period during which the individual assesses the job's suitability (i.e., the degree to which the job allows one to implement one's self-concept fully). There may be several job changes before the individual stabilizes and feels comfortable and secure in his or her career choice. Following this stabilization and commitment, the individual puts effort into "climbing the corporate ladder," so to speak. Advancement in one's career becomes of paramount importance when people reach their 30s and 40s. This is generally considered to be the time of peak performance. When people reach their late 40s and 50s, individuals, having accomplished much in their careers, attempt to preserve their accomplishments in the face of competition from younger, achievement-oriented colleagues (those most likely in the advancement stage). When people reach their 60s, physical and mental skills begin to slow, work activities change, and individuals begin to look toward nonwork activities for self concept implementation and satisfaction. Disengaging from work, and adjusting to retirement are major developmental tasks during these years.

Super's (1957) research led to the definition of different career patterns for men and women. The four types of career patterns that characterized men were:

1. The stable career pattern—Following the completion of school, the individual goes into a job for the remainder of his working life.

2. Conventional career pattern—Following the completion of school, the individual tries out a number of jobs, and then enters stable employment.

3. Unstable career pattern—Following the completion of school, the individual tries out a series of trial jobs, secures a stable job, and then returns to trial jobs, resulting in no permanent occupation.

4. Multiple-trial career pattern—Following the completion of school, the individual takes many trial jobs, all of insufficient duration to indicate a predominant type of work or the establishment of a career.

The seven types of career patterns Super (1957) identified for women were:

1. Stable homemaking career pattern—Following the completion of school, the woman gets married without performing any significant paid, outside of the home work.

2. Conventional career pattern—Following the completion of school, and after working for a short period of time, the woman gets married and embarks on a career as a full-time homemaker.

3. Stable working career pattern—Following the completion of school, the woman goes into a job for the remainder of her working life.

4. The double-track career pattern—Following the completion of school, the woman secures a job and functions as a homemaker.

5. The interrupted career pattern—Following the completion of school, the woman follows a pattern of work, marriage, raising of children, and return to work.

6. The unstable career pattern—Following the completion of school, the woman embarks on a career pattern similar to that of unstable career-oriented men, except with the inclusion of homemaking and childrearing responsibilities.

7. Multiple-trial career pattern—This pattern is the same for women as it is for men.

Certainly, the percentage of people following each of these career patterns has changed considerably over the years. The percentage of women following the stable working and double track patterns has probably increased, whereas the number of women following the stable homemaking career has probably declined. Nevertheless, these typical patterns provide professionals with information useful to their provision of career planning assistance.

Decision-Making Theories

Decision-making theories highlight the factors that influence individual choice about careers and often suggest a model by which these decisions *should* be made. The following section of this chapter will discuss three notable career decision-making theorists: H. B. Gelatt, John Krumboltz, and Vincent Harren.

H. B. Gelatt's Decision-Making Model

H. B. Gelatt was one of the first theorists to outline a theory of decision making that could be applied by professionals assisting clients in making vocational choices (Clarke, Gelatt, & Levine, 1965; Gelatt, 1962). Gelatt advocates use of a rational, step-by-step decision-making process to make vocational decisions. His theory is based upon the concepts of value, defined as the desirability of an object or outcome, and probability, defined as the likelihood that a given event will occur. The theory is based upon the earlier work of Bross (1953). As Bross had suggested, the decision-making process proposed by Gelatt involves a predictive system (a system used to assess alternatives, possible outcomes, and probabilities), a value system (a means by which possible outcomes can be weighted as to importance or desirability), and a decision criterion (a way to integrate and select an appropriate course of action). Four basic categories of information are necessary to make an informed decision: knowledge of possible alternative actions, possible outcomes of each of these actions (i.e., what is likely to happen if each of these alternative actions is implemented), a knowledge of the probability that each action will result in the expected outcome (i.e., how likely it is that each of the predicted outcomes associated with each alternative action will actually occur, if the action is implemented), and relative preferences (i.e., how desirable each of the predicted outcomes is).

Gelatt suggests that two types of decisions can be reached after all information has been processed: a terminal decision and an investigatory decision. An investigatory decision is one in which more information is needed before a final decision can be made. Hence, an investigatory decision requires that the decision maker generate additional information about options, and resequence through the various decision-making steps. A terminal decision is a decision that is eventually implemented by the decision maker. However, the term *terminal* may be inappropriate for describing the true nature of this decision. Although a terminal decision is one that is implemented (and, hence, the decision maker is forced to confront the inevitable consequences of this decision), it is not irreversible. That is, at some later point in time, the decision maker will assess the suitability of the decision (i.e., Did the decision result in the predicted outcomes? Am I satisfied with the decision that I made? etc.). If, based upon this assessment, the decision maker is dissatisfied with the terminal decision, he or she will consider making another decision that will, in essence, reverse the initial one.

Consider, for example, a high school student who, after processing and weighing the college options, decides to go to a large, urban university because of the university's status, and because of the availability of cultural and recreational opportunities in the urban area. After the freshman year, the student finds he or she is dissatisfied with the lack of individual attention students at this large university receive from faculty, the faculty's emphasis on research and graduate-level teaching rather than undergraduate education, the lack of personalization, and the high crime rate in the area. The student simply decides to reverse this terminal decision by transferring to a smaller university, in a suburban or rural, low crime area, at which faculty see their primary mission as undergraduate education rather than research, and at which class size is considerably smaller. Obviously, this involves a new decision and requires that the individual resequence through the steps in the decision-making model. Thus, it is important to recognize that no decisions are "terminal" from the perspective of being irreversible. Also, this scenario clearly illustrates the developmental nature of Gelatt's model. That is, decisions are not perceived to be static events that occur at a single point in time, but are perceived to be developmental in nature. The decision-making process is the process of making a series of decisions that are influenced by the past and have impact on decisions made in both the immediate and distant future.

A similar model proposed by Hohenshil, Levinson, and Buckland-Heer (1985) is depicted in Table 2-1. Following an identification of the decision to be made (Step 1), information about both the individual and the educational and work environment is collected via assessment (Step 2). This information is then used to identify realistic career options for the individual (Step 3). These options are explored and prioritized (Step 4). The individual then begins to pursue his or her preferred career option via coursework and work experiences (Step 5). The appropriateness of the preferred career option is continually evaluated by the individual as he or she progresses through the courses and work experiences (Step 6). Assuming the option continues to be viewed as appropriate, it is pursued (Step 7). However, if it is no longer viewed as appropriate for the individual, a secondary option is identified and pursued instead (Step 4).

Table 2-1.
Career Planning Model (Hohenshil, Levinson, and Buckland-Heer, 1985)

Step 1 — *Determine Decision to be Made*
  — Depends upon student's level of educational and psychological development

Step 2 — *Collect Appropriate Information*
  — Internal Information
        Interests
        Aptitudes
        Values
        Aspirations
        Achievement
        Personality
        Small/large motor coordination
  — External information
        Types of occupations available
        Personal requirements for entry
        Educational requirements
        Economic & social consequences
        Relation of curriculum to various career options
        Application process for entrance

Step 3 — *Generate Alternative Career Options*

Step 4 — *Select Primary Alternative & Specify Secondary Alternatives*

Step 5 — *Reality Testing in Sheltered Environment*
        School courses
        Co-op programs
        Simulated work experience
        Observation

Step 6 — *Evaluate Results of Reality Testing*

Step 7 — *Continue to Pursue Primary Alternative*
        or
        Return to Step 4 to consider secondary career alternatives

Note. From *Best Practices in School Psychology* (p. 217) by T. H. Hohenshil, E. M. Levinson, and K. Buckland-Heer, 1985. Kent, OH: National Association of School Psychologists. Copyright 1985 by National Association of School Psychologists. Reprinted by permission.

Krumboltz' Social Learning Theory

Social learning theory, as proposed by Krumboltz (1979), a colleague of Gelatt's, attempts to explain how educational and vocational skills and preferences develop and how decisions are made in each of these areas.

The theory, based upon the work of Bandura (1977) and others, utilizes behavioral and learning principles, such as reinforcement, punishment, and modeling, to explain vocational choice.

Four major factors are believed to influence career choice:

1. Genetic endowment and special abilities — Inherited characteristics like sex, race, physical appearance and coordination, and special skills that may develop as a result of genetic predisposition are all believed to have a role in career choice. Depending upon these factors, eventual functioning in certain careers may either be facilitated or restricted. For example, the history of sex and racial discrimination in employment practices may either increase or decrease the likelihood of a female (or male) being employed in a given occupation.

2. Environmental conditions and events — Factors like the types of jobs and job-training opportunities available; organizational employment practices and regulations; labor laws; technological developments; neighborhood, community, and educational influences; natural events like earthquakes and floods; or availability (or lack thereof) of natural resources will all influence eventual occupational selection and functioning to some extent. These are all well beyond the control of the individual, but will influence the individual nonetheless.

3. Learning experiences — All previous learning experiences that have occurred as a result of environmental interaction have some degree of influence on career choice. *Instrumental* learning experiences refer to those experiences in which the individual acts on the environment to produce some consequence. Learning is based upon the consequences experienced. Educational and occupational skills are learned this way. *Associative* learning experiences refer to those experiences in which the individual reacts or responds to external environmental stimuli. Learning via classical conditioning or via modeling are examples of associative learning.

4. Task approach skills — These are skills that an individual has developed over time that s/he uses when approaching any new task or activity. Examples of task approach skills are abilities, values, work habits, emotional responsiveness, or cognitive processes. These task approach skills influence the outcome of the tasks or problems confronted by the individual and are, themselves, modified by these experiences.

Based upon the relatively unique set of experiences an individual has throughout his or her life, one develops:

1. Self-observation generalizations — Overt or covert evaluations of one's actual or perceived performance on tasks. These are made on the basis

of learned standards and may or may not be accurate. Self-observation generalizations are, in a sense, self-perceptions that are used to make judgments about the probabilities for success in a given occupation. For example, if a person were to possess the competencies necessary for successful performance in a given occupation, but constantly compared him- or herself to others who possessed superior competencies, he or she might conclude that he or she did not possess the necessary competencies and, hence, might rule out that occupational choice. Self-observation generalizations are crucial to occupational choice.

2. Task approach skills—Abilities, values, work habits, cognitive processes, emotional responsiveness, etc., used to make overt and covert predictions about future events and influence the development of self-observation generalizations.

3. Actions—Implementations of behavior that produce certain consequences influencing future behavior. Examples are applying for admission into a training program, or changing jobs.

Thus, Krumboltz suggests that genetically determined traits and abilities interact with environmental conditions and learning experiences to influence the development of self-observational generalizations and task approach skills. These self-observation generalizations and task approach skills are used to make decisions and to take actions, the outcomes and consequences of which modify these characteristics and influence later decisions and actions. From a more practical and pragmatic perspective, social learning theory suggests that individuals are more or less likely to choose a particular occupation depending upon whether they have been positively reinforced (experienced positive consequences) or punished (experienced negative consequences) as a result of having engaged in activities and tasks associated in some way with that particular occupation *and/or* whether they have observed a respected and important other person reinforced or punished as a result of having engaged in activities and tasks associated in some way with that occupation.

In assisting clients in making career decisions, Krumboltz and Baker (1973) recommended that the client and counselor follow the following steps:

1. Define the problem and the client's goals.
2. Agree mutually to achieve counseling goals.
3. Generate alternative problem solutions.
4. Collect information about alternatives.
5. Examine the consequences of the alternatives.
6. Reevaluate goals, alternatives, and consequences.

7. Make a decision or tentatively select an alternative based on new developments and new opportunities.

8. Generalize the decision-making process to new problems.

Krumboltz and Hamel (1977) revised and simplified this model so as to render it appropriate for use with high school and college students. This revised model, called DECIDES, includes the following seven steps:

1. Define the problem.

2. Establish an action plan.

3. Clarify values.

4. Identify alternatives.

5. Discover probable outcomes.

6. Eliminate alternatives systematically.

7. Start action.

Social learning theory contains several implications for those professionals involved in establishing school-based vocational assessment and counseling programs. Among the implications cited by Krumboltz, Mitchell, and Jones (1976) are:

1. Career selection is a lifelong process that is influenced by a long and complex sequence of learning experiences, environmental events, and decisions.

2. Due to the complex factors influencing career selection, it is virtually impossible to predict any one individual's career choice.

3. Career indecision is a natural result of not having had sufficient career-relevant learning experiences, or of having had learning experiences that have resulted in the development of maladaptive behavior.

4. The responsibility of those professionals involved in assisting individuals in making vocational decisions is to help the individual learn a rational sequence of career decision-making skills, arrange an appropriate sequence of career-relevant exploratory experiences, and teach the individual how to evaluate the personal consequences of those learning experiences.

Harren's Decision-Making Model

Harren (1979a) proposed a decision-making model that was originally targeted to college students, but has since been used with high school students as well (Buck & Daniels, 1985). The theory is based partially upon the work of Tiedeman and his associates (Miller & Tiedeman, 1972; Tiedeman & O'Hara, 1963), partially upon the decision-making theory of Janis and Mann (1977), and partially upon the developmental theory of Chickering (1969). Harren's model is a theory of decision making that attempts to explain how decision making may vary among individuals as a function of the characteristics of the decision maker, the context in which the decision is being made, and the type of decision being made. As depicted in Figure 2-5, the model consists of four major components: decision-maker characteristics, developmental tasks, decision-making conditions, and the decision-making process.

Figure 2-5.
Harren Career Decision-Making Model

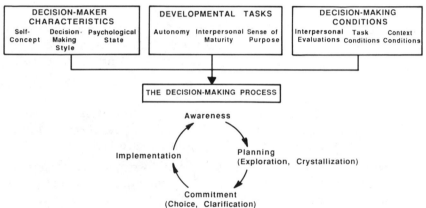

Note. Reprinted from the *Manual for the Assessment of Career Decision Making (ACDM)* by V. A. Harren, 1985, Los Angeles, CA: Western Psychological Services. Copyright 1985 by Western Psychological Services. Reprinted by permission.

Decision-making process.   Harren suggests that the process of decision making involves progression through four sequential stages: awareness, or the point at which one acknowledges the need or desire to make a decision; planning, or the stage at which one gathers, explores, and processes data relevant to making the decision; commitment, or the stage at which one commits to a course of action; and implementation, or the stage during which one carries out the actions necessary to implement the decision.

Decision-making characteristics.   Harren suggests that the decision-making process outlined above is influenced by three major characteristics of the individual making the decision: self-concept, psychological state, and decision-making style. Self-concept refers to "vocationally relevant attitudes or traits which the person attributes to him or herself" (Harren, 1979b; p. 124). Psychological state refers to the degree of anxiety and other emotionality evoked in the decision maker as a function of other decision-making characteristics or conditions. Style refers to the manner in which an individual characteristically responds to decision-making situations. Harren identifies three decision-making styles: rational, intuitive, and dependent.

Rational — This decision-making style is characterized by a logical, systematic processing of facts and other bits of information.

Intuitive — This decision-making style is characterized by reliance on feelings, emotions (intuition), and "gut reactions."

Dependent — This decision-making style is characterized by denial of personal responsibility, and reliance on others in decision making.

Decision-making tasks. Harren believes that one's ability to make successful decisions depends, in part, on the individual having accomplished certain developmental tasks. These developmental tasks, adapted from Chickering (1969), are: autonomy, interpersonal maturity, and sense of purpose.

Autonomy — Autonomy involves the capacity to be relatively free of the need for emotional support and approval of others, and of possessing the capacity to engage in self-directed behavior.

Interpersonal maturity — Interpersonal maturity refers to the capacity to develop mutually satisfying, trusting, and intimate relationships with others, and to possess the capacity for making long-term commitments.

Sense of purpose — Sense of purpose refers to the individual's awareness of goals and conscious planning of activities designed to accomplish those goals.

Decision-making conditions. Harren believes that the conditions under which a particular decision is to be made influence the decision-making process. Specifically, he cites the following conditions: interpersonal evaluations, task conditions, and context conditions.

Interpersonal evaluations — Interpersonal evaluations refer to the positive and negative reactions the decision maker receives from others.

Task conditions — Task conditions refer to the type of decision (i.e., decision-making task) being made by the individual.

Context conditions — Context conditions refer to the decision-maker's interpersonal relationships and the role that significant others play in the decision-making process.

The aspect of Harren's model that has received considerable research attention has been the formulation of the three decision-making styles proposed. Research studies have suggested that most individuals use some combination of the three styles proposed; however, one style may dominate the decision-making processes of an individual. Studies have suggested that rational decision-making styles lead to greater certainty and more satisfying decisions than do the other styles, that the intuitive decision-making style is somewhat less effective than is the rational style, and that the dependent style tends to lead to the least satisfying decisions (Buck, 1981; Harren, 1979a; Harren, Kass, Tinsley, & Moreland, 1978, 1979; Lunneborg, 1978; Moreland, Harren, Krimsky-Montague, & Tinsley, 1979; Rubinton, 1980). Buck and Daniels (1981) have suggested that dependent decision makers, in particular, may need some form of intervention or assistance with decision making and with the developmental tasks associated with the decision-making process. In order to assist professionals in assessing decision-making style, Buck and Daniels (1985) have developed the *Assessment of Career Decision Making*, an instrument based upon Harren's model.

A SYNTHESIS OF THEORIES

As you read through this chapter and were exposed to the different theoretical perspectives offered by the theorists discussed, you may have noticed some similarities. In fact, you may have said to yourself that several of the theorists seemed to be making the same points about the career development process, except using slightly different terms to describe components of the process or simply emphasizing different aspects of the process. It is fair to say that there is considerable overlap among the different theoretical perspectives discussed in this chapter, although fundamental differences exist as well. The following points are offered as a synthesis of the various theories discussed in this chapter:

1. Career development is a lifelong process that is influenced by both environmental and genetic factors.

2. Career development is a rather systematic process characterized by progression through a series of hierarchical stages, each of which has associated with it certain developmental tasks or objectives.

3. The career development process entails a series of ongoing, interrelated decisions that must be made by individuals. Decisions influence the career development of the individual, and the decision-making process itself is influenced by vocational/career experiences.

4. Personality development/traits assume an important role in career development/choice. Because different people possess different traits, and

because different traits are required for success in different occupations, certain types of people are best suited for certain types of occupations.

5. Self-concept, one's feeling about oneself (whether an accurate representation of one's personality characteristics and traits or not), influences career development and choice.

6. How well an individual adjusts to work is at least partially determined by the extent to which that individual is satisfied with the work, and the extent to which that individual performs the work well. Both job satisfaction and job performance may be influenced by the "match" that exists between one's personality traits and self-concept, and the demands and requirements inherent in one's work environment.

7. Because personality traits, self-concept, and demands inherent in the work environment all change somewhat over time, adjustment to a particular job or occupation is also likely to change over time, hence, rendering career development/choice a process characterized by continuous adjustment and readjustment.

CAREER DEVELOPMENT AMONG INDIVIDUALS WITH DISABILITIES

Little research has been conducted on the career development processes that characterize individuals with disabilities. The theoretical perspectives discussed in this chapter were meant to be applied to the general population and, as such, may have only limited application to those with disabilities. Osipow (1976) has suggested, for example, that the career development process among individuals with disabilities is less likely to be systematic, and is more likely to be stressful than is the career development process of individuals without disabilities. He also suggested that the career options of individuals with disabilities are likely to be more limited than are those for individuals without disabilities and are likely to be overly influenced by each individual's disability.

Because the theories discussed in this chapter attempt to explain factors that influence the career development of the general population, application of each of them in full to individuals with disabilities would clearly be inappropriate. The career development process among individuals with disabilities may not be nearly as orderly and as systematic as is suggested by developmental theory. Many individuals with disabilities have been restricted in their vocational exploration and limited in terms of their range of experiences. As a function of this, these individuals may progress through the developmental stages cited by Super and others at a slowed rate, or not at all. Although the developmental tasks cited in each of these stages *may* be equally applicable to individuals with disabilities, the ages at which these developmental tasks are confronted may deviate significantly from what is true for those without disabilities.

As do most trait-factor approaches, Holland's (1985) theory emphasizes testing, the provision of occupational information, and a process of "matching" the individual to a particular job. This perspective's emphasis on testing and on a self-directed approach to career guidance renders it inappropriate for many individuals with disabilities. As will be discussed in a future chapter, the utility of a test-match-place orientation to the vocational assessment and programming of individuals with severe disabilities has been seriously questioned. Likewise, the self-directedness inherent in decision-making theory limits its usefulness with many individuals with disabilities, especially those who lack the cognitive and intellectual capabilities required for independent use of occupational information.

Although inappropriate when applied in full, each of the theories discussed in this chapter offers a perspective that can be modified and adapted for use with individuals with disabilities. Age ranges aside, developmental theory would seem to suggest that increasing self- and occupational awareness, facilitating occupational exploration, implementing an occupational choice, and facilitating adjustment within that occupation would be sequentially appropriate developmental tasks for all individuals regardless of disability. The ages at which these tasks may be appropriate for a given individual may deviate significantly from what is the norm and may be influenced by type and severity of disability, and range of occupational and life experience. Decision-making theory may be most appropriately applied within this developmental framework at logical decision points, such as the time at which decisions need to be made about which occupational areas a particular individual should further explore, which of these are realistic options, and which of these options should be pursued. Although individuals with disabilities may not be able to apply such a decision-making approach independently, those assisting these individuals can utilize decision-making theory as a guide, and can involve the individual in the process to the maximum extent possible.

Trait-factor approaches seem to have their greatest utility within this decision-making framework, specifically in terms of identifying realistic options for individuals with disabilities. Testing and other forms of assessment can be utilized to identify the specific traits possessed by the individual and to determine how these traits compare to the traits required for successful adjustment to various occupations and jobs. From such an assessment, realistic options can be identified. The social learning perspective offered by Krumboltz would seem to have its greatest utility in training individuals with disabilities to function within a previously identified and appropriate occupational training program or job. The behavioral and learning principles that form the foundation of social learning theory can be used to aid in acquisition of the skills necessary to complete the vocationally appropriate developmental tasks specified in developmental theory. In Figure 2-6 the interrelationship among and application of the various career development theories discussed are shown as applied to individuals with disabilities.

Figure 2-6.
*Interrelationships Among and Application of
Vocational Theories to Individuals with Disabilities*

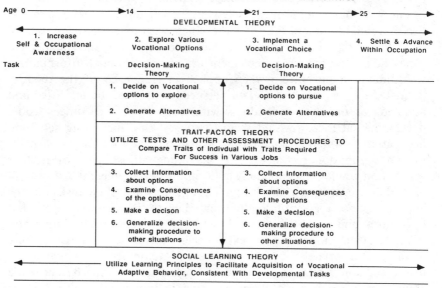

SUMMARY

Career development theory provides a foundation for the design and implementation of vocational assessment programs. It provides guidance as to what individual traits should be assessed and at what point in a student's educational career these traits are most appropriately evaluated. Career development theory also provides users of assessment results with a basis for the interpretation of these data and increases the likelihood that assessment results will be validly interpreted.

The various theoretical perspectives reviewed suggest that career development is a continuous, ongoing process. Assessment programs must reflect this characteristic and must be dynamic rather than static in nature. Career development theory offers guidelines as to the career-related objectives and tasks confronting students at given points in their educational careers.

Assessment programs must be developed with these age-appropriate developmental tasks in mind and should permit an assessment of the extent to which an individual student has mastered these career-related objectives. An individual student's inability to master career development objectives in a timely fashion may indicate a need for career assistance and for more involved vocational intervention.

Career development theory also provides direction relative to the traits that need to be assessed and considered when making vocational decisions. Clearly, the theoretical perspectives reviewed in this chapter emphasize the importance of personality traits, self-concept, and decision-making skills in the career development process. Hence, an assessment of a student's personality traits (e.g., interests, abilities, temperaments, values, work habits) and of the extent to which the student possesses a realistic understanding and acceptance of these traits (self-concept) and is capable of utilizing a rational decision-making approach to make realistic and informed career decisions should form the basis for the development of any vocational assessment program. In summary, career development theory provides a foundation upon which vocational assessment programs, and any career-related interventions that emanate from such assessment, should be established and implemented.

REFERENCES

Bandura, A. (1977). *Social learning theory.* Englewood Cliffs, NJ: Prentice-Hall.

Borgen, F. H., Weiss, D. J., Tinsley, H. E., Dawis, R. V., & Lofquist, L. H. (1972). Occupational reinforcer patterns: Vol. II. *Minnesota Studies in Vocational Rehabilitation, No. XXIX.* Minneapolis: Industrial Relations Center, University of Minnesota.

Bross, I. D. (1953). *Design for decision.* New York: Macmillan.

Buck, J. N. (1981). Influence of identity and decision-making style on the career decision-making process (Doctoral dissertation, Southern Illinois University at Carbondale, 1981). *Dissertation Abstracts International, 42,* 2027A. (University Microfilms No. 81-22, 622)

Buck, J. N., & Daniels, M. H. (1981). The importance of career in adult development. In V. A. Harren, M. H. Daniels, & J. N. Buck (Eds.), *New directions for student services: Facilitating students' career development.* San Francisco: Jossey-Bass.

Buck, J. N., & Daniels, M. H. (1985). *Manual for the assessment of career decision making.* Los Angeles: Western Psychological Services.

Buehler, C. (1933). *Der mensch liche lebenslauf als psychologisch es problem.* Leipzig: Hirzel.

Chickering, A. W. (1969). *Education and identity.* San Francisco: Jossey-Bass.

Clarke, R., Gelatt, H. B., & Levine, L. A. (1965). A decision-making paradigm for local guidance research. *Personnel and Guidance Journal, 44,* 40-51.

Cole, J. A. (1975). *A study of person-environment interactions in a school system.* Unpublished master's thesis, University of Melbourne.

Coles, R. (1978). Work and self-respect. In E. H. Erikson (Ed.), *Adulthood.* New York: Norton.

Dawis, R. V., England, G. W., & Lofquist, L. H. (1964). A theory of work adjustment. *Minnesota Studies in Vocational Rehabilitation*, No. XV. Minneapolis: Industrial Relations Center, University of Minnesota.

Dawis, R. V., Lofquist, L. H., & Weiss, D. J. (1968). A theory of work adjustment. A revision. *Minnesota Studies in Vocational Rehabilitation,* No. XXIII. Minneapolis: Industrial Relations Center, University of Minnesota.

Dore, R., & Meacham, M. (1973). Self-concept and interests related to job satisfaction of managers. *Personnel Psychology, 26,* 49-59.

Elton, C. F. (1971). The interaction of environment and personality: A test of Holland's theory. *Journal of Vocational Behavior, 2,* 114-118.

Gay, E. G., Weiss, D. J., Hendel, D. D., Dawis, R. V., & Lofquist, L. H. (1971). Manual for the Minnesota Importance Questionnaire. *Minnesota Studies in Vocational Rehabilitation,* No. XXVIII. Minneapolis: Industrial Relations Center, University of Minnesota.

Gelatt, H. B. (1962). Decision making: A conceptual frame of reference for counseling. *Journal of Counseling Psychology, 9,* 240-245.

Ginzberg, E., Ginsburg, S. W., Axelrad, S., & Herma, J. L. (1951). *Occupational choice: An approach to a general theory.* New York: Columbia University Press.

Gottfredson, G. D. (1977). Career stability and redirection in adulthood. *Journal of Applied Psychology, 62,* 436-445.

Gottfredson, G. D. (1981, August). *Why don't interests predict job satisfaction better than they do?* Paper presented at American Psychological Association Convention, Los Angeles, CA.

Gottfredson, G. D., Holland, J. L., & Ogawa, G. D. (1982). *Dictionary of Holland occupational codes.* Palo Alto, CA: Consulting Psychologists Press.

Greenhaus, J. H. (1971). Self-esteem as an influence on occupational choice and occupational satisfaction. *Journal of Vocational Behavior, 1,* 75-83.

Harren, V. A. (1979a). A model of career decision making for college students. *Journal of Vocational Behavior, 14,* 119-133.

Harren, V. A. (1979b). *The influence of sex roles and cognitive styles on the career decision making of college men and women* (Project Final Report, Project No. NIEG-76-0079). Carbondale: Southern Illinois University.

Harren, V. A., Kass, R. A., Tinsley, H. E. A., & Moreland, J. R. (1978). Influence of sex role attitudes and cognitive styles on career decision making. *Journal of Counseling Psychology, 25,* 390-398.

Harren, V. A., Kass, R. A., Tinsley, H. E. A., & Moreland, J. R. (1979). Influence of gender, sex role attitudes and cognitive complexity on gender-dominant career choices. *Journal of Counseling Psychology, 26,* 227-234.

Hener, T., & Meir, E. I. (1981). Congruency, consistency and differentiation as predictors of job satisfaction within the nursing occupation. *Journal of Vocational Behavior, 18,* 304-309.

Hohenshil, T. H., Levinson, E. M., & Buckland-Heer, K. (1985). Best practices in vocational assessment for handicapped students. In J. Grimes & A. Thomas (Eds.), *Best practices in school psychology.* Washington, DC: National Association of School Psychologists.

Holland, J. L. (1966). *The psychology of vocational choice.* Waltham, MA: Blaisdell.

Holland, J. L. (1968). Explorations of a theory of vocational choice: IV. Vocational preferences and their relation to occupational images, daydreams, and personality. *Vocational Guidance Quarterly,* published in four parts in Summer, Autumn, and Winter issues.

Holland, J. L. (1973). Some practical remedies for providing vocational guidance for everyone. *Center for the Study of Social Organization of Schools,* 163.

Holland, J. L. (1985). *The Self-Directed Search professional manual — 1985 edition.* Odessa, FL: Psychological Assessment Resources.

Isaacson, L. E. (1986). *Career information in counseling and career development* (4th ed.). Boston: Allyn and Bacon.

Janis, I. L., & Mann, L. (1977). *Decision making: A psychological analysis of conflict, choice and commitment.* New York: Free Press.

Kalanidi, M. S., & Deivasenapathy, P. (1980). Self-concept and job satisfaction among the self-employed. *Psychological Studies, 25*(1), 39-41.

Katz, M. (1963). *Decision and values: A rationale for secondary school guidance.* New York: College Entrance Examination Board.

Krumboltz, J. D. (1979). A social learning theory of career decision making. In A. M. Mitchell, G. B. Jones, & J. D. Krumboltz (Eds.), *Social learning and career decision making.* Cranston, RI: Carroll Press.

Krumboltz, J. D., & Baker, R. (1973). Behavioral counseling for vocational decisions. In H. Borow (Ed.), *Career guidance for a new age.* Boston: Houghton Mifflin.

Krumboltz, J. D., & Hamel, D. A. (1977). *Guide to career decision making skills.* New York: College Entrance Examination Board.

Krumboltz, J. D., Mitchell, A. M., & Jones, G. B. (1976). A social learning theory of career selection. *The Counseling Psychologist, 6,* 71-80.

Lofquist, L. H., & Dawis, R. V. (1984). *A psychological theory of work adjustment.* Minneapolis: Industrial Relations Center, University of Minnesota.

Lunneborg, P. W. (1978). Sex and career decision-making styles. *Journal of Counseling Psychology, 25,* 299-305.

Maslow, A. H. (1954). *Motivation and personality.* New York: Harper & Row.

Meir, E. I., & Erez, M. (1981). Fostering a career in engineering. *Journal of Vocational Behavior, 18,* 115-120.

Miller, A. L., & Tiedeman, D. V. (1972). Decision making for the '70s: The cubing of the Tiedeman paradigm and its application in career education. *Focus on Guidance, 5,* 1-16.

Moreland, J. R., Harren, V. A., Krimsky-Montague, E., & Tinsley, H. E. A. (1979). Sex role self-concept and career decision making. *Journal of Couseling Psychology, 26,* 329-336.

Morrow, J. M., Jr. (1971) A test of Holland's theory. *Journal of Counseling Psychology, 18,* 422-425.

Mount, M. K., & Muchinsky, P. M. (1978). Concurrent validation of Holland's hexagonal model with occupational workers. *Journal of Vocational Behavior, 13,* 84-100.

Nafziger, D. H., Holland, J. L., & Gottfredson, G. D. (1975). Student-college congruency as a predictor of satisfaction. *Journal of Counseling Psychology, 22,* 132-139.

Norris, W., Hatch, R. N., Engelkes, J. R., & Winborn, B. B. (1979). *The career information service* (4th edition). Chicago: Rand McNally.

Osipow, S. H. (1976). Vocational development problems of the disabled. In H. Rusalem & D. Malikan (Eds.), *Contemporary vocational rehabilitation.* New York: New York University Press.

Parsons, F. (1909). *Choosing a vocation.* Boston: Houghton Mifflin.

Roe, A. (1949). Analysis of group Rorschachs of biologists. *Journal of Projective Techniques, 13,* 25-43.

Roe, A. (1950). Analysis of group Rorschachs of physical scientists. *Journal of Projective Techniques, 14,* 385-398.

Roe, A. (1951). A psychological study of eminent physical scientists. *Genetic Psychology Monograph, 43,* 121-239.

Roe, A. (1952). Analysis of group Rorschachs of psychologists and anthropologists. *Journal of Projective Techniques, 16*(2). (Whole No. 352)

Roe, A. (1956). *The psychology of occupations.* New York: Wiley.

Roe, A., & Siegelman, M. (1964). The origin of interests. *APGA Inquiry Studies,* No. 1. Washington, DC: American Personnel and Guidance Association.

Rubinton, N. (1980). Instruction in career decision making and decision-making styles. *Journal of Counseling Psychology, 26,* 581-588.

Sears, S. (1982). A definition of career guidance terms: A National Vocational Guidance Association perspective. *Vocational Guidance Quarterly, 31,* 137-143.

Seligman, L. (1980). *Assessment in developmental career counseling.* Cranston, RI: Carroll Press.

Snyder, C. D., & Ferguson, L. W. (1976). Self-concept and job satisfaction. *Psychological Reports, 38*(2), 603-610.

Super, D. (1957). *The psychology of careers.* New York: Harper & Row.

Super, D. E. (1942). *The dynamics of vocational adjustment.* New York: Harper.

Tiedeman, D. V., & O'Hara, R. P. (1963). *Career development: Choice and adjustment.* New York: College Entrance Examination Board.

Vandergoot, D. (1987). Placement and career development in rehabilitation. In R. M. Parker (Ed.), *Rehabilitation counseling.* Austin, TX: Pro-Ed.

Walsh, W. B., & Lewis, R. O. (1972). Consistent, inconsistent, and undecided career preferences and personality. *Journal of Vocational Behavior, 2,* 309-316.

Weinrach, S. G. (1979). *Career counseling: Theoretical and practical perspectives.* New York: McGraw-Hill.

Weiss, D. J., Dawis, R. V., England, G. W., & Lofquist, L. H. (1967). Manual for the Minnesota Satisfaction Questionnaire. *Minnesota Studies in Vocational Rehabilitation,* No. XXI. Minneapolis: Industrial Relations Center, University of Minnesota.

Werner, W. E. (1974). Effect of role choice on vocational high school students. *Journal of Vocational Behavior, 4,* 77-84.

Wiggins, J. D. (1976). The relation of job satisfaction to vocational preferences among teachers of the educable mentally retarded. *Journal of Vocational Behavior, 4,* 13-18.

Wiggins, J. D., & Westlander, D. L. (1977). Expressed vocational choices and later employment compared with Vocational Preference Inventory and Kuder Preference Record-Vocational Scores. *Journal of Vocational Behavior, 11,* 158-165.

3 GENERAL CONSIDERATIONS IN ASSESSMENT

Vocational assessment is a process whereby human traits (e.g., intelligence, personality characteristics, vocational interests, aptitudes) are measured, and inferences (e.g., vocational recommendations) are made about an individual based upon these measurements. The accuracy of the assessment process is largely influenced by the accuracy of the measuring devices used and the skills of the individual administering the measures. To illustrate the importance of these two factors, suppose you are having your blood pressure taken as part of a comprehensive physical examination. If the apparatus used to take your blood pressure is faulty (it yields inaccurate measures), you may be incorrectly diagnosed as having high (or low) blood pressure. As a function of this, you may be unneccesarily placed on medication which, over a period of time, may have a negative impact on your health (obviously, faulty equipment could also lead to dangerously high or low blood pressure going undetected.) Similarly, if the apparatus is not faulty, but the measures yielded are misread or misinterpreted by inadequately trained medical personnel, your health may also be adversely affected.

Vocational assessments can be viewed in a similar fashion. If faulty or inaccurate instruments are used to gather vocational assessment data, and measures from these instruments are used in vocational planning, it is likely that a student's vocational development will be negatively affected as a result of the inappropriate programming that will emanate from use of inaccurate data. However, accurate instruments may yield accurate measures but do not, in and of themselves, guarantee that results will be interpreted and used accurately by professionals involved in the vocational assessment process. Only in the hands of competent and skilled assessment professionals may accurate vocational assessment instruments yield data that may significantly and positively contribute to a student's vocational development.

The purpose of this chapter is to review basic considerations in assessment, all of which are important in ensuring that (a) the assessment techniques selected to be used in a vocational assessment program will yield relatively accurate measures and (b) the measures emanating from these assessment techniques will be interpreted and used in an appropriate manner. Basic assumptions underlying assessment practice, psychometric properties of measuring devices (reliability, validity, standardization of norm-referenced tests), and situational and background variables likely to influence assessment results will be discussed. The chapter will conclude with a discussion of issues that need to be considered when selecting, using, and interpreting assessment data; ethical and legal considerations in assessment; and with a discussion of the unique issues surrounding the use of computerized assessment techniques.

TESTING VS. ASSESSMENT

At the outset, it is important to distinguish between what is meant by *testing* and *assessment*. According to the joint committee of the American Psychological Association, the American Educational Research Association, and the National Council on Measurement in Education (as cited in Salvia & Ysseldyke, 1985), a test "may be thought of as a set of tasks or questions intended to elicit particular types of behaviors when presented under standardized conditions, and to yield scores that have desirable psychometric properties" (p. 4). Salvia and Ysseldyke (1978) suggest that a test is simply a set of questions (or tasks), administered in a standardized manner, that yields a score (the end product of the test). In contrast, assessment refers to a much broader and more comprehensive data-gathering process designed to assist professionals in making decisions about individuals. Thus, tests may be considered data-gathering tools that can be used as part of an assessment. Examples of other tools that can be used to gather data as part of an assessment are interviews, observations, rating scales/checklists, work samples, and simulated work experiences. These other data-gathering techniques will be discussed in Chapter 4.

Although the term *test* will be used routinely in this chapter, you should understand that, in most instances, the issues that pertain to selecting and interpreting tests also apply to the selection and use of other assessment tools and to interpreting the data yielded thereby. That is, concerns about reliability and validity (to be discussed in this chapter) are as important when considering the use of rating scales, interviews, work samples, and observations as they are when considering the use of tests. Information presented in this chapter should be interpreted accordingly.

ASSUMPTIONS UNDERLYING ASSESSMENT

Salvia and Ysseldyke (1991) identify five basic assumptions that underlie all valid assessments of students. If any of the following assumptions are not met, assessment results may be invalid.

The Person Administering a Test Is Skilled

When test scores are interpreted and used by transdisciplinary teams in vocational planning, there is an inherent assumption that the test was administered, scored, and interpreted accurately. However, this usually depends upon the training, experience, and skills possessed by the person administering the test. The test administrator must be knowledgeable about general assessment practices and must also be familiar with the administration guidelines of the test being used. In examining this issue, several questions should be answered including: Is the test administrator knowledgeable about situational factors (to be discussed shortly) that are likely to affect test performance, and does (s)he arrange the testing conditions so as to elicit an optimum but representative level of performance? That is, has adequate rapport been established? Are distractions reduced? Are the lighting, temperature, and ventilation adequate, and so on? Is the test administrator knowledgeable about the specific "rules" or guidelines inherent in administering, scoring, and interpreting the particular test being used? How much experience does the test administrator have in administering this (or other) tests? The less experienced and skilled an individual is, both in regard to general testing and assessment practice, as well as in regard to administering, scoring, and interpreting the particular test being used, the less likely it is that accurate results will be obtained from the test.

As Salvia and Ysseldyke (1991) infer, each member of a transdisciplinary assessment team should recognize and operate within the confines of their training and expertise. Although several members of the team may have been trained in and may be knowledgeable about general assessment practice, team members may have varying levels of expertise with different kinds of tests. For example, psychologists may be more experienced in administering, scoring, and interpreting intelligence and personality tests, whereas vocational evaluators may be more experienced in administering, scoring, and interpreting vocational aptitude and interest tests. Prior training, experience, and expertise of the various professionals serving on the transdisciplinary vocational assessment team should be considered when assigning testing (and other assessment) responsibilities. In many states, the administration of certain tests requires that an individual possess a certain license or certification. These requirements should also be considered when assigning testing (and other assessment) responsibilities to team members.

Error Will Be Present

All educational, psychological, and vocational measures contain some degree of error. Hence, test scores should not be interpreted rigidly and should be interpreted with some degree of flexibility. *No* test score is a *perfectly accurate* measure of the trait being assessed. Rarely do psychological, educational, or vocational tests yield perfectly stable and consistent measures. Unfortunately, the scale I use to weigh myself in the morning is a good example of a less than "perfectly accurate measure." When I get on and off the same scale twice in rapid succession, I generally get two different readings (these days, anywhere between 145–148 lbs.). Have I actually gained or lost weight in that nanosecond? Of course not! What is my actual weight? Who knows? Please understand that if I had only weighed myself once, I would have only received one reading and might have been tempted to assume that this one reading was the *one* perfectly accurate estimate of my weight. However, I know my scale yields different measures upon multiple weighings, and I know I can never be sure which of these different measures (if any) is my current weight. Therefore I take multiple weighings, average them, and consider the average an estimate of my current weight.

Due to the error inherent in them, psychological, educational, and vocational tests will yield different scores when administered several times to the same student. Thus, we can never be sure that the score obtained on a test is the *one* score that perfectly accurately estimates the degree to which the student currently possesses the trait being measured by the test. Hence, we must treat scores as estimates and interpret these scores with some degree of flexibility. The reliability of a test (to be discussed later) estimates the extent to which the test produces stable and consistent scores. The more stable the results of a test, the more closely an obtained score resembles the student's current "true" score on what is being measured. As we will see, reliability estimates can be combined with a score yielded by a test to construct a *confidence interval* within which we can be confident the student's current "true" score on the test falls.

Because of the lack of precision with which we typically measure human traits, an attempt should be made to confirm the results of one assessment tool designed to measure a particular trait with the results of another assessment tool (preferably administered by a different member of the transdisciplinary vocational assessment team) designed to measure the *same* trait. For example, an attempt should be made to confirm the results of a pencil-and-paper vocational interest survey by interviewing the student and the student's parents and by observing the student during free (leisure) time. If the results of the test are consistent with the information gleaned from interviews and observations, more confidence can be placed in the test results than would have been the case if only the test had been used to measure interests. This "triangulation" of data-gathering techniques will be discussed in more detail in the next chapter.

Acculturation Is Comparable

Scores yielded by standardized norm-referenced tests are a reflection of how a particular student performed in comparison to students who made up the normative sample of the test. In order for this comparison to be fair (and, hence, for the score to be a fairly accurate measure of a particular trait), the background experiences of the child being tested must be comparable to the background experiences of the children who comprise the reference (norm) group. If acculturation of the tested individual differs markedly from the acculturation of the individuals comprising the norm group of the test, performance comparisons are inappropriate and unfair, and the score yielded by the test may be misleading.

Consider, for example, the differences in the backgrounds between mentally retarded individuals and individuals of average intelligence. Compared with individuals of average intelligence, mentally retarded individuals tend not to be provided with the same range or diversity of experiences and tend not to profit or learn as well from their experiences. Unfortunately, many vocational interest inventories are normed on only nonhandicapped populations and exclude mentally retarded students from their standardization samples. Because interests are to some extent dependent on experience, and because mentally retarded individuals have experienced less (and profited and learned less from these experiences) than nonhandicapped individuals of the same age, use of such interest inventories with mentally retarded individuals yields misleading results.

Whereas the nonhandicapped students who comprise the norm group have had a wide variety of experiences that have led to the development of interest patterns (which are then reflected in their test performance), the mentally retarded individual lacks comparable experiences (and, hence, hasn't developed the same range of interests). In comparison, then, the mentally retarded individual is at a considerable disadvantage in demonstrating interests on the test and tends to demonstrate considerably less interest across inventory areas. Practically speaking, administering an interest inventory normed on nonhandicapped individuals to a mentally retarded individual often results in a uniform pattern of low interest scores across all interest areas. Such low scores are more reflective of limited experience or exposure than of limited interest and probably should be interpreted as such. A fairer comparison would be to compare the interests of the mentally retarded individual to the interests of other mentally retarded students of the same age. Assuming that the background experiences of the mentally retarded students comprising the norm group were roughly comparable to those of the student being tested, scores would be more reflective of interests than of experiential differences. The point made here is that it is unfair to compare students whose background and experiences are markedly different. When selecting a standardized norm-referenced test for use with a particular student, it is important to ensure that the background and experiences of the students comprising the norm group do not differ markedly from those of the students to whom the test is being administered.

Behavior Sampling Is Adequate

Would you consider a test composed of only simple addition problems to be a "mathematics" achievement test? Because the field of mathematics comprises more than simple addition, such a test does not adequately represent all that we believe mathematics to be. Hence, such a test could not be considered to be a test of mathematics. It would best be described as a test of addition.

When we interpret a test score, we are assuming that the score is reflective of what the test purports to measure. We assume that scores from intelligence tests reflect "intelligence," scores from interest inventories reflect "interests," and so on. However, this assumption is true only when the test adequately samples all behavior we typically associate with the construct being measured by the test. A test that only requires a student to read printed words aloud is best thought of as a test of "oral reading" rather than a test of "reading," because we typically associate reading with the ability to comprehend and understand the printed word, as well as the ability to read aloud. As Salvia and Ysseldyke (1991) suggest, we can not rely on a test's name in defining what the test measures. We must analyze the content of the test and ensure that the items adequately reflect the trait or traits supposedly being measured. This issue of content validity will be discussed later in more detail.

Present Behavior Is Observed, Future Behavior Is Inferred

Can we ever be sure that what we observe to be true today will also be true tomorrow? Obviously, there is no guarantee that this will be the case. We must remember, then, that test scores reflect what was true (we hope!) about a particular student at the time of testing. When we use these test scores at a later point in time for educational and vocational planning, we are inferring that what was true about the student at the time of testing is still true. Without readministering the test, however, we can never be certain that this is the case. For example, we may administer an interest inventory to a student toward the end of a school year and, based upon the results, recommend that the student be placed in a particular vocational education program the following year. When we do this, we must remember that we are inferring that the student's interests the following year will be the same as (or at least similar to) what they were on the day of testing. Without such an assumption, test scores are of limited value.

When using scores in this manner, however, we must understand (a) the extent to which scores on the test tend to fluctuate or change over time (this issue of test-retest reliability will be discussed later) and (b) the extent to which the trait being assessed by the test tends to change over time. For example, interests tend to be relatively unstable in junior high school and tend to stabilize in high school. Therefore, results of interest assessments need to be interpreted and used more cautiously at one level than at the other. Relatedly, scores on tests that tend to yield inconsistent results over time also need to be interpreted more cautiously than do those that yield more consistent results over time.

SITUATIONAL AND BACKGROUND FACTORS THAT INFLUENCE ASSESSMENT RESULTS

Once, prior to having surgery on a set of impacted wisdom teeth, a dental technician took my blood pressure. Curious as to what my blood pressure was, I asked. I was slightly alarmed at the response, in that my systolic pressure was considerably higher than it had ever been in my life. Afraid that I was on the verge of "the big one" (a heart attack), I remarked, "Isn't that a little high?" "Not when you are about to have some of the most painful oral surgery of your life," replied the technician. Thank God she didn't take *another* blood pressure reading! I've since learned that systolic pressure readings are somewhat more variable than are diastolic readings and are more influenced by situational and environmental variables. My interpretation of the score (and alarm) was simply the result of my lack of knowledge regarding the influence of situational and background factors on blood pressure readings.

In order to interpret assessment data properly, professionals must be aware of the various situational and background factors that may ultimately influence a student's performance on a particular test. Test scores should always be interpreted in light of such factors. The purpose of the following section is to discuss some of the factors likely to influence student test performance that must be considered by professionals when interpreting test scores.

Physical Environment

The physical environment in which testing is done is likely to influence test performance. Adequate lighting, heating, and ventilation must be present in order for a student to perform at an optimum level on a test. If a student is tested in a room where there are lots of other people, or lots of interesting and colorful wall hangings, students may be easily distracted and may respond to items in a haphazard and inconsistent manner. Instead of being motivated to perform optimally, students may be motivated to explore the "exciting" or "active" environment in which they now find themselves. Generally, movement and distractions should be eliminated, and in group testing the examiner should be as unobtrusive as is possible. To summarize, professionals must ensure that testing is done in a reasonably sized room in which adequate heating, lighting, and ventilation are present, and in which few distractions are evident.

Emotional Climate

Emotional climate refers to the degree of comfort a student feels in a testing situation. Although this is partially the result of the physical environment (a cramped and dark room can lead students to feel uncomfortable) and the student's personality (passive, withdrawn, and insecure students are likely to be uncomfortable despite other factors), it will be largely influenced by the relationship the professional has established with the student immediately prior to testing. In order to encourage optimum test performance, professionals must make the student feel at ease. This can be done by interacting informally with the student prior to initiating formal testing. Students can be asked what their interests are, what they do in their free time, or what they plan to do when they finish school. Students are often curious (and sometimes worried) about the testing experience. Hence, they should be told what the purpose of the testing is and how the results will be used. Students should be given the opportunity to ask any questions they may have about the testing, and should be given honest and direct answers. They should also be tested at a time that is convenient for them, if possible. (Testing students at undesirable times can lead to resentment, which may diminish motivation and lead to less than optimal test performance.) Generally, students should not be tested during lunch period, recess, gym class, or during an assembly or special program. Professionals should provide the student with lots of encouragement throughout the testing, but must do so without compromising the standardized testing procedures. Although students should not be provided with feedback as to the accuracy or desirability of their responses (this will bias their responding and may invalidate the testing), they should be praised for their effort.

Administration Practices and Test Usage

The type of test used (e.g., norm referenced vs. criterion referenced, paper-and-pencil vs. experiential, objective vs. open ended, group vs.

individual), the number of students administered the test at a given time, and the amount of testing done in any one sitting (without break) will also influence test performance. Some students may perform optimally on individually administered tests (perhaps because they need encouragement or continual monitoring) but not on group tests. Similarly, some students may be highly motivated to perform experiential tasks (work samples, for example) but "turned off" to paper-and-pencil tasks such as interest inventories. Because attention span varies, some students may experience fatigue quickly and may need more frequent breaks than other students in order to perform at an optimum level on a particular test. For these reasons, different assessment tools, preferably administered by different professionals, should be utilized to measure a given trait. (See the discussion of triangulation of data techniques in the next chapter.)

Examiner Skill

As alluded to previously, the expertise possessed by the examiner will influence the test score derived. Skill in organizing and arranging the test materials and test environment, skill in administering and scoring the test, and in motivating the student and managing the student's behavior will influence student test performance and, ultimately, the score derived from the test. Especially important in the administration of a standardized norm-referenced test is adherence to the standard administration procedures. Any deviation from these procedures is likely to result in invalid results.

Current and Past Life Circumstances of the Student

Assessment results must be considered in light of the current and past life circumstances experienced by the student. That is, the student's current health and nutrition, family life, and attitude at the time of testing, for example, are all likely to affect student performance on assessment measures. Similarly, significant events in the student's past such as deaths, divorces, or serious illnesses are also likely to influence his or her test performance. These factors must all be considered when interpreting and using assessment results. For these reasons, complete medical, social, and developmental histories should be a part of all comprehensive school-based vocational assessments.

PSYCHOMETRIC ISSUES IN ASSESSMENT

In order to understand and interpret assessment results properly, one must have a general understanding of basic descriptive statistics and psychometric and measurement principles. This section will briefly discuss measures of central tendency, measures of dispersion, normal curve theory, and correlation. It will also discuss the means by which standardized norm-referenced tests are developed, the various types of scores yielded by norm-referenced assessment instruments (and how these scores are interpreted), reliability (including a discussion of standard error of measurement and confidence intervals), and validity.

Basic Descriptive Statistics

It is necessary to have a basic understanding of descriptive statistics in order to evaluate and interpret the psychometric properties properly of instruments that might be considered for use (or are currently being used) in vocational assessment programs. The following discussion of measures of central tendency, measures of dispersion, normal curve theory, and correlation are not meant to be exhaustive. Rather, they are introductory in nature and meant to provide readers with an initial base of information pertinent to their understanding of the more complex topics of score interpretation, reliability, and validity.

Measures of Central Tendency

There are three common measures of central tendency: the mode, the median, and the mean. The mode is simply the most frequently occurring score in any distribution of scores. The median is the middle point in a set of scores and the point in a distribution where 50% of the scores lie above and 50% of the scores lie below the point. The mean is the arithmetic average of all the scores in the distribution. It is computed by simply adding up all of the scores in the distribution and dividing this sum by the number of scores in the distribution.

Consider the following set of scores: 1, 3, 5, 6, 7, 9, 9, 9, 10. The mode of this distribution is 9 (it occurs most frequently). The median of this distribution is 7 (half the scores are above 7 and half the scores are below 7). The mean of this distribution is 6.55 (the sum of these scores is 59; 59 divided by 9 scores = 6.55).

Measures of Dispersion

The more spread out scores are in a distribution, the less adequate is a measure of central tendency as a description of the set of scores. Measures of dispersion provide information about the degree of variability inherent in a set of scores and, combined with a measure of central tendency, provide a better understanding of the scores. There are three common measures of dispersion: the range, the variance, and the standard deviation. The range is simply the distance between the highest and lowest scores in the distribution (to compute the range, one simply subtracts the lowest score in the distribution from the highest score in the distribution). The range for the distribution 1, 3, 5, 6, 7, 9, 9, 9, 10 is 9 (10 − 1 = 9).

Both the variance and the standard deviation are statistical measures that provide information about the degree of spread or variability inherent in a distribution of scores. The standard deviation, which is a frequently cited statistic in test manuals, is the square root of the variance. (Conversely, the variance is equal to the standard deviation squared.) The computational formula for standard deviation is provided in Figure 3-1.

Normal Curve

Ever notice that there are so few people who are geniuses and so few people who are mentally retarded, and that most people have intelligence that falls somewhere in the middle of these two extremes? The reason for this is that intelligence, like so many other human and psychological traits, is normally distributed in the population. Simply put, most of us have an average amount of, any given trait. Very few of us have a lot of, or very little of, any given trait.

The "normal curve" (shown in Figure 3-2) pictorially represents the phenomenon of normal distribution and clearly depicts the notion that "most" people possess about an average amount of whatever is being measured. When we are measuring traits that we believe are normally distributed in the population, we can be relatively certain that a given percentage of "cases" (individuals) will fall between any two points in the distribution. For example, we know that roughly 68% of all cases will fall within one standard deviation of the mean (that is, ± one standard deviation from the mean). Similarly, we can be relatively sure that roughly 95% of cases will fall within two standard deviations of the mean. We also know that approximately 34% of all cases will fall between the mean and one standard deviation above the mean, and that approximately 13% of cases will fall between one and two standard deviations above the mean. The further away from the mean (average) one goes, the fewer cases one will find.

Correlation

Correlations assist in determining the degree of association or relationship that exists between variables. Correlation coefficients (symbolized by *r*) range between −1.00 and +1.00. The plus/minus sign in front of the value indicates the nature of the relationship that exists between the

Figure 3-1.
Computational Formula for Standard Deviation

$$S = \sqrt{\frac{\Sigma (X - \bar{X})^2}{N - 1}}$$

Where: Σ = sum of

X = raw score

$\bar{X}$ = mean

N = number of scores

Example. Find the standard deviation for the following distribution:
1, 2, 3, 4, 5

1) Compute the $\bar{X}$.

$$\bar{X} = \frac{\Sigma X}{N} = \frac{15}{5} = 3$$

2) Compute $(X - \bar{X})^2$ for each score.
$(1 - 3)^2 = 4$
$(2 - 3)^2 = 1$
$(3 - 3)^2 = 0$
$(4 - 3)^2 = 1$
$(5 - 3)^2 = 4$

3) Sum the scores computed in #2, divide this by the number of scores in the distribution, and take the square root of this number.

$$S = \sqrt{\frac{10}{5 - 1}}$$

$$S = \sqrt{\frac{10}{4}}$$

$$S = \sqrt{2.5}$$

$$S = 1.58$$

variables. A plus sign represents a positive relationship, meaning that high scores on one variable are associated with high scores on another variable and that low scores on one variable are associated with low scores on another variable. Intelligence and academic achievement are positively correlated. That is, the more intelligent a student is, the greater are the

Figure 3-2.
The Normal Curve

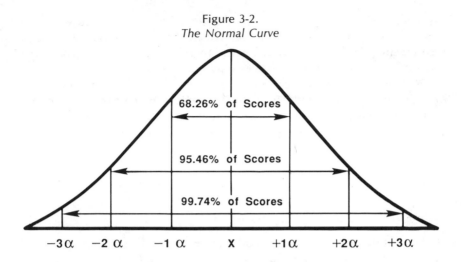

academic gains that student makes over a given period of time. Less intelligent students demonstrate smaller academic gains over the same period of time.

A minus sign in front of a correlation coefficient means that an inverse or negative relationship exists between variables. This means that high scores on one variable are associated with low scores on another variable, and that low scores on one variable are associated with high scores on the other variable. This summer, I've been pleased to learn that golf scores and golf handicaps are inversely related to the frequency with which one plays golf. That is, the more I've played, the lower my scores and handicap have become (and, by the way, low scores mean better golf).

The absolute value of the correlation coefficient (the number regardless of the sign in front of it) is reflective of the strength of the relationship that exists between variables. For example, two variables that correlate − .95 are more strongly related than are two variables that correlate + .90 (because .95 > .90; remember, the sign only depicts the *nature* of the relationship between variables).

Correlations by themselves provide limited information about cause–effect relationships. That is, two variables may be correlated but may not be directly related in a cause–effect way. Consider that there may be a positive relationship between ice cream sales and the homicide rate in New York City. As ice cream sales increase, the homicide rate increases. As ice cream sales decrease, the homicide rate decreases. Does ice cream cause homicide? Messrs. Carvel, Breyers, and Baskin & Robbins surely hope not! It certainly is unlikely that ice cream causes homicide despite the mathematical relationship that may exist between these two variables. It is more likely that a third variable, like temperature, may cause both to vary. That is, as the temperature increases, both the homicide rate and ice cream sales may increase. As the temperature decreases, both the homicide rate and ice cream sales may decrease.

Although correlations provide limited information about cause-and-effect relationships, they have predictive value. When two variables are highly correlated, one can be used to make predictions about the other. Because intelligence and academic achievement are highly correlated, we can (and do) use intelligence test scores to make predictions about how students will achieve in school.

Norm-Referenced Test Development

Norm-referenced instruments allow a respondent's performance to be compared to that of a specific group of individuals. In contrast, criterion-referenced instruments assess the extent to which an individual has mastered a particular set of, for example, skills or concepts. The majority of instruments that are typically used in school-based vocational assessment programs are norm referenced. Hence, the following discussion pertains largely to these types of instruments.

The development of norm-referenced tests usually involves the following steps:

1. Identification of Test Domain
   The first step in norm-referenced test construction is the selection of a topic around which test items are to be developed.

2. Identification of Test Purpose
   The second step in norm-referenced test construction is defining the purpose of the test. Usually, this will also involve identification of the test's target population. For example, a mathematics test may have the purpose of measuring math achievement (the degree to which one has acquired and mastered math concepts and skills) or math aptitude (the degree to which one has the potential to learn math concepts and skills). Similarly, the test may be developed for children and adolescents (ages 5–17, grades K–12) or for adults (ages 18 or above).

3. Test Items Are Written
   Test items are written based upon the test domain specified, the test's intended purpose, and the test's target population. It is particularly important to ensure that the test items adequately sample all behaviors associated with the test domain. To determine whether "behavior sampling" is adequate (or whether the test possesses content validity), a panel of experts in the field most closely associated with the domain of the

test will review the test items and render a judgment about the adequacy of item representativeness. (See discussion of behavior sampling and content validity elsewhere in this chapter.)

4. Field Testing Is Completed

Field testing involves administering test items to a sample of people who are representative of all those individuals for whom the test is to be used. A sample is representative of a population if the sample possesses the same characteristics as the population and possesses these characteristics to the same degree (or in the same proportion) as the population. Representativeness will be discussed later in more detail.

5. Item Analysis Is Completed

Following field testing, all test items are analyzed. An attempt is made to identify "good" items and "bad" items. Good items are items that are not too easy and not too hard for the sample of intended users. Good items are also items that produce the greatest variability of scores. Generally, these are items that are answered correctly by between 40% to 60% of the sample. If too high or too low a percentage of students in the sample answered the item correctly, the item would not adequately differentiate between high- and low-achieving students. Hence, an item analysis results in the discarding of certain items and a formulation of a set of final test items likely to result in optimum differentiation of students on the trait assessed by the test.

6. The Test Is Normed

The final list of items is administered to a (norm) group representative of those for whom the test was designed. This step is similar to field testing except that the final set of test items is used, and the sample of students on whom the test is normed is larger and generally more representative of the intended population than is the sample used in the field testing.

7. Norm Tables Are Constructed

Norm tables are constructed that allow an individual's score to be compared to all, or a selected group of, individuals upon whom the test was normed. For each age and grade range for which a table of norms is to be developed, the raw score mean and standard deviation are computed for all students of that age or grade in the normative sample. Based upon these raw score means and standard deviations (in combination with normal curve theory), norm tables are developed that assign certain standard scores to raw scores. These norm tables are then used to convert raw scores to standard scores, percentile ranks, or age or grade equivalents. These different types of scores will be discussed shortly.

8. Studies of Reliability and Validity Are Conducted
   The final step in norm-referenced test development is the initiation of reliability and validity studies (reliability and validity will be discussed shortly).

Adequacy of Norms

The adequacy of test norms depends upon several factors: the representativeness of the norm sample, the number of cases in the norm sample,
and the relevance of the norms (Salvia & Ysseldyke, 1978).

Representativeness

Of particular importance in norm-referenced test development is the
degree to which the sample used to develop the norms of a test is representative
of the population for whom the test was designed. As mentioned previously,
representativeness refers to the degree to which the sample used to develop
a test's norms "represents" the population for whom the test will be used.
More specifically, a sample is representative of a population if it possesses
the same characteristics as the population and possesses these characteristics
to the same degree or in the same proportion as does the population. As
Salvia and Ysseldyke (1991) state, representativeness hinges on two questions: Does the norm sample contain the same kinds of people as the population that the norms are intended to represent, and are the various kinds
of people present in the same proportion in the sample as they are in the
population of reference?

In evaluating representativeness, one must compare the demographic
characteristics of the normative sample with the demographic characteristics
of the test's target population. If the two are highly similar, one can conclude that the normative sample is probably representative of the target
population. If there are major discrepancies between the demographic
characteristics of the normative sample and target population, one must
conclude that the norms are probably not representative of the population and, hence, are inappropriate to use. According to Salvia and Ysseldyke
(1991), the demographic characteristics most important to consider are:
age, grade, sex, race, acculturation of parents, geographic region, and intelligence. Most test authors, in the test's manual, will provide evidence
of representativeness by comparing the norm sample and population on
these and other characteristics.

Number of Subjects

Norms that are developed from small samples of individuals are likely
to be unstable and inaccurate. Hence, adequate norms depend on whether

adequate numbers of individuals exist in the norm sample. Salvia and Ysseldyke (1991) suggest that a minimum of 100 individuals should exist in any norm sample. They suggest that if a test spans multiple years or grades and if norms are developed for different ages or grades, at least 100 individuals per age or grade should be present in the normative sample. Simply put, for each set of norm tables developed, a minimum of 100 subjects is needed.

Relevance of the Norms

According to Salvia and Ysseldyke (1991), relevance of norms refers to the extent to which the norms provide comparisons that are relevant given the purpose of the test. An achievement test that was designed to compare the math achievement of a 4th-grade student in Podunk County Schools to all 4th-graders nationally would need to have national norms. However, if the test was designed to compare a 4th-grader in Podunk to all 4th-graders in Podunk, it would need to possess local (Podunk) norms. Thus, one must assure that the norm group is one that allows comparisons to be made that are consistent with the purpose and nature of the test.

Types of Scores

Age and Grade Equivalents

Age equivalents and grade equivalents are derived by determining the average raw scores achieved by students of a particular age or students in a particular grade. If the average raw score of all students who are 6 years 3 months of age on a particular test is 36, then all students who take the test and achieve a raw score of 36 are assigned an age equivalent of 6 years 3 months. Similarly, if the average raw score of all students who are in their 3rd month of 11th grade and who take the test is 75, then any student who achieves a raw score of 75 on the test will be assigned a grade equivalent of 11.3 (3rd month of 11th grade). Hence, age equivalents and grade equivalents indicate that the student taking the test achieved a raw score equal to the average raw score achieved by students of that age or in that grade and who were included in the test's standardization sample.

As Sattler (1990) and Salvia and Ysseldyke (1991) have summarized, age and grade equivalents are problematic for several reasons. First, they are usually derived by interpolation and extrapolation, rather than by actually testing children who are of a particular age or who are in a particular grade. That is, in norming a test, I may include students who are beginning the 10th and 11th grades in my standardization sample. If the 10th-graders achieve an average raw score of 50, and the 11th-graders achieve an average raw score of 62, I may establish the following grade equivalents (assuming a 10-month school year):

Raw Score	Grade Equivalents
50	10.0
56	10.5
62	11.0

The problem with this is that I have not included any students in their 5th month of 10th grade in my standardization sample, do not know precisely what raw score they would achieve on the test, and am simply estimating the raw score they might have achieved had they been tested. Hence, grade and age equivalents are often estimates (based on interpolation and extrapolation) and are often imprecise measures. These estimates are also based on the assumption that growth in the particular skill being measured is constant throughout the school year. This may be a false assumption. That is, the rate of growth made in the first 5 months of the school year may be greater than is the growth made in the last 5 months. If this were the case, the extrapolated grade equivalents listed above would be in error.

Several other problems exist with age and grade equivalents. These include the following:

1. Grade equivalents encourage comparisons with inappropriate groups. For example, a 7th-grader who achieves a grade equivalent of 11.0 on a reading test should not be thought of (although frequently is thought of) as possessing reading skills characteristic of beginning 11th-graders. The two students share only one thing in common: the raw score they achieved on the reading test. It is erroneous to assume that the 7th-grader "reads like an 11th-grader," or possesses reading skills and strategies characteristic of average 11th-grade students. The students may have used very different cognitive strategies in achieving the same raw score on the test.

2. Grade-equivalent scores depend on promotion and retention practices and on the particular curricula in different grades in a given school. To assume that a 3rd-grade student who achieves a grade equivalent of 5.2 on a nationally standardized reading test could function successfully in a 5th-grade reading class in Podunk Elementary School would be naive and most likely incorrect. Because 5th-grade students in Podunk may be above (or below) the national average in reading, they might score at the 7th- (or 3rd-) grade level on this particular test. Without testing 5th-graders in Podunk we have no way of knowing precisely how *they* would score on this particular test. It is inappropriate to assume that they would achieve an average grade equivalent of 5.0. Hence, it is problematic to use grade equivalent scores on nationally standardized tests to make decisions about the grade in which a student should be placed in a particular school.

3. Some age- or grade-equivalent scores have little practical value. For example, of what value is a grade equivalent of 14.3 or an age equivalent of 20-4 to school personnel?

Other problems exist with age- and grade-equivalent scores in addition to the ones summarized here. For these reasons, age and grade equivalents should be used cautiously if at all. Percentile ranks and standard scores should be used instead of age and grade equivalents when interpreting test performance.

Percentile Ranks

Percentile ranks are scores that allow us to determine a particular student's performance in comparison to a normative sample. A percentile rank is the point in a distribution at or below which a given percentage of individuals fall. For example, if a student's performance on a test was measured to be at the 95th percentile, it would mean that the student's performance on the test equaled or exceeded 95% of all students included in the normative sample of the test. Assuming that the normative sample of the test was representative of all students nationally, and that the norms used were based upon students of a similar age, we could conclude that the student's performance on the test equaled or exceeded 95% of all students his or her age in the country.

Percentile ranks have the advantage of being relatively clear-cut and easy to understand. For this reason, they are useful scores to provide to parents and other laypeople who have a limited understanding of psychometrics.

Standard Scores

Standard scores are scores that have a "standard" mean and standard deviation. Several different types of standard scores exist. The z score is a standard score with a mean of 0 and a standard deviation of 1. T scores are standard scores with a mean of 50 and a standard deviation of 10. Deviation IQs are standard scores with a mean of 100 and a standard deviation of 15 or 16 depending upon the intelligence test used to derive the score. (The Wechsler Intelligence Scales use a standard deviation of 15, the Stanford-Binet Intelligence Scale uses a standard deviation of 16.) These various standard scores are interchangeable with one another and with percentile ranks, and provide essentially the same type of information: how an individual's test performance compares with individuals who comprise the normative sample of the test. For example, a student who scored exactly one standard deviation above the mean on a particular test could be assigned any one of the following scores: z score of 1, T score of 60, deviation

IQ of 115 (Wechsler Scale) or 116 (Stanford-Binet), and/or a percentile rank of 84. These scores are all equivalent, all indicate an individual's relative standing in comparison to the test's normative sample, and may generally be used interchangeably. If the mean and standard deviation of a distribution are known, a z score can be computed for any score in that distribution. Figure 3-3 provides the formula for computing z scores. The formula for computing other standard scores from z scores is provided in Figure 3-4.

Figure 3-3.
Formula for Z Score Computation

$$Z = \frac{X - \bar{X}}{S}$$

Where: X = raw score

$\bar{X}$ = mean

S = standard deviation

Example. In a distribution with a mean of 10 and a standard deviation of 2, what is the Z score associated with a raw score of 5?

$$Z = \frac{5 - 10}{2}$$

$$\frac{-5}{2}$$

$$-2.50$$

Stanines

Stanines are standard score bands that divide the distribution into nine parts. The percentages of scores at each stanine are 4, 7, 9, 12, 17, 20, 17, 12, 7, and 4, respectively. Figure 3-5 depicts the relationship among percentiles, standard scores, and stanines.

Reliability

Reliability refers to the degree of consistency and stability inherent in scores yielded by a measuring instrument. Reliable measures are dependable, stable, consistent, predictable, and accurate. When measures are reliable we say that they are relatively free from error.

Figure 3-4.
Computational Formula for Standard Scores

$$SS = \bar{X}_{SS} + (S_{SS})\ (Z)$$

Where: $\bar{X}$ = Mean

SS = Standard Score

S = Standard Deviation

Z = Z score

Example. Convert Z score of 2 to T score ($\bar{X}$ = 50, S = 10)

SS = 50 + (10) (2)

= 50 + 20

= 70

Example. Convert Z score of 2 to GRE score ($\bar{X}$ = 500, S = 100)

SS = 500 + (100) (2)

= 500 + 200

= 700

Example. Convert Z score of 2 to Wechsler IQ equivalent ($\bar{X}$ = 100, S = 15)

SS = 100 + (15) (2)

= 100 + 30

= 130

As previously stated, scores that come from educational and psychological tests are never perfectly accurate measures of the trait being measured. There is always some degree of error inherent in these scores. (Remember how I described getting two different weights when I weigh myself twice in rapid succession? This is due largely to error inherent in the scale.) It is this error that causes scores to vary for one individual from one test administration to another. The less reliable an instrument is, the more error will be present in the scores yielded by that instrument, and the less accurate these scores will be.

When we measure a human trait using a test or other measuring device, we assume that there is one number (score) that perfectly accurately estimates the extent to which the individual possesses the trait being measured. This hypothetical number is termed the *true score*. However, when we actually measure the trait with less than perfectly accurate measuring devices, we

Figure 3-5.

Normal Curve, Percentiles, and Selected Standard Scores

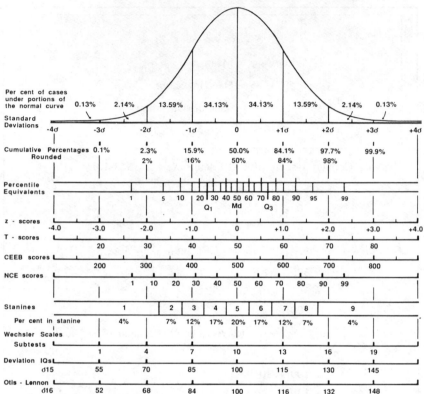

Note. From *Test Service Notebook 148,* issued by The Psychological Corporation. Originally published as *Test Service Bulletin* No. 48, 1955, and updated to include Normal Curve Equivalents, September, 1980. Reprinted by permission of The Psychological Corporation.

obtain a score that is only an estimate of the true score. This "obtained score" possesses some degree of error that causes it to deviate somewhat from the true score. Hence,

$$\text{Obtained Score} = \text{True Score} + \text{Error}$$

The degree to which the obtained score deviates from the true score depends upon how accurate or reliable the measuring instrument is (that is, how much error it possesses). By determining the instrument's reliability, we can estimate the extent to which error will cause obtained scores to deviate from true scores on the test. Hence, by estimating reliability, we can determine how accurate our estimates are. Obviously, instruments that lack adequate reliability possess too much error to allow accurate measurement estimates to be made. Therefore, tests that possess less than adequate reliability are relatively useless and should not be used. Scores yielded by unreliable tests are very poor estimates of the trait being measured.

Three methods exist for estimating a test's reliability: Test-retest, alternative forms, and internal consistency. Each of these methods yields a reliability coefficient symbolized by *r*. Reliability coefficients range from .00 (indicating the absence of reliability) to 1.00 (indicating perfect reliability). The closer the reliability coefficient is to 1.00, the more accurate are the scores yielded by the test.

Test-Retest Reliability

When assessing reliability using this procedure, we administer the same test to the same group of people at two different points in time. The two sets of scores are then correlated. As such, test-retest reliability is an estimate of the stability of scores over time. Usually, the interval between test administrations is rather short (often 2 weeks or so). With such a short interval, we can be relatively sure that the people being tested have not changed much in terms of the trait being measured. Hence, any changes reflected in the scores of an individual from one testing to the next should be a function of error inherent in the test (rather than a true change in the trait being measured). However, with most tests, a "practice effect" will inflate scores on the second testing if the interval between administrations is too short.

Again, consider the scale I use to weigh myself. When I get on and off the scale twice in rapid succession, I know the trait the scale is measuring (my weight) has not changed. Hence, any change in scores is reflective of measurement error inherent in the scale, rather than a true change in my weight. Obviously, the longer the interval is between weighings, the greater the likelihood that changes in scores may actually be reflective of changes in the trait being measured (that is, I may gain or lose weight over time). For this reason, shorter testing intervals generally yield higher reliability estimates than do longer testing intervals when test-retest procedures are used to assess reliability.

Alternate Form Reliability

This form of reliability is assessed by using two equivalent forms of the same test. One group of individuals is given Form A of the test followed by Form B of the test. The other group of individuals is given Form B of the test followed by Form A of the test (alternating the order of administration of the two forms of the test controls for any systematic inflation of scores on any one form of the test due to practice). Scores from the two forms of the test are then correlated to yield a reliability coefficient for the test. Obviously, a disadvantage of this type of reliability is that two equivalent forms of the test must be developed.

Internal Consistency Reliability

This form of reliability is based upon one administration of the test to one group of individuals. Split-half procedures for estimating internal consistency reliability involve splitting the test into two equivalent forms and correlating the scores from each of the two forms. The most common method for splitting a test into two equivalent forms is to divide the test into even-numbered items and odd-numbered items. If it is assumed that the test items are hierarchically arranged by difficulty and that all of the items are measuring the same trait, then it can be assumed that item 1 is essentially equivalent to item 2 (both are measuring the same trait and are of the same difficulty level), that item 3 is essentially equivalent to item 4, and so on. It is important to note that internal consistency reliability estimates are inappropriate to use for timed tests, and do not estimate changes that may occur over time. Hence, estimations of both internal consistency reliability and test-retest reliability should be considered when evaluating tests. Other methods for measuring internal consistency reliability exist as well and are based upon intercorrelations among all comparable parts of the same test (Sattler, 1990). Formulas such as the Kuder-Richardson Formula 20 and Cronbach's Alpha are examples of other methods that are often used to estimate the internal consistency of tests.

When evaluating a test's reliability, one should consider the type of reliability provided as well as the reliability coefficients. Ideally, evidence of several forms of reliability (i.e., test-retest to assess stability, and internal consistency to assess consistency) should be provided. Although reliability coefficients of .90 or higher are considered to be good, coefficients of .80 or higher are generally considered to be adequate (Sattler, 1990).

Factors That Affect Reliability

Several factors are likely to influence the reliability of a test. One factor that influences reliability is test length. The longer the test is (the more items the test contains), the more reliable the test will be. It is unlikely that a very short test will be an accurate measure of a trait. As mentioned previously, the length of time that passes between test administrations in test-retest reliability studies also influences reliability estimates. The shorter this interval is, the higher the resulting reliability coefficient is likely to be. Guessing will also influence reliability estimates. The more respondents guess on a test, the more chance and luck (rather than the trait being assessed by the test) will influence scores. Hence, guessing will lower reliability estimates. Clarity of test items and test administration consistency will also affect reliability. If test items are poorly written and ambiguous, they may be interpreted differently by different people and, as a consequence, will be responded to differently. Under these circumstances, differences in scores will not be due to differences in the trait being measured by the test, but will instead be due to the item being interpreted differently. Similarly, the setting in which the test is administered, and the directions used to administer the test are also likely to influence test scores. If these vary from one situation to another, test scores are likely to vary as a result, and reliability estimates will be negatively affected.

Standard Error of Measurement

The standard error of measurement (SEM) uses the reliability coefficient of a test to estimate the amount of error inherent in any individual score on the test. In theory (but not practice), the standard error of measurement is the standard deviation of the distribution of error scores. Because error scores are computed by subtracting obtained scores from true scores for a group of individuals who have been administered the test, and because we can *never* know what the true scores are of these individuals, the SEM can not be computed by simply taking the standard deviation of error scores. (Error scores can't be computed because we do not know what each individual's true score is.) Therefore, the SEM is computed by multiplying the standard deviation of the test by the square root of one minus the reliability coefficient of the test (the reliability coefficient being an estimate of the error of the test). The standard error of measurement is directly related to the reliability of a test. The more reliable the test, the lower the standard error of measurement; the lower the reliability of a test, the higher the standard error of measurement. The value of the standard error of measurement is that it, in conjunction with an individual's obtained score on a test, can be used to construct a score interval in which we can assume with a certain degree of confidence the individual's true score falls. By constructing such intervals, we can more precisely and more accurately communicate an individual's performance on a test.

Confidence Intervals

The standard error of measurement provides the basis for the establishment of a confidence interval. The following is the formula for computing a confidence interval:

$$\text{Confidence Interval} = \text{Obtained Score} \pm z(\text{SEM})$$

Thus, to compute the confidence interval, one must know the student's obtained score on the test, the standard error of measurement of the test, and the z score associated with the degree of confidence one has selected for the score interval. A range of scores can be constructed that represents any level of confidence desired. Although a statistics book can be consulted to determine the z score associated with any confidence interval, most professionals construct score intervals that represent 68%, 95%, and 99% confidence levels. The z scores associated with each of these confidence levels are:

Confidence Level	z score
68%	1.00
95%	1.96
99%	2.58

Example — Assume a student had been administered a test of mechanical aptitude, and obtained a *T* score of 50. Assume further that the SEM of the test (in *T* score units, the score around which the confidence interval is to be constructed) is 3. Construction of the 68%, 95%, and 99% confidence intervals would be as follows:

$$68\% \text{ CI} = 50 \pm (1.00)\ (3)$$
$$= 50 \pm 3$$
$$= 47\text{--}53$$

$$95\% \text{ CI} = 50 \pm (1.96)\ (3)$$
$$= 50 \pm 5.88$$
$$= 44.12\text{--}55.88$$

$$99\% \text{ CI} = 50 \pm (2.58)\ (3)$$
$$= 50 \pm 7.74$$
$$= 42.26\text{--}57.74$$

Notice that as our degree of confidence increases, the score interval increases as well. That is, we can be 68% confident that the student's true score falls between 47 and 53; we can be 95% confident that the student's true score falls between 44.12 and 55.88; and we can be 99% confident that the student's true score falls between 42.26 and 57.74. Stated in slightly different terms, there is a 68% chance that the score interval 47–53 contains the student's true score, and so on. Notice that the larger a test's standard error of measurement is, the larger the score interval will be for any given confidence level. Thus, the more reliable a test is, the lower the standard error of measurement will be for that test, the smaller will be the score interval for any given confidence level, and the greater the degree of precision one will possess when estimating a student's true score. As Sattler (1990) has indicated, it is particularly important to report confidence intervals when reporting test scores, so that other professionals who gain access to these scores will understand that an obtained score on a test is simply an *estimate* of the degree to which the student tested possesses the trait being assessed by the test.

Validity

Whereas reliability refers to the extent to which a measuring instrument is consistent, stable, accurate, and free of error, validity refers to the extent to which the instrument measures what it purports to measure. At first glance, it may seem as if a test cannot be accurate (reliability) if it does not measure what it says it measures (validity). However, a test may be a perfectly accurate measure of something *other* than what it purports to measure. Again, consider the scale on which I weigh myself. Assume that it is perfectly accurate and measures with no error ($r = 1.00$). Now, further assume that the manufacturer of the scale contends that the scale measures intelligence! Although a perfectly accurate measure of something (weight), the scale does not measure what it (or its developer) says it measures. Although the scale is reliable, it is not a valid measure of intelligence. Hence, there is no guarantee that a reliable test is valid. However, a test that has been shown to be valid is also reliable. For this reason, reliability coefficients always exceed validity coefficients. Three types of validity exist: content validity, criterion-related validity (consisting of both concurrent validity and predictive validity), and construct validity.

Content Validity

Content validity refers to the extent to which items on a test are representative of the domain the test purports to measure. Clearly, a test that contains only addition problems can not be considered a valid test of mathematics achievement because the domain of mathematics entails more than simple addition. Thus, the items on this hypothetical test do not adequately represent the domain of mathematics, and the test can not be considered to possess adequate content validity.

Content validity is not assessed via statistical methods. Rather it is typically assessed by a panel of experts in the field represented by the test. Thus, to assess the content validity of a newly developed test of mathematics achievement, the test would be subjected to the scrutiny of experts in the field of mathematics. These experts would objectively evaluate whether the test items were appropriate given the purpose and nature of the test, and whether the test contained enough information to measure what it intended to measure. Their judgments would be used as evidence of the test's content validity.

Criterion-Related Validity

This form of validity assesses the relationship between test scores and some criterion believed to be related to the construct measured by the test. There are two types of criterion-related validity: concurrent validity and predictive validity. Concurrent validity assesses the extent to which test scores are related to some currently available criterion measure. For example, to assess the concurrent validity of an individually administered intelligence test, I might correlate scores on this test with scores on a previously administered intelligence test that may be on file in the school office. Assuming the previously administered test has been demonstrated to be valid, it would be an appropriate criterion to use to judge the validity of the individually administered test (because the two tests supposedly measure the same construct). If the individually administered test is a valid measure of intelligence, scores on it should be highly correlated with scores on the previously administered (and validated) group intelligence test. If the two sets of scores are not highly correlated, I can only conclude that the two tests are not measuring the same construct. Because I have ensured that the criterion was a valid measure of the construct of intelligence, I can only conclude that the poor correlation between the two measures means that the individually administered test does not measure the same construct and hence is not a valid measure of intelligence.

Predictive validity refers to the correlation between a test and a criterion in which there is a time lapse between administration of the test and performance on the criterion measure. Because intelligence tests predict school achievement rather well, a test presumed to measure intelligence ought to correlate reasonably well with measures of school achievement. Hence, to establish the predictive validity of a test presumed to measure intelligence, I could administer it to a group of students today and correlate these scores with some measure of school performance gathered at the end of the school year. A strong correlation between these two measures means that the test scores can be used to predict school achievement. Because intelligence tests have been shown to be valid for this purpose, I can only assume that this test is a valid measure of intelligence.

When evaluating criterion-related validity, one must consider the type of validity evidence provided (concurrent or predictive) and the associated validity coefficients. As Gay (1987) has suggested, however, there is no "magic number" that a validity coefficient should reach. Generally, the higher the validity coefficient, the more valid the instrument is. Hence, professionals who are considering selecting instruments for possible use in a vocational assessment program should compare the validity evidence of several instruments that could be utilized to assess a particular trait and base their evaluation on this comparison.

Construct Validity

This type of validity assesses the extent to which a test actually measures the psychological construct it purports to measure. Construct validity is usually assessed statistically by using a procedure known as factor analysis. This procedure allows one to determine how many different "things" (factors) are actually being measured by a particular test. This can then be compared to what we know about the nature of the construct purportedly being measured by the test to determine if the structure of the test (as assessed by factor analyses) resembles the theoretical and empirical structure of the construct. For example, we believe that the construct of intelligence is composed of at least two factors: a verbal reasoning factor and a nonverbal problem-solving factor. That is, Intelligence = Verbal Reasoning + Nonverbal Problem Solving. If, when factor-analyzing a test that purportedly measures intelligence, we find that the test possesses two factors (measures two "things"), and that these factors resemble verbal reasoning and nonverbal problem solving, then we have provided some evidence for the construct validity of the intelligence test.

EVALUATING TESTS

As is apparent in the preceding pages, both practical and technical issues need to be considered when evaluating tests for possible use in a school-based vocational assessment program. From a practical standpoint, issues such as the ease with which the test can be administered, the clarity of the directions provided, the ease of scoring, and the attractiveness and durability of the test materials must all be considered. From a technical standpoint, the process used to standardize the test and the nature, size, and representativeness of the test's norms (and the appropriateness of the norm sample, given the intended use of the test) must all be considered. Likewise, the reliability and validity of the test must also be evaluated. An outline of the various factors that should be considered when evaluating tests is provided in Table 3-1.

ISSUES IN COMPUTERIZED ASSESSMENT

A gradual but steady shift from the use of paper-and-pencil instruments to the use of computerized assessment instruments has occurred within the last 10 years. Computerized assessment has numerous advantages over traditional forms of assessment. Because computers are particularly fast and efficient in processing complex information, many practitioners have begun to use computerized assessment instruments to save time, to simplify tasks, and to eliminate the human error typically associated with hand-scoring

Table 3-1.
Suggested Outline for Test Evaluation

Note. The following outline contains basic features applicable to nearly all tests. Additional features are undoubtedly noteworthy in the case of particular tests. A good preparation for one's own evaluation of tests should include a thorough reading of the APA *Standards for Educational Psychological Tests* and a perusal of a sample of test reviews in the *Mental Measurements Yearbooks*.

A. General Information:
  1. Title of test (including edition and forms if applicable)
  2. Author(s)
  3. Publisher, date of publication
  4. Time required to administer
  5. Cost (booklets, answer sheets, other test materials, available scoring services)

B. Brief Description of Purpose and Nature of Test:
  1. General type of test (e.g., individual or group, performance, multiple aptitude battery, interest inventory)
  2. Population for which designed (age range, type of person)
  3. Nature of content (e.g., verbal, numerical, spatial, motor)
  4. Subtests and separate scores
  5. Type of items

C. Practical Evaluation:
  1. Qualitative features of test materials (e.g., design of test booklet, editorial quality of content, ease of using, attractiveness, durability, appropriateness for examinees)
  2. Ease of administration
  3. Clarity of directions
  4. Scoring procedures
  5. Examiner qualifications and training
  6. Face validity and examinee rapport

D. Technical Evaluation:
  1. Norms:
  Type (e.g., percentiles, standard scores)
  Standardization samples, nature, size, representativeness, procedures followed in obtaining sample, availability of subgroup norms (e.g., age, sex, education, occupation, region)
  2. Reliability:
  Types and procedure (e.g., retest, parallel-form, split-half, Kuder-Richardson), including size and nature of samples employed
  Scorer reliability if applicable
  Equivalence of forms
  Long-term stability when available

(continued)

Table 3-1.
(Continued)

3. Validity:
   Appropriate types of validation procedures (content, criterion-related
     predictive or concurrent, construct)
   Specific procedures followed in assessing validity and results obtained
   Size and nature of samples employed

E. Summary Evaluation: Major strengths and weaknesses of the test,
   cutting across all parts of the outline

Note. From *Psychological Testing* (4th ed.) (pp. 705-706) by A. Anastasi, 1976, New York: Macmillan. Copyright 1976 by Macmillan. Reprinted by permission.

responses. As Brown (1990) and Sampson (1983) have indicated, computerized assessment instruments are frequently cost effective, increase administration and scoring efficiency and accuracy, and yield positive responses from clients. Several studies have suggested that clients actually prefer computer-administered instruments over paper-and-pencil instruments (Miller, Karriker, & Springer, 1986; Reardon, Bonnell, & Huddleston, 1982; Reardon & Loughead, 1988).

However, several concerns exist regarding the adaptation of paper-and-pencil instruments to computerized formats and the general use of computerized instruments. Hofer and Green (1985) have suggested that "computer-linked factors might change the nature of the task so dramatically that one could not say that the computerized and conventional paper-and-pencil versions of the test are measuring the same construct" (p. 828). That is, once a paper-and-pencil instrument is computerized, essentially a whole new instrument has been created. Hence, one can never be sure that the computerized form of the instrument maintains the same psychometric (and other) characteristics as did the paper-and-pencil version of the instrument. Duthie (1984) suggested that there may be cognitive differences associated with responding to paper-and-pencil versus computerized versions that may actually alter test performance. For example, computers may evoke affective and emotional responses in individuals that are not evoked by traditional paper-and-pencil instruments, and that may modify or alter responding. Similarly, the equipment used to administer a computerized version of a test is likely to vary from one situation and setting to another. This variability may also contribute to differences in test performance. All of these factors combined suggest that the reliability, validity, and normative information relevant to the traditional paper-and-pencil instrument may not apply to the computerized version of the same instrument. Hofer and Green (1985) have suggested that "interpretation of computer-obtained data should be rejected if there are plausible reasons for expecting nonequivalence" (p. 832). Although several studies have suggested that paper-and-pencil tests can be adapted to computerized formats without altering their psychometric qualities and without affecting scores (Lukin, Dowd, Plake, & Kraft, 1985; Wilson, Genco, & Yager, 1985), comparability of scores should not automatically be assumed. Another concern that has been expressed about computerized assessment instruments pertains to the "rules" used by the computer program to "make decisions" about clients. Frequently, these decision rules (which are based upon statistical algorithms and are used to classify or categorize clients based upon their responses) are not clearly explained or published (Brown, 1990). Therefore, analyzing the validity of test interpretations becomes problematic.

Several ethical concerns exist in regard to the use of computerized assessment instruments. Zachary and Pope (1984) have suggested that computers create an aura of objectivity that may not be justified. Unfortunately, users of computerized assessment instruments and clients who have been administered computerized tests often assume that the interpretive statements generated by these instruments are perfectly objective and accurate. Instead, users of such instruments should treat interpretive statements generated by computers as hypotheses that must be supported or refuted with additional data. Additionally, the ease with which computers generate reports and interpretive statements is frequently an invitation for unqualified professionals to use such instruments. This too increases the risk of inappropriate use and interpretation of data generated by computerized assessment instruments. Zachary and Pope (1984) have suggested that client welfare should be of paramount concern to developers, users, and distributors of computerized assessment instruments and that procedures should be in place to ensure that only qualified professionals can purchase and use such instruments.

Users of computerized instruments should evaluate these instruments separately from their paper-and-pencil counterparts, and should require the same evidence of technical adequacy that they demand of any assessment instrument. To this end, the American Psychological Association (APA) has published *Guidelines for Computer-Based Tests and Interpretations* (APA, 1985) which list standards to be adhered to by all participants in computerized assessment, including the test developer, test user, and test taker. Standards that computerized assessment instruments should meet are included. As Brown (1990) has noted, of particular interest is the inclusion of standards requiring test developers to provide specific information on the validity studies that have been conducted on the test, and the statistical algorithms underlying such validation. Vocational assessment personnel who are considering the use of computerized asssessment instruments should review these standards and should base their selection of instruments upon such standards.

ETHICAL AND LEGAL CONSIDERATIONS IN ASSESSMENT

Vocational assessment personnel have an obligation to conduct their assessments in a manner consistent with good legal and ethical practice. To that end, professionals involved in school-based vocational assessment programs must be familiar with the legal and ethical guidelines that govern the administration and use of assessment instruments, the interpretation of assessment data, and the maintenance and dissemination of assessment information. Although this section will summarize some of the major issues that need to be considered and addressed by assessment personnel, this discussion is not meant to be exhaustive. For a more detailed description of ethical standards governing assessment practice, readers are referred to *Standards for Educational and Psychological Testing* (American Psychological Association, American Educational Research Association, & National Council on Measurement in Education, 1985) and *Ethical Standards for Psychologists* (American Psychological Association, 1979).

Salvia and Ysseldyke (1991) summarize several ethical issues that need to be considered by assessment personnel. First, assessment personnel must assume responsibility for the consequences of their work. Those who assess students and use assessment results to make decisions about students are assuming an enormous responsibility, in that the decisions made are likely to have a major impact upon the life of the student. Assessment personnel must understand this and must make every effort to ensure that their assessment results are used in an appropriate manner. Second, assessment personnel must recognize the limits of their competence, and must function within these limits. In some instances, this may mean refusing to perform certain assessment activities that others request they perform. Third, assessment personnel must make every effort to ensure that assessment results are held in the strictest confidence. Assessment results should not be discussed informally with others who have no legitimate educational interest in the student or who are not directly involved in using the assessment data in decision making. Confidentiality should only be breached when there is a clear and imminent danger to the student or society. In general, parental permission should be secured prior to initiating an assessment, and reports of assessment results should only be released with the permission of the individual tested or the individual's parents or guardian (if the individual is a minor). Fourth, professionals involved in assessment must make every effort to maintain test security. Test items should not be revealed to others, and assessment material should be stored in a safe and secure location.

As vocational assessment becomes increasingly more common, the possibility of lawsuits based on discrimination, inaccurate test interpretation, and use of tests by unqualified persons, becomes increasingly more likely (Barrett, 1987). As such, Barrett (1987) has compiled a list of legal considerations for those conducting vocational assessments. As summarized by Maddy-Bernstein (1990), this list includes the following:

1. The purpose of the assessment should be clear.
2. There should be a written analysis of the specific training program or job the assessment is designed to measure.
3. Those administering the assessment should be able to cite evidence that the assessment instruments used were free of bias and discrimination.
4. The validity and reliability of the instruments used should be familiar to the test user.
5. The evaluator and others involved in the assessment process should be properly licensed or certified to perform the assessment activities they are being asked to perform.
6. Those involved in the assessment process should understand normative data and should be certain that the tests they utilize have representative and appropriate norm groups.
7. Assessments should be conducted in a way so as to eliminate ethnic and racial discrimination and bias.
8. Assessment professionals must keep abreast of new procedures and instruments.

SUMMARY

The effectiveness of school-based vocational assessment programs depends, in part, on the accuracy of the tests and other data-gathering procedures employed within the program, and on the expertise of the personnel responsible for gathering and interpreting the data. If the data-gathering procedures employed in an assessment program lack adequate validity, or possess norms that are inappropriate given the purpose and nature of the assessment, the data are unlikely to contribute positively to a student's educational or vocational programming. In fact, use of invalid data poses a substantial risk to students, in that use of these data may well result in inappropriate vocational placements being enacted. Similar problems are likely to occur if valid data are incorrectly interpreted or utilized.

This chapter has provided an overview of both practical and psychometric issues that need to be considered when selecting and using tests and other data-gathering procedures in a vocational assessment program. Consideration of these issues by professionals involved in establishing and implementing school-based vocational assessment programs is a must for those interested in establishing effective programs. Should the reader be interested in additional information on the topics discussed in this chapter, the following references may be consulted:

Cohen, R., & Swerdlik, M. (1991). *Psychological testing: An introduction to tests and measurements* (2nd ed.). Mountain View, CA: Mayfield.

Gronlund, N. E., & Linn, R. L. (1990). *Measurement and evaluation in teaching* (6th ed.). New York: Macmillan.

Kubiszyn, T., & Borich, G. (1987). *Educational testing and measurement: Classroom application and practice.* Glenview, IL: Scott Foresman.

REFERENCES

American Psychological Assocation. (1979). *Ethical standards for psychologists.* Washington, DC: Author.

American Psychological Association. (1985). *Guidelines to computer-based tests and interpretations.* Washington, DC: Author.

American Psychological Assocation, American Educational Research Association, & National Council on Measurement in Education. (1985). *Standards for educational and psychological testing.* Washington, DC: American Psychological Association.

Anastasi, A. (1976). *Psychological testing* (4th ed.). New York: Macmillan.

Barrett, S. P. (1987). The legal implications of testing. In P. LeConte (Ed.), *Using vocational assessment results for effective planning.* Stevens Point, WI: The Department of Public Instruction.

Brown, D. T. (1990). Computerized techniques in career assessment. *Career Planning and Adult Development Journal, 6*(4), 27-36.

Duthie, B. (1984). A critical examination of computer-administered psychological tests. In M. D. Schwartz (Ed.), *Using computers in clinical practice.* New York: Hawthorne.

Gay, L. R. (1987). *Educational research: Competencies for analysis and application* (3rd ed.). Columbus, OH: Merrill.

Hofer, P. J., & Green, B. F. (1985). The challenge of competency and creativity in computerized psychological testing. *Journal of Consulting and Clinical Psychology, 53*, 826-838.

Lukin, M., Dowd, E. T., Plake, B., & Kraft, R. (1985). Comparing computerized versus traditional psychological assessment. *Computers in Human Behavior, 2*, 49-58.

Maddy-Bernstein, C. (1990). Special considerations regarding career assessment for special groups. *Career Planning and Adult Development Journal, 6*(4), 37-40.

Miller, M. J., Karriker, C. S., & Springer, T. P. (1986). A comparison of two approaches to counselor-free exploration. *Journal of Employment Counseling, 23*, 167-175.

Reardon, R. C., Bonnell, R. O., & Huddleston, M. R. (1982). Self-directed career exploration: A comparison of CHOICES and the Self-Directed Search. *Journal of Vocational Behavior, 20*, 22-29.

Reardon, R., & Loughead, T. (1988). A comparison of paper-pencil and computer versions of the Self-Directed Search. *Journal of Counseling and Development, 67,* 249-252.

Salvia, J., & Ysseldyke, J. E. (1978). *Assessment in special and remedial education.* Boston, MA: Houghton-Mifflin.

Salvia, J., & Ysseldyke, J. E. (1985). *Assessment in special and remedial education* (3rd ed.). Boston, MA: Houghton-Mifflin.

Salvia, J., & Ysseldyke, J. E. (1991). *Assessment* (5th ed.). Boston: Houghton-Mifflin.

Sampson, J. P. (1983). Computer-assisted testing and assessment: Current status and implications for the future. *Measurement and Evaluation in Guidance, 15,* 293-299.

Sattler, J. (1990). *Assessment of children* (3rd ed.). San Diego: Author.

Wilson, F., Genco, K., & Yager, G. (1985). Assessing the equivalence of paper-and-pencil vs. computerized tests: Demonstration of a promising methodology. *Computers in Human Behavior, 2,* 265-275.

Zachary, R. A., & Pope, K. S. (1984). Legal and ethical issues in the clinical use of computerized testing. In M. D. Schwartz (Ed.), *Using computers in clinical practice.* New York: Hawthorne.

4 VOCATIONAL ASSESSMENT TECHNIQUES AND STRATEGIES

A variety of assessment techniques and strategies can and should be employed to gather data within a transdisciplinary school-based vocational assessment program. Ideally, several *different* assessment techniques designed to assess the *same* trait should be utilized by *different* assessment team members. This "triangulation" of data and data sources principle is based upon the multitrait–multimethod (MTMM) approach to multifactored assessment advocated by Gresham (1983). This chapter will discuss the MTMM approach and its application to the transdisciplinary vocational assessment process. Additionally, the various assessment techniques that can be utilized by TVA team members when gathering information about a student will be reviewed. Included in this chapter will be a discussion of paper-and-pencil tests, interviews, observations, work samples, and situational assessment techniques. Advantages and disadvantages of each of these assessment techniques will be reviewed, and suggestions for effective use of these techniques will be presented.

Figure 4-1.
Experiential Continuum

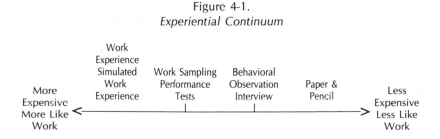

As Figure 4-1 indicates, the assessment techniques to be discussed in this chapter can be organized according to two dimensions: cost and relationship to real work. For the most part, those vocational assessment techniques that are most like real work (work samples or situational assessment techniques, for example) are more expensive and time consuming than are those that are less like real work. Relatedly, those assessment techniques that are more similar to real work tend to possess less desirable psychometric characteristics than do the other assessment techniques listed. However, the "face" validity of work samples or situational assessment techniques is high. As a consequence, students may be more motivated to perform these activities than they are paper-and-pencil tests and may be more honest and realistic in their responding to these techniques.

Transdisciplinary vocational assessment programs should encompass the entire range of assessment techniques and strategies depicted in Figure 4-1. In selecting assessment techniques for use, several issues need to be considered including the type of information desired, cost and time factors, and psychometric properties. These issues were discussed in the previous chapter.

A MULTITRAIT-MULTIMETHOD APPROACH TO ASSESSMENT

Traditional psychoeducational assessment, as practiced by school personnel, has been plagued by several problems, including the use of technically inadequate tests and the use of assessment measures that yield inappropriate, insufficient, or educationally irrelevant information (Gresham, 1983). The use of technically inadequate assessment instruments has been particularly problematic in the field of vocational assessment. Unfortunately, many vocational assessment instruments in use today lack adequate psychometric properties (i.e., they have been subjected to inadequate standardization and norming procedures, possess unacceptable reliability and validity, etc.). Gresham (1983) has suggested the use of a multitrait–multimethod (MTMM) approach to assessment as a means of overcoming these problems. This method is based on Campbell and Fiske's (1959) multitrait–multimethod means of establishing the construct validity of psychological and educational tests.

Validity is the extent to which an instrument measures what it purports to measure. A common method for assessing a test's validity is to determine the extent of agreement or convergence between it and another method used to assess the same trait. For example, to assess test A's validity as a measure of intelligence, I might correlate scores on it with scores on a valid measure of intelligence. If, for a group of individuals, scores on test A "agree" with (are similar to) scores on the already validated measure of intelligence, I might infer that test A is a valid measure of intelligence.

If the two sets of scores are very different, I might assume that the two tests are measuring different traits and that test A is not a valid measure of intelligence. Relatedly, a test may be judged to lack validity if it "agrees" (correlates) with a test that is intended to measure a different trait. For example, if the scores from test A correlate highly with scores on a measure of adaptive behavior, I might infer that test A is not a valid measure of intelligence (but might be a valid measure of adaptive behavior).

Scores from measuring instruments are often affected by variables other than the trait being assessed by the instrument. Sometimes scores are more influenced by the person administering the instrument or the type of assessment device being used than by the trait being assessed. For example, when being interviewed about their interests, students may respond one way to their parents and a different way to their guidance counselor. In such an instance, the results of the interview may be a function of the "interviewer" rather than of the trait being assessed by the interview (interests). Similarly, the interests a student demonstrates when responding to a paper-and-pencil interest inventory may be very different from the interests a student demonstrates when actively involved in a work sample. In this case, the results of the interest assessment may be a function of the assessment technique being utilized (interview vs. work sample) rather than the trait being assessed (interests).

Campbell and Fiske (1959) use the terms *trait variance* and *method variance* to differentiate between the extent to which scores on a measuring instrument are influenced by (a) the trait being assessed and (b) the method used to assess the trait. Clearly, it is desirable to have trait variance exceed method variance. That is, we want the results of an assessment to be a function of the trait being assessed and not the method used to assess the trait. Campbell and Fiske (1959) have suggested that convergent validity can be established through an MTMM matrix. That is, the validity of the scores yielded by use of various assessment techniques can be evaluated by using multiple techniques (methods) to assess multiple traits and then evaluating the extent to which these various scores agree with one another. Validity exists when there are higher correlations between *different* methods of assessing the *same* trait than there are between the same methods of assessing different traits. For example, we would expect to find the correlation between interest inventory results and an assessment of interests via interviewing to be higher than the correlation between aptitudes and interests using the same method (paper-and-pencil test). If we were to find the opposite to be true, we would have to assume that the results were more influenced by the method of assessment than the trait being assessed. In summary, different methods of measuring the same trait should converge on that trait and should account for more variance in measurement than the same method of measuring different traits (Gresham, 1983).

The MTMM approach to assessment can be applied within TVA programs to "assess" the validity of the assessment techniques being utilized and to improve the reliability and validity of the overall assessment process. In particular, the MTMM approach can be used to overcome the problem of technically inadequate tests. For example, assume that an interest inventory possessing less than desirable reliability and validity was used in an assessment and that the results indicated high interest in automotive mechanics. Although it would be inadvisable to place much confidence in the interest inventory results alone, assume that the student had also indicated high interest in automotive mechanics in an interview with the guidance counselor and had been observed rebuilding car engines by parents and teachers. That multiple methods of assessing interests (test, interviews, observations) all yielded similar results suggests that the interest inventory results, in this instance, may be reliable and valid. Had there not been agreement among the results of these different assessment techniques, the validity of the assessment would be in question, and considerably less confidence could be placed in the results.

Relatedly, the extent to which assessment data may be a function of the individual gathering the data (or the interaction between the student and the data gatherer) can also be evaluated by ensuring that different team members are responsible for gathering similar information about a student using similar assessment techniques. That is, if both a school psychologist and a teacher were to interview a student about his or her interests, and both were to conclude that the student was interested in automotive mechanics, greater confidence could be placed in this conclusion than would be the case if only the school psychologist had interviewed the student. In contrast, if the teacher and school psychologist formed different conclusions from interviewing the student, considerably less confidence could be placed in this data. In this instance, one might infer that the student's responses may have been influenced by the interviewer.

Ideally, different TVA assessment team members should be asked to gather similar information about a student using multiple assessment techniques. For example, a school psychologist could be asked to assess a student's vocational interests by interviewing the student and by administering an interest inventory. A guidance counselor could also be asked to assess the student's interests by interviewing the student's parents and by observing the student in various shop classes. Should the results of this interest assessment conducted by different team members using different sources of information and different assessment techniques agree (converge), considerable confidence can be placed in the results. Given such convergence, it is unlikely that the results of the assessment were overly influenced by either the method used to measure interests or the individual conducting the assessment.

PAPER-AND-PENCIL TESTS

As was apparent in the preceding chapter, many factors must be considered when evaluating the adequacy of tests and when interpreting scores obtained from them. Both practical and technical issues need to be considered when evaluating tests for possible use in a school-based vocational assessment program. From a practical standpoint, issues such as the cost of the test, the ease with which the test can be administered, the clarity of the directions provided, the ease of scoring, and the attractiveness and durability of the test materials all must be considered. From a technical standpoint, the process used to standardize the test and the nature, size, and representativeness of the test's norms (as well as the appropriateness of the norm sample, given the intended use of the test) must all be considered. Likewise, the reliability and validity of the test must be evaluated. An outline of the various factors to be considered when evaluating tests was provided in the previous chapter (Table 3-1). Readers can obtain information about all published tests from two major sources: the *The Ninth Mental Measurements Yearbook* (MMY) (Mitchell, 1985) and *Test Critiques* (Keyser & Sweetland, 1984–1985). Reviews of several tests designed to measure a variety of different traits will be presented in Chapter 5. Many of the issues that need to be considered in order to ensure the appropriate use and interpretation of tests were discussed in the previous chapter and will not be repeated here.

Pencil-and-paper tests have been developed to measure a variety of human traits including intelligence, academic achievement, personality, interests, and aptitudes. Paper-and-pencil tests are of two types: criterion referenced and norm referenced. Criterion-referenced tests are used to identify an individual's status with respect to an established standard of performance and, as such, to determine the student's mastery of certain skills (Sattler, 1988). For example, a criterion-referenced test may be used to determine how many competencies a student has acquired in a vocational training program and, hence, to determine whether that student has gained the competencies necessary for entry-level employment in the area, or is ready to progress on to the next level course in the training sequence. Statements such as "John has mastered 85% of the skills taught in Automotive Mechanics I" can be made with criterion-referenced tests. In contrast, norm-referenced tests compare an individual's performance to other individuals (rather than to a particular standard of performance). Statements like "John's interest in automotive mechanics exceeds 90% of all other students his age across the country" can be made on the basis of norm-referenced tests.

Advantages

Pencil-and-paper tests have numerous advantages. They provide objective measures of certain aspects of behavior and frequently possess adequate reliability and validity. Standardized norm-referenced tests provide a means of comparing the performance of one student with another student, or of evaluating a student's progress over time. Because they allow for comparisons to be made, tests are useful in selecting students for certain programs. For example, intelligence tests are often used to assist in determining which students should be placed in a program for gifted and talented students, and vocational aptitude tests are often used to assist in determining in which vocational training program a particular student should be placed. Norm-referenced tests are also useful for evaluating school programs, data from which can be used to recommend program development or changes. Norm-referenced test data can also be used for accountability purposes in documenting that a certain level of learning has occurred.

Disadvantages

Norm-referenced tests have been criticized for a variety of reasons. They frequently create tension and anxiety in students, that interferes with their performance, and are often used to label and categorize students in ways that do them harm (Sax, 1980). Tests have also been said to discriminate against minorities (Sax, 1980), although this has been debated (Reschly, 1990; Sattler, 1988). Another criticism is that tests have been said to penalize very bright and creative students in that unique or innovative responses are often penalized and scored as incorrect. Tests do not effectively assess the intellectual or cognitive processes underlying test responses and usually measure a very limited range of skills or abilities. Last, tests are not at all like real work and, from a vocational assessment standpoint, lack adequate face validity.

INTERVIEWS

An interview can be defined as a verbal and nonverbal interaction with more than one person working toward a common goal (Murphy, 1985). Although it is often perceived to be similar to a conversation, an interview and a conversation differ in that an interview has a clear focus, is more structured, and is planned and organized ahead of time. According to Sattler (1988), the essential difference between an interview and a conversation is that an interview involves an impersonal interaction that has a mutually agreed upon purpose and has formal, clearly defined rules governing the interaction.

Several different types of interview formats exist. Standardized interviews are highly structured procedures that are often used when the same information is to be collected from several different people. Topics to be discussed are established ahead of time and are discussed in a set order. Questions are asked using the same wording, and the entire interview process is held constant from one individual to another. Often, standardized interviews have a means by which interviewee responses are quantified or scored according to some scale. In standardizing the interview process, individuals can be compared with one another based upon their responses. Differences in responses are not likely to be overly affected by the interview process, because it does not vary from one individual to another. Many standardized tests, such as the Wechsler Intelligence Scale for Children – Revised, are considered to be standardized interviews.

A structured interview format specifies the topics and questions that are to be discussed during the interview, but allows the interviewer considerable flexibility in sequencing and elaborating upon the issues to be addressed. Issues may be addressed in any order, and questions may be asked in any way. In contrast, an unstructured interview does not specify ahead of time the type of information desired, or the topics or questions to be addressed. Few if any restraints are placed upon the interviewer using an unstructured interview format.

Conducting Effective Interviews

The ability to conduct effective interviews is dependent upon several factors including the extent to which the interview has been planned and organized ahead of time, the interviewer's ability to establish rapport with the interviewee, the interviewer's interpersonal/social and communication skills, and the interviewer's ability to process and evaluate information effectively.

Planning and Organization

Prior to conducting the interview, the interviewer should gather information about the interviewee and should identify (if possible) the specific area(s) of concern to be addressed. Based upon the background information gathered, an informal interview plan should be developed. This plan should identify the purpose of the interview, the major issues to be addressed, and potential questions that may be asked of the interviewee. The interviewer should also prepare a means of organizing and recording the information obtained during the interview. In establishing a plan for conducting the interview, a method for assessing the reliability and validity of the interview should be developed. For example, reliability may be assessed by comparing responses to multiple (but similar) questions on the same topic that are asked at different times during the interview. Other methods for assessing the reliability and validity of interview data will be discussed shortly and should be considered when planning the interview. An interview plan provides the interviewer with the structure necessary to establish direction and to maintain control of the interview.

Establishing Rapport

Because an interview is an interaction between two people, its success is somewhat dependent upon how well the two people "get along." It is unlikely that an interview will be an effective means of gathering reliable and valid data unless a positive relationship is established between the interviewer and the interviewee. The early phases of an interview should be devoted to establishing rapport. Establishing rapport means building a sense of trust and confidence, and developing an open means of communication. This can be done by maintaining eye contact and a relaxed and comfortable posture, speaking slowly and calmly, and by using a warm and expressive tone of voice. Rapport can also be facilitated by being non-judgmental and accepting of what is said, demonstrating interest in what is said (by nodding or asking questions, for example), and by being sensitive to and understanding of feelings that are expressed. When establishing rapport during the early stages of an interview, controversial or emotion-laden issues should be avoided, and the interviewer should attempt to focus upon general and nonthreatening concerns. In many respects, the interviewer's ability to establish and maintain rapport is dependent upon his or her interpersonal and communication skills.

Interpersonal and Communication Skills

Interpersonal and communication skills underlie the success of any social interaction and, as such, greatly influence the success of any interview. Effective communication is dependent upon being able to see, hear, feel, listen, and speak. Although seeing, hearing, and feeling are purely sensory processes, effective listening and speaking require specific skills.

The ability to listen is a key factor in the interview (Benjamin, 1981) and requires that the interviewee be given one's full attention. A good listener is attentive to the thoughts and feelings expressed by the interviewee and to the language used in expressing these thoughts and feelings. How thoughts and feelings are expressed is just as important as what is expressed. Thus, the interviewer must pay attention to the tone of voice used by the interviewee and the rate and intensity of the interviewee's speech. All of these may provide clues about the interviewee's true thoughts and feelings. The interviewer must also be attentive to the nonverbal cues (e.g., gestures, posture, tremors, blushing) communicated by the interviewee, as well as his or her mood and personal appearance. In many respects, effective interviewing is enhanced by pertinent observation.

Effective speaking (communication) is dependent upon using appropriate words to communicate ideas or to phrase questions, being able to clarify ambiguous or nondescriptive terms used by the interviewee, and encouraging appropriate responses or additional information (by the nodding of the head, use of "uh-huh," or the use of prompts such as "tell me a little more about that"). Being able to formulate effective questions is a particularly important part of interviewing. Questions should be short and simple, should not be capable of being answered as "yes" or "no," and should not be coercive or leading (i.e., "don't you think it was wrong to . . ."). Being able to ask questions at the right time (i.e., not asking potentially embarrassing questions until after rapport and trust have been established) is also an important component of effective interviewing. Communicating concern and interest by restating, rephrasing, or summarizing what the interviewee has said not only assists in establishing rapport, but also reinforces and encourages the interviewee.

Ability to Process and Evaluate Information

The ability to process and evaluate the information provided by an interviewee quickly often determines the course and success of an interview. That is, the interviewer must be able to judge when sufficient information on a particular topic has been obtained and another topic should be addressed, when discrepancies between verbal and nonverbal communication indicate that certain statements should be considered suspect and that a particular issue should be explored further, when a topic has become uncomfortable and threatening and the topic should be changed, and when a previously neglected but important topic is raised by the interviewee and should be immediately pursued. The ability to be flexible during the course of an interview, and to "change gears" and to alter the previously developed interview plan in the face of newly uncovered information, is a particularly important interviewer skill.

Advantages of Interviews

Interviews have numerous advantages as a data-gathering strategy. Edelbrock, Costello, Dulcan, Kalas, and Conover (1985) have noted that structured interviews can reduce the variability of information typically gathered during the diagnostic process and can boost diagnostic reliability. As Sattler (1988) has indicated, interviews provide an opportunity for professionals to motivate a student to provide information the student would not have ordinarily and otherwise volunteered, and to gather information about students that may not be obtainable in any other way. The interview also affords the professional an opportunity to clarify misunderstandings or ambiguities, to obtain a chronology or history of events, and to learn about a student's perceptions of events and issues. As Hughes (1989) has indicated, developing an understanding of the subjective experience of the student is important because the student's interpretation of his or her experiences (whether accurate or not) will affect his or her behavior. The interview is an extremely flexible data-gathering strategy that can be modified or changed at a moment's notice to accommodate and integrate any new information. It also can be used to gather information about a wide range of topics and, as such, is extremely versatile.

Disadvantages

The interview also possesses some disadvantages as an assessment tool. Reliability and validity are difficult to establish, and interviewer and interviewee biases may distort the information obtained. Interviews are often time consuming to conduct and require skills that some professionals do not possess. Hence, many professionals may need to have training in order for them to conduct interviews effectively. Some type of training is usually required to administer the many published, standardized interviews on the market today.

Reliability and Validity of Interviews

The reliability and validity of interviews are difficult to establish and are influenced by many factors, including the interviewer, the interviewee, the type of interview conducted, the conditions under which the interview took place, and the interaction among all of these factors. Although flexibility and versatility may be the interview's greatest strength, these characteristics may also bias the information gathered. Bias and error can be introduced by both the interviewer or the interviewee. The interviewer can unintentionally encourage certain types of responses (and, relatedly, discourage other types of responses) by communicating approval, disapproval, or expectancies either verbally (by the manner in which questions are asked) or nonverbally (by facial expressions or gestures). By failing to establish satisfactory rapport, the interviewer may inhibit the interviewee from sharing important information. Recording errors and forming inappropriate and incorrect inferences are other errors often made by interviewers.

Relatedly, interviewee bias may also affect the accuracy of interview data. Interviewees sometimes purposely distort events that may make them look bad. At other times, interviewees may not accurately remember events, or may unconsciously color these in some way. Interviewees may also have difficulty communicating ideas and events, or may use language that leads the interviewer to form inaccurate impressions.

Although they may be difficult and time consuming to implement, methods exist for assessing the reliability and validity of interview data. Reliability can be assessed by:

— determining the extent to which the information provided by the interviewee is consistent over the course of the interview (i.e., Is what the interviewee says at the beginning, middle, and end of the interview consistent?);

— determining the extent to which interview data gathered at one time is consistent with interview data gathered at another time (i.e., If a student is interviewed on two separate days, how consistent is what the student says on each day?);

— determining the extent to which information obtained from the interviewee is consistent with information obtained from another informant (i.e., Is what the student says consistent with what the student's parents and teachers say?);

— determining the extent to which the information obtained by one interviewer is consistent with the information gained from another interviewer (i.e., Is what the student says to the school psychologist consistent with what the student says to his or her teacher?).

Validity can be assessed by:

— determining the extent to which information obtained from the interview is consistent with information obtained from using other data gathering strategies (i.e., Are the interview data consistent with observational data and test data?);

— determining the extent to which the interview data accurately predict some expected outcome (i.e., Do the interview data accurately predict the effectiveness of a specific vocational placement?).

OBSERVATION

Observation is the process of gathering information through one's senses. Much information can be gained about a student's interests, aptitudes, and work habits by simply watching and listening to the student. However, unsystematic and poorly planned observations are likely to yield inaccurate information. Ideally, observation of a student's behavior should take place in a variety of settings, be conducted at different times, and be completed by several different team members. The use of multiple observers and different observational settings can assist in determining the reliability and validity of the observational data gathered and also increases the representativeness of the behavior observed.

Behavior can be described according to several dimensions. These include frequency, duration, latency, and intensity. Frequency refers to the number of times a particular behavior occurs in a specified period of time (e.g., "During the first 15 minutes of shop class, John disrupted his co-worker four times"). Duration refers to the length of time a particular behavior persists (e.g., "John's disruptions lasted an average of 45 seconds"). Latency refers to the length of time that passes between the presentation of a stimulus and the occurrence of a behavior (e.g., "Fifteen seconds after being told by the instructor to begin working on the project, John complied"). Intensity refers to the magnitude or severity of an observed behavior (e.g., "John disrupted his co-worker"; "John disrupted several students"; "John disrupted the entire class"). Observations may be designed to measure any of these behavioral dimensions.

Observational Recording Methods

Behavior can be recorded on a continuous or discontinuous basis. Continuous recording is a process in which all behavior occurring during a set period of time is recorded. Narrative recording is an example of a continuous recording procedure. Using narrative recording, an observer keeps a running record of student behavior. Everything the student does during the observational session is recorded. Based upon this, a sequence analysis, designed to determine antecedents (causes) or consequences (potential reinforcers) of specific behaviors, can be conducted. Continuous recording and sequence analysis are most often conducted during the initial stages of assessment to determine if a student's behavior requires further study. Although continuous recording procedures may be efficient when recording low-frequency behaviors, they tend to be inefficient when recording high-frequency behaviors. Because they are often time consuming, continuous recording procedures are best used as screening tools to identify specific student behaviors in need of further observation and study (McLoughlin & Lewis, 1986).

Interval recording, also known as time-sampling procedures, requires that the observational period be divided into specific intervals. The observer notes whether behavior occurs during each interval. Several different time-sampling methods exist for observing and recording behavior: whole interval recording, partial interval recording, point-time interval sampling, and momentary time sampling.

In whole interval recording, an observation session is divided into intervals of equal length. A behavior is scored as having occurred only when it occurs throughout the entire interval. In partial interval recording, an observation session is also divided into intervals of equal length. However, a behavior is judged to have occurred if it occurs during any part of the interval. (Thus the behavior may commence before the interval begins and the behavior may cease before the interval ends, but as long as the behavior occurs sometime during the interval, the behavior is scored as having occurred.)

In point-time sampling, a behavior is scored only when it occurs at a designated time during an interval. In momentary time sampling, if the behavior is occurring at the last moment of the interval, an occurence is recorded. If the behavior is not occurring at the last minute of the interval, an occurrence is not recorded.

Event recording and ratings recording are two other types of recording procedures. In event recording, each instance of a particular behavior or event is observed and recorded, and frequency, duration, intensity and latency may be measured. In ratings recording, behavior is observed, and rated on a Likert-type scale. Table 4-1, adapted from Sattler (1988), summarizes the characteristics, advantages, and disadvantages of these different observational recording methods.

Salvia and Hughes (1990) have studied the accuracy of different recording procedures and have concluded that:

—Both whole interval and partial interval sampling procedures provide inaccurate estimates of duration and frequency. Whole interval recording overestimates the frequency and underestimates the prevalence of a behavior. Partial interval recording usually underestimates the frequency and overestimates the prevalence of a behavior.

—Momentary time sampling provides an unbiased estimate of prevalence, but underestimates the frequency of behavior.

Planning the Observation

According to Salvia and Ysseldyke (1991), six steps should be followed when preparing for and conducting systematic observations. These steps include the following: defining a target behavior, selecting the setting(s) in which behavior will be observed, selecting an observation schedule, developing recording procedures, and selecting a means of observation.

Defining a Target Behavior

The behavior to be observed must be described in objective and measurable terms. This description should clearly identify which behavior qualifies as an "occurrence." This "operational definition" of a behavior should allow behavior to be measured accurately enough so that two independent observers can agree as to when the behavior did and did not

Table 4-1.
Observational Recording Methods

Recording Method	Types	Applications	Data	Advantages	Disadvantages
Narrative recording Behavior is comprehensively described	Anecdotal recording Anything that appears noteworthy is recorded. Running record Observer makes an on-the-spot description of behaviors.	Is useful as a precursor to more specific and quantifiable observations Helps in the development of hypotheses about factors controlling target behaviors Provides an in-depth picture of behavior	No specific quantitative data, although the record can be analyzed for various occurrences of behavior	Provides a record of child's behavior and general impressions Maintains original sequence of events Facilitates discovering critical behaviors and noting of continuing difficulties Requires a minimum of equipment	Is not well suited to obtaining quantifiable data Is costly in terms of time and person power Is difficult to validate Is time consuming May be insensitive to critical behaviors Produces findings with limited generalizing
Interval recording Observational period is divided into brief segments or intervals; observer notes whether a behavior occurs in each interval.	Partial-interval time sampling Behavior is scored only once during the interval, regardless of duration or frequency of occurrence. Whole-interval time sampling Behavior is scored only when it lasts from the beginning to the end of the interval.	Is useful for behaviors that are overt or easily observable, that are not clearly discrete, and that occur with reasonable frequency (for example, reading, working, roughhousing, smiling, playing with toys)	Number of intervals in which target behaviors did or did not occur	Defines important time-behavior relationships Facilitates checking inter-observer reliability Maintains standard observation conditions in an economical way Enhances attention to specific behaviors Allows for flexibility in recording large numbers of behaviors	Provides somewhat artificial view of behavior sequence May lead observer to overlook important behaviors Usually tells little about quality of behaviors or situation Provides numbers that are usually not related to frequency of behaviors

(continued)

Table 4-1.
(Continued)

Recording Method	Types	Applications	Data	Advantages	Disadvantages
	Point-time interval sampling Behavior is scored only when it occurs at a designated time during the interval. *Momentary time interval sampling* Behavior is scored only when it occurs at the end of the interval. *Variable interoccasion interval time sampling* Behavior is scored only when it occurs at designated random time intervals.				Is not sensitive to very low-frequency behaviors and, in point-time sampling, behaviors of short duration
Event recording Each instance of a specific behavior (event) is observed and recorded.	*Event* Observer waits for preselected behavior to occur and then records its occurrence. *Duration* Observer determines the amount of time that elapses between the beginning and the end of the behavior.	Is useful for behaviors that have clearly defined beginnings and endings, such as spelling words correctly, rocking movements, asking questions, and speech errors	Number of occurrences of the behavior—frequency count Also, in some cases, rate of behavior, duration of behavior (time), intensity of behavior (if built into code), latency of behavior (time)	Facilitates detection of low-frequency behaviors Facilitates study of many different behaviors in an economical and flexible manner	Provides artificial view of behavior sequence and breaks up continuity of behavior Is not suited to recording nondiscrete behaviors Presents difficulties in establishing reliability

(continued)

Table 4-1.
(Continued)

Recording Method	Types	Applications	Data	Advantages	Disadvantages
	Intensity Behavior is divided into various degrees of intensity, and behavior of each degree is recorded separately. *Latency* Observer determines the amount of time that elapses between the initiation of the request and the onset of behavior.			Provides information about the frequency with which behavior is performed and changes in behavior over time	Limits quantification of the hows and whys associated with behavior Makes comparison across sessions difficult if the length of the observation period is not constant
Ratings recording Behavior is observed and then rated on various scales.	5-point scales 7-point scales Other dimensional scales	Is useful for evaluating more global aspects of behavior and for quantifying impressions	Scale value (or number or score) on rating scale	Allows for the recording of many different behaviors in an economical manner Allows for the rating of many individuals and the group as a whole Permits rating of subtle aspects of behavior Facilitates statistical analysis	Uses scale values which may be based on unclear assumptions May have low reliability Does not allow for recording of important quantitative dimensions Does not allow for recording of antecedent and consequent events

Note. From *Assessment of Children* (3rd ed.) (pp. 506-507) by J. Sattler, 1988. San Diego: Author. Copyright 1988 by Jerome Sattler. Reprinted by permission.

occur. If behavior is not clearly defined, the observational data gathered are likely to be inaccurate, and faulty inferences and inappropriate educational and vocational decisions about the student may be made (Epps, 1985).

As an example, Epps (1985) uses the construct "impulsivity." Behavior that may be described and labeled as impulsive by one observer may not be labeled as impulsive by another observer. Thus, to standardize what is meant by impulsivity, observers may define it as "responding to a question before 5 seconds has elapsed." Although this definition in and of itself may be inadequate (i.e., additional descriptors of this type may need to be added to represent the full range of impulsivity), it has the advantage of defining the behavior in objective and measurable terms. With this type of definition, different observers are likely to agree when impulsive behavior has and has not occurred. As such, the reliability of the observational process will be enhanced.

Select the Setting(s) in Which the Behavior Is to Be Observed

In order to determine if the behavior in question is confined to a specific setting or not, Salvia and Ysseldyke (1991) recommend that observations be conducted in at least three different settings. Observing in multiple settings also increases the likelihood that observational results will be representative (typical) of the student's behavior, thus increasing the validity of the overall observational process. To assess a student's work habits, for example, one might want to observe a student in an academic class, a vocational class, and in a work setting. When behavior is observed in multiple settings, an assessment can be made of the extent to which the behavior is situationally specific (confined to one setting) or not. That is, if disruptiveness is apparent in only one setting and not others, one might hypothesize that external, situational variables (like teasing by other students in that class) may be causing the behavior. However, if disruptiveness is apparent in all observation settings, one might hypothesize that internal, personality variables (like anger or impulsivity) may be responsible for the behavior. Although inferring the cause(s) of behavior using observational methods is difficult, this determination clearly has intervention and remediation implications.

Select an Observation Schedule

The scheduling of an observation involves choosing a session length (i.e., how much time will be spent in one sitting observing the student in a particular setting) and deciding between continuous and discontinuous observation. Ideally, several observations should be conducted at different times in each setting. This increases the representativeness of the behavior observed and increases the reliability and validity of the overall observational process.

Developing Recording Procedures

Both the type of recording schedule to be used (i.e., whole interval, partial interval, momentary) and the forms to be used during the observation must be decided upon. The forms to be used will depend upon the type of recording process selected.

Selecting a Means of Observation

Although human observers may be the most common and preferred means of observation, the use of electronic devices, such as videotape recorders, can be used as well. If human observers are used, several observers should be employed. Even if behavior is to be videotaped, more than one professional should be involved in reviewing the videotape and recording the behavior. The use of multiple observers will allow for an assessment of the reliability of the observation.

Carrying out the Observations

Observations should be conducted in an unobtrusive fashion. During the observation, the observer should assess potential problems (i.e., behavior is inadequately described, sampling and recording procedures are inefficient) and should strive to rectify these problems.

Advantages of Observation

Epps (1985) has identified numerous advantages of observation, including the following:

—Correct use of behavioral observation provides objective, reliable, and valid data that strengthen inferences made about students from the use of other assessment techniques. For example, observing a student competently repairing a carburetor strengthens the inference of "high aptitude in auto mechanics" that may have been made based upon scores from an aptitude test.

—Observations provide a methodology to measure an infinite number of nonacademic behaviors. Although tests are generally limited to measuring one specific trait, observations can be used to measure many traits. Based upon an observation, for example, inferences can be made about a student's interests, aptitudes, work habits, etc. Few other assessment techniques have such versatility.

—Observations can be conducted in a way so as to allow social comparisons to be made. For example, if we are concerned that John's work habits (time on task, for example) are poor in comparison to other students, we might observe the amount of time both John and Suzy (who has been identified by the instructor as an "average" worker) spend on a particular work task. By comparing these two sets of observational data, we can determine the extent to which John's work habits deviate from those of an average student (Suzy). For a procedure to calculate such a deviation, Epps (1985) recommends that readers consult Deno and Mirkin (1977).

—Observations allow events and conditions that precede, accompany, or follow the behavior of interest to be analyzed. This analysis may assist in identifying reinforcers of undesirable behavior and in developing interventions designed to eliminate behavior that may threaten successful vocational adjustment. Such an analysis may assist in determining the causes of behavior.

Additionally, Sattler (1988) has suggested that:

—Observations provide a picture of a student's spontaneous behavior in natural settings and allow for a comparison to behavior in more contrived settings like a test situation.

—Observations allow for verification of the accuracy of parent and teacher reports regarding student behavior.

—Observations of behavior provide information on students that may not be gained in other ways from uncooperative students.

Disadvantages and Problems of Observing Behavior

Several common problems exist in behavioral observation. Despite the attempt to observe *naturally* occurring behavior, the presence of an observer creates an *artificial* situation and may influence the student being observed. That is, students may change the way they normally behave when they detect the presence of an observer. This phenomenon has been labeled *reactivity*. That people change the way they normally act when they realize they are being observed has been well documented and is often referred to as the *Hawthorne effect*. Hence, it is important to conduct observations in an unobtrusive manner and to desensitize students to any observers or observational equipment that may be introduced into the observational setting.

The values and expectations that observers possess may also bias their observations. That is, observers are more likely to notice and record behaviors they expect to notice and believe should be noticed than they are other behaviors. This expectancy bias has also been well documented. Relatedly, the first impressions observers form about a student often bias their later judgments and ratings of the student. (These phenomena have been termed the *primacy* and *halo effects*.) Also, some observers tend to be overly generous and lenient when recording occurrences of behavior, whereas others tend to be overly strict. All of these biases threaten the validity of the observational data generated.

Although conducting a well-planned and systematic observation may be difficult enough, defining the behavior to be observed and inferring *why* the behavior occurred is often more problematic. "Aggressive" behavior can be defined in many different ways. Is calling out an answer in class "aggressive"? Is accidentally hitting another child "aggressive"? Is name calling "aggressive"? An inexact definition of behavior is likely to reduce the reliability and validity of the observational data gathered. Relatedly, professionals often want to know *why* a student behaves the way he or she does, not just *how* the student behaves. Although observational data may validly describe *how* a student behaves, using it to determine *why* the student behaves that way is much more difficult. Unfortunately, one can not observe the thoughts or feelings that may cause behavior to occur. These must be inferred from the observations made. As Kerlinger (1973) has said, a basic weakness of the observer is, despite being accurate in observing what occurred, the observer may make very inaccurate inferences about why behavior occurred. The more the burden of interpretation is placed upon the observer, the less valid obtained data are likely to be.

Unless multiple observations are made at various times in different settings, the observer may fail to obtain a representative and generalizable sample of behavior. If an unrepresentative sample of behavior is obtained, it is likely that inaccurate inferences will be made, and inappropriate programming (based upon these inferences) will be enacted. Hence, obtaining valid observational data can be time consuming.

Last, one of the most vexing problems affecting the accuracy of observations is the inaccurate recording of correctly observed behavior (Salvia & Ysseldyke, 1991). Recording errors often occur because observers are unfamiliar with the recording system being used, have insufficient time to record what they have observed, or experience a lapse in attention and concentration frequently referred to as *observer drift* (Salvia & Ysseldyke, 1991).

Many of the problems that plague the use of observations can be eliminated by developing clear, objective, and precise definitions of behaviors; developing systematic rules and procedures for conducting observations; using well-trained observers; and establishing observational sessions that are not overly long. Brown (1983) has offered several additional guidelines for conducting useful and accurate observations:

1. Specify in advance the student characteristic(s) to be observed.
2. Observe specific behaviors.
3. Focus on a small number of characteristics and behaviors.
4. Make observations as unobtrusively as possible.
5. Obtain as many observations as possible.
6. Use several observers.

Additionally, Sattler (1988) suggests that observers can reduce their obtrusiveness by:

— Making several visits to the observational setting before the scheduled observation takes place, so students become accustomed to the observer's presence.

— Avoiding eye contact or interaction with the student being observed, and ensuring that a rationale for the observer's presence has been provided to students by the teacher.

— Positioning themselves so they have a good view of the student, but are away from the ordinary paths of movement in the setting.

— Shifting their attention from one student to another so as to deflect attention away from the student being observed.

— Entering and leaving the setting when it is least disruptive to do so.

Reliability and Validity of Observations

Unlike published tests for which reliability and validity data are usually available, this type of data is usually not available for observations and must instead be gathered by the observer. As has been inferred, reliability and validity of observations are influenced by the observer, the observational setting, the instruments used in the observation, the student being observed, and the interactions among these sources (Sattler, 1988). Several methods exist for estimating the reliability of observational data: interobserver reliability or agreement, test-retest reliability, and internal consistency reliability.

Estimates of interobserver reliability are based on scores of two or more observers who record the same information while simultaneously and independently observing the same child (Sattler, 1988). The agreement between or among raters is assessed using one of several statistical procedures. The higher the percentage of agreement between or among raters, the greater the reliability of the data.

Reliability can also be assessed by determining the stability or consistency of the observed behavior over time. This can be done by correlating the frequency with which behavior was observed by a single observer on one occasion, with the frequency with which the same behavior was observed by that same observer on another occasion. The greater the consistency and stability of the observed behavior over time, the more reliable the data are presumed to be.

Internal consistency reliability procedures can also be used to assess the reliability of observations. An observation session can be divided into two equal parts (even intervals and odd intervals, for example), and the frequency with which behavior occurs during each half of the session can be compared. For a more elaborate description of methods for assessing the reliability of observational data, complete with computational formulas and examples, readers are referred to Sattler (1988, pp. 510-518).

The validity of observational data is more difficult to assess than its reliability and is more often assumed than determined via statistical means (Sattler, 1988). In considering the validity of observational data, one should consider the extent to which these data are consistent with data gathered from the use of other assessment techniques designed to measure the same trait. Additionally, it should be considered whether the operational definition of the behavior to be observed constitutes a satisfactory and functional definition of the trait being assessed. One should also consider whether the observed behavior accurately reflects the student's behavior in other situations as reported by teachers and parents.

WORK SAMPLES

A work sample is "a well defined work activity involving tasks, materials and tools which are identical or similar to those in an actual job or cluster of jobs . . . and are used to assess an individual's vocational aptitude, worker characteristics and vocational interest" (VEWAA-CARF Vocational Evaluation and Work Adjustment Standards with Interpretation Guidelines and VEWAA Glossary, 1978, p. 20). For example, a masonry work sample might require a student to mix cement and build a brick wall. An occupational foods work sample might require a student to prepare and serve a meal. An automotive work sample might require a student to change a tire or adjust a carburetor. There are several different types of work samples: cluster trait work samples, indigenous work samples, job samples, simulated work samples, and single trait work samples (McCray, 1982).

Cluster Trait Work Samples

A cluster trait work sample is a single work sample designed to assess a group of traits necessary to perform a variety of related jobs. Although this type of work sample may allow performance to be generalized to a number of related jobs, it does not look like real work and, as such, possesses less face validity and may be less motivating to students than are other types of work samples.

Indigenous Work Samples

An indigenous work sample is designed to assess the essential traits of an occupation as it currently exists in a specific community. This type of work sample has the advantage of being highly realistic and of incorporating local industrial standards into the assessment process. However, it has the disadvantage of representing only one job.

Job Sample

A job sample is a work sample taken in its entirety from industry and requires use of the exact tools, materials, procedures, and industrial work standards that exist in the job. Like the indigenous work sample just discussed, this type of work sample has the advantage of being highly realistic and of incorporating industrial standards into the assessment process. However, it has the disadvantage of representing only one job.

Simulated Work Sample

A simulated work sample attempts to replicate the essential requirements and tools of a job as it is performed in industry. Although it may not be quite as realistic as indigenous work samples or job samples, it is usually less expensive.

Single Trait Work Sample

A single trait work sample assesses a single trait or characteristic necessary for the performance of a specific job or a series of related jobs. Although it tends to be rather inexpensive, this type of work sample resembles a psychometric test more than it does real work.

The administration of an individual work sample often takes several hours and usually consists of a demonstration/training phase and an assessment phase. During the demonstration/training phase, the student is trained to perform certain work tasks. Tasks may be demonstrated by an evaluator, or the student may be exposed to an audio-video presentation combined with text material. Following this, the student is usually afforded an opportunity to practice the task and receive feedback on his or her performance. A set amount of time is usually specified for this practice and feedback. Following this demonstration/training phase, the student performs the task and is evaluated. Evaluation often consists of tallying the number of errors made by the student and determining the amount of time taken to complete the task. The student's performance is usually compared to age-based norms or industrial standards.

Many commercially prepared work sampling systems have been developed and are available for purchase and use. Each of these systems is composed of several individual work samples, each of which is designed to assess a different occupational area. The administration of an individual work sample often takes several hours. The administration of an entire commercially prepared work sampling system may take as long as 1 or 2 weeks. As such, these systems are time consuming and extremely expensive. (These systems usually cost several thousand dollars each.)

Several factors should be considered when selecting a work sampling system for purchase and use. First, the work sampling system should contain work samples that correspond to jobs available in the local community, and for which there is training available locally. Second, the work sampling system should be appropriate for use with the specific student population targeted for services. Third, the work sampling system should possess acceptable psychometric properties. Readers are referred to Botterbusch (1982) for a detailed evaluation of several work sampling systems. Table 4-2 provides an outline that can be used when evaluating the suitability of a particular work sampling system.

Advantages

Power (1984) has cited several advantages of work samples including the following: (a) they provide students with an opportunity to explore and try out various jobs in a rather controlled setting; (b) they allow aspects of "jobs" to be brought into school and classroom settings; (c) they are more like real work than are interest or aptitude tests and, hence, may be more motivating to students; and (d) they can be used to assess a variety of traits including interests, aptitudes, and work habits. Additionally, work samples require minimum academic skills, and provide direct and immediate feedback to students (Swanson & Watson, 1982).

Disadvantages

Sax (1973) and Power (1984) have cited several disadvantages of work samples including the following: (a) they emphasize quality and quantity of production rather than personality factors, (b) they provide a superficial assessment of interest and aptitude in that the conditions (environment)

Table 4-2.
Vocational Evaluation System Outline

1. *Development*
    a. Sponsor—The organization that originally funded or financed the development of the vocational evaluation system.
    b. Target Group—What specific populations, such as disadvantaged, mentally retarded, or physically handicapped, was the system designed to serve?
    c. Basis of the System—What theoretical or organizational principle, such as the *Dictionary of Occupational Titles,* was used as a basis for development?

2. *Organization*
    a. Name and Number of Work Samples—How many work samples does the system contain? What are the names of the work samples?
    b. Grouping of Work Samples—What is the arrangement of the individual work samples within the system? Are several work samples grouped in a hierarchy or is each work sample independent?
    c. Manual—What are the organization and contents of the manual(s)? Does it provide all the details that the evaluator needs to know in order to use the system?

3. *Physical Aspects*
    a. Packaging of the Work Samples—How are work samples packaged for sale? Does each work sample "stand alone" or must tools and equipment be shared with other work samples?
    b. Durability—How durable are the tools and equipment in the system? If the system uses audiovisual components, how prone to breakdown are they?
    c. Expendable Supplies—How much and what type of expendable supplies (e.g., wood, paper, wire) are needed per client?
    d. Replacement—To what degree can supplies and materials (e.g., tools, nuts and bolts, colored chips) be obtained locally or must they be ordered from the developer?

4. *Work Evaluation Process*
    a. Preliminary Screening—What information is needed or what decisions must be made before a client can be administered the system?
    b. Sequence of Work Sample Administration—In what order are the work samples administered?
    c. Client Involvement—To what extent is the client informed of his/her progress during the course of administration? What type, if any, of formal feedback is given to the client after the entire battery has been administered? What type of contact does the client have with the evaluator?
    d. Evaluation Setting—Does the general environment attempt to simulate industry, produce a classroom atmosphere, or resemble a formal testing situation?
    e. Time to Complete the Entire System—How long does it take the average client to complete all the work samples in the system?

(continued)

Table 4-2.
(Continued)

---

5. *Administration*

   a. Procedures—Are the purposes of each work sample, materials needed, layout, and general instructions clearly given so that there is little chance of misinterpretation?

   b. Method of Instruction Giving—How does the client receive his/her instructions for the work samples in the system, for example: oral demonstration, written instructions, or audiovisual?

   c. Separation of Learning/Performance—Does the work sample have separate practice (learning) and performance periods: Are there definite criteria (e.g., three correct assemblies; the lines drawn within ± 1/16 inch) that must be met before the client can progress from a practice period to a performance period?

   d. Providing Assistance to the Client—What procedures are there for giving extra or additional instruction, demonstration or feedback after the period of initial instructions?

   e. Repeating Work Samples—What provisions are made for the re-administration of some work samples and what is the purpose of re-administration?

6. *Scoring and Norms*

   a. Timing—What are the procedures for timing the client?

   b. Timing Interval—When does the evaluator start timing the client and when does he stop? Are there specific cut-offs or does the client continue until the work sample is completed?

   c. Time Norms—What is the procedure for reporting the time score for each work sample?

   d. Error Scoring—What procedures, such as a random check of some parts, general rating of overall quality, or a comparison to standards, are used for determining errors?

   e. Scoring Aids—What use is made of overlays, templates, models, etc., to make scoring more accurate and easier for the evaluator?

   f. Quality Norms—What procedures are used for reporting the number of errors, quality ratings, etc., for each work sample? What, if any, type of a rating system is used?

   g. Emphasis in Scoring—Does the system emphasize time or errors in the scoring process or are both given equal weight?

7. *Observation of Clients*

   a. Work Performance—Are work performance factors (e.g., fine finger dexterity, color perception) listed for the system and are specific work performance factors given for each work sample?

   b. Work Behaviors—Are work behaviors (e.g., ability to follow instructions, communication with supervisors) defined for the system and are specific work behaviors to be observed for each work sample?

   c. Recording System—What procedures does the system have for the recording, describing, and rating of observed work performance and work behaviors?

(continued)

Table 4-2.
(Continued)

---

   d. Frequency of Observation—How often and to what extent is the evaluator to observe and record client behavior?

8. *Reporting*
   a. Forms—What forms for recording time and quality, work performance, work behavior, etc., are used for each work sample in the system?
   b. Final Report Format—What information is included in the final report and what type of format (e.g., rating scales, free narration) is used to present the information? Is a final report format and/or example given in the work sample manual?

9. *Utility*
   a. Vocational Exploration—Does the system provide experiences that the client can readily relate to real jobs?
   b. Vocational Recommendations—Are training and job recommendations specific or general? How are they related to the DOT or other job classification systems? Can extended evaluation work adjustment, etc., be recommended as a result of this sytem?
   c. Counselor Utilization—Can the system provide the counselor or referring agency with useful information and to what extent is the counselor involved in the process?

10. *Training in the System*
    a. Training Required—Is formal training required before the system is sold?
    b. Training Available—Is formal training available? Where is it available?
    c. Duration—How much time is required for training?
    d. Follow-up—Is technical assistance available after purchase and training?

11. *Technical Considerations*
    a. Norm Base—On what types of populations (e.g., client, employed workers, general populations) was the system normed, and are these norm groups clearly defined? Are norm groups of adequate size for practical use? Are predetermined time standards, such as Methods-Time-Measurement, used?
    b. Reliability—What empirical evidence is there to demonstrate that the system and its component work samples give reliable or consistent results? Are the research methods, sample sizes, etc., described in enough detail to permit the user to judge the meaningfulness of any data?
    c. Validity—What content, construct, or empirical validity data are available to indicate that the system really does what it claims, such as make more realistic choices, job and/or training success, etc.? Are research methods, sample sizes, etc., described in enough detail to permit the user to judge the meaningfulness of any data?

Note. Reprinted from *A Comparison of Vocational Evaluation Systems* (2nd ed.) (pp. 5–8) by K. F. Botterbusch, 1982. Menomie, WI: Materials Development Center, Stout Vocational Rehabilitation Institute, University of Wisconsin - Stout. Copyright 1982 by Materials Development Center, Stout Vocational Rehabilitation Institute. Reprinted by permission.

surrounding performance of the job are usually not replicated by the work sample, (c) they are expensive and time consuming to utilize, and (d) they often lack acceptable psychometric properties; as such, there is no assurance that work samples accurately predict performance in specific jobs.

SITUATIONAL ASSESSMENT

Situational assessment techniques are designed to assess a student's interests, aptitudes, or work habits in a real or simulated work situation. Information about the student is gathered from peers and supervisors via use of observation, interviews, and rating scales. Although work samples are sometimes considered to be a type of situational assessment, they are discussed separately in this chapter given their popularity and extensive use. Several different types of situational assessment techniques exist. The situational assessment techniques to be discussed here include simulated job stations, production work situations, on-the-job evaluations, job tryouts, and evaluation in a vocational training setting.

Simulated Job Station

A simulated job station is a work setting designed to simulate an actual job. Job stations have been frequently used in the military (a flight trainer is an example of a job station) and in business and industry to assess potential job functioning. They possess the following characteristics:

1. All aspects of a job (not just aspects of jobs) or a work process are replicated as realistically as possible.
2. Students are not necessarily paid for the work they perform.
3. The work setting is controlled by a vocational evaluator or assessment professional.
4. The job station is located in a school or other vocational evaluation facility.

Simulated job stations not only include all job tasks, but also incorporate the environmental, physical, and social characteristics of a job. As such, they are extremely realistic and offer a great deal of face validity. Although they are costly to develop, they are not as expensive to maintain and operate as are many other situational assessment techniques.

Production Work Situation

A production work situation is a method of evaluating students via the use of actual industrial work brought into the evaluation facility. It is possible for the evaluation staff to vary all the customary conditions of the real job in an effort to discover difficulties that prevent the student from working effectively. According to McCray (1982), the production work situation possesses the following characteristics:

1. The student is placed on tasks in which wages are paid when finished, and saleable products are produced.

2. The student works in a production-oriented manufacturing or service environment where performance standards with regard to quality, quantity, etc., have been clearly established.

3. The production situation can be varied by the evaluation staff in conjunction with the production staff, to observe the student's reactions to such changes.

Although the production work situation can be an extremely useful assessment technique, it possesses two major disadvantages (McCray, 1982): (1) It is dependent on the production program having an adequate supply of materials and an ongoing demand for the product, and (2) excessive pressure to maintain exacting production schedules and to ensure quality control safeguards usually accompanies it. For a description of a modified production work situation developed for emotionally disturbed high school students, readers are referred to Levinson (1984).

On-The-Job Evaluation

On-the-job evaluation provides one of the most realistic means available of assessing a student's vocational functioning. Because students are placed in an actual job, the establishment of this evaluation technique necessitates a close working relationship between school staff and local employers. Placement on the job is temporary and for evaluation purposes only. In most cases, the student is supervised by the employer rather than vocational assessment personnel while on the job. On-the-job evaluation possesses the following characteristics:

1. The student is not necessarily paid.

2. The evaluation is designed to benefit the student not the employer.

3. The evaluation/placement will not necessarily result in employment.

4. The employer does not necessarily experience any real immediate benefit.

5. The student does not displace or fill any vacant worker slots.

6. The student's performance is supervised and evaluated by the employer and/or the evaluation staff.

7. The student is given the opportunity to experience all aspects of a specific job in a real work setting.

There are numerous advantages to on-the-job evaluation (Poor and co-workers, 1975): Business and industry are actively involved in the assessment process, no additional financial investment is required for equipment or personnel, job tryouts are realistic and motivating to students, and the evaluation process may eventually result in employment (i.e., the employer may hire the student following the evaluation). Prior to initiating on-the-job evaluation, employers should be apprised of a student's strengths, weaknesses, and special needs, and a means of establishing ongoing communication between the employer and school staff should be developed. Although it is a desirable assessment technique, on-the-job evaluations are sometimes difficult to establish because of insurance laws, regulations regarding minimum wage, and safety hazards. Relatedly, some employers do not have the time necessary to observe and supervise students who are placed.

Job Tryout

A job tryout is a form of situational assessment in which a student is placed in an actual job in the community, with the understanding that the student may not necessarily succeed, and will be provided with help and assistance if needed. Success or failure provides both the student and assessment professional with information that can assist in making additional employment decisions. Job tryouts possess the following characteristics:

1. Wages are paid to the student.
2. The placement is primarily designed to benefit the employer.
3. The student becomes an employee.
4. The work setting is controlled by the employer.

Job tryouts possess many of the same advantages and disadvantages as on-the-job evaluation.

Evaluation in a Vocational Training Setting

This form of situational assessment is conducted in any setting that provides some type of vocational training and possesses the following characteristics:

1. The student is not paid.
2. The student is placed in an existing vocational training program.

3. The placement is designed to benefit the student.

4. The evaluation setting is controlled by vocational assessment personnel and the vocational instructor.

5. The placement does not necessarily result in entry into the vocational training program.

Advantages and Disadvantages of Situational Assessment

Situational assessment techniques have numerous advantages. They closely resemble real work and as such may be particularly motivating to students. However, they are extremely time consuming and difficult to establish and tend to be rather expensive to operate. Additionally, situational assessment strategies usually require extensive coordination and cooperation with employers and instructors.

SUMMARY

A variety of assessment techniques should be employed within a school-based vocational assessment program. Ideally, a multitrait–multimethod approach to multifactored assessment, in which different assessment team members are responsible for assessing similar student traits using different assessment methods, should be integrated into the data-gathering process. This approach has the advantage of allowing professionals to assess the reliability and validity of the assessment data gathered, and to compensate for the use of instruments that lack adequate psychometric characteristics. This chapter has discussed the advantages and disadvantages of paper-and-pencil tests, interviews, observations, work samples, and situational assessment techniques and has identified some of the problems typically associated with use of each of these strategies. Relatedly, suggestions have been made for effective use of each of the assessment methods discussed. Professionals should base their choice of an assessment method on the type of information desired, the relative advantages/disadvantages of each assessment method in gathering the type of information desired, and their own comfort and expertise with each technique. Should the reader be interested in additional information on the topics discussed in this chapter, the following references may be consulted:

Gresham, F. M. (1983). Multitrait-multimethod approach to multifactored assessment: Theoretical rationale and practical application. *School Psychology Review, 12*(1), 26-34.

Salvia, J., & Hughes, C. (1990). *Curriculum-based assessment: Testing what is taught.* New York: Macmillan.

Salvia, J., & Ysseldyke, J. E. (1991). *Assessment* (5th ed.). Boston: Houghton-Mifflin.

Sattler, J. (1988). *Assessment of children*. San Diego, CA: Author.

REFERENCES

Benjamin, A. (1981). *The helping interview* (3rd ed.). Boston: Houghton-Mifflin.

Botterbusch, K. F. (1982). *A comparison of commercial vocational evaluation systems* (2nd ed.). Menomonie, WI: Materials Development Center, Stout Vocational Rehabilitation Institute.

Brown, F. G. (1983). *Principles of educational and psychological testing* (3rd. ed.). New York: Holt, Rinehart, & Winston.

Campbell, D. T., & Fiske, D. W. (1959). Convergent and discriminant validation by the multitrait-multimethod matrix. *Psychological Bulletin, 56*, 81-105.

Deno, S. L., & Mirkin, P. K. (1977). *Data-based program modification: A manual*. Reston, VA: Council for Exceptional Children.

Edelbrock, C., Costello, A. J., Dulcan, M. K., Kalas, R., & Conover, N. C. (1985). Age differences in the reliability of the psychiatric interview of the child. *Child Development, 56*, 265-275.

Epps, S. (1985). Best practices in behavioral observation. In A. Thomas & J. Grimes (Eds.), *Best practices in school psychology*. Kent, OH: National Association of School Psychologists.

Gresham, F. M. (1983). Multitrait-multimethod approach to multifactored assessment: Theoretical rationale and practical application. *School Psychology Review, 12*(1), 26-34.

Hughes, J. N. (1989). The child interview. *School Psychology Review, 18*(2), 247-259.

Kerlinger, F. N. (1973). *Foundations of behavior research* (2nd ed.). New York: Holt, Rinehart, & Winston.

Keyser, D. J., & Sweetland, R. C. (Eds.). (1984-85). *Test critiques* (Vols. 1-4). Kansas City: Test Corporation of America.

Levinson, E. M. (1984). A vocationally oriented secondary school program for the emotionally disturbed. *Vocational Guidance Quarterly, 33*(1), 76-81.

McCray, P. M. (1982). *Vocational evaluation and assessment in school settings*. Menomonie, WI: Research and Training Center, Stout Vocational Rehabilitation Institute, University of Wisconsin-Stout.

McLoughlin, J. A., & Lewis, R. B. (1986). *Assessing special students* (2nd ed.). Columbus, OH: Merrill.

Mitchell, J. V. (Ed.). (1985). *The ninth mental measurements yearbook*. Lincoln: University of Nebraska, Buros Institute of Mental Measurement.

Murphy, J. P. (1985). Best practices in interviewing. In A. Thomas & J. Grimes (Eds.), *Best practices in school psychology*. Kent, OH: National Association of School Psychologists.

Poor, C., et al. (1975). Vocational assessment potential. *Archives of Physical Medicine and Rehabilitation, 56*, 33-36.

Power, P. W. (1984). *A guide to vocational assessment*. Baltimore: University Park Press.

Reschly, D. (1990). Best practices in intellectual assessment. In A. Thomas & J. Grimes (Eds.), *Best practices in school psychology II*. Washington, DC: National Association of School Psychologists.

Salvia, J., & Hughes, C. (1990). *Curriculum-based assessment: Testing what is taught*. New York: Macmillan.

Salvia, J., & Ysseldyke, J. E. (1985). *Assessment in special and remedial education* (3rd ed.). Boston: Houghton-Mifflin.

Salvia, J., & Ysseldyke, J. E. (1991). *Assessment* (5th ed.). Boston: Houghton-Mifflin.

Sattler, J. (1988). *Assessment of children* (3rd ed.). San Diego, CA: Author.

Sax, A. (1973). Work samples. In W. Crow (Ed.), *Positions on the practice of vocational evaluation*. Washington, DC: Vocational Evaluation and Work Adjustment Association.

Sax, G. (1980). *Principles of educational and psychological measurement and evaluation* (2nd ed.). Belmont, CA: Wadsworth.

Swanson, H. L., & Watson, B. L. (1982). *Educational and psychological assessment of exceptional children*. St. Louis, MO: C.V. Mosby.

VEWAA-CARF. (1978). *Vocational evaluation and work adjustment standards with interpretation guidelines and VEWAA glossary*. Menomonie, WI: University of Wisconsin-Stout, Stout Vocational Rehabilitation Institute, Materials Development Center.

5 VOCATIONAL ASSESSMENT DOMAINS AND INSTRUMENTATION

As discussed in the preceding chapters, transdisciplinary school-based vocational assessment (a) involves a variety of school and community-based professionals, (b) utilizes a variety of assessment techniques and strategies, and (c) requires that assessment information be gathered in a variety of domains, including intelligence, academic achievement, personality, occupational social skills/adaptive behavior, interests, aptitudes, and career maturity. Whereas the preceding chapter focused on data-gathering techniques and strategies that may be utilized in vocational assessment programs, this chapter will focus on the domains that should be assessed as part of a transdisciplinary school-based assessment and the instruments that may be employed to assess each of these domains. Each section in this chapter will define and describe a specific assessment domain and will provide a brief summary of assessment instruments that can be utilized to assess the domain.

INTELLIGENCE

No other area of assessment has generated as much attention and been the subject of as much controversy as has that of intelligence (Salvia & Ysseldyke, 1991). Numerous definitions of the construct have been proposed, and a variety of intelligence tests based on these different definitions have emerged. To some extent, the failure to develop a universally accepted definition of intelligence has been responsible for the widespread controversy that has plagued the assessment of intelligence over the years (Miller & Reynolds, 1984). Although no clear consensus of agreement exists regarding a definition of intelligence, most intelligence tests are validated based on the extent to which they can predict academic achievement. That is, although different intelligence tests may sample slightly different behaviors (believed by the authors of the test to be associated with "intelligence"), "valid" measures of intelligence are judged to be those that accurately predict school achievement. In fact, most intelligence tests are used for this purpose. Thus, a practical, albeit not universally accepted, definition of "intelligence" is academic or scholastic aptitude. Relatedly, intelligence can be considered to be a measure of one's ability to learn and to profit from experience. Intelligence has also been defined as one's capacity to learn, one's ability to adapt adequately to the environment, and one's ability to solve a variety of problems quickly and effectively (Sax, 1980).

It is important to note that different intelligence tests sample slightly different behaviors and measure slightly different skills. That is, authors of intelligence tests often subscribe to slightly different definitions of intelligence, and construct their tests accordingly. Therefore, it is important to remember that scores from different intelligence tests are not necessarily interchangeable, and that use of a particular intelligence test implies acceptance of a particular definition of the construct.

Generally, factor-analytic studies have suggested that most intelligence tests measure two or three relatively distinct factors. These have been labeled by some experts as verbal reasoning/comprehension (a measure of one's ability to use language to solve problems), perceptual organization (a measure of one's nonverbal, manual/manipulative problem-solving ability), and memory (one's ability to remember, pay attention, concentrate, and remain free from distractions).

Most theorists believe that intelligence is a function of the interaction between heredity and environment, although the relative influence of each of these two factors has been the source of considerable debate. As Sattler (1988) has suggested, reliable measures of intelligence can be obtained from at least 4 or 5 years onwards, and scores generally become more stable as children become older. The stability of IQ scores over time is generally attributed to the invariance of genetic factors and the relative stability of the environment for any particular individual (Sattler, 1988).

Intelligence has been related to educational and occupational attainment as far back as the 1930s. Morris and Levinson (in press) conducted a comprehensive review of over 50 years of research investigating the relationship between intelligence and occupational/vocational functioning. Despite some contradictory findings, some patterns emerged for individuals with and without disabilities.

For individuals without disabilities, it was found that:

1. Minimum and median/mean IQ levels associated with success in occupations exist, although there is considerable overlap between the IQ

levels associated with different occupations. (Table 5-1 summarizes these data, drawn from several studies reviewed by Morris & Levinson, in press.)

2. Training and performance in clerical occupations have displayed the highest correlations with IQ.

3. IQ is correlated with number of years of schooling and occupational status and prestige.

4. The assessment of intelligence as a measure of academic/scholastic success has utility as a predictor of success in occupational training, especially in higher level occupations where considerable postsecondary education is required for entry into the occupation. The higher one's IQ, the greater the likelihood that the individual will be able to complete the educational requirements necessary for entry into high-level, high-status occupations.

5. IQ is correlated with vocational/career maturity and with more accurate self-knowledge. The higher one's IQ, the more likely it is that expressed and realistic interests will be congruent.

6. Intelligence is related to type of vocational interest, and to a willingness to pursue selected occupations.

For individuals with disabilities, it was found that:

1. IQ is predictive of successful release from institutions and with selective placement into occupations.

2. Mentally retarded individuals with higher IQs are more likely to find and keep jobs as long as they do not exhibit deficits in behavioral, social, and attitudinal skills that are viewed negatively by employers.

3. IQ is related to the integration of sensory input, error rates, and reaction time.

4. Performance IQ or a combination of performance (nonverbal) subtests has been most predictive of success in low-level occupations.

Recent research has investigated the relationship between intelligence test scores and aptitude tests, and has primarily focused upon the Wechsler Intelligence Scale for Children (WISC; 1974) and the General Aptitude Test Battery (GATB; U.S. Department of Labor, 1983). These studies have suggested that there is considerable overlap between these measures. Miller (1978) found that WISC–GATB subtests correlated highly and, using a linear regression model, was able to use intelligence test scores to glean useable information about the vocational aptitudes of individuals included in the study. Similarly, Heinlein (1987) found that the factor structure

Table 5-1.

Mean IQ of Selected Occupations and Training Sites by Source

Mean IQ by SD	Source					
	a.	b.	c.	d.	e.	f.
< −4.5 IQ 32.5			Light Factory Worker Domestic Worker Garden Worker			
−4.0 IQ 40			Assembly Worker			
−3.5 IQ 47.5			Laundry Worker Cook Stock Worker	Laundry Worker		
−3.0 IQ 55			Clerical Worker General Houseworker Painter	Sales Clerk Sheltered Workshop	Restaurant Worker Laundry Worker Hotel Housekeeper Janitor Factory Worker Dishwasher	
−2.5 IQ 62.5	Teamster		Salesman Janitor	Truck Driver Sewing Machine Operator		
−2.0 IQ 70						
−1.5 IQ 77.5				Bartender Carpenter		
−1.0 IQ 85	Barber Beautician			Teamster Farm Worker Lumberjack		Nurse's Aide Cable Assembler Stock Clerk
−0.5 IQ 92.5	Butcher Carpenter Foreman Shipping Clerk Foundrymen Unskilled Laborer		Tractor Driver Painter Hospital Orderly Construction Machine Operator Stonemason Cook Well Driller			
x = 100	Contractor Mortician Nurse Baker Clerical Worker Dress Maker Mechanic Plumber Stenographer Letter Carrier		Welder Plumber Automotive Mechanic Bricklayer Carpenter Woodworker Machine Operator Chauffeur			LPN Electrician Auto Mechanic Distribution Clerk
+0.5 IQ 107.5	Artist Dentist Acountant Business Manager Draftsmen Housewife Salesmen Teacher Firemen	Personal Service Worker	Foremen Meat Cutter Optician Sheet Metal Worker Diesel Mechanic Auto Body Repairmen Pattern Maker			Radiology Technician Teller

(continued)

Table 5-1.
(Continued)

Mean IQ by SD	Source					
	a.	b.	c.	d.	e.	f.
+1.0 IQ 115	Author Architect Business 　Executive College Professor Lawyer Physician Librarian Policemen	Bookkeeper Clerk Skilled Labor	Tool Maker LPN Printer Dental Lab 　Technician Machinist Policemen Sales Clerk Salesmen File Clerk Surveyor			Nurse Draftsmen Accountant
+1.5 IQ 122.5	Chemist General 　Engineer Druggist Photographer	Teacher Business 　Executive Salesmen	Bookkeeper Stenographer Pharmacist Draftsmen Reporter Postal Clerk Writer Teacher Lawyer Auditor			
+2.0 IQ 130	College 　Administrator CPA Cabinet Maker Plasterer	Engineer Accountant	Accountant Mechanical 　Engineering 　Student Medical Student Chemist Electrical 　Engineering 　Student			
+2.5 IQ 137.5						General 　Practitioner Engineer
+3.0 IQ 145						Mathematician

Source: a—Proctor (1935); b—Wechsler (1958); c—Super and Crites (1962); d—Wolfensberger (1967); e—Brickley, Browning, and Campbell (1982) / Brickley, Campbell, and Browning (1985); f—Gottfredson (1984).

Note. Reprinted from "Intelligence and Occupational/Vocational Adjustment: A Literature Review" by T. Morris and E. Levinson (in press), *Journal of Counseling and Development*. Copyright American Association of Counseling and Development. Reprinted with permission. No further reproduction authorized without written permission of American Association for Counseling and Development.

of the Wechsler Adult Intelligence Scale (WAIS) was similar to the factor structure of the GATB.

More recently, Faas and D'Alonzo (1990) found several Wechsler Adult Intelligence Scale - Revised (WAIS-R) scores to be significant predictors of job success among learning disabled adults. Specifically, the subtests of information, digit span, vocabulary, comprehension, and similarities and both the Verbal and Full Scale IQs were found to be significantly associated with job success. The comprehension subtest and Verbal IQ were found to be the best predictors of positive school-to-work adjustment in this learning disabled sample. In a related study using the Non-Reading Aptitude Test Battery (NATB), Watkins (1980) found several significant correlations between aptitude measures and WISC-R Verbal, Performance, and Full Scale IQs. Highest correlations were found for the following aptitude–IQ pairs: general learning aptitude–Verbal IQ, Performance IQ, and Full Scale IQ; verbal aptitude–Verbal IQ; form perception–Performance IQ and Full Scale IQ. Hypothesized relationships between Wechsler intelligence test scores and vocational aptitudes and vocational training programs, drawn from two sources, are presented in Tables 5-2 and 5-3, respectively.

Several other studies have found significant associations among Wechsler intelligence test scores and various vocational outcome measures. Hartzell and Compton (1984) found that age and Full-Scale IQ were the best predictors of job success in a California learning disabled sample. Wechsler (1958) found significant correlations between Performance IQs and scores on two different mechanical comprehension tests. Webster (1974) found significant correlations between workshop clients' achievement ratings and WAIS Performance and Full Scale IQs and the object

Table 5-2.
Overlap Among GATB and WAIS-R Abilities and Aptitudes

Canonical Composite	WAIS-R	GATB
Set 1: Verbal Cluster	Information Vocabulary Comprehension Block Design	G: General V: Verbal N: Numerical S: Spatial
Set 2: Perceptual-Motor Cluster	Block Design Object Assembly	F: Finger Dexterity M: Manual Dexterity P: Form Perception S: Spatial
Set 3: Psychomotor Cluster	Digit Span Arithmetic Digit Symbol	S: Spatial P: Form Perception Q: Clerical Perception K: Motor Coordination

Note. From "Aptitude Testing in Career Assessment" by C. F. Capps, W. E. Heinlein, and F. W. Sautter, 1982, *Career Planning and Adult Development Journal,* Winter. Reprinted by permission from the *Career Planning and Adult Development Journal.*

Table 5-3.
*Hypothesized Relationships Between Wechsler Subtests
and Occupational Training Programs*

Socially Oriented Occupations	*Data-Oriented Occupations*
Information	Arithmetic
Comprehension	Digit Span
Vocabulary	Digit Symbol
Picture Arrangement	Picture Completion
Trade & Industrial Occupations	*Marketing Education*
Arithmetic	Information
Picture Completion	Comprehension
Block Design	Vocabulary
Object Assembly	Picture Arrangement
Business Education (Bookkeeping/Accounting/Computer)	*Business Education (Secretarial/Typing/Receptionist)*
Arithmetic	Comprehension
Digit Span	Digit Span
Digit Symbol	Vocabulary
Picture Completion	Digit Symbol
	Picture Completion
Drafting	*Electronics*
Arithmetic	Arithmetic
Digit Symbol	Block Design
Picture Completion	Digit Symbol
Block Design	Object Assembly
Object Assembly	Picture Completion
Child Care—Human Services	*Carpenter/Plumber*
Comprehension	Arithmetic
Vocabulary	Picture Completion
Picture Arrangement	Block Design
	Object Assembly

Note. From T. H. Hohenshil and W. E. Heinlein, personal communication, 1984.

assembly and block design subtests for four different samples of individuals with disabilities. McCarthy (1976) found significant correlations between sheltered workshop performance and Verbal, Performance, and Full Scale IQs for trainable mentally retarded clients. In the latter study, Performance IQ correlated highest with sheltered workshop performance. Several other studies have identified significant correlations between Wechsler intelligence test scores and vocational test performance (Webster, 1974), parent ratings of interests (Matheny, Dolan, & Krantz, 1980), class rank assigned to students by teachers in vocational-technical schools (Warren & Gardner, 1981), and scores on a measure of career maturity (Palmo & Lutz, 1983). Tables 5-4 and 5-5 summarize some of this research.

As Sattler (1988) has said, "The IQ has a larger collection of correlates predictive of success in a wide variety of human endeavors than does any other variable" (p. 78). Clearly, some general trends regarding the relationship between intelligence and vocational functioning are apparent in the literature. However, it is important to understand that in most instances, the relationships uncovered, although significant, are generally modest at best. The exception to this is the relationship between intelligence and academic achievement, which correlate in the .70s. Therefore, although intelligence test data may allow assessment personnel to make reasonably accurate predictions about school performance and, to a lesser extent, understand the vocational potential of students, intelligence test data should be utilized in combination with other data and should never be interpreted in isolation.

In summary, research suggests that intelligence test scores may be better predictors of vocational training than of actual performance in specific occupations and may be better at predicting functioning in clerical occupations than in other occupations. Similarly, Performance IQs seem to be better predictors of vocational training than are Verbal or Full Scale IQs. Research has also suggested that intelligence is associated with vocational/career maturity and with educational attainment.

Given these findings, vocational assessment team members may wish to confine their use of intelligence test scores to making recommendations for vocational training and may wish to weigh Performance IQs more heavily than they do Verbal IQs when doing so (although this will depend upon the type of vocational training being considered). Team members may also wish to utilize intelligence test scores to assess the potential need for vocational assistance and intervention. Students scoring low on intelligence tests are less likely to demonstrate mature career decision-making skills and are more likely to need assistance in vocational planning. This appears to be particularly true of students scoring low on verbal measures of intelligence, who are less likely to progress far in the educational system (given the system's emphasis on verbal ability). Thus, a low Full Scale IQ, combined with a Verbal–Performance discrepancy in favor of the performance scale may suggest a high need for vocational planning assistance, the inappropriateness of considering occupations that require post-secondary education, and the potential to succeed in vocational-technical programs.

Table 5-4.

Relationship of Wechsler Intelligence Test Scores to Occupational Factors

Study	N	Population	Instrument	Dependent Variable	Correlation
Wechsler (1958)	94	General	W-B I: PIQ	Bennett Mechanical Comprehension Test	.35*
				Kuder Mechanical Interest	.31*
		Psychiatric Residents	W-B I: VIQ	Over All Competence	.38***
Webster (1974)			WAIS	Workshop Achievement Evaluator's Rating	
	40	Neurologically Impaired	FSIQ		.27
			PIQ		.51*
			BD/OA		.52*
	40	Character Disorder	FSIQ		.39**
			PIQ		.48*
			BD/OA		.51*
	40	Neurotics	FSIQ		.54*
			PIQ		.60*
			BD/OA		.29
	40	Psychotics/Functional	FSIQ		.37*
			PIQ		.52*
			BD/OA		.47*
	160	Combined	FSIQ		.40*
			PIQ		.51*
			BD/OA		.42*
McCarthy (1976)	48	TMR: Ages 20 & 21	WAIS:	Sheltered Workshop Performance	
			VIQ		.31**
			PIQ		.71*
			FSIQ		.59*
Webster (1979)	180	Psychiatric Outpatients	WAIS:	Vocational Test Performance	
			PIQ		.52**

NOTE: When patients were classified as Neurologically Impaired, Mentally Retarded, Neurotic, Physically Handicapped, and Psychotic, the FSIQ or PIQ entered into the multiple regression procedure on the first step.

Study	N	Population	Instrument	Dependent Variable	Correlation
Matheny, Dolan, & Krantz (1980)	148	White 15 Year Olds	WISC:	Parent Interviews	
			FSIQ	Interests: Females	.56*
				Males	.14
				Responsibilities: Females	.27*
				Males	.31*
Warren & Gardner (1981)	75	Disabled Students: Vocational-Technical Schools	WISC: FSIQ	Class Rank Assigned by Teachers	.63*
Palmo & Lutz (1983)	120	Economically Disadvantaged: Age 16-22	WAIS: Selected Factors	Career Maturity Inventory	*see inset
Shapira, Cnaan, & Cnaan (1985)	34	Residents in Institutions in Israel	WAIS:	Success in Assembly of Toys:	
				Performance Time	06
				Productivity	.23
				Effort Evaluation	−.15

CMI[1]	KY	KAJ	CAJ	LA	WSTD	AS
WAIS:						
VIQ	.53*	.66*	.50*	.53*	.53*	.50*
PIQ	.32*	.53*	.31*	.39*	.35*	.43*
FSIQ	.48*	.66*	.46*	.52*	.50*	.51*
Information	.53*	.65*	.44*	.47*	.47*	.44*
Comprehension	.44*	.51*	.43*	.45*	.44*	.42*
Similarities	.42*	.57*	.41*	.48*	.42*	.40*
Vocabulary	.57*	.66*	.54*	.56*	.54*	.55*

* p < .01
** p < .05
*** Not Reported

[1]KY = Knowing Yourself; KAJ = Knowing About Job; CAJ = Choosing A Job; LA = Looking Ahead; WSTD = What Should They Do; AS = Attitude Scale.

Note. Reprinted from "Intelligence and Occupational/Vocational Adjustment: A Literature Review" by T. Morris and E. Levinson (in press), *Journal of Counseling and Development.* Copyright American Association of Counseling and Development. Reprinted with permission. No further reproduction authorized without written permission of American Association for Counseling and Development.

Table 5-5.

*Correlation Between Various Intellectual Measures
and Selected Occupational Variables*

Study	Instrument	Subjects	Dependent Variable	Correlation	
				Training	Placement
Albin (1973)	Unknown	Sheltered Workshop Clients	Production		.145***
Ghiselli (1973)	Various, e.g.,	Executives & Administrators	Success	.27	.30
	Otis &	Foreman	Success	.31	.28
	Wessman	All Managers	Success	.29	.29
		General Clerks	Success	.47	.28
		Recording Clerks	Success	.46	.26
		Computing Clerks	Success	.52	.25
		All Clerks	Success	.47	.28
		Sales Clerks	Success		−.03
		Salesman	Success		.33
		All Sales Occupations	Success		.19
		Protective Occupations	Success	.42	.22
		Service Occupations	Success	.42	.27
		Vehicle Operators	Success	.18	.16
		Mechanical Repairmen	Success	.41	.23
		Electrical Workers	Success	.49	.29
		Structural Workers	Success	.31	.25
		Processing Workers	Success	.46	.24
		Complex Machine Workers	Success	.26	.26
		Machine Workers	Success	.35	.19
		All Trades & Crafts	Success	.41	.25
		Machine Tenders	Success	−.31	.21
		Bench Workers	Success	.27	.18
		Inspectors	Success	.24	.21
		Packers & Wrappers	Success	.49	.18
		Gross Manual Workers	Success	.25	.22
		All Industrial Workers	Success	.38	.20
		9-12 Grade Students	Vocational Maturity	Males	Females
Tseng & Rhodes (1973)	Educational Development Series:				
	IQ			.39*	.27*
	Verbal Ability			.30*	.24*
	Nonverbal Ability			.18***	.13
McCall (1977)	Stanford-Binet: Age 5	Fels Longitudinal Study Subjects	Attained Adult Occupation: Hollingshead Score	.15	.38
Flynn (1980)	Not reported	National Longitudinal Survey: Young Men's Cohort	Occupational Status		
		White Low I.Q.		.049****	
		White Average I.Q.		.303**	
		Black Low I.Q.		−.054****	
		Black Average I.Q.		.124****	
Malgady, Blacher, Davis, & Towner (1980)	Not reported	Developmental Center: Adolescents & Adults	Initial Placement Recommendation	.36*	
			1 Year Placement Success	.29*	
				Training	Placement
Albin (1973)	Unknown	Sheltered Workshop Clients	Production		.145****

(continued)

Table 5-5.
(Continued)

Study	Instrument	Subjects	Dependent Variable	Correlation Training	Placement
Gottfredson (1984)	GATB, G Factor	Unknown	Work with Complex Things	.00	
			Vigilance with Machines	.00	
			Operating Machines	–.01	
			Catering to People	.00	
			Selling	.00	
			Using Success	.00	
Hunter & Hunter (1984)	GATB Ability Composite	Meta-Analysis Study, 32, 124 Subjects	Selection for Entry-Level Jobs	.53	
Linn (1986)	Job Knowledge as Measure for General Cognitive Ability	Medical Technicians Black White	Over All Supervisory Rating	.45 .25	
		Cartographic Technicians Black Hispanic White		.28 .42 .36	

* *p* < .001.
** *p* < .01.
*** *p* < .05.
**** *Nonsignificant.*

Note. Reprinted from "Intelligence and Occupational/Vocational Adjustment: A Literature Review" by T. Morris and E. Levinson (in press), *Journal of Counseling and Development.* Copyright American Association of Counseling and Development. Reprinted with permission. No further reproduction authorized without written permission of American Association for Counseling and Development.

That mean IQ levels differ for various occupational groups, that IQ is associated with educational attainment, and that educational attainment is associated with occupational status suggests the appropriateness of using intelligence test data to assess the probability of successfully completing the educational requirements associated with different occupations. Jencks et al. (1979) analyzed 11 major studies and determined that "academic ability" explained approximately 37% of the variance in educational attainment and 27% of the variance in occupational status. It can be said that the higher one's IQ, the greater the probability that the individual has the potential to complete the educational requirements necessary to gain employment in high-status occupations, most of which require more formal education.

It is clear that additional research needs to be done in order to enable vocational assessment team members to utilize intelligence test data more confidently in vocational planning. Research needs to be done with different school populations and should focus upon the extent to which intelligence test scores can predict success in various vocational training programs. Until such research is completed, however, vocational assessment personnel should interpret and utilize intelligence test data cautiously and should attempt to confirm any hypotheses generated from intelligence test data with other assessment information. The proper administration, scoring, and interpretation of intelligence tests requires extensive training in cognitive and intellectual development, and in measurement theory and psychometrics. As such, the use of intelligence tests should generally be restricted to psychologists.

Tests of Intelligence

Wechsler Scales

David Wechsler has authored three different measures of intellectual ability targeted at different age groups. The Wechsler Adult Intelligence Scale - Revised (WAIS-R; Wechsler, 1981) is designed for use with individuals 16 years of age or older. The Wechsler Intelligence Scale for Children - Third Edition (WISC-III; Wechsler, 1992) is an updated version of the Wechsler Intelligence Scale for Children - Revised (1974; WISC-R) and is designed to assess the intelligence of individuals ages 6–16 years. The Wechsler Preschool and Primary Scale of Intelligence - Revised (WPPSI-R; 1989) is intended for use with children 3 to 7 years of age. Although the three scales are used with different age groups, they are similar in form and content.

All three scales are point scales and include both verbal and performance subtests. The three tests sample similar behaviors, although differences in format exist. The following is a listing of the subtests included in the various Wechsler scales, and a very brief description of what each subtest measures:

Information — assesses the ability to answer specific questions; assesses one's general fund of knowledge;

Comprehension — assesses practical knowledge, social judgment, common sense, and reasoning;

Similarities — assesses verbal concept formation;

Arithmetic — assesses numerical reasoning ability;

Vocabulary — assesses the ability to define words;

Digit Span — assesses immediate recall of orally presented numbers; assesses attention and concentration;

Sentences — assesses the ability to repeat sentences verbatim (included only on the WPPSI-R); assesses short-term recall;

Picture Completion—assesses the ability to differentiate essential from nonessential details;

Picture Arrangement—assesses nonverbal reasoning ability and the ability to plan and organize;

Block Design—assesses visual-motor coordination and perceptual organization;

Object Assembly—assesses perceptual organization ability and the ability to synthesize a whole from its parts;

Coding (Digit Symbol on WAIS-R; Animal Pegs on WPPSI-R)— assesses visual-motor coordination, speed of mental operation, and short-term visual recall;

Mazes—assesses visual motor planning and organization;

Geometric Design—assesses perceptual and visual motor organization abilities (included only on the WPPSI-R);

Symbol Search (WISC-III only)—assesses speed of information processing.

For each subtest, raw scores are converted to standard scores, which have a mean of 10 and a standard deviation of 3. Scores on verbal subtests are combined to compute a Verbal IQ, which has a mean of 100 and a standard deviation of 15. Similarly, scores on the performance subtests are combined to yield a Performance IQ, which has a mean of 100 and a standard deviation of 15. A Full Scale IQ can then be obtained from a combination of these two scores. IQs for the full scale also have a mean of 100 and a standard deviation of 15.

Nationally stratified random samples were used in the standardization of all three Wechsler scales. The WAIS-R was standardized on 1,880 adults. The WISC-III was standardized on 2,200 children ages 6 to 16 years. The WPPSI-R was standardized on 1,700 children ages 3 to 7 years. Reliability for all three scales, though variable by subtests and age, is generally excellent. Average reliability coefficients for the Full Scale IQs are .96 for the WPPSI-R, .96 for the WISC-III, and .97 for the WAIS-R.

The WAIS-R reports no evidence of validity. However, validity studies for the original WAIS combined with the similarity between the WAIS and WAIS-R are used to support the WAIS-R's validity. Eighty percent of the items overlap on the two scales. The WISC-III manual contains results of studies designed to determine the relationship between it and the WPPSI-R, the WAIS-R, and the WISC-R (the previous edition of the WISC-III). Correlations for the Verbal, Performance, and Full Scale IQ scores are generally in the .80s. Scores on the WISC-III are generally 2–7 points lower than are scores from the WISC-R, with scores on the performance scale demonstrating a greater disparity (average of 7 points lower on the WISC-III) than scores on the verbal scale (average of 2 points lower on the WISC-III). The validity of the WPPSI-R has been supported via correlations with the WPPSI, WISC-R, and Stanford-Binet intelligence scales. Correlations between the WPPSI-R and these instruments were found to be .87, .85, and .74, respectively. Additionally, the McCarthy Scales of Children's Abilities General Cognitive Index correlated .81 with the WPPSI-R.

In general, the Wechsler scales are considered to possess numerous assets, including high reliability, good validity, excellent standardization, good administration procedures, detailed manuals, and an extensive research and clinical basis (Sattler, 1988). They are extremely popular, frequently used, and highly respected instruments. However, as Salvia and Ysseldyke (1991) have noted, reliabilities of many subtests are low. Hence, some subtest scores should not be used as a basis for making placement decisions. Test users should consult the test manual and examine individual subtest reliabilities before interpreting and using individual subtest scores.

Stanford-Binet IV

The Stanford-Binet Intelligence Scale, originally developed in 1905, has undergone numerous revisions over the years. The most recent edition, the fourth edition (S-B IV), was published in 1986 and was authored by Robert Thorndike, Elizabeth Hagen, and Jerome Sattler. The S-B IV is individually administered, and encompasses an age range of 2 years through adult. The test is a point scale with 15 separate subtests grouped into four areas: verbal reasoning, quantitative reasoning, abstract/visual reasoning, and short term memory. Several subtests are included within each of these areas.

Each subtest yields raw scores that are converted to standard age scores (SAS), which have a mean of 50 and a standard deviation of 8. These subtest scores are combined into area scores (which have a mean of 100 and a standard deviation of 16) and are used to compute an overall composite IQ score (which has a mean of 100 and a standard deviation of 16).

The test was normed on a sample of 5,013 individuals from ages 2 through adult. Internal consistency reliabilities are excellent for the composite score (.97) but less satisfactory for individual subtest scores (.73 to .94). Stability coefficients are satisfactory for the composite score (.90), but inadequate for several of the subtest scores (.28 to .86). Validity studies comparing the S-B IV with other intelligence tests have indicated satisfactory concurrent validity (median correlation, .80) (Sattler, 1988).

The S-B IV is said to possess numerous assets, including good validity, high reliabilities, excellent standardization, and good administration procedures (Sattler, 1988). However, factor-analytic studies have suggested that different factor structures underlie the instrument at different age ranges. Because these studies do not wholly support the structure and organization of the test (i.e., some scores computed for certain age individuals should not be interpreted), users of the instrument are referred to Sattler (1988) for more detailed information on interpreting scores yielded by this instrument. Because different subtests are employed for different individuals, the test is somewhat limited in its ability to monitor intellectual changes in specific individuals over time. It also requires more time to administer than do other individually administered tests of intelligence (Salvia & Ysseldyke, 1991).

Kaufman Assessment Battery for Children

The Kaufman Assessment Battery for Children (K-ABC; Kaufman & Kaufman, 1983) is an individually administered test of both intelligence and academic achievement for children ages 2½ through 12½ years. There are four global scales, the product of which has a mean of 100 and a standard deviation of 15. The sequential processing scale emphasizes problem solving of a serial or temporal nature. The simultaneous processing scale assesses a holistic or global problem-solving approach. The mental processing composite is a combination of the sequential and simultaneous processing scales and yields an overall estimate of intellectual functioning. The achievement scale emphasizes knowledge of facts, and assesses language and school-related skills. A nonverbal scale can be administered to children who are hearing impaired, speech and language disordered, or non–English speaking.

Split-half reliability coefficients for the four global scales range from .86 to .97 for the different age groups. To demonstrate the test's validity, the authors briefly summarize more than 40 correlational studies using a diverse sampling of 2,000 subjects. Sattler (1988) has summarized numerous concerns about the K-ABC and has suggested that it not be used as the primary instrument for identifying the intellectual abilities of normal or exceptional students. Relatedly, Salvia and Ysseldyke (1991) have noted that the test was adequately standardized, possesses adequate reliability, but presents no data to validate it "as a measure of learning potential, for use in educational placement and planning, for clinical assessment, or for neurological assessment" (p. 499).

Woodcock-Johnson Psycho-Educational Battery

The Woodcock-Johnson Psycho-Educational Battery (Woodcock & Johnson, 1989), developed in 1978, is an individually administered test for individuals from 3 to adult. The instrument is designed to assess cognitive ability, scholastic aptitude, academic achievement, and interests. The instrument contains 27 subtests, which are organized into three parts. The first part contains 12 subtests assessing cognitive ability and specific scholastic aptitudes. Part 2 contains 10 subtests assessing academic achievement. The third part assesses specific scholastic and nonscholastic interests. The subtests yield raw scores, which can be converted into cluster scores. The cluster scores can then be converted to percentile ranks, grade scores, age scores, standard scores, and instructional ranges.

The instrument was normed on a school-aged sample of 3,900 individuals and 832 preschoolers and adults. Split-half reliability measures range between .62 to .95 on the various subtests. According to Salvia and Ysseldyke (1991), the battery was adequately standardized, and the data in the manual provide support for both the reliability and validity of the instrument. However, they indicate that the reliabilities of the subtests and other clusters are so variable that these scores should probably not be used in educational decision making.

Slosson Intelligence Test

The Slosson Intelligence Test (SIT; Slosson, 1983) is a brief intelligence test similar in nature to early editions of the Stanford-Binet. The test is designed as a basic screening instrument, is verbally oriented, and takes approximately 15 to 20 minutes to administer. No age range is reported; however, items range from the .5-month level to the 27-year level. Raw scores are obtained and may be transformed into IQs, percentile ranks, normal curve equivalents, T scores, or stanines. The IQ scores have a mean of 100 and a standard deviation of 16.

The standardization sample was composed of 1,109 individuals. However, no demographic data are reported on this sample. Consequently, the extent to which the standardization sample is nationally representative of the population is unknown. Test-retest reliability is reported to be .97. Correlations with the WISC have been reported to be .75 with the Full Scale IQ, .82 with the Verbal IQ, and .62 with the Performance IQ (Sattler, 1988). Salvia and Ysseldyke (1991) have suggested that the Stanford-Binet Intelligence Scale (the test upon which the SIT was based) should be used instead of the SIT, because it provides a more in-depth and qualitative evaluation of intelligence.

Otis-Lennon School Ability Test

The Otis-Lennon School Ability Test (OLSAT; Otis & Lennon, 1982) is the fifth revision of this scale since 1918. The test is designed as a group-administered test for use in grades 1 through 12. Two forms (R and S) are available at five levels: Primary I, Primary II, Elementary, Intermediate, and Advanced. The two forms encourage beginning- and end-of-the-year testing.

Behaviors assessed at the various levels include: following directions, defining words, detecting similarities and differences, classifying, sequencing, quantitative reasoning, and completing analogies. Raw scores can be converted into standard scores, a School Ability Index (which has a mean of 100 and a standard deviation of 16), and age stanines. The OLSAT was standardized on approximately 130,000 children in grades 1 through 12 from 70 school systems across the country.

Internal consistency reliability coefficients for both grade and age level exceed .93. Test-retest reliability for different grades ranges between .84 to .92. Predictive validity studies have yielded correlations ranging between .36 and .64. Salvia and Ysseldyke (1991) have concluded that although the test possesses adequate internal consistency, evidence of score stability and validity is quite limited.

ACADEMIC ACHIEVEMENT

Because different vocational training programs and jobs require different skill levels in such academic areas as reading and mathematics, the assessment of academic achievement should be an integral component of any comprehensive vocational assessment program. As new jobs are created, it is likely that the academic skills required to perform these jobs will increase. As Johnson and Packer (1987) have stated, "new jobs in service industries will demand much higher skill levels than the jobs of today. Very few jobs will be created for those who cannot read, follow directions, and use mathematics" (p. xiii).

Achievement tests have the purpose of measuring scholastic accomplishment. Generally, tests are considered to be achievement tests if they measure learning that has occurred as a result of experiences in a specific learning situation (such as a classroom or a training program) and when the focus of the test is on assessing what has been learned (Brown, 1983). Given this function, one of the most important considerations when selecting a test of achievement is whether the test possesses adequate content validity. That is, there must be an adequate match between the skills assessed by the test and those taught in the specific instructional or training program. If the skills assessed by a test do not adequately measure what a student was taught in a class or program, the test will not be a valid measure of the extent to which the student profited (learned) from that class or program.

There are several types of achievement tests. Achievement tests can be norm referenced or criterion referenced, individually administered or group administered, and can be unidimensional (measures achievement in only one area, such as reading) or multidimensional (measures achievement in a variety of areas, such as reading, mathematics, and spelling). For the most part, group-administered, multidimensional achievement tests tend to be superior to individually administered, unidimensional tests from a psychometric and practical perspective. In contrast to the latter, the former have greater breadth and scope and tend to be more cost and time efficient. Because they can be administered to large numbers of students at a time, group-administered multidimensional achievement tests also tend to have larger and more representative standardization samples. For this reason, these types of tests are frequently adopted by school districts for school-wide testing programs. School personnel who are considering including academic achievement testing in their vocational assessment programs should evaluate the tests already being administered in their districts. In many instances, the results of these tests (which are likely to be found in a student's cumulative file) will provide an adequate measure of achievement in a variety of academic areas. The use of such data may eliminate the need for individual achievement testing by vocational assessment personnel and allow for a more efficient use of personnel time.

Several prominent studies over the years have investigated the relationship between academic achievement and vocational outcomes. For the most part, these studies have suggested that there is a significant association between these variables. Biller (1987) reviewed several studies investigating the relationship between academic achievement and occupational status attainment. The studies reviewed suggested that academic achievement measures were better predictors of occupational status attainment than were intelligence tests; that achievement tests given in the 6th grade predicted educational attainment, occupational status, and earnings as well as tests given later; and that mathematics achievement was a better predictor of later vocational success than were other measures of achievement (including reading achievement).

Although the studies reviewed by Biller (1987) should be interpreted cautiously in light of their instrumentation and methodological limitations, several other studies have yielded similar findings. For example, Ansley and Forsythe (1983) found that standardized achievement test scores could be used to predict college grade point average and graduation status (graduated/not graduated) and that, although the predictability of these achievement test scores increased from grade 4 to grade 12, the increase in predictability over these grades was moderate at best. Ansley and Forsythe concluded that any of the achievement measures (even those from grade 4) could be used to help in predicting future academic performance in college. Schmitt (1978) found achievement to be the strongest predictor of educational choice among a sample of high school graduates in the

Midwest. Similarly, Wolf (1983) found that achievement measured by the GED (Test of General Educational Development) proved to be a valid predictor of first semester grade point average at a 2-year college. Church (1977) found that academic achievement measured by the California Achievement Test correlated positively with the mean job level aspired to by Anglo and Navaho high school students. Relatedly, Schill, McCartin, and Meyer (1985) found that grade point average in high school was significantly correlated with employment among adolescents.

Several studies have indicated that reading and math achievement are correlated with success in vocational training. Zurawell and Das (1982) studied factors associated with success in an automotives training program and found that whereas math achievement correlated significantly with grade received in the course, reading comprehension and reading vocabulary did not. In contrast, Goldstein (1977) found that scores on the Nelson Reading Test along with age and number of years of formal education completed were significant predictors of vocational education course completion.

In summary, research has indicated that academic achievement is correlated with educational attainment and occupational status. As such, achievement test scores can be used to assess the probability that a student will successfully complete the postsecondary educational requirements necessary for entry into many high-status occupations. Relatedly, achievement test data can be used to assess the extent to which a student has mastered the academic skills necessary for success in a given vocational training program. However, one must remember that, in many cases, deficiencies in the academic skills necessary for success in a given vocational training program and/or occupation can be compensated for via use of alternative instructional methods. For example, a student who may have difficulty learning carpentry because of an inability to read the textbook used in the class can be provided with audiotapes of the book. Although achievement test data may be useful in identifying potential obstacles to success in vocational training, data should not necessarily be used to rule out training programs or occupations for students.

Tests of Achievement

Wide Range Achievement Test - Revised

The Wide Range Achievement Test - Revised (WRAT-R; Jastak & Wilkinson, 1984) is an individually administered scale of achievement for ages 5 to adult. The purpose of the WRAT-R is to measure what the authors refer to as "codes" that are necessary to learn basic skills. The instrument contains two levels (one level for each of two different age ranges) and takes approximately 20 to 30 minutes to administer. There are three subtests at each level: reading, spelling, and arithmetic. Raw scores obtained from the subtests can be converted to grade equivalents and standard scores. Standard scores can be converted to percentiles, stanines, scaled scores, or T scores.

Standardization of the WRAT-R included a sample of 5,600 individuals from 5 years to 74 years 11 months. However, the standardization procedures are inadequately described in the test manual. Hence, the degree to which the standardization sample is nationally representative of the population is unknown. The authors fail to report traditional reliability coefficients, and validity is limited to data reported on earlier editions of the WRAT. The test also assesses a very limited range of academic skills. For these and other reasons, Reynolds (1986) has argued that the WRAT-R is psychometrically inadequate and has strongly urged that it not be used.

Peabody Individual Achievement Test - Revised

The Peabody Individual Achievement Test - Revised (PIAT-R; Markwardt, 1989) is an individually administered test for students ages 5 years to 18 years 11 months. The test contains two composite scores (total reading and total test) and one optional composite score (written language). There are a total of six subtests: general information, reading recognition, reading comprehension, mathematics, spelling, and written expression. Raw scores are calculated for each composite and can be converted to grade equivalents, age equivalents, standard scores, percentile ranks, normal curve equivalents, and stanines.

A total of 1,563 students, kindergarten through grade 12, were included in the standardization sample. The authors report that the sample was stratified according to geographic region, socioeconomic status, and race or ethnic group. Reliability coefficients for the subtests are generally in the .90s. Concurrent validity was determined by correlating the PIAT-R with the Peabody Picture Vocabulary Test - Revised (Dunn, 1981). Resulting correlations ranged between .50 and .72. Salvia and Ysseldyke (1991) have concluded that the test is adequately standardized, and possesses acceptable internal consistency reliability. Given its response format, the PIAT-R is a particularly good instrument for use with students who have upper mobility problems or limited use of arms and hands.

California Achievement Tests

The California Achievement Tests (CAT; Tiegs & Clark, 1970) are a set of norm-referenced tests that assess skill development in seven content areas in kindergarten through grade 12. The skills measured include reading, spelling, language, mathematics, study skills, science, and social studies. Two forms of the test, Form E and Form F, are used to assess skills at 11 and 8 levels, respectively.

The CAT yields five different scores for interpretation: percentile ranks, stanines, grade equivalents, normal curve equivalents, and scaled scores. Machine scoring is available through the publisher. The instrument can be hand scored as well.

Two sets of norms are available (Fall of 1984 and Spring of 1985) for grades kindergarten through 12. A total of 300,000 students comprised the Fall sample and 230,000 students comprised the Spring sample. A stratified random sample was obtained from students in public, private, and Catholic schools.

The test's technical manual reports internal consistency coefficients of greater than .80 for all but two subtests (science and social studies). The reliabilities of these two subtests are .68 and .66, respectively. Limited validity data are reported in the test manual. Salvia and Ysseldyke (1991) indicate that although the test was adequately standardized, data supporting the test's internal consistency reliability and validity are limited.

Iowa Tests of Basic Skills

The Iowa Tests of Basic Skills (ITBS; Hileronymous, Hoover, & Lindquist, 1986) comprise both a norm-referenced and criterion-referenced test designed to measure skills in vocabulary, reading, language, work study, listening, and mathematics. The test also contains two supplementary subtests in science and social studies. The ITBS is a group-administered test for use in grades kindergarten through 9. There are 10 levels of the ITBS, with two forms for each level.

The ITBS was standardized using a stratified national sample of 332,000 students, 14,000 at each grade level. Internal consistency reliability coefficients for the ITBS range from .67 to .95. However, the word analysis and mathematics subtests are the only subtests that have adequate reliability on which to base screening decisions of students at the kindergarten and 1st-grade levels. No stability data are presented for the 1986 edition. There are no data on construct or concurrent validity of the ITBS; validity is based on previous editions of the ITBS. Salvia and Ysseldyke (1991) conclude that the standardization of the ITBS is exemplary; however, because internal consistency reliability is variable, they recommend that users of the test check the reliability for the grades and subtests for which the test is going to be used.

Metropolitan Achievement Tests

The most recent edition (the sixth edition) of the Metropolitan Achievement Test (MAT6; Prescott, Balow, Hogan, & Farr, 1984) is composed of two sets of tests—Survey and Diagnostic. The Survey battery is a group-administered test of achievement that measures skills in reading, mathematics, language, social studies, and science. Both norm-referenced and criterion-referenced interpretations are available in eight overlapping levels for grades kindergarten through 12. Reading, mathematics, and language make up the Diagnostic test battery. The purpose of the diagnostic test is to aid school personnel in instructional planning and in evaluating specific parts of the curriculum. The Diagnostic battery can also be interpreted as a norm-referenced or criterion-referenced measure in six nonoverlapping levels from grades K.5 to 12.9.

Raw scores and nine different types of derived scores including scaled scores, percentile ranks, grade equivalents, normal curve equivalents, performance indicators, instructional reading levels, independent reading levels, frustration reading levels, and instructional mathematics levels can be obtained. Standardization of the MAT6 included more than 200,000 students. However, there is no evidence that the sample was a stratified random sample representative of the general population.

The MAT6 manual provides data on internal consistency and alternate-form reliability. Generally, the data suggest that the test is reliable from grade 3 onward (Salvia & Ysseldyke, 1991). Validity judgments are to be made by the user in testing the extent to which the test adequately samples what has been taught in the school's curriculum.

SRA Achievement Series

The SRA Achievement Series (Naslund, Thorpe, & LeFever, 1978) is a group-administered, norm- and criterion-referenced battery designed to assess skill development in reading, mathematics, language arts, social studies, science, and use of reference materials. The SRA series is designed for use in grades kindergarten through 12. There are eight (A-H) nonoverlapping levels of the test.

Raw scores from the SRA series can be transformed into grade equivalents, stanines, national and local percentiles, and national percentile bands. The stratified standardization sample included 83,681 students in 383 schools (Spring of 1978) and 129,900 students in 457 schools (Fall of 1978).

Three measures of reliability are reported: internal consistency, alternate forms, and test-retest. Internal consistency coefficients are reported to range from .54 to 94; alternate form coefficients range from .70 to .88;

and test retest coefficients range from .66 to .91 for the majority of the subtests. Validity is demonstrated via correlations with course grades and other achievement tests (coefficients range from .43 to .93). Salvia and Ysseldyke (1991) conclude that the test was appropriately standardized, possesses adequate validity, and possesses reliability suitable for screening purposes.

Stanford Achievement Test Series

The Stanford Achievement Test Series (Gardner, Rudman, Karlsen, & Merwin, 1982) contains three different measures: the Stanford Early School Achievement Series (SESAT), the Stanford Achievement Test (SAT), and the Test of Academic Skills (TASK). The tests are both norm and criterion referenced and are group administered. The SESAT covers kindergarten and 1st grade; the SAT covers 1st grade through 9th grade; and the TASK covers 8th grade through community college.

The series contains 10 levels with 5 to 11 subtests at each level. The behaviors sampled in each series include: sounds and letters, word study skills, word reading, sentence reading, reading comprehension, vocabulary, listening to words and stories, listening comprehension, spelling, language/English, mathematics, concepts of numbers, mathematics computation, mathematics application, science, social science, and environment. The series also contains special editions for assessing blind and deaf students.

Scores obtained on all forms can be transformed into stanines, grade-equivalent scores, percentiles, age scores, and various standard scores. Standardization of the Stanford Series was done simultaneously with the Otis-Lennon School Ability Test. Approximately 450,000 students were used in the standardization sample. Reliability coefficients range from .76 to .96. In assessing the test's content validity, the authors state that they submitted test items to different groups of subject-matter experts, measurement experts, minority group persons, and teachers for screening and editing of test items. Overall, Salvia and Ysseldyke (1991) state that the standardization, reliability, and validity of the test are adequate for screening purposes.

Basic Achievement Skills Individual Screener

The Basic Achievement Skills Individual Screener (BASIS; Sonnerschein, 1983) is an individually administered instrument designed to provide both norm-referenced and criterion-referenced information. The BASIS assesses skills in reading, mathematics, spelling, and writing for students in grades 1 through 12. Test items are administered in clusters that reflect the curriculum of a specific grade. Scores are intended to be used to derive placement suggestions.

Scores obtained from the BASIS can be expressed as standard scores, percentile ranks, stanines, grade equivalents, age equivalents, and normal curve equivalents. The BASIS was standardized on a representative sample of 3,200 students in grades 1 through 12. Internal consistency reliability coefficients exceed .90 for all four subtests. All test-retest reliabilities exceed .80. According to the authors, content validity was established by selection of items and item match to grade level. Additionally, the BASIS was correlated with several unspecified achievement tests. Resultant correlations ranged between .30 and .72. Salvia and Ysseldyke (1991) state that the validity of the test is adequate, reliability is suitable for screening purposes, but that the test's norms may now be outdated.

Woodcock Reading Mastery Tests - Revised

The Woodcock Reading Mastery Test (WRMT-R; Woodcock, 1987) is an individually administered test designed for use with individuals from kindergarten to college and with adults up to 75 years of age. There are two alternative forms of the test, G and H, with six and four subtests, respectively. Form H excludes the readiness subtests. The subtests include: visual-auditory learning, letter identification, word identification, word attack, word comprehension, and passage comprehension. These six tests are organized into three clusters: the readiness cluster, composed of the visual-auditory learning and letter identification subtests; the basic skills cluster, made up of the word identification and word attack subtests; and the reading comprehension cluster, made up of the word comprehension and passage comprehension subtests.

Scores obtained on the WRMT-R include grade equivalents, age equivalents, relative performance indices, instructional ranges, percentile ranks, and standard scores. The standardization sample of the WRMT-R included 6,089 students in 60 geographically diverse areas stratified according to sex, race, community size, ethnic origin, and type of college. Internal consistency reliability coefficients exceed .80 for all clusters. The manual provides no evidence for test-retest reliability. Content validity is based upon expert judgment and the Rasch scaling procedure used in constructing the instrument. Concurrent validity was assessed by correlating the WRMT-R with the reading subtests of the Woodcock-Johnson Psycho-Educational Battery. Salvia and Ysseldyke (1991) report that the test was adequately normed and possesses adequate evidence of internal consistency reliability and validity. Although they indicate that the test lacks test-retest reliability data, they compliment the test's updated norms and new diagnostic aids.

Stanford Diagnostic Reading Test

The Stanford Diagnostic Reading Test (SDRT; Karlsen & Gardner, 1985) is a group-administered test designed to measure strengths and weaknesses in reading by assessing the skills of decoding, vocabulary, comprehension, and reading rate. The SDRT contains four levels with two parallel forms (G and H) at each level. The grade ranges of the four levels of the tests are 1.5 through 3.5 for the Red level, 2.5 through 5.5 for the Green level, 4.5 through 9.5 for the Brown level, and 9 through 13 for the Blue level.

The SDRT is both norm referenced and criterion referenced. Student responses can be either hand or machine scored. The SDRT yields six different scores; raw scores can be transformed into "Progress Indicators," percentile ranks, stanines, grade equivalents, and scaled scores. Progress Indicators are criterion-referenced scores that indicate mastery or lack of mastery of an age-related skill.

The standardization sample of the SDRT included a stratified random sampling with socioeconomic status, school system enrollment, and geographic region as variables. Internal consistency reliability coefficients are .80 or higher for all but two subtests (the reliabilities of these subtests are .79 and .76). Alternate form reliabilities range from .66 to .78. Criterion-related validity coefficients range from .67 to .88 at the Red level, .68 to .87 at the Green level, .69 to .87 at the Brown level, and .64 to .74 at the Blue level. Salvia and Ysseldyke (1991) indicate that this instrument was exceptionally well standardized and possesses adequate reliability. They note that, as is true with other achievement measures, validity must be measured against the content of the local curricula.

KeyMath Revised: A Diagnostic Inventory of Essential Mathematics

The KeyMath Revised: A Diagnostic Inventory of Essential Mathematics (KeyMath-R; Connolly, 1988) is an individually administered instrument for use with children ages 5 through 13. The KeyMath-R provides assessment in three areas: basic concepts, operations, and applications. There are 13 strands measured in the subtests. Basic concepts include numeration, rational numbers, and geometry. Operations assesses addition, subtraction, multiplication, division, and mental computation. Applications assesses measurement, time and money, estimation, interpreting data, and problem solving. There are two forms of the instrument, A and B, each containing 258 items.

Raw scores can be converted to standard scores, percentile ranks, stanines, normal curve equivalents, grade equivalents, and age equivalents. The standardization sample of the KeyMath-R included 873 students in kindergarten through 8th grade at 22 test sites in 16 states. The normative sample was stratified on the basis of geographic region, grade, sex, race or ethnic background, and level of parental education.

Alternate-form reliability correlations for the two forms range from the .50s to the .70s for the subtests, the low .80s for the area scores, and the .90s for the total test score. Split-half reliabilities for the subtests are mostly in the .70s (.80s for the area scores and .90s for the total test score). Reliability coefficients based upon the Rasch model fall within the .70s and .80s for all subtests. The coefficients are in the low to middle .90s for the area scores and total test score. Internal consistency reliability ranges from the low .30s to the mid-.90s.

Content validity of the KeyMath-R was assessed by identifying essential mathematics content and prevailing curricular trends. Nationally recognized experts were consulted in the test's development. Correlations with the original KeyMath range from the .80s to mid-.90s. Salvia and Ysseldyke (1991) have indicated that although the standardization of the test was generally adequate, low reliabilities of subtests prevent users from making inferences about a student's instructional strengths and weaknesses based upon subtest and domain scores.

Stanford Diagnostic Mathematics Test

The Stanford Diagnostic Mathematics Test (SDMT; Beatty, Gardner, Madden, & Karlsen, 1985) is a group-administered, norm-referenced instrument for use with individuals in grades 2 through 12. There are four overlapping levels of the SDMT (Red, Green, Brown, and Blue). The SDMT contains three subtests: number system and numeration, computation, and applications. Each subtest yields content- and norm-referenced scores. Content-referenced scores can also be converted to progress indicators, which are designed to assist in identifying individuals who are capable of making satisfactory progress in a mathematics program. The norm-referenced scores can be converted to percentiles, stanines, normal curve equivalents, grade equivalents, and scaled scores.

The manual does not specify the number of subjects used in the standardization sample, or the number of school districts used. Internal consistency reliability of the total score exceeds .90 except for grade 4. No stability data are reported. Similarly, no data on the reliability of the progress indicators are provided. The manual fails to describe how items were selected and there is only limited evidence of the concurrent validity of the instrument. The SDMT was correlated with the Stanford Achievement Test with resulting correlations ranging between .64 and .89. No evidence of the validity of the progress indicators is provided. Salvia and Ysseldyke (1991) indicate that the test has an inadequate description of norms and that lack of subtest reliability limits the instrument's use as a diagnostic tool.

PERSONALITY

As was suggested in Chapter 2, many career development theorists argue that vocational choice is a function of personality, and that aspects of personality (self-concept, for example) may be influenced by work experiences. As such, personality characteristics are important to assess when conducting comprehensive vocational assessments. However, as Brown (1990) has suggested, personality assessment has not been widely used in vocational/career counseling, despite the widespread acceptance of the important role personality plays in vocational/career development.

Personality can be defined as a relatively permanent set of characteristics and traits that remain fairly stable over time (Baron & Greenberg, 1990). In that the traits and characteristics that comprise one's personality include things like interests, skills, and values, inclusion of personality as a separate topic in this chapter is somewhat redundant. That is, in separately discussing the assessment of intelligence, interests, and aptitudes, we are, in a sense, discussing the assessment of specific components of personality.

A variety of methods exist for assessing personality: projective techniques, rating scales, self-report measures, and observational procedures (Salvia & Ysseldyke, 1991). Projective techniques employ ambiguous stimuli, responses to which are thought to provide information about an individual's thoughts, feelings, and needs. Theoretically, individuals project aspects of their personalities in their responses. Rating scales are similar to checklists and require that a "significant other" (someone who is thoroughly familiar with the person being rated) rate the extent to which specific behaviors are exhibited. Often, rating scales attempt to assess the frequency, duration, and intensity of behaviors. Self-report measures are similar to rating scales. Individuals who are being assessed are asked to respond to items designed to identify the frequency, intensity, or duration of specific behaviors or feelings. Observational measures are systematic procedures designed to identify specific behaviors as they unfold naturally in the environment.

As Brown (1990) has indicated, personality tests used to make vocational decisions fall into two broad categories: tests that measure the "normal" personality and "clinical" tests that measure maladjustment or psychopathology. The former provide information on a person's motives, values, attitudes, and other characteristics, profiles from which can be used to describe the kind of person one is. This information can be compared to the requirements and demands of different jobs to assist in decision making. The Self-Directed Search and 16 PF are examples of "normal" personality measures. "Clinical" measures are specifically designed to detect patterns of pathology and are frequently used to screen people in or out of stressful jobs such as air traffic controller or police officer. The Minnesota Multiphasic Personality Inventory is an example of such a clinical test.

Unfortunately, personality assessment is fraught with problems. As Salvia and Ysseldyke (1991) indicate, most personality assessment devices possess inadequate norms, and provide little evidence of reliability or validity. For this reason, they suggest that school personnel refrain from using personality measures altogether. Although it is true that many personality assessment devices possess inadequate psychometric characteristics, newer objective assessment devices and rating scales are increasingly becoming available with acceptable psychometric characteristics. Even though projective techniques should be used cautiously if at all (because of their inadequate psychometric properties), school-based personnel should consider the inclusion of objective personality assessment devices in their transdisciplinary vocational assessment programs. As with instruments used to assess other traits important to comprehensive vocational assessment, professionals should ensure that only those personality assessment instruments with acceptable reliability, validity, and standardization be incorporated into assessment programs.

Personality assessment data can be used to identify the degree to which traits possessed by an individual will either assist or inhibit training and eventual vocational functioning in a particular occupation. Research has indicated that some personality assessment data can be used to predict both job satisfaction and job performance (Holland, 1985a). Holland (1985a) has argued that the choice of a vocation is simply the expression of personality and has demonstrated that individuals who choose similar occupations have similar personalities. He believes that interests are a reflection of personality and that, consequently, interest inventories are measures of personality. Although Holland's theory is often conceptualized as a theory of "vocational personalities," it is more often categorized as a theory of career development and, as such, is discussed in detail in Chapter 2. Because the Self-Directed Search (an instrument based upon Holland's theory) is typically categorized as a vocational interest inventory, it will be reviewed in a later section of this chapter.

Research has investigated the extent to which specific personality assessment devices can be effectively used to assess aspects of vocational functioning. Timmerman (1975) found that after assigning a trait-scoring system to a sentence completion form, scores could be used effectively to predict employer ratings. Edwards (1977) found promising results in a study involving the use of a peer rating system designed to predict job and school performance. Students and workers were divided into work groups. After a period of time, each was given a set of 16 personality descriptors and a list of the others in their group. The members were instructed to choose four individuals from the group for each trait. The results suggested that group peer rating was an effective method for developing reliable measures of personality for use in predicting performance. Hafner and Fakouri (1984) compared the content of early recollections to subsequent career choice. College students in accounting, secondary education, and psychology were asked to recall incidents in their childhood. Scoring was based upon themes, characters, and concerns. Education students' early recollections most often involved the school setting. Psychology students reported themes that related to fear or anxiety-provoking situations. Accounting students reported early recollections that showed internal control and low frequencies of references to people or animals.

Personality Tests

Minnesota Multiphasic Personality Inventory

The Minnesota Multiphasic Personality Inventory (MMPI; Hathaway & McKinley, 1967) is designed to assess personality characteristics that are indicative of psychological abnormality. The inventory is designed for adults 16 years or older with at least a 6th-grade reading ability. The MMPI consists of 10 scales: hypochondriasis, depression, hysteria, psychopathic deviate, masculinity-femininity, paranoia, psychasthenia, schizophrenia, hypomania, and social. Additionally, three validity scales are included: the lie scale, the infrequency scale, and the correction scale. The examinee responds to 550 statements in a "yes," "no," or "cannot say" fashion.

Raw scores of the MMPI can be converted to standard scores with a mean of 50 and a standard deviation of 10. Scores of 79 or above are indicative of a problem. The MMPI may also be computer scored and computer interpreted. New norms were constructed in 1983, which included responses from 1,408 individuals from ages 18 through 99 years. Streiner (1986) suggests that caution should be exercised when using the newer norms, and ideally they should be used in conjunction with the original norms.

The 1967 manual reports test-retest reliability coefficients ranging from .50 to .90, and internal consistency coefficients of over .90 for certain scales. Validity of the original scale was determined by comparing clinical diagnosis and successful predictions of the MMPI. The MMPI is a popular and frequently used clinical instrument by psychologists.

Minnesota Multiphasic Personality Inventory - 2

The Minnesota Multiphasic Personality Inventory - 2 (MMPI-2; Butcher, Dahlstrom, Graham, Tellegren, & Kaemmer, 1989) is a newer version of the MMPI. A 567-item test with a true-false format, the

MMPI-2 may be administered by audiocassette tape, paper and pencil, or IBM-compatible computer. It can be administered individually or to a group and requires at least an 8th-grade reading level. The MMPI-2 is composed of 13 basic scales—lie, infrequency, correction, hysteria, depression, hypochondriasis, psychopathic deviate, masculinity/femininity, paranoia, psychasthenia, schizophrenia, hypomania, and social introversion—which only require the administration of the first 370 items to evaluate. In addition, 15 new content scales have been developed for the MMPI-2, including: anxiety, fears, obsessiveness, depression, health concerns, bizarre mentation, anger, cynicism, antisocial practices, type A, low self-esteem, social discomfort, family problems, work interference, and negative treatment indicators. Raw scores obtained from the MMPI-2 can be converted to T scores.

Standardization of the MMPI-2 included a sample of 2,600 individuals ranging in age from 18 to 90. However, there was an underrepresentation of individuals from the Hispanic and Asian-American subgroups as compared to the 1980 U.S. census. Reliability coefficients have been found to range from .67 to .92 for males and .58 to .91 for females. Holden (1991) cited the following disadvantages of the MMPI-2: the lack of data for adolescents below the age of 18 and the increase in the required reading level from the 7th- (on the original MMPI) to the 8th-grade level (on the MMPI-2).

Burks' Behavior Rating Scale

The Burks' Behavior Rating Scale (BBRS; Burks, 1969), for use with children in grades 1 through 9, is designed to identify patterns of pathological behavior in children already having behavior difficulties at home or in school. The BBRS is a preliminary device designed to facilitate differential diagnosis by measuring the severity of observed negative symptoms. The scale contains 19 subscales that measure excessive self-blame, anxiety, withdrawal, dependency, poor ego strength, physical strength, coordination, intellectuality, academics, attention, impulse control, reality contact, sense of identity, anger control, suffering, sense of persecution, aggressiveness, resistance, and social conformity.

An adult rater who knows the child well describes the child's behavior according to 1 of 5 descriptive statements (which range from not noticing the behavior to noticing the behavior to a very large degree). The scores are calculated and recorded on a profile sheet. The respective score can fall within one of three ranges: not significant, significant, or very significant.

Test-retest reliability was determined by the rating of 95 disturbed children by their teachers. The resulting coefficients ranged between .60

to .83. Content validity was assessed by 22 school psychologists and 200 teachers who reviewed the scale. Lerner (1985) suggests that the BBRS, when used with other sources of information about a child, can be a valuable tool for differentially diagnosing children with problems.

Sixteen Personality Factor Questionnaire

The Sixteen Personality Factor Questionnaire (16 PF; Cattell, Eber, & Tatsuoka, 1970) was designed for use with high school, college, and general adult populations. It is an instrument designed to assess 16 "source traits" of an individual. There are five forms of the 16 PF: A, B, C, D, and E. The instrument contains a forced-choice format that yields scores of 16 bipolar primary factors: reserved/outgoing, concrete/abstract thinking, affected by feelings/emotionally stable, not assertive/dominant, serious/enthusiastic, expedient/conscientious, shy/venturesome, tough/tender minded, trusting/suspicious, practical/imaginative, forthright/shrewd, self-assured/apprehensive, conservative/experimenting, group dependent/self-sufficient, undisciplined/self-disciplined, and relaxed/tense.

Test-retest reliabilities range from .45 to .93 for forms A and B; and from .67 to .86 for forms C and D. Validity of the 16 PF as reported in the manual is limited. Bolton (1978) suggests that the 16 PF compares favorably with other personality inventories, although the manual contains serious deficiencies.

Basic Personality Inventory

The Basic Personality Inventory (BPI) (Jackson, 1989) is a questionnaire consisting of 240 true/false items appropriate for use with adolescents and adults. It is composed of 12 scales and takes approximately 35 minutes to complete. The BPI can be hand scored and results can be graphed on a profile form. Raw scores are converted to T scores.

The adolescent norm group consisted of 2,000 persons between the ages of 12 and 18. The extent to which these norms are nationally representative of the adolescent population, however, is questionable. Average internal consistency reliability coefficients for the scales, computed for various samples, range between .69 and .78. An average test-retest reliability coefficent reported in the manual, based upon two studies with 1-month intervals, was .75. In summary, LaVoie (1991) has indicated that the BPI possesses barely adequate reliability and questionable validity. However, he applauds the instrument's approach to the measurement of normal and pathological personality and adjustment and suggests that with additional research the BPI may "take its place in the front rank of measures that are important for clinical practice" (p. 42).

Prout-Strohmer Assessment System

The Prout-Strohmer Assessment System (PSAS; Prout & Strohmer, 1989) is a multimethod, multitrait system composed of two component parts, the Prout-Strohmer Personality Inventory (PSPI) and the Strohmer-Prout Behavior Rating Scale (SPBRS). The purpose of the PSAS is to assess emotional and behavioral problems of adolescents and adults (age 14 years and up) in the mildly mentally retarded and borderline intelligence ranges (IQs in the 55 to 83 range).

The PSPI is an individually administered self-report instrument containing 162 items with a "yes/no" format. The inventory is administered verbally with all words at or below the 4th-grade reading level. Administration time is approximately 30 minutes and scores from six clinical scales — depression, low self-esteem, anxiety, thought/behavior disorder, impulse control, and total pathology — and two validity scales — lie scale and response set indicator — may be obtained.

The SPBRS is a 135-item rating scale that is completed by someone familiar with the individual. Items are rated on a continuum from 0 (never observed/reported) to 3 (often observed/reported). Administration time is approximately 15 minutes. Scores from 12 clinical scales — anxiety, depression, withdrawal, low self-esteem, somatic concerns, thought/behavior disorder, physical aggression, noncompliance, distractibility, hyperactivity, verbal aggression, and sexual maladjustment — and two global factors — externalizing and internalizing disorders — are produced.

Approximately 700 subjects, from seven states and Canada, were used in the norming sample for both the PSPI and the SPBRS. Reliability coefficients for the PSPI range from .81 to .96, whereas coefficients of .90 to .97 have been obtained for the SPBRS. Test-retest reliabilities of .80 and above have been reported for the PSPI. Interrater reliabilities across settings of .70 and above have been reported for the SPBRS. Validity studies have indicated significant correlations between the PSPI and the Beck Depression Inventory and between both the PSPI and SPBRS and clinical diagnoses, involvement with behavior plans, use of psychotropic medications, level of independent living, vocational placement, vocational performance, and other counselor ratings of adjustment. Possible areas of application for the PSAS include: vocational placement and decision making, planning for residential placement, referral to mental health services, treatment monitoring, and diagnostic assessment.

ADAPTIVE BEHAVIOR

Adaptive behavior can be defined as the effectiveness or degree to which an individual meets the standards of personal independence and social responsibility (Grossman, 1983), or the extent to which individuals adapt themselves to the expectations of nature and society (Salvia & Ysseldyke, 1991). According to Reschly (1990), adaptive behavior is composed of four major domains: independent functioning, social functioning, functional academic competencies, and vocational/occupational competencies.

Independent Functioning—This domain includes an assessment of skills such as toileting, feeding, dressing, traveling within the community, and shopping. It also includes an assessment of communications skills, use of leisure time, and degree of need for supervision.

Social Functioning—This domain includes an assessment of social skills, including greeting, communication, expressing feelings, sharing, sensitivity, interacting with others, and avoidance of situationally inappropriate or obnoxious behavior.

Functional Academic Competencies—This domain includes an assessment of literacy skills, knowledge of time and number concepts, and other cognitive competencies necessary for independent functioning.

Vocational/Occupational Competencies—This domain includes an assessment of work habits and behaviors, knowledge of careers and work, and the specific skills necessary for successful job performance.

Adaptive behavior is particularly important to assess with students who have disabilities (whose inability to function independently or interact appropriately are major obstacles to employment) and is a required component of the assessment of mentally retarded students. Information gleaned from adaptive behavior assessment can assist TVA team members in identifying the skills a student must be taught in order to make a successful adjustment to both work and community living. Because people often lose jobs because of affective or social deficiencies rather than technical incompetence (Hooper, 1980), an assessment of social functioning is an especially important component of a comprehensive vocational assessment.

Tests of Adaptive Behavior

The Vineland Adaptive Behavior Scale

The Vineland Adaptive Behavior Scale (VABS; Sparrow, Balla, & Cicchetti, 1984) is an individually administered instrument used to assess the personal and social adaptability of individuals. The VABS is a revision of the Vineland Social Maturity Scale. The scale is administered to an informant who is familiar with the individual being assessed. There are three versions of the VABS: Interview Edition, Survey Form; Interview

Edition, Expanded Form; and Classroom Edition. The survey and expanded forms are administered in an interview format and are utilized with caregivers of individuals ages birth to 18 years 11 months. The survey form contains 577 items. The classroom edition is a questionnaire completed by teachers of children ages 3 to 12 years 11 months. All three forms assess the following domains: communication, daily living skills, socialization, and motor. The interview form also assesses maladaptive behavior.

Domain and composite raw scores can be transformed to standard scores, percentile ranks, age equivalents, and adaptive levels. A total of 3,000 individuals were used in the standardization of the interview editions. The sample was stratified on the basis of age, sex, community size, geographic region, parental education, and race or ethnicity. Split-half reliabilities range from .83 to .94. Test-retest reliability coefficients fall in the .80s and .90s. Interrater reliability is extremely high and was measured to be between .96 and .99.

Content validity of the instrument, as stated by the authors, was assessed via an intensive review of the child development literature and via the author's own personal clinical experiences. Holden (1984) has suggested that the VABS has remedied faults of the previous scale and commended the authors for their thorough and elaborate standardization of the instrument. Salvia and Ysseldyke (1991) have concluded that although reliability of the scales varies, the test was adequately normed and appears to possess adequate validity.

AAMD Adaptive Behavior Scale for Children and Adults

The AAMD Adaptive Behavior Scale for Children and Adults (AAMD; Nihara, Foster, Shellhaas, & Leland, 1974) is individually administered to an informant who is familiar with the child or adult being assessed. It is intended to provide information about "personal independence in daily living." There are two parts to the scale. Part 1 requires the informant to rate 66 items across 10 domains: independent functioning, physical development, economic activity, language development, numbers and time, domestic activity, vocational activity, self-direction, responsibility, and socialization. Part 2 contains 44 items in 14 domains: violent and destructive behavior, antisocial behavior, rebellious behavior, untrustworthy behavior, withdrawal, stereotyped behavior and odd mannerisms, inappropriate interpersonal manners, unacceptable vocal habits, unacceptable or eccentric habits, self-abusive behavior, hyperactive tendencies, sexually aberrant behavior, psychological disturbance, and use of medication.

Raw scores are converted to deciles. A high decile rank in Part 1 indicates the presence of more adaptive behavior, whereas a high decile score in Part 2 indicates less adaptive behavior. Although designed for use with a variety of persons with disabilities, normative information for this instrument is based only on an institutionalized population of retardates. Interrater reliability coefficients range from .71 to .93 for Part I and .37 to .77 for Part 2. Salvia and Ysseldyke (1991) contend that the instrument possesses questionable content validity and was subjected to poor standardization procedures. They indicate that the test now possesses outdated norms, presents no evidence of stability or internal consistency reliability, and probably should not be used as a norm-referenced device.

Scales of Independent Behavior

The Scales of Independent Behavior (SIB; Bruininks, Woodcock, Weatherman, & Hill, 1984) constitute a 226-item, multidimensional measure of functional independence and adaptive behavior for individuals of all ages. The instrument is designed as a structured interview. It takes approximately 45 to 60 minutes to administer in the complete form and 10 to 15 minutes to administer in the short form. The SIB is composed of four separate scales: (1) Broad Independence Scale—which consists of 14 subscales comprising 4 clusters of independence (motor skills, social and communication skills, personal living skills, and community living skills); (2) Short Form Scale—a 32-item, brief measure of broad independence; (3) Early Development Scale—a 32-item developmental measure designed for individuals with severe disabilities and those up to 3 years of age; and (4) Problem Behaviors Scale—an assessment of eight areas of personal and social adjustment. Raw scores from the scales may be converted into part scores and cluster scores. Cluster scores can be converted into age equivalents, percentile ranks, standard scores, stanines, normal curve equivalents, and instructional functioning scores.

Standardization of the SIB included a stratified, randomly selected sample of 1,800 subjects ranging in age from infancy to over 40 years of age. In addition, over 1,000 handicapped and nonhandicapped individuals were sampled, as well as nearly 5,000 subjects tested with both the SIB and the Woodcock-Johnson Psycho-Educational Battery. Reliability coefficients for the scales are generally in the .80s to .90s, with only a few test-retest coefficients (4 out of 20) dropping into the .70s. The SIB is also reported to possess good content validity. However, Harrington (1985) indicates that the SIB technical manual provides no factor analytic or predictive validity studies.

San Francisco Vocational Competency Scale

The San Francisco Vocational Competency Scale (SFVCS; Freeman & Levine, 1968) is individually administered to an informant who is familiar with the individual being assessed. The SFVCS was developed to assess mentally retarded adults in sheltered workshop settings. Four areas of vocational competence are assessed: motor skills, cognition, responsibility, and social-emotional behavior. The informant rates the assessee's competence on 30 items. A vocational competency score is yielded by summing scores for each item. The total score is then converted to percentiles.

The norm group contained 562 mentally retarded individuals from 45 workshops around the country. Internal consistency reliability coefficients are reported to be .95 and test-retest coefficients are reported to be .85. No evidence of validity is reported in the manual. Power (1984) suggests that the SFVCS has value as a general screening device, which can be used to assess an individual's readiness for placement in work settings, assist in program evaluations, and assist with instructional planning.

Camelot Behavioral Checklist

The Camelot Behavioral Checklist (CBC; Foster, 1977) is a norm- and criterion-referenced instrument used to evaluate adaptive behavior of moderately and severely retarded individuals. The test contains 399 items organized into 10 domains and 40 subdomains. The 10 domains include: self-help, physical development, home duties, vocational behavior, economic behavior, independent travel, numerical skills, communication skills, social behaviors, and responsibility.

The checklist is completed by an informant familiar with the individual being assessed. The test items are answered "yes" (the task can be performed by the individual) or "no" (needs training). The manual provides no data as to the standardization sample's characteristics. Interrater reliability of the CBC domain scores ranges from .79 to .98. Interrater reliability for the entire instrument has been estimated to be .93. Construct validity was assessed via correlation with instruments such as the Leiter, Stanford-Binet, WISC, and WAIS. These correlations ranged from .33 to .50. Gory (1985) has suggested that the CBC has limited prescriptive capabilities; however it may be used to profile an individual's skills, make comparisons to the norm sample, and measure progress.

Social and Prevocational Information Battery

The Social and Prevocational Information Battery (SPIB; Halpern, Raffeld, Irvin, & Link, 1975) contains a group of individually administered tests used to identify deficiencies in adaptive behavior of educable mentally retarded individuals in grades 7–12. The test items are presented orally to the student(s). The battery consists of nine tests containing 26 to 30 items each. A total of 240 of the 277 test items are answered in a "true or false" format. The response sets for the remaining 37 items are two pictorial representations of an answer from which the student must choose. Raw scores can be converted to percentile ranks for interpretation.

The standardization sample consisted of 700 junior high and 1,100 senior high school educable mentally retarded students in Oregon. Kuder-Richardson reliabilities ranged from .65 to .82 for the various subtests. Reliability of the total battery ranged from .94 to .93. Meyers (1978) states, "the use of the SPIB will be well received, though some reservations must be expressed" (p. 1527). Although validity evidence is acceptable, some of the scale scores have insufficient reliability, and the standardization sample is extremely limited.

Vocational Adaptation Rating Scale

The Vocational Adaptation Rating Scale (VARS; Malgady, Barcher, Davis, & Towner, 1980) is a measure of maladaptive behavior that might jeopardize the employment status of severely, moderately, and mildly retarded workers in a vocational setting. It is designed to be completed by employment supervisors or vocational teachers. The VARS contains 133 items that comprise six general domains: verbal manners, communication skills, attendance and punctuality, interpersonal behavior, respect for property, rules and regulation, and grooming and personal hygiene. The VARS is scored on a 4-point rating scale ("never," "sometimes," "often," "regularly"). The instrument yields a frequency score and a severity score.

Interrater reliability coefficients range from .40 to .72. Internal consistency reliabilities of .86 to .93 have been reported. Concurrent validity was assessed by comparing the VARS to the Adaptive Behavior Scale and the San Francisco Vocational Competency Scale. The VARS has a computer program designed for scoring, interpretation, and providing information on educational planning. Malgady, Barcher, Davis, and Towner (1980) have reported that the VARS is a promising instrument with ecological validity for the vocational evaluation of retarded workers.

VOCATIONAL INTERESTS

The assessment of vocational interests is an integral component of an overall assessment of an individual's vocational development needs and, as such, is a major focus of professionals providing vocational assistance to individuals. Interests can be defined as constellations of likes and dislikes, and as positive and negative reactions to stimuli (Super & Crites, 1962). Three types of interests exist. Expressed interests are the likes and dislikes people express when simply asked about what they do and do not enjoy. Expressed interests are easily assessed in a clinical interview.

Manifest interests are the likes and dislikes evidenced by the activities in which individuals voluntarily engage. Manifest interests can be assessed by clinical interview or via observation. Inventoried interests are the likes and dislikes reflected on standardized interest inventories. When assessing interests, all three types of interests should be assessed by the professional.

Interests have been found to be a major determinant of college major and occupational choice (Scharf, 1970; Thomas, Morrill, & Miller, 1970) and to exert a greater influence on occupational choice than do aptitudes (Scharf, 1970). Whereas aptitudes seem to influence performance in an occupation, interests appear to influence the degree of satisfaction an individual experiences in a particular occupation and the length of time he or she remains in that occupation. The relationship between interests and aptitudes is not generally high. Interests have consistently been found to be a predictor of job satisfaction, but have not been found to be consistently related to occupational success. Hence, it is important to assess both interests and aptitudes in a comprehensive vocational assessment so as to prevent students from selecting occupations they like, but in which they are unable to perform well.

Vocational development theorists have generally indicated that interests tend to be relatively unstable during childhood and early adolescence, and are greatly influenced by factors such as family and social background, peer group interests, and educational and recreational experiences. Once adolescents reach their middle teens, however, interests seem to stabilize enough to play a major role in vocational planning. Seligman (1980) has identified numerous purposes, uses, and goals of interest assessment. Among these are translating likes and dislikes into occupational terms, providing insight into academic and occupational satisfaction or dissatisfaction, broadening and increasing the appropriateness of occupational and academic options, and facilitating conflict resolution and realistic decision making.

Interest inventories are developed using one of two widely used methods. The first of these methods, termed the "people-similar" approach, compares the likes and dislikes of the test-taker with the likes and dislikes of satisfied workers in a particular occupation. The second method, termed the "activity-similar" approach, assesses the degree to which the test-taker likes or dislikes activities typically performed in various occupations. The predictive validity of interest inventories is generally assessed by comparing inventoried interests with subsequent occupational choice and determining the rate of correct predictions over a specified period of time. Concurrent validity is generally assessed by correlating the scores obtained on one interest inventory with the scores obtained by the same group of individuals on another interest inventory. Reliability of interest inventories is assessed using conventional internal consistency and test-retest procedures. Both the reliability and validity of interest inventories, particularly those using a "people-similar" approach, are relatively good.

In selecting an interest inventory for use, several factors should be considered. Because interest inventories sample different occupational areas and levels, the vocational goals and aspirations of the student must be considered when selecting an instrument. Certainly, it would be inappropriate to utilize an instrument that samples interest in professional and managerial occupations (requiring a minimum of 4 years of postsecondary education) with a student who has neither the aptitude for nor the interest in such occupations. Similarly, some interest inventories yield scores that reflect interest in broad occupational areas (and are, therefore, more useful in encouraging occupational exploration rather than decision making), whereas others yield scores reflecting interest in specific occupations (and are, therefore, more useful in decision making). Hence, the purpose in using the interest inventory will influence the selection of an instrument.

Several factors should be considered when interpreting interest inventory results. First, how results are interpreted depends upon the method used in developing the inventory (people-similar vs. activity-similar approach). Second, interest inventory results are strongly influenced by experience. If a student has never experienced an activity or occupation, he or she is unlikely to express an interest in it. Consequently, it is important to differentiate between low interest scores reflective of lack of experience and those reflective of lack of interest. Finally, students must be counseled as to the difference between intrinsic and extrinsic sources of satisfaction, and its relationship to interest inventory results. Interest inventories assess only intrinsic sources of satisfaction and indicate the likelihood that an individual will enjoy certain work. However, extrinsic sources of satisfaction such as salary or advancement opportunities will also influence one's overall satisfaction with a job.

In conclusion, interest assessment is an important part of a comprehensive vocational assessment program. When selecting interest inventories for use, professionals must consider the instrument's psychometric characteristics, the nature and types of occupations surveyed, the instrument's cost and scoring options, and the goal or purpose of the assessment. Interpretation of interest inventory results depends upon several factors including the degree to which the client has experienced the activities surveyed and the method used to develop the interest inventory.

Vocational Interest Inventories

Career Assessment Inventory

The Career Assessment Inventory (CAI; Johansson, 1982) was originally designed to assist those individuals who were not interested in attending a college or university, but who were interested in immediate vocational entry. The new expanded, Enhanced Version of this instrument, however, is also directed toward individuals who seek professional careers and is constructed to encompass a wide range of occupations. This version has been described as an above-average vocational assessment inventory that is empirically based and suitable for the general population (McCabe, 1988). The 1986 version was constructed to eliminate sex bias by combining sex occupational scales.

The Enhanced Version, organized according to Holland's Occupational Themes, contains 370 items (the original CAI contained 305 items). Rounds (1989) notes that the manual fails to discuss standard methods for coding the themes or their relationship to Holland's comprehensive occupational classification. These six general themes are divided into 25 Basic Interest Area Scales (BIA). The themes incorporate 111 Occupational Scales that match interests to personality types of persons employed in that occupation. The test also includes administrative indices, which describe response tendencies of the individual, as well as four nonoccupational scales.

The norm groups on which scores are based contain a sample of 900 adults (450 males and 450 females). In contrast, norms on the original CAI were based upon a sample of 1,500 adults. The manual describes in detail the selection of criterion groups for each of the occupational themes including the size, date, and collection methods. Reported coefficients range from .80 to .96 and indicate adequate stability. However, there are no test-retest reliability coefficients available for periods longer than 3 months. Evidence of content, construct, and concurrent validity is also presented in the manual and suggests the CAI to be a relatively valid instrument.

The manual discusses the construction of the scales and provides a description of psychometric properties, but lacks information to assist individuals in using the results to find satisfying occupations (Rounds, 1989). McCabe (1988) commends the CAI for its clarity, its minimization of sex bias, and its ease of administration and interpretation of results. The inventory requires machine scoring, which renders it a rather expensive device for selective individual use; however, it can be cost effective for large groups (Spitzer & Levinson, 1988). Mail-in scoring is available with a maximum 24-hour turnaround.

Career Occupational Preference System

The Career Occupational Preference System (COPS; Knapp & Knapp, 1984), formerly known as the California Occupational Preference System, contains 168 job activity items and measures interests on two levels (professional and skilled) in 14 interest areas (known as occupational clusters). The job activities are presented clearly, and individuals (7th grade through adult) respond to each activity by marking a 4-point Likert scale: L—Like very much; l—Like moderately; d—Dislike moderately; D—Dislike very much. Each of the 14 clusters has 12 items and each item is scored on a similar scale. Raw scores are converted into percentile ranks for each occupational cluster.

The test was normed on students in grades 7–12 and community college students. Because of poor written documentation, Bauernfeind (1988) suggests the development of local norms when using this instrument. Split-half and test-retest coefficients range from the .70s to the .90s. These coefficients indicate satisfactory stability. However, the COPS has been criticized for its lack of validity evidence (Hansen, 1978; Layton, 1978).

Reviews of this instrument vary. In spite of the lack of technical studies, the questionnaire is realistically presented, easily scored, and enjoyable for high school and college students (Bauernfeind, 1988). Other reviewers have suggested that the COPS inventory is not suitable for individuals with a reading level below the 8th grade or individuals interested in unskilled jobs (Spitzer & Levinson, 1988).

Harrington-O'Shea Career Decision-Making System

The Harrington-O'Shea Career Decision Making System (CDM; Harrington-O'Shea, 1982) is an interest inventory that incorporates an assessment of abilities, job values, future plans, course subject preferences, and interests. The CDM is based on Holland's Theory of Vocational Personalities and Work Environments. There are 120 job activity items, 20 for each of Holland's six Vocational Interest Areas. (These six areas are renamed crafts, scientific, arts, social, business, and clerical.) The instrument can be self-, computer, or machine scored.

The results of each section in the CDM are transferred to a summary profile that produces a vocational code, based on Holland's theory. Although the directions are clear, some reviewers have suggested that the CDM requires at least a 7th-grade reading ability and strong motivation to complete the inventory accurately (Manuele, 1988). An interpretive folder is included, which enables the individual to use the instrument without professional assistance.

Evidence of reliability and validity is included in the CDM manual. Norm groups were composed of students in grades 7–12 and college freshmen. Internal reliability coefficients of about .90 are reported for all scales. Short-term test-retest coefficients range from .75 to .94. Reliability of the self-scoring procedure is reported to be .98. This suggests that the instrument can be self-scored accurately by examinees. Concurrent validity of the Interest Survey was supported via correlation with the Strong-Campbell Interest Inventory.

Reviews of the CDM have generally been favorable, although some have suggested the need for more research on the reliability and validity of the instrument (Droege, 1988; Manuele, 1988; Westbrook, Rogers, & Covington, 1980; Willis, 1978, 1983). In praising the CDM, Manuele (1988) has suggested that the CDM is more comprehensive and offers better interpretive information than does the Self-Directed Search (Holland, 1985b).

Jackson Vocational Interest Survey

The Jackson Vocational Interest Survey (JVIS; Jackson, 1977), designed to assist in the educational and vocational planning of adolescents and adults, assesses a broad range of vocational interests. The JVIS contains 289 pairs of preferred interest activities, grouped into 34 scales of 17 items each. The instrument can be hand scored in about 10 minutes or computer scored (which is preferred because it provides additional information). Standard scores are provided for the 34 Basic Interest Scales.

Norms are provided for adolescents in grades 9–12 and college students. The manual gives separate and combined norms for males and females. The lack of description of socioeconomic status representation in the standardization sample suggests the possibility of cultural bias (Davidshofer, 1988b; Spitzer & Levinson, 1988). Reliability coefficients range from .70 to .91. Although support for the JVIS's validity is presented in the manual, more extensive research is needed on the psychometric properties of the instrument before it will be able to compete with other instruments (Brown, 1989; Shepard, 1989).

Reviews of the JVIS commend its time and cost efficiency, its minimization of stereotyping, and its tendency to direct attention of the individual to broad areas of interests rather than to specific occupations (Brown, 1989: Davidshofer, 1988b; Shepard, 1989; Spitzer & Levinson, 1988). Disadvantages of the instrument include its time requirements (attention span and fatigue become factors), the confusion caused by "forced-choice items," and inconclusive psychometric data (Davidshofer, 1988b; Spitzer & Levinson, 1988; Thomas, 1985).

Kuder Form DD Occupational Interest Survey - Revised

The Kuder Occupational Interest Survey Form DD, Revised (KOIS; Kuder & Diamond, 1985), is intended to be used as a measure of occupational and college major interests. The KOIS compares preferred interests of the examinee with the interest patterns of successful individuals in specific occupations and college majors. There are a total of 119 occupational scales, 48 college major scales, 10 traditional Kuder interest scales, and 8 experimental scales. The KOIS must be machine scored.

Norms are provided for both males and females for occupational and college major scales. Two other scales, Dependability (which is a verification of obtained scores) and Vocational Interest Estimates (a rank of estimates for preferences of activities), are also included in the norm groups. Test-retest reliability coefficients for the Vocational Interest Estimates range from .70 to .84. Although the predictive validity data presented in the manual are supportive, Herr (1989) and Tenopyr (1989) state that additional research should be done on the predictive validity of this instrument to ensure its usefulness.

Overall, the 1985 revision of the KOIS is an improvement over other versions. The instrument is relatively time efficient, and the inclusion of an audiotape, designed to explain the interpretation of the inventory, is helpful. A booklet, *Expanding Your Future,* and worksheet are designed to assist the individual in identifying occupational possibilities from the scales. Herr (1989) has suggested that a revision of the worksheet and booklet are needed to keep it current. In summary, the KOIS can be described as a useful instrument in assessing vocational and college preferences.

Kuder General Interest Survey - Form E

The Kuder General Interest Survey, Form E (KGIS; Kuder, 1975), is an instrument designed to measure broad vocational interests. The categories measured include: outdoor, mechanical, computational, scientific, persuasive, artistic, literary, musical, social service, and clerical. A Verification Scale is also included and is designed to check the honesty of responses. The KGIS is designed for students from grade 6 through college, can be administered in groups or individually, and can be scored by hand or machine. The hand-scored version uses pins and corrugated paper, which make it difficult for the test-taker to change an answer. This response format is, therefore, not recommended.

Norms are based upon 9,819 students in grades 6-12. There were four norm groups: males grade 6-8, males grades 9-12, females grades 6-8, and females grades 9-12. Reliability coefficients are reported to be .70 or above. The manual is written in a rather technical manner and may confuse a novice who is unfamiliar with evaluating psychometric data (Williams & Williams, 1988). Reviewers have noted that there are no predictive validity data presented on this form (Kirk & Frank, 1983; Williams & Williams, 1988).

Self-Directed Search

The Self-Directed Search (SDS; Holland, 1985b) is a popular, frequently used, self-administered, self-scored, and self-interpreted guide for students and adults in need of career planning assistance. It is appropriate for use with high school students, college students, and adults. Reading level of the instrument is estimated to be between 7th and 8th grade; however, a Form E(asy) version of the instrument is available and has an estimated 4th-grade reading level. The SDS can be administered individually or in groups and takes approximately 30 minutes. A computerized version of the instrument and Spanish and Vietnamese editions are also available. The 96-page Professional Manual provided with the SDS is comprehensive and provides information about the origins of Holland's theory, a description of administration and scoring practices, practical applications and uses of the SDS, and case studies illustrating use. Technical characteristics of the instrument are also included in this manual. The SDS is used in conjunction with an "Occupations Finder," a booklet that lists a variety of occupations and their associated Holland code types. A *Dictionary of Holland Occupational Codes,* 2nd edition (Gottfredson & Holland, 1989), provides a comprehensive listing of 12,860 occupations and their associated code types and is available for separate purchase and use.

The SDS asks students to list their occupational daydreams and to use the Occupations Finder to list the associated Holland code, and to indicate whether they like or dislike a variety of activities to indicate whether they can competently perform a variety of activities, and whether they are interested in a variety of occupations. Students are also asked to rate themselves on six abilities. Students then collate their responses in a manner that organizes their responses by Holland types. This collation yields a three-letter summary code (each letter reflecting one of Holland's six personality types) believed to be reflective of the student's personality. Using the Professional Manual, raw scores for each of the six types can be converted into percentile ranks. Conversion tables are provided for high school and college students by sex. Students are then instructed to use the Occupations Finder to identify occupations congruent with every possible ordering of the obtained three-letter code. Following this, students are provided with some basic interpretive guidelines, how and where to get additional information on careers, and a listing of some useful references.

The Professional Manual (Holland, 1985b) provides reliability and validity data for the 1971, 1977, and 1985 editions of the SDS. For brevity, only data relative to the 1985 edition will be presented. Internal consistency reliability coefficients are presented for each SDS scale for three different age groups broken down by sex. Generally, these coefficients cluster in the .70s and .80s. Coefficients for the summary score are considerably higher and range between the mid-.80s and low .90s. Although no test-retest reliability data are provided for the 1985 edition, stability of scores is inferred based upon (a) the test-retest reliability data presented for the 1977 edition of the test, and (b) the high correlations between scores of the 1977 and 1985 editions. Validity data presented in the Professional Manual suggest that the validity of the SDS is adequate and comparable to other vocational interest inventories. Other studies have supported this contention (Dolliver, 1975; Hanson, Noeth, & Prediger, 1977; Hughes, 1972; O'Neil, Magoon, & Tracey, 1978; Touchton & Magoon, 1977; Wiggins & Westlander, 1977). Research has suggested that the SDS is valid for males and females (Gottfredson & Holland, 1975), for African Americans (Kimball, Sedlacek, & Brooks, 1973), and Mexican Americans (Turner & Horn, 1975), as well as for Caucasions. Other research on the SDS summarized in the Professional Manual (Holland, 1985b) suggests that use of the SDS increases the number of vocational options a person is considering, increases satisfaction with a vocational aspiration, and increases self-understanding.

Scores derived from the SDS can be used in a variety of ways. First, raw scores can be converted into percentile ranks to determine the percentage of a population (high school students in grades 10–12, college students, employed adults) who possess characteristics associated with a particular personality type to a greater or lesser extent than does the client. This assists in determining the extent to which the client may be more or less interested in occupations associated with specific personality types, as compared to his or her peers. The three-letter code derived from the SDS can then be used to access occupations (using either the Occupations Finder, or the *Dictionary of Holland Occupational Codes*) that are congruent with the client's personality (as reflected in their three-letter code). Holland suggests that the sequencing of letters in the three-letter code be juxtaposed and reordered; that is, that different combinations of the three-letter code be constructed so as to access a greater number of viable occupational options. However, this practice is most appropriate when there are no significant differences between scores associated with each of the types. Holland suggests that, based upon the standard error of difference scores, scale differences of less than 8 should be regarded as trivial because they are within the limits of measurement error. Thus, resequencing only those scales between which no significant difference exists, and then using those code combinations to access occupational options, would seemingly be a sounder practice. These codes can also be used to access information about various occupations (for exploration purposes) given that many counseling and career centers organize their information according to Holland code types.

The SDS possesses several strengths. Given the number and variety of alternatives that can be identified, the risk of premature narrowing of options and inappropriate decision making is reduced. Because counselors and other school-based professionals typically involved in providing vocational services to students are often familiar with Holland's theory and the SDS, results can be easily used by these other professionals. The instrument is based upon a sound, empirically validated theoretical framework and possesses adequate technical characteristics. Because the instrument is self-administered and self-scored, administration and scoring require little time. Use of the SDS is both a time- and cost-efficient way of gathering vocationally relevant data.

Although the reading requirement of the SDS may negate its use with some secondary school students with disabilities, Form-E (4th-grade reading level) can be used in its place. Studies have attested to this form's reliability (Wirtenberg, 1979) and appropriateness of use with learning disabled high school students (Maddux & Cummings, 1986). A computerized form of the SDS is available as well. Use of the computerized form of the instrument can further minimize a professional's workload, particularly in regard to error checking, generation of interpretive hypotheses, and identification of viable occupational options. One study has confirmed the equivalence of scores generated by the paper-and-pencil and computerized forms of the instrument (Reardon & Loughead, in press). Finally, the instrument provides data that allow one to identify a broad spectrum of relevant occupational options and is therefore appropriate for use with a diverse population of both college-bound and non–college bound students.

Although administration of the SDS is simple and easy, interpretation and use of its results are more difficult. Some knowledge of Holland's theory and interpretive strategies is necessary. However, such knowledge can be easily gleaned from the SDS Professional Manual. The SDS should not be used with students who have severe disabilities. (The vocational assessment literature indicates that the trait-factor approach upon which the SDS is based is clearly inappropriate for these individuals and that an environmental assessment approach based upon developmental theory is more appropriate with this population.) Similarly, caution should be exercised in use of the SDS with some students who have moderate disabilities. The reading requirement and self-scoring nature of the instrument may render it inappropriate for use without some modification. Last, the SDS is essentially a self-report scale and requires that individuals have adequate self-understanding and, to a lesser extent, adequate understanding of the world of work. Even though the instructions are concise and easy to follow, many reviewers have suggested that scores should be double-checked by trained personnel to reduce the possibility of self-scoring errors (Bodden, 1986; Campbell, 1988; Daniels, 1989; Manuele, 1989). In spite of the concerns of self-scoring error, many reviewers have found the SDS and its computerized version to be a well-constructed instrument that can be used by a diverse population (Bodden, 1986; Campbell, 1988; Daniels, 1989; Manuele, 1989; McKee & Levinson, 1990; Spitzer & Levinson, 1988).

Strong-Campbell Interest Survey

The Strong-Campbell Interest Inventory (SCII; Campbell & Hansen, 1985) has a 60-year history of use as a vocational interest tool. The SCII is designed to measure interests in professional, technical, nonprofessional, and vocational-technical occupational areas. The inventory contains 325 items written at a 6th-grade reading level. All scoring is done by machine. The computer-generated profile contains three kinds of scales: Holland's Six Vocational Personality types, 23 Basic Interest Scales, and 207 Occupational Scales (which compare an individual's interests to those of satisfied persons in various occupations).

The norm groups contain a representative sample of the population, collected through extensive national data. Extensive reliability and validity data are available for the SCII (Layton, 1985). The manual provides evidence of construct, content, and concurrent validity. Test-retest reliability for the various scales ranges from the .80s to .90s.

The construction of the SCII, based on recent research done by Jo-Ida Hansen, has been quite extensive. Many reviewers have commended Hansen on this research (Borgen, 1988; Layton, 1985; Spitzer & Levinson, 1988; Westbrook, 1985). Hansen's (1984) *User's Guide for the SVIB-SCII* is a useful interpretive manual because of its introduction and coverage of areas such as special populations, adult vocational change, and minorities and cultures. The availability of the SCII in many foreign languages is also a positive feature of this instrument. In summary, reviews of the SCII have been very favorable (Anastasi, 1982; Borgen, 1988; Layton, 1985; Tzeng, 1985; Westbrook, 1985).

Wide Range Interest-Opinion Test

The Wide Range Interest-Opinion Test (WRIOT; Jastak & Jastak, 1979) is a nonreading instrument designed to sample a wide range of work activities from unskilled labor and technical occupations to professional and managerial positions. It contains 150 triads of pictures and uses a forced choice format requiring respondents to select a most and least preferred activity. Designed for persons aged 5 through adult, it can be administered individually or to groups in about 40 minutes. The 26 scales include 18 basic interest scales and 4 scales related to response bias. The WRIOT can be hand or machine scored.

Norms are divided into seven age groups and include children, adolescents, and adults. The groups include 15% minorities, at all educational levels. However, norms are not reported for special populations. Items are not sex stereotyped, and the scales have high internal consistency. (Split-half reliability estimates are high, ranging from .82 to .95.) No test-retest reliability estimates are reported. With the exception of adequate interscale correlations between the WRIOT and the Geist Picture Interest Inventory (Geist, 1964), evidence of validity is lacking.

Because the WRIOT is designed to identify interest preferences in a wide range of work activities for special populations, it addresses an important need. However, the lack of both test-retest reliability and validity data, and the absence of information on how special populations actually perform on the test, diminish one's confidence in the instrument. For these reasons, reviews have generally been unfavorable (Hsu, 1985; Manuele, 1985; Zytowski, 1983). However, the WRIOT is one of the few instruments currently available for use (without modification) for low reading mentally retarded and learning disabled populations who are capable of performing higher-level job activities.

Reading Free Vocational Interest Inventory—Revised

The Reading Free Vocational Interest Inventory—Revised (RFVII; Becker, 1981) was developed to provide information on interest patterns of mentally retarded and learning disabled persons from ages 13 through adult. Pictorial illustrations of people performing jobs, arranged in 55 triads, are presented in a forced-choice format. The instrument, which is designed to be administered to individuals or to groups, can be completed in approximately 20 minutes and is easily hand scored. The range of occupations is at the unskilled, semiskilled, and skilled levels and covers 11 occupational areas.

The RFVII was the subject of a national standardization that included educable mentally retarded and learning disabled males and females in grades 7 through 12, and mentally retarded adults in sheltered workshops and vocational training centers. Normative data were collected in a manner that ensured representativeness. Test-retest reliabilities over a 2-week period are acceptable for all groups (.70s and .80s). Content validity was assessed by determining the degree to which various study teams agreed on classifications of the pictures. Concurrent validity was studied by comparing correlations between the RFVII and the Geist Picture Interest Inventory (Geist, 1964). Product moment correlations were significant at or beyond the .05 level for 36 of the 45 correlations in the groups of mentally retarded males (n = 154) and for 38 of 45 correlations in the groups of mentally retarded females (N = 148) (Becker, 1981, p. 45). Occupational (Status) validity (not to be confused with predictive validity, but rather a form of construct validity) (Diamond, 1983) was studied by comparing the highest scores of mentally retarded males and females and sheltered workshop clients in the 11 occupational groups. Reportedly, each group of workers scored higher on the scale representing their own occupation than they did on other scales.

The development of national norms and the elimination of sex bias are the major improvements in the 1981 edition of the instrument. The status of the instrument's validity has been questioned (Diamond, 1988; Domino, 1978; Holden, 1985). However, Holden (1985) has found the instrument to be very useful with adolescents and adults in a rehabilitation workshop setting. The RFVII does provide an easy method for exploring interest patterns for special populations of nonreaders. Because additional validity studies are needed, caution should be exercised in interpreting results. Some learning disabled examinees may profit from an interest inventory that has a wider range of occupational selections, such as the audiocassette version of the CAI or the WRIOT.

Geist Picture Interest Inventory—Revised

The Geist Picture Interest Inventory—Revised (GPII-R; Geist, 1982) was developed to identify vocational interests of individuals from 8th grade through adult, especially culturally limited and educationally deprived individuals. Separate male and female booklets contain illustrations that are presented in forced-choice format and arranged in 27 triads for females and 44 triads for males. The GPII-R can be administered to individuals or to groups in about 20 to 40 minutes. The written questions require a 4th-grade reading level. Areas of interest are scored in terms of broad fields of interest (11 male and 12 female areas). A separate motivation questionnaire is intended to identify reasons behind choices.

Male form test-retest reliability coefficients for each interest area vary considerably, with a median in the .60s. Although the manual reports "high statistical significance" for female form test-retest correlation, little evidence of this is presented. In general, the GPII-R provides a quick method to identify interest areas of individuals who otherwise may not have the stamina, motivation, or verbal resources to engage in vocational exploration. The GPII-R may be useful as a screening instrument to identify broad areas of interest, particularly with adolescents and adults of limited verbal ability. The short length of the test makes it feasible for an examiner to read the written questions to persons with a reading level below the 4th grade.

Occupational Aptitude Survey and Interest Schedule - Second Edition: Interest Schedule (OASIS-2 IS)

The Second Edition of the Occupational Aptitude Survey and Interest Schedule (Parker, 1991; OASIS-2) is an instrument designed to assist students in pairing their interests and abilities with potential occupational choices. The OASIS-2 is separated into two distinct sections. The Aptitude Survey assesses the abilities of the student, while the Interest Schedule assesses the level of interest certain activities and occupations hold for the student. As stated by Parker (1991), the purpose of the OASIS-2 IS is to "assist students in Grades 8 through 12 in self-exploration, vocational exploration, and career development" (pp. 2-3) and, as part of this process, to assist them in "an inventorying of their interests" (p. 3). The OASIS-2 IS assesses interest in 12 areas: artistic, scientific, nature, protective, mechanical, industrial, business detail, selling, accommodating, humanitarian, leading-influencing, and physical performing. A student profile is obtained from scoring that indicates the student's level of interest in each of these areas as compared to the standardization sample. Raw scores are converted to percentiles and stanines. Norms tables were derived from a nationally representative standardization sample of 1,398 students enrolled in 8th through 12th grades.

Parker (1991) reports that individual items within the 12 areas all have correlations over .30 for interrelatedness, which is well over the acceptable standard of .20. Alpha reliability coefficients are provided for each of the 12 scales by three grade levels (8th, 10th, 12th) and by sex. Coefficients generally cluster in the high .80s and low .90s. Test-retest reliability with a 2-week interval computed on data from 54 junior and senior high school students ranged between .72 and .91 for the 12 scales. Through factor analysis and a detailed comparison of items with the *Guide for Occupational Exploration,* Parker (1991) provides additional evidence of the construct and content validity of the OASIS-2 IS. Although little evidence of the criterion-related validity of the OASIS-2 IS is presented in the manual, a recent study of Levinson, Rafoth, and Lesnak (in submission) found statistically significant and moderately high correlations between OASIS-2 IS and Self-Directed Search scales.

Tables 5-6 and 5-7, respectively, provide a summary of the characteristics of several interest inventories and provide a listing of recommended instruments (taken from Spitzer & Levinson, 1988).

VOCATIONAL APTITUDES

Aptitudes can be defined as specific capacities or abilities that are necessary to learn or adequately perform a task or job duty (Isaacson, 1986). Aptitude tests are designed to predict a person's ability to learn or profit from an educational experience and/or the likelihood of a person's success in a given occupation or course of study (Seligman, 1980). Aptitude tests are most often used to select individuals for placement in specific educational or vocational training programs or jobs.

Some confusion exists as to the differences between aptitude and achievement tests. Aiken (1985) has differentiated the two by suggesting that aptitude measurement focuses on the future whereas achievement measurement focuses on the past. That is, Aiken believes that achievement tests measure how much one has profited from past learning experiences, whereas aptitude tests allow predictions to be made about how one will perform in certain situations in the future. Although traditional definitions of aptitude have suggested that it is intrinsic to an individual and that aptitude tests essentially measure innate abilities, more contemporary

Table 5-6.
Characteristics of Career Interest Inventories

Characteristic	Interest Inventory			
	Career Assessment Inventory	*COPS SYSTEM Inventory*	*Harrington-O'Shea CDM*	*Jackson Vocational Interest Survey*
Publisher/ Distributor	National Computer Systems	Edits Educational and Industrial Testing Service	American Guidance Service	Research Psychologists Press
Estimated Time	35 min	25 min	40 min	50 min
Age/Grade Range	8th to Adult	7th to Adult	7th to Adult	7th to Adult
Scoring Procedure	Machine	Hand/ Machine	Hand/ Machine	Hand/ Machine
Administration	Individual/ Group	Individual/ Group	Individual/ Group	Individual/ Group
Available Languages	English	English, Spanish, Braille	English, Spanish	English, French, Spanish Booklet Only
Occupations Assessed	Immediate Entry, Technical, Some Professional	Professional and Skilled	Abilities, Job Values, Future Plans, Interests	Broad Interest Categories

(continued)

Table 5-6.
(Continued)

Characteristic	Interest Inventory			
	Kuder General Interest Survey Form E	*Kuder Form DD Occupational Interest Survey*	*Self-Directed Search*	*Strong Interest Inventory*
Publisher/ Distributor	Science Research Associates	Science Research Associates	Psychological Assessment Resources	Consulting Psychologists Press
Estimated Time	50 min	35 min	40 min	30 min
Age/Grade Range	6th to Adult	10th to Adult	Ages 15 to 70	8th to Adult
Scoring Procedure	Hand/ Machine	Machine	Hand/ Machine	Machine
Administration	Individual/ Group	Individual/ Group	Individual	Individual
Available Languages	English	English	French, English, Dutch, Chinese, Vietnamese, Japanese, Arabic, Afrikaans, Danish	English, French, Spanish, Hebrew, German, Slovak
Occupations Assessed	Broad Interest Categories	Wide Range of Occupational Scales and College Majors	Wide Range of Interests and Abilities	Advanced Technical, College or Postgraduate

Note: Some Definitions

Professional: Four-year college or university and possibly graduate school or professional school (e.g., Lawyer, Teacher, Psychologist).

Technical: Specialized training beyond high school, usually one or two years in a technical school or trade college (e.g., Dental Assistant, Electronic Technician, Paralegal Assistant).

Managerial: Undergraduate degree, and possibly postgraduate degree or specialized training for higher level positions (e.g., Sales Manager, Government Administrator, Bank Manager).

Skilled: Graduation from high school required or preferred; requires apprenticeship or on-the-job training, and specific trade instruction (e.g., Auto Mechanic, Carpenter, Plumber).

Unskilled: Entry-level positions, some high school required or preferred; usually trained on the job (e.g., General Laborer, Service Station Attendant, Stock Room Clerk).

Note. From "Career Interest Assessment Techniques" by E. Levinson and L. Folino, 1990-91, *Career Planning and Adult Development Journal,* Winter, pp. 10-11. Reprinted by permission from the *Career Planning and Adult Development Journal.*

Table 5-7.
Recommended Instruments According to Educational Level, Vocational Goal, and Reading Level

Educational Level	Educational Goal	Reading Level	Recommended Instrument(s)	Rationale/Remarks
High School (10-12)	College Bound	High	SDS	Considers a wide variety of occupational areas; is based upon a well-researched theory of vocational choice; can be self-administered and self-scored resulting in time savings
		High	KOIS	Inclusion of college major scales makes it particularly appropriate for juniors and seniors; possesses adequate psychometric characteristics, requires machine scoring.
		Low	CDM (audio cassette)	Considers a wide variety of occupational areas, eliminates reading, can be self-administered and self-scored reliably; includes occupational information which is updated every two years.
		Low	KOIS	Recommended for students with a 6th-grade reading level, includes college major scales, possesses adequate psychometric characteristics, requires machine scoring.
	Non-College Bound	High	SDS	Considers a wide variety of occupational areas; is based upon a well-researched theory of vocational development; can be self-administered and self-scored.
		High	CAI	Designed specifically for non-college bound students; cheap but expensive to administer and score; requires machine scoring; possesses adequate psychometric characteristics.
		Low	CAI (audio cassette)	Designed specifically for non-college bound students; eliminates reading requirement; can be modified for use with blind and mentally retarded students, cheap but expensive to score.
		Low	CDM (audio cassette)	Considers a wide variety of occupational areas, eliminates reading, can be self-administered and self-scored reliably, includes occupational information which is updated every two years.

(continued)

Table 5-7.
(Continued)

Educational Level	Educational Goal	Reading Level	Recommended Instrument(s)	Rationale/Remarks
Junior High School (7-9)	College Bound	High	JVIS	Assesses broad interest areas which encourage further exploration; use with low socioeconomic groups is questionable; possesses excellent psychometric characteristics; lengthy administration time.
		Low	CDM (audio cassette)	Considers a wide variety of occupational areas, eliminates reading, can be self-administered and self-scored reliably; includes occupational information which is updated every two years.
			SDS (Form E)	Requires a 4th-grade reading level; considers a wide variety of occupational areas; is based upon a well-researched theory of vocational choice; can be self-administered and self-scored.
	Non-College Bound	High	JVIS	Assesses broad interest areas which encourage further exploration; use with low socioeconomic groups is questionable; possesses excellent psychometric characteristics; lengthy administration time.
			SDS	Considers a wide variety of occupational areas which encourages exploration; is based upon a well-researched theory of vocational choice; can be self-administered and self-scored resulting in time savings.
		Low	RFVII*	Pictorially based and requires no reading; standardization on mentally retarded and learning disabled populations; limited range of occupations surveyed; validity has been questioned.
			CDM (audio cassette)	Considers a wide variety of occupational areas, eliminates reading, can be self-administered and self-scored reliably; includes occupational information which is updated every two years.

*Recommended with reservation; caution is advised regarding interpretation.
Note. High reading level = above 6th grade. Low reading level = 6th grade or below.
Note. From "A Review of Selected Vocational Interest Inventories for Use by School Psychologists" by D. Spitzer and E. Levinson, 1988, *School Psychology Review, 4,* 678-692. Reprinted by permission of the National Association of School Psychologists.

theorists disagree. Anastasi (1982), for example, believes that aptitude, achievement, and intelligence tests all measure "developed abilities" and none measures the specific manner in which the abilities are developed. She argues that it is incorrect to infer that aptitude tests measure innate abilities. Anastasi suggests a practical difference between achievement and aptitude tests. She believes that aptitude tests tend to assess the cumulative experiences of daily living whereas achievement tests tend to assess the effects of more formal "standardized" and "controlled" learning experiences like academic coursework. As discussed previously, there is some recent research suggesting a considerable overlap between what is measured by multidimensional aptitude tests and what is measured by intelligence tests. Readers who are interested in a brief review of this research are referred to the section of this chapter that discusses intelligence.

Seligman (1980) suggests that aptitudes begin to take a definable shape in childhood and then remain fairly stable thoughout the adolescent and adult years. Whereas interests seem to relate to the degree of satisfaction one may experience in a given occupation, aptitudes seem to relate to the level of performance one may demonstrate in an occupation. The relationship between interests and aptitudes is not high and may vary considerably from one individual to another. That is, whereas one individual may develop an interest in tasks that he or she performs well, another may demonstrate the opposite tendency. Hence, both interests and aptitudes need to be considered when assisting students in making vocational decisions.

Aptitude assessments can assist in determining the degree to which a student has the potential to satisfy specific training or occupational demands. However, they may not necessarily predict success or performance because motivation (effort), personality characteristics, or social skills, for example, will also ultimately influence one's performance on a task. As Parker (1987) has suggested, for occupations that are clerical, service, trades and crafts, and industrial, potential for training may be predicted rather well by intelligence and aptitude tests; however, the prediction of job proficiency is much more tenuous.

Most multidimensional aptitude tests tend to measure a common set of aptitudes. These include the following:

G — General Learning Ability: the ability to understand instructions and underlying principles; the ability to reason and make judgments. This measure is closely related to doing well in school and is frequently used to predict potential success in college.

V — Verbal: the ability to understand the meaning of words and ideas associated with them and to use them effectively; to comprehend language, to understand relationships among words, to understand meanings of whole sentences and paragraphs, and to present information or ideas clearly.

N — Numerical: the ability to perform arithmetic operations quickly and accurately.

S — Spatial: the ability to comprehend forms in space and understand the relationships of planes and solid objects, similar to what is done in blueprint reading and solving geometry problems; frequently described as the ability to visualize objects of 2 or 3 dimensions, or to think visually of geometric forms.

P — Form Perception: the ability to perceive pertinent details in objects or in pictorial or graphic material; to make visual comparisons and discriminations and to see slight differences in shapes and shadings of figures and widths and lengths of lines.

Q — Clerical Perception: the ability to perceive pertinent detail in verbal or tabular material; to observe differences in copy; to proofread words and numbers, and to avoid perceptual errors in arithmetic computation.

K — Motor Coordination: the ability to coordinate eyes and hands or fingers rapidly and accurately in making precise movements with speed; to make movement responses accurately and quickly.

F — Finger Dexterity: the ability to move the fingers and manipulate small objects with the fingers quickly and accurately.

M — Manual Dexterity: the ability to move the hands easily and skillfully; to work with the hands in placing or turning motions.

Vocational Aptitude Batteries

General Aptitude Test Battery

The General Aptitude Test Battery Forms C and D (GATB) is a group-administered test designed by the United States Employment Service (1983) for use in occupational counseling. The battery was originally designed in 1947 and has undergone numerous revisions. It is among the most frequently used tests on the market today. The current version of the GATB consists of 12 subtests and measures nine aptitudes: general learning ability, verbal aptitude, numerical aptitude, spatial aptitude, form perception, clerical perception, motor coordination, finger dexterity, and manual dexterity. The GATB can be machine or hand scored. Raw scores are converted to standard scores which have a mean of 100 and a standard deviation of 20.

Through an extensive validation program, Occupational Aptitude Patterns (OAPs) and Specific Aptitude Test Batteries (SATBs) have been established for 66 work groups that encompass several thousand occupations. OAPs are minimum cut off scores on the two, three, or four most important aptitudes for clusters of similar occupations. SATBs are cutoff scores that have been established for specific occupations. Occupational success is predicted for individuals who score above the cut off score for all critical aptitudes associated with a particular occupation. OAPs are provided for adults, 10th-graders, and 9th-graders and are linked to the Guide for Occupational Exploration (GOE; U.S. Depoartment of Labor, 1979). (For more information on the use of OAPs and SATBs, the reader is referred to a discussion of the use of interest and aptitude test data that appears later in this chapter.) Validity studies, using OAPs and SATBs, are presented for over 400 occupations. However, many of these studies are plagued by rather small sample sizes (Borgen, 1983).

Test-retest reliability coefficients for the GATB subtests range from .80 to .90. Considerable validity evidence is available on the GATB. Kirnan and Geisinger (1986) suggest that the test is technically adequate but possesses several shortcomings including a need for the inclusion of new occupations and a restandardization.

USES Nonreading Aptitude Test Battery

The USES Nonreading Aptitude Test Battery (NATB; United States Employment Service Office, 1982) is a nonreading alternative to the GATB and is intended for use with individuals with limited reading skills. The NATB adds the following new subtests to the nine subtests already included in the GATB: picture-word matching; oral vocabulary; coin matching; design completion; tool matching; three dimensional space; form matching; coin series; name comparison; and mark making, placing, turning, assembling, and disassembling.

The GATB standardization sample included individuals between 15 and 59 years of age. The manual presents no evidence of reliability. Validity of the NATB is based upon its apparent similarity to the GATB. Kamphaus (1985) describes the NATB as having questionable standardization and as lacking evidence of validity and reliability.

Differential Aptitude Test

The Differential Aptitude Test, Forms V and W (Bennett, Seashore, & Wesman, 1982), is designed for use with children in grades 8–12. The DAT contains eight subtests: verbal reasoning, numerical ability, abstract reasoning, clerical speed and accuracy, mechanical reasoning, space relations, spelling, and language usage. It can be machine scored or hand scored. Raw scores can be converted to percentiles that can be plotted graphically on a profile chart for visual presentation of the student's performance. Separate sex norms are provided in the manual. However, both sets of norms may be used in determining percentile ranks.

Generally, reliability coefficients for all grade levels and both sexes are in the low .90s. Considerable evidence of the DAT's validity is presented in the test manual. Validity is based on correlations with standardized achievement batteries, other aptitude tests, course grades in specific subjects, college-level courses, and success in post–high school job training programs. Pennock-Roman (1985) states that the test is "psychometrically sound, easy to administer, and useful for academic counseling and research on cognitive aptitudes" (p. 242).

Occupational Aptitude Survey and Interest Schedule - Second Edition: Aptitude Survey (OASIS-2 AS)

The OASIS-2 AS (Parker, 1991) is designed to "assist students in Grades 8 through 12 in their career search by providing them with information regarding their relative strengths in several aptitude areas related to the world of work" (p. 1). The instrument consists of five subtests which yield scores in six aptitude areas: general ability, verbal aptitude, numerical aptitude, spatial aptitude, perceptual aptitude, and manual dexterity. Administration time is approximately 40 minutes. Raw scores on each subtest are converted to percentiles and stanine scores.

The OASIS-2 AS was standardized on 1,398 students in grades 8 through 12 in 11 states. The sample was chosen to be representative of the school-aged population in these grades. Data are provided that attest to the representativeness of the norm sample by geographical region, gender, race, and domicile (urban/rural). Reliability coefficients are provided for each subtest by grade and generally cluster in the .80s and .90s (the exception is the spatial relations subtest, which possesses reliability coefficients in the .70s for grades 8–10). The concurrent validity of the OASIS-2 AS is supported via correlations with the GATB. Correlations between related subtests range between .74 and .85. Additional evidence of the instrument's validity is provided in the OASIS-2 AS manual.

Armed Services Vocational Aptitude Battery Form 14

The Armed Services Vocational Aptitude Battery – 14 (ASVAB; United States Department of Defense, 1984) is intended for use with individuals ages 16–23. A total of 334 multiple-choice items are presented in 10 subtests. The subtests are: general science, arithmetic reasoning, word knowledge, paragraph comprehension, numerical operations, coding speed, auto shop information, math knowledge, mechanical comprehension, and electronic information.

The Battery must be machine scored with scores reported for seven subtest composites. The composites include: academic ability; verbal; math; mechanical and crafts; business and clerical; electronics and electrical; and health, social, and technology. Scores are reported in the form of percentiles based upon grade norms, grade/sex cohort norms, grade/opposite sex norms, and youth population norms.

The ASVAB was standardized on a stratified sample of 12,000 individuals. Internal consistency reliability coefficients range from .81 to .92 for the subtests. Alternate-form reliability coefficients for the seven composites range from .90 to .95. Concurrent validity data on the ASVAB are contained in the manual with correlation coefficients ranging from .50 to .60 with grades in training school. Correlation between the academic ability composite and grades is about .40.

System for Assessment and Group Evaluation

The System for Assessment and Group Evaluation (SAGE; Train-Ease Corporation, 1982) is a measure of attitudes, aptitudes, and interests related to the *Dictionary of Occupational Titles* (4th edition) and other U.S. Labor Department publications. Aimed primarily at secondary school students, the SAGE can be modified and used with most types of disabilities. The SAGE takes approximately 3 hours to administer and is composed of four basic parts:

Vocational Interest Inventory (VII) is an untimed, 152-item test that evaluates the person's interests in 12 interest areas. Fairly high validity coefficients were reported with the Singer Experimental Vocational Choice Index, and KR-20 reliabilities range from .60s to .80s.

Vocational Aptitude Battery (VAB) is a paper-and-pencil and apparatus test that measures 11 aptitude areas. Raw scores can be converted into percentiles or scaled scores. High test-retest and internal consistency reliabilities have been reported, as well as high correlations with the General Aptitude Test Battery.

Cognitive and Conceptual Abilities Test (C-CAT) is a 54-item test that reflects the U.S. Department of Labor's General Educational Development scale and consists of three parts — reasoning, mathematics, and language. The subtests were developed based on samples from two groups of high school students and one group of adults from New Jersey and Pennsylvania. Reported KR-20 reliabilities are fairly high.

Assessment of Work Attitudes (AWA) is a 30-item attitude scale that covers 20 common work attitude categories.

According to Botterbusch (1982a), the SAGE possesses one major flaw—its sample size; however, its benefits are numerous. The SAGE may be electronically or manually scored and all instructions are written at the 4th-grade level. Results are directly related to training or occupations and are easily interpreted by the client or evaluator.

COMBINED USE OF INTEREST AND APTITUDE DATA

Interest and aptitude data can be combined and used to generate potentially suitable occupational areas for students to explore. Interests should initially be assessed to identify pertinent occupational areas. Aptitudes should then be assessed. An aptitude pattern (a profile of the student's strengths and weaknesses) can then be constructed. This profile can then be compared to the "aptitude pattern" believed to be necessary for success in specific occupations within each high-interest area. In so doing, high-interest occupational areas in which the student demonstrates potential for successful performance can be identified.

Through an extensive validation program conducted by the United States Employment Service (USES), Occupational Aptitude Patterns (OAPs) and Specific Aptitude Test Batteries (SATBs) based upon GATB test scores have been established for 66 work groups that encompass several thousand occupations. OAPs are minimum cutoff scores on the two, three, or four most important aptitudes for clusters of similar occupations. SAPs are cutoff scores that have been established for specific occupations. Occupational success is predicted for individuals who score above the cutoff score for all critical aptitudes associated with a particular occupation. OAPs and SATBs were developed by testing large numbers of workers in a given occupation (between 18–54 years of age) and identifying the point on each aptitude measure above which two thirds of the workers fell. This level is believed to be the minimum level necessary for success in the occupation. (Eliminating the lowest one third was believed to eliminate the less satisfactorily performing workers.)

In the interpretive system developed by the USES, there are three levels of predicted success: high, medium, and low. Standards for each of these three levels follow:

High Predicted Success—The individual's scores on all critical aptitudes composing the OAPs are above the minimum cutoff score.

Medium Predicted Success—The individual's scores on all critical aptitudes composing the OAPs are above the minimum cutoff score *only* when the standard error of measurement is added to the individual's aptitude score.

Low Predicted Success — The individual's score on any one critical aptitude composing the OAP is more than one standard error below the minimum cutoff score for that aptitude.

As an example, assume that a student has demonstrated high interest in plumbing and drafting. Assume that the SATBs for these two occupations are S-90, P-85, M-85 and G-105, N-100, S-100, respectively. Assume that the student achieved the following scores on the GATB (the standard error of measurement for each aptitude score is listed in parentheses): G-95 (6), V-75 (6), N-98 (6), S-95 (8), P-102 (8), Q-99 (9), K-103 (8), F-92 (10), and M-94 (10). Based on this data, the student would receive a "High Predicted Success" rating for plumbing (because the student's scores on S, P, and M exceed the cutoff scores for these critical aptitudes in plumbing) and would receive a "Low Predicted Success" rating for drafting (because the student's score on G falls more than one standard error below the minimum cutoff score on this critical aptitude).

CAREER MATURITY

Career maturity can be considered to be the extent to which an individual possesses the knowledge and skills necessary to make realistic and informed vocational choices. Super (1957) was one of the first theorists to discuss the concept of vocational maturity. He identified the dimensions of vocational maturity as: orientation to vocational choice (the extent to which one is concerned with career choice and is actively seeking out occupational resources and information), information and planning about preferred occupation (the extent to which one has gathered information about a preferred occupation and the degree to which planning involving that occupation has been conducted), consistency of vocational preference (the extent to which one's occupational preferences are consistent and stable over time), crystalization of traits (the degree to which one has developed realistic attitudes toward work, stable interests, etc.), and wisdom of vocational preferences (the degree to which there is a match between one's occupational preferences and abilities, interests, work habits, etc.). In an elaboration upon this definition of vocational maturity, Super and Thompson (1979), based upon research conducted with the *Career Development Inventory*, suggested that six dimensions comprised career maturity: extent of planning, use and evaluation of resources in occupational exploration, career decision making, career development information, world of work information, and information about a preferred occupation.

Seligman (1980) has suggested that career maturity, regardless of the stage or age involved, is characterized by a number of life-long processes including increasing realism of career goals, increasing self-awareness, increasing congruence between self-image and career goals, increasing competence in career planning, improving career-related attitudes, increasing knowledge of relevant career options, and increasing productivity and satisfaction. Although there has been considerable discussion about the various traits associated with career maturity, it is relatively clear that individuals who demonstrate a high level of career maturity are individuals who have adequate understanding of themselves (understand their interests, skills, values, etc.), adequate understanding of the world of work (understand the various requirements and demands that exist in occupations, understand and appreciate the rewards of work, etc.), and are capable of using this information to make necessary career choices via application of a rational decision-making style.

Career Maturity Inventories

Career Maturity Inventory

The Career Maturity Inventory (CMI) (Crites, 1978) is designed for use with individuals in grades 6–12. The inventory consists of an attitude scale and a knowledge test. The two forms of the attitude scale contain true/false questions. Form A-2 is a screening scale and Form B-1 is a counseling form. There are five subscores computed on Form B-1: decisiveness in, involvement in, independence in, orientation to, and compromise in career decision making. Raw scores on each scale can be transformed to percentiles and standard scores.

Internal consistency and test-retest reliability coefficients for form A-2 range from .73 to .75. Internal consistency coefficients for Form B-1 range from .50 to .72 for the subscales.

The Knowledge scale of the CMI contains five subtests: self-appraisal, occupational information, goal setting, planning, and problem solving. Raw scores for this scale can be converted to percentile ranks and standard scores. Internal consistency reliability coefficients range from .58 to .90 for the subtests.

Frary (1988) indicates that the CMI has flaws but well-documented psychometric properties. Additionally, he states that, "The CMI seems to cover most closely what needs to be measured" (when assessing career maturity) (p. 185).

Career Development Inventory

The Career Development Inventory (CDI) (Super, Thompson, Lindeman, Jordan, & Myers, 1981) has two forms, a School Form (grades

8–12) and a College and University Form. Each form contains two parts and consists of 120 items. The subtests that comprise Part One are: career planning, career exploration, decision making, and world of work information. Part Two is designed to assess "knowledge of preferred occupational group." A total of eight scaled scores are obtained from the CDI; four are based on the subtests from Part One. Scores for career development attitudes, career development knowledge, and career orientation are based on combining scores for several of the subtests.

The standardization sample of the CDI included over 5,000 high school students and over 1,800 college students. Test-retest reliability coefficients on the School Form ranged from .36 to .90 for the eight scales. Coefficients for the career development attitudes, career development knowledge, and career orientation scales ranged from .74 to .84. Evidence for both content and construct validity is presented in the CDI Technical Manual.

WORK SAMPLING

As discussed in the previous chapter, work samples are samples of real work performed by students under the supervision of a trained vocational evaluator. Work sampling systems are generally composed of several work samples (designed to evaluate one's ability to function in several occupational areas), each of which usually requires 2–3 hours of administration time. Student performance is evaluated by comparison with age-based norms and industrial standards. Several work sampling systems are reviewed in the following section.

Work Sampling Systems

Jewish Employment Vocational Services Work Sample System

The Jewish Employment Vocational Services Work Sample System (JEVS) (Vocational Research Institute, 1973a) is intended for use with unemployed/underemployed individuals who have physical and mental disabilities and is used in constructing vocational placement and training plans. The system has 28 work samples that are associated with 10 Worker Trait Group Arrangements in the *Dictionary of Occupational Titles*. The descriptive evaluation obtained from the JEVS includes a 10-page narrative report covering worker characteristics, fundamental abilities, time and quality scores, and vocational training/placement recommendations.

Assessment with the JEVS requires approximately 5–7 six-hour days. The types of scores reported for the JEVS are raw scores for production time and "product" errors. The normative sample used for the JEVS included 1,122 individuals from rehabilitation centers in 32 states. Validity studies are limited and no reliability studies have been done. Flanagan (1983) reports that the JEVS provides excellent information to vocational evaluators regarding strengths and weaknesses of clients; however, he expresses concerns about the validity and reliability of the system.

Vocational Information and Evaluation Work Samples

The Vocational Information and Evaluation Work Samples (VIEWS) (Vocational Research Institute, 1973b) is designed for use with individuals 14 years of age and up who are classified as mildly, moderately, or severely mentally retarded. Administration of the system requires approximately 4–7 five-hour days. The work evaluation process has three phases for each work sample: demonstration, training, and production.

Each work sample is scored according to specific standards. The final report contains the following information on each client: general observations, interpersonal relations, training, worker characteristics, recommendations, and a profile sheet containing work sample results. This report is oriented toward counselor use in making vocational recommendations.

A renorming of the VIEWS took place in 1979 and was based on 452 mentally retarded individuals ages 15 to 61. No reliability or validity data are available on the VIEWS.

Vocational Interest Temperament and Aptitude System

The Vocational Interest Temperament and Aptitude System (VITAS; Vocational Research Institute, 1979) is intended for use with individuals with an 11th-grade education or less who are economically/educationally disadvantaged. The VITAS contains 21 independent work samples based on 16 work groups. Administration of the entire system requires approximately 3 five-hour days. Scoring procedures of the VITAS are similar to that of the JEVS and VIEWS.

The final report presents information on: physical description, attendance and punctuality, verbal ability, interpersonal behavior skills, vocational recommendations by work groups, recommendations for supportive services, and a profile of all work sample time and ratings.

Two norm samples are reported for the VITAS. The 1980 norms contained 325 persons with a median age of 25. The 1981 norms contained 220 individuals with a median age of 15.2. No validity or reliability data are presented. Botterbusch (1982b) indicates that many of the work samples are modifications of the JEVS system. He cites two major problems with the VITAS: a lack of client occupational information and a failure to make any real distinction between learning and performance.

McCarron-Dial System

The McCarron-Dial System (MDS) (McCarron & Dial, 1986) is intended for use with mentally retarded, emotionally disturbed, learning disabled, cerebral palsied, head injured, or socially/culturally disadvantaged individuals. The system assesses an individual's ability to function in a variety of work settings using a combination of individually administered psychological tests and observations in a work setting.

Psychological tests used on the MDS are the Peabody Picture Vocabulary Test-Revised (PPVT-R), Bender Visual Motor Gestalt Test (BVMGT), Behavior Rating Scale (BRS), Observational Emotional Inventory (OEI), Haptic Visual Discrimination Test (HVDT), and the McCarron Assessment of Neuromuscular Development (MAND). Intelligence tests, such as the Wechsler scales or Stanford-Binet, may also be used.

Scores on the MDS are expressed in time, quality, or as a combination of these two dimensions. All scores can be converted to percentiles or *T* scores and plotted on a profile sheet. Norming information is available for adults with mental retardation as well as for other groups on some tests. Computerized reports are available via user-purchased software or by sending the data to McCarron-Dial Evaluation Systems.

Test-retest reliability coefficients are mostly in the high .80s and .90s. Predictive validity studies conducted by the authors are encouraging. However, as Peterson (1988) has suggested, "Since the system does not assess any specific vocational skills or involve individuals in identifiable work tasks, occupational exploration and direct observation of work skills is limited" (p. 257).

Hester Evaluation System

The Hester Evaluation System (Hester, 1981) is intended for use with individuals who have physical and mental disabilities. The system, based on the Data-People-Things (DPT) hierarchy, contains 26 separate performance and paper-and-pencil tests. Total administration time is approximately 5 hours.

Raw scores are transformed to scale scores using a 1 to 6 scale, with a score of 6.0 being the highest score. Computer-generated reports of the assessment contain: demographic information, scores for each test, client level of functioning with the DPT hierarchy, and specific DOT job titles. Information on the Hester standardization sample is limited. Test-retest reliability coefficients for the Hester range from .72 to .95. Few data are presented regarding the validity of the system. However, one concurrent validity study was done with dentists in which 80% "would have been recommended to enter dentistry." Botterbusch (1982b) has criticized the author's inability to provide data on the instrument's technical characteristics.

Singer Vocational Evaluation System

The Singer Vocational Evaluation System (Singer, 1971) is designed to assist in vocational and occupational exploration and is intended for use with special needs individuals 17 to 30 years old. The Singer is intended to identify vocational abilities, vocational interests, and work tolerances that are necessary for vocational training.

The system contains a series of 24 work sampling stations that represent jobs found in the DOT. Scoring is based upon the amount of time needed to complete a task and the number of errors made. Test-retest reliability studies conducted by Cohen and Drugo (1976) yielded coefficients of .61 and .71.

Micro-Tower System

The Micro-Tower System (Institute for the Crippled and Disabled, 1977) is designed for use with special needs individuals. It is a group-administered aptitude test that contains 13 work samples in five major groups: Motor, Spatial, Clerical Perception, Numerical, and Verbal. Administration of the entire system requires approximately 15 to 20 hours. Each work sample contains five steps: occupational orientation, basic instructions, practice period, timed evaluation, and self-evaluation. Instructions are administered by audiocassette and are coordinated with a demonstration by the evaluator.

Raw scores obtained are transformed to percentiles and plotted on a profile sheet. The final report is also accompanied by a summary report and recommendations. Norms are based upon 19 groups that range in size from 40 to approximately 1,300. Test-retest, alternate-form, and internal consistency reliability coefficients range from .74 to .97. Construct validity is reported in the manual and is based upon intercorrelations among the work samples. The technical manual also reports correlations with the General Aptitude Test Battery (GATB).

SUMMARY

Transdisciplinary vocational assessment involves a variety of school and community-based professionals, utilizes a variety of assessment techniques and strategies, and requires that assessment information be gathered in a variety of domains. This chapter focused upon the assessment of intelligence, academic achievement, personality, vocational interests, vocational aptitudes, adaptive behavior, and career maturity, all of which should be assessed in a transdisciplinary school-based vocational assessment. Each section of this chapter defined and described a specific assessment domain, and provided brief summaries of assessment instruments that can be utilized by assessment personnel to assess each domain. As discussed in previous chapters, instruments should be selected based upon their purpose and usefulness, their psychometric properties, their cost and administration time, and other practical and logistical considerations. It is hoped that those professionals involved in selecting instruments for use in a transdisciplinary vocational assessment program will find the descriptions contained in this chapter helpful in identifying instruments for use in their programs.

REFERENCES

Aiken, L. R. (1985). *Psychological testing and assessment* (5th ed.). Boston, MA: Allyn & Bacon.

Albin, T. J. (1973). Relationship of IQ and previous work experience to success in sheltered employment. *Mental Retardation, 11*(3), 26.

Anastasi, A. (1982). *Psychological testing* (5th ed.). New York: Macmillan.

Ansley, T. N., & Forsyth, R. A. (1983). Relationship of elementary and secondary school achievement test scores to college performance. *Educational and Psychological Measurement, 43*(4), 1103-1112.

Baron, R. A., & Greenberg, J. (1990). *Behavior in organizations: Understanding and managing the human side of work* (3rd ed.). Boston, MA: Allyn & Bacon.

Bauernfeind, R. H. (1988). A review of the Career Occupational Preference System Interest Inventory. In J.T. Kapes & M.M. Mastie (Eds.), *A counselor's guide to vocational assessment instruments*. Alexandria, VA: National Vocational Development Association.

Beatty, L. S., Gardner, E. G., Madden, R., & Karlsen, B. (1985). *The Stanford Diagnostic Mathematics Test* (3rd ed.). San Antonio, TX: The Psychological Corporation.

Becker, R. L. (1981). *Revised Reading-Free Vocational Interest Inventory Manual*. Columbus, OH: Elbern.

Bennett, G. K., Seashore, H. G., & Wesman, A. G. (1982). *The Differential Aptitude Test, Forms V and W*. Cleveland: The Psychological Corporation.

Biller, E. F. (1987). *Career decision making for adolescents and young adults with learning disabilities: Theory, research and practice*. Springfield, IL: Charles C. Thomas.

Bodden, J. L.(1986). The Self-Directed Search. In D.J. Keyser & R. C. Sweetland (Eds.), *Test critiques*. Kansas City: Test Corporation of America.

Bolton, B. F. (1978). A review of the 16 Personality Factor Questionnaire. In O. K. Buros (Ed.), *The eighth mental measurements yearbook*. Highland Park, NJ: The Gryphon Press.

Bolton, B. (1985). Discriminant analysis of Holland's occupational types using the Sixteen Personality Factor Questionnaire. *Journal of Vocational Behavior, 27*, 210-217.

Borgen, F. H. (1983). A review of the USES General Aptitude Test Battery. In J. T. Kapes & M. M. Mastie (Eds.), *A counselor's guide to vocational guidance instruments*. Falls Church, VA: National Vocational Development Association.

Borgen, F. H. (1988). A review of the Strong-Campbell Interest Inventory. In J. T. Kapes & M. M. Mastie (Eds.), *A counselor's guide to career assessment instruments*. Alexandria, VA: National Vocational Development Association.

Botterbusch, K. F. (1982a). SAGE—System for Assessment and Group Evaluation. *Vocational Evaluation and Work Adjustment Bulletin, 15*(1), 32-34.

Botterbusch, K. F. (1982b). A review of the Hester Evaluation Systems. In *A comparison of commercial vocational evaluation systems* (2nd ed.). Menomonie, WI: Materials Development Center, Stout Vocational Rehabilitation Institute.

Botterbusch, K. F. (1982c). A review of the Vocational Interest Temperament and Aptitude System. In *A comparison of commercial vocational evaluation systems* (2nd ed.). Menomonie, WI: Materials Development Center, Stout Vocational Rehabilitation Institute.

Brickley, M., Browning, L., & Campbell, K. (1982). Vocational histories of sheltered workshop employees placed in projects with industry and competitive jobs. *Mental Retardation, 20*(2), 52-57.

Brickley, M., Campbell, K., & Browning, L. (1985). A five year follow-up of sheltered workshop employees placed in competitive jobs. *Mental Retardation, 23*(2), 67-73.

Brown, D. T. (1989). A review of the Jackson Vocational Interest Survey. In J. C. Conoley & J. J. Kramer (Eds.), *The tenth mental measurements yearbook*. Lincoln: The Univrsity of Nebraska Press.

Brown, F. G. (1983). *Principles of educational and psychological testing* (3rd ed.). New York: Holt, Rinehart, & Winston.

Brown, M. B. (1990). Personality assessment in career counseling. *Career Planning and Adult Development Journal, 6*(4), 22-26.

Burks, H. (1969). *Burks' Behavior Rating Scales*. Los Angeles: Western Psychological Services.

Butcher, J. N., Dahlstrom, W. G., Graham, J. R., Tellegren, A., & Kaemmer, B. (1989). *MMPI-2 Manual*. Minneapolis: University of Minnesota Press.

Campbell, D. P., & Hansen, J. C. (1981). *Manual for the Strong-Campbell Interest Inventory* (3rd ed.). Stanford, CA: Stanford University Press.

Campbell, N. J. (1988). A review of the Self-Directed Search. In J. T. Kapes & M. M. Mastie (Eds.), *A counselor's guide to career assessment instruments*. Alexandria, VA: National Vocational Development Association.

Cattell, R. B., Eber, H., & Tatsuoka, M. (1970). *Sixteen Personality Factor Questionnaire*. Champaign, IL: Insititute for Personality and Ability Testing.

Church, A. G. (1977). Academic achievement, IQ, level of occupational plans, and self-concepts for Anglo and Navaho school students. *Psychology, 14*, 24-40.

Cohen, C., & Drugo, J. (1976). Test-retest reliability of the Singer Vocational Evaluation System. *The Vocational Guidance Quarterly, 24*(3), 263-270.

Connolly, A. J. (1988). *KeyMath-Revised: A Diagnostic Inventory of Essential Mathematics.* Circle Pines, MN: American Guidance Service.

Crites, J. O. (1978). *Administration and use manual for the Career Maturity Inventory* (2nd ed.). Monterey, CA: CTB/McGraw-Hill.

Daniels, H. (1989). A review of the Self-Directed Search. In J. C. Conoley & J.J. Kramer (Eds.), *The tenth mental measurements yearbook.* Lincoln: The University of Nebraska Press.

Davidshofer, C. O. (1988a). A review of the Career Occupational Preference System Interest Inventory. In J. T. Kapes & M. M. Mastie (Eds.), *A counselor's guide to career assessment instruments.* Alexandria, VA: National Vocational Development Association.

Davidshofer, C. O. (1988b). A review of the Jackson Vocational Interest Survey. In J. T. Kapes & M. M. Mastie (Eds.), *A counselor's guide to career assessment instruments.* Alexandria, VA: National Vocational Development Association.

Diamond, E. E. (1983). A review of the AAMD-Becker Reading Free Vocational Interest Inventory. In J. T. Kapes & M. M. Mastie (Eds.), *A counselor's guide to career assessment instruments.* Alexandria, VA: National Vocational Development Association.

Dolliver, R. H. (1975). Concurrent prediction from the Strong Vocational Interest Blank. *Journal of Counseling Psychology, 22,* 199-203.

Domino, G. (1978). Review of AAMD-Becker Reading Free Vocational Interest Inventory. In O.K. Buros (Ed.), *The eighth mental measurements yearbook.* Highland Park, NJ: The Gryphon Press.

Droege, R. C. (1988). A review of the Harrington-O'Shea Career Decision Making System. In J. T. Kapes & M. M. Mastie (Eds.), *A counselor's guide to career assessment instruments.* Alexandria, VA: National Development Association.

Dunn, L. M. (1981). *Manual for the Peabody Picture Vocabulary Test—Revised.* Circle Pines, MN: American Guidance Service.

Edwards, R. (1977). Personal traits and success in schooling and work. *Educational and Psychological Measurement, 37,* 125-138.

Faas, L. A., & D'Alonzo, B. (1990). WAIS-R scores as predictors of employment success and failure among adults with learning disabilities. *Journal of Learning Disabilities, 23,* 311-316.

Flanagan, W. M. (1983). A review of the Jewish Employment Vocational Service Work Sample System. In J. T. Kapes & M. M. Mastie (Eds.), *A counselor's guide to vocational guidance instruments.* Falls Church, VA: National Vocational Guidance Association.

Foster, R. (1977). *Camelot Behavioral Checklist.* Lawrence, KS: Author.

Frary, R. B. (1988). A review of the Career Maturity Inventory. In J. T. Kapes & M. M. Mastie (Eds.), *A counselor's guide to career assessment instruments* (2nd ed.). Alexandria, VA: The American Association for Counseling and Development.

Freeman, E., & Levine, S. (1968). *San Francisco Vocational Competency Scale.* San Antonio, TX: The Psychological Corporation.

Geist, C. R. (1982). Social avoidance and distress as a predictor of perceived locus of control and level of self-esteem. *Journal of Clinical Psychology, 38*(3), 611-613.

Ghiselli, E. E. (1973). The validity of aptitude tests in personnel selection. *Personnel Psychology, 26,* 461-477.

Geist, H. (1964). *The Geist Picture Interest Inventory.* Beverly Hills, CA: Stanford University Press.

Goldstein, W. J. (1977). Vocational education: Predicting success and failure among disadvantaged adults. *Dissertation Abstracts International, 38*(3), 1468B.

Gory, E. L. (1985). A review of the Camelot Behavioral Checklist. In J. V. Mitchell, Jr. (Ed.), *The ninth mental measurements yearbook.* Lincoln: The University of Nebraska Press.

Gottfredson, L. S. (1984). The role of intelligence and education in the division of labor. *Center for Social Organization of Schools Report, Johns Hopkins University, 355,* p. 162.

Gottfredson, G. D., & Holland, J. L. (1975). Vocational choices of men and women: A comparison of predictors from the Self-Directed Search. *Journal of Counseling Psychology, 22,* 28-34.

Gottfredson, G. D., & Holland, J. L. (1989). *Dictionary of Holland occupational codes* (2nd ed.). Odessa, FL: Psychological Assessment Resources.

Grossman, H. J. (Ed.). (1983). *Classification in mental retardation.* Washington, DC: American Association of Mental Deficiency.

Hafner, J., & Fakouri, E. (1984). Early recollections and vocational choice. *Individual Psychology: Journal of Adlerian Theory, Research, and Practice, 40,* 54-60.

Halpern, A. S., Raffeld, P., Irvin, L. K., & Link, R. (1975). *Social and Prevocational Information Battery.* Monterey, CA: CTB/McGraw-Hill.

Hansen, J. C. (1978). A review of the California Occupational Preference System. In O. K. Buros (Ed.), *The eighth mental measurements yearbook.* Highland Park, NJ: The Gryphon Press.

Hanson, G. R., Noeth, R. J., & Prediger, D. J. (1977). The validity of diverse procedures for reporting interest scores: An analysis of longitudinal data. *Journal of Counseling Psychology, 24,* 487-493.

Harrington, R. G. (1985). Scales of independent behavior. In D. J. Keyser & R. C. Sweetland (Eds.), *Test critiques.* Kansas City: Test Corporation of America.

Harrington, T. F., & O'Shea, A. J. (1982). *Manual for the Harrington-O'Shea Career Decision Making System.* Circle Pines, MN: American Guidance Service.

Hartzell, H. E., & Compton, C. (1984). Learning disability: 10-year follow-up. *Pediatrics, 74,* 1058-1064.

Hathaway, S., & McKinley, J. (1967). *Minnesota Multiphasic Personality Inventory.* Cleveland: The Psychological Corporation.

Heinlein, W. E. (1987). *Clinical utility of the Wechsler scales in psychological evaluations to estimate vocational aptitude.* Unpublished doctoral dissertation, Virginia Polytechnic Institute and State University, Blacksburg, VA.

Herr, E. L. (1989). A review of the Kuder Occupational Interest Survey, Revised (Form DD). In J. C. Conoley & J. J. Kramer (Eds.), *The tenth mental measurements yearbook.* Lincoln: The University of Nebraska Press.

Hester, E. (1981). *Hester Evaluation Systems.* Chicago, IL: Evaluation Systems.

Hileronymus, A. N., Hoover, H. D., & Lindquist, E. F. (1986). *Iowa Tests of Basic Skills.* Chicago: Riverside.

Holden, R. H. (1984). A review of the Vineland Scale. In D. J. Keyser & R. C. Sweetland (Eds.), *Test critiques.* Kansas City: Test Corporation of America.

Holden, R. H. (1985). Reading-Free Vocational Interest Inventory Revised. In D. J. Keyser & R. C. Sweetland (Eds.), *Test critiques.* Kansas City: Test Corporation of America.

Holden, R. H. (1991). Minnesota Multiphasic Personality Inventory - 2. In D. J. Keyser & R. C. Sweetland (Eds.), *Test critiques.* Austin, TX: Pro-Ed.

Holland, J. L. (1985a). *A theory of vocational personalities and work environments.* Englewood Cliffs, NJ: Prentice-Hall.

Holland, J. L. (1985b). *The Self-Directed Search professional manual — 1985 edition.* Odessa, FL: Psychological Assessment Resources.

Hooper, P. G. (1980). Guidance and counseling: Potential impact on youth unemployment. *Journal of Career Education, 6,* 270-287.

Hsu, L. M. (1985). Review of the Wide Range Interest Opinion Test. In J. V. Mitchell, Jr. (Ed.), *The ninth mental measurements yearbook.* Lincoln: The University of Nebraska Press.

Hughes, H. M., Jr. (1972). Vocational choice, level, and consistency: An investigation of Holland's theory in an employed sample. *Journal of Vocational Behavior, 2,* 377-388.

Hunter, J. E., & Hunter, R. F. (1984). Validity and utility of alternative predictors of job performance. *Psychological Bulletin, 96*(1), 72-98.

Isaacson, L. E. (1985). *Basics of career counseling.* Boston, MA: Allyn & Bacon.

Institute for Crippled and Disabled. (1977). *Micro-Tower.* New York: ICD Rehabilitation and Research Center.

Jackson, D. N. (1977). *Jackson Vocational Interest Survey Manual.* Goshen, NY: Research Psychologists Press.

Jackson, D. N. (1989). *Basic Personality Inventory manual.* Port Huron, MI: Sigma Assessment Systems.

Jastak, J. F., & Jastak, S. R. (1979). *Wide Range Interest Opinion Test Manual.* Wilmington, DE: Guidance Associates of Delaware.

Jastak, S., & Wilkinson, G. S. (1984). *Wide Range Achievement Test-Revised.* Wilmington, DE: Jastak Associates.

Jencks, C., Bartlett, S., Corcoran, M., Crouse, J., Eaglesfield, D., Jackson, G., McCelland, K., Mueser, P., Olneck, M., Schwartz, J., Ward, S., & Williams, J. (1979). *Who gets ahead? The determinants of economic success in America.* New York: Basic Books.

Johansson, C. R. (1982). *Manual for Career Assessment Inventory, Second edition*. Minneapolis, MN: NCS Interpretive Scoring Systems.

Kamphaus, R. W. (1985). A review of the USES Nonreading Aptitude Test Battery. In J. V. Mitchell, Jr. (Ed.), *The ninth mental measurements yearbook*. Lincoln: The University of Nebraska Press.

Karlsen, B., & Gardner, E. (1985). *Stanford Diagnostic Reading Test* (3rd ed.). San Antonio, TX: The Psychological Corporation.

Kaufman, A. S., & Kaufman, N. L. (1983). *K-ABC: Kaufman Assessment Battery for Children*. Circle Pines, MN: American Guidance Service.

Kimball, R. L., Sedlacek, W. E., & Brooks, G. C. (1973). Black and white vocational interests in Holland's Self-Directed Search (SDS). *Journal of Negro Education, 42,* 1-4.

Kirk, B. A., & Frank, A. C. (1983). A review of the Kuder General Interest Survey-Form DD. In J. T. Kapes & M. M. Mastie (Eds.), *A counselor's guide to career guidance instruments*. Falls Church, VA: National Vocational Guidance Association.

Kirnan, J. P., & Geisinger, K. F. (1986). A review of the General Aptitude Test Battery. In D. J. Keyser & R. C. Sweetland (Eds.), *Test critiques*. Kansas City: Test Corporation of America.

Knapp, R. R., & Knapp, L. (1984). *COPS Interest Inventory Technical Manual*. San Diego, CA: EDITS.

Kuder, F. (1975). *General Interest Survey (Form E) O-Manual*. Chicago, IL: Science Research Associates.

Kuder, F., & Diamond, E. E. (1985). *Kuder DD Occupational Interest Survey, Revised*. Chicago: Science Research Associates.

LaVoie, A. L. (1991). A review of the Basic Personality Inventory. In D. J. Keyser & R. C. Sweetland (Eds.), *Test critiques* (Vol. 8). Austin, TX: Pro-Ed.

Layton, W. L. (1978). Review of COPS. In O.K. Buros (Ed.), *The eighth mental measurements yearbook*. Highland Park, NJ: The Gryphon Press.

Layton, W. L. (1985). A review of the Strong-Campbell Interest Inventory. In J. V. Mitchell, Jr. (Ed.), *The ninth mental measurements yearbook*. Lincoln: The University of Nebraska Press.

Lerner, J. V. (1985). A review of Burks' Behavior Rating Scales. In D. J. Keyser & R. C. Sweetland (Eds.), *Test critiques*. Kansas City: Test Corporation of America.

Levinson, E. M., Rafoth, B., & Lesnak, L. (in submission). *A criterion related validity study of the OASIS-2 Interest Schedule*.

Linn, R. L. (1986). Comments on the g factor in employment testing. *Journal of Vocational Behavior, 29,* 438-444.

Maddux, C. D., & Cummings, R. E. (1986). Alternate form reliability of the Self-Directed Search - Form E. *Career Development Quarterly, 35,* 136-140.

Malgady, R. G., Barcher, P. R., Davis, J., & Towner, G. (1980). Validity of the Vocational Adaptation Rating Scale: Prediction of mentally retarded workers' placement in sheltered workshops. *American Journal of Mental Deficiency, 84*(6), 633-640.

Manaster, G. J., & Perryman, T. P. (1974). Early recollections and occupational choice. *Journal of Individual Psychology, 30*(2), 232-237.

Manuele, C. A. (1985). Wide Range Interest Opinion Test. In J. V. Mitchell, Jr. (Ed.), *The ninth mental measurements yearbook*. Lincoln: The University of Nebraska Press.

Manuele, C. A. (1988). A review of the Harrington-O'Shea Career Decision Making System. In J. V. Mitchell, Jr. (Ed.), *The ninth mental measurements yearbook, supplement*. Lincoln: The University of Nebraska Press.

Manuele, C. A. (1989). A review of the Self-Directed Search. In J. C. Conoley & J. J. Kramer (Eds.), *The tenth mental measurements yearbook*. Lincoln: The University of Nebraska Press.

Markwardt, F. C. (1989). *Peabody Individual Achievement Test - Revised*. Circle Pines, MN: American Guidance Service.

Matheny, A. P., Dolan, A. B., & Krantz, J. Z. (1980). Cognitive aspects of interests, responsibilities, and vocational goals in adolescence. *Adolescence, 15*(58), 301-311.

McCabe, S. P. (1988). A review of the Career Assessment Inventory. In J. T. Kapes & M. M. Mastie (Eds.), *A counselor's guide to career assessment instruments*. Alexandria, VA: National Center Development Association.

McCarron, L. T., & Dial, J. G. (1986). *McCarron-Dial System*. Dallas, TX: McCarron-Dial Evaluation Systems.

McCarthy, W. (1976). Exploration of skills associated with successful performance of retarded individuals in a sheltered workshop. *Educational Training of the Mentally Retarded, 11*(1), 23-31.

McKee, L. M., & Levinson, E. M. (1990). A review of the computerized version of the Self-Directed Search. *Career Development Quarterly, 38*, 325-333.

Meyers, C. E. (1978). A review of the Social and Prevocational Information Battery. In O. Buros (Ed.), *The eighth mental measurements yearbook*. Highland Park, NJ: The Gryphon Press.

Miller, J. T. (1978). A study of WISC subtest scores as predictors of GATB occupational aptitude patterns for EMH students in a high school occupational orientation course. *Dissertation Abstracts International, 38*(12-A7), 7272.

Miller, T. L., & Reynolds, C. R. (1984). The KABC [Special Issue]. *The Journal of Special Education, 18*(3).

Morris, T., & Levinson, E. M. (in press). Intelligence and occupational/vocational adjustment: A literature review. *Journal of Counseling and Development*.

Myers, C. E. (1978). A review of the Social and Prevocational Information Battery. In O. K. Buros (Ed.), *The eighth mental measurements yearbook*. Highland Park, NJ: The Gryphon Press.

Naslund, R. A., Thorpe, L. P., & LeFever, D. W. (1978). *SRA Achievement Series*. Chicago: Science Research Associates.

Nihira, K., Foster, R, Shellhaas, M., & Leland, H. (1974). *AAMD Scale* (rev. ed.). Washington, DC: American Association of Mental Deficiency.

O'Neil, J. M., Magoon, T. M., & Tracey, T. J. (1978). Status of Holland's investigative personality types and their consistency levels seven years later. *Journal of Counseling Psychology*, 25, 530-535.

Otis, A., & Lennon, D. (1982). *The Otis-Lennon School Ability Test*. San Antonio, TX: The Psychological Corporation.

Palmo, A. J., & Lutz, J. G. (1983). The relationship of performance on the CMI to intelligence with disadvantaged youngsters. *Measurement and Evaluation in Guidance, 16*(3), 139-148.

Parker, R. M. (1991). *Occupational Aptitude Survey and Interest Schedule - Second Edition*. Austin, TX: Pro-Ed.

Parker, R. M. (1987). Multifactor aptitude and achievement tests. In B. Bolton (Ed.), *Handbook of measurement and evaluation in rehabilitation*. Baltimore, MD: Paul H. Brookes.

Pennock-Roman, M. (1985). A review of the Differential Aptitude Test. In D. J. Keyser & R. C. Sweetland (Eds.), *Test critiques*. Kansas City, MO: Test Corporation of America.

Peterson, M. (1988). A review of the McCarron-Dial System. In J. T. Kapes & M. M. Mastie (Eds.), *A counselor's guide to career assessment instruments* (2nd ed.). Alexandria, VA: National Career Development Association.

Power, P. W. (1984). *A guide to vocational assessment*. Baltimore: University Park Press.

Prescott, G. A.; Balow, J. H., Hogan, T. R., & Farr, R. C. (1984). *Metropolitan Achievement Test 6: Survey Battery*. San Antonio, TX: The Psychological Corporation.

Proctor, W. M. (1935). Intelligence and length of schooling in relation to occupational levels. *School and Society, 42*(1093), 783-786.

Prout, T., & Strohmer, D. (1989). *Prout-Strohmer Assessment System*. Schnectady, NY: Genium.

Reardon, R., & Loughead, T. (in press). A comparison of the paper-pencil and computer versions of the Self-Directed Search. *Journal of Counseling and Development*.

Reschly, D. J. (1990). Best practices in intellectual assessment. In A. Thomas & J. Grimes (Eds.), *Best practices in school psychology II*. Washington, DC: National Association of School Psychologists.

Reynolds, C. (1986). Wide Range Achievement Test (WRAT-R), 1984 edition. *Journal of Counseling and Development, 64*, 540-541.

Salvia, J., & Ysseldyke, J. E. (1991). *Assessment* (5th ed.). Boston: Houghton-Mifflin.

Sattler, J. (1988). *Assessment of children* (3rd ed.). San Diego: Author.

Sax, G. (1980). *Principles of educational and psychological measurement and evaluation* (2nd ed.). Belmont, CA: Wadsworth.

Scharf, R.(1970). Relative importance of interest and ability in vocational decision making. *Journal of Counseling Psychology, 17*, 258-262.

Schill, W. J., McCartin, R., & Meyer, K. (1985). Youth employment: Its relationship to academic and family variables. *Journal of Vocational Behavior, 26*, 155-163.

Schmitt, N. (1978). Achievement level and sex differences in levels of interests and the interest-educational choice relationship. *College Student Journal, 12*, 167-173.

Seligman, L. (1980). *Assessment in developmental career counseling*. Cranston, RI: Carroll Press.

Shapira, Z., Cnann, R. A., & Cnann, A. (1985). Mentally retarded workers' reactions to their jobs. *American Journal of Mental Deficiency, 90*(2), 160-166.

Shepard, J. W. (1989). A review of the Jackson Vocational Interest Survey. In J. C. Conoley & J. J. Kramer (Eds.), *The tenth mental measurements yearbook*. Lincoln: The University of Nebraska Press.

The Singer Company. (1971). *Vocational evaluation systems*. Morris, IL: New Concepts Corporation.

Slosson, R. L. (1983). *Slosson Intelligence Test (SIT) and Oral Reading Test (SORT) for Children and Adults*. East Aurora, NY: Slosson Educational Publications.

Sonnerschein, J. L. (1983). *Basic Achievement Skills Individual Screener*. Cleveland, OH: The Psychological Corporation.

Sparrow, S. S., Balla, D. A., & Cicchetti, D. V. (1984). *Vineland Adaptive Behavior Scales*. Circle Pines, MN: American Guidance Service.

Spitzer, D., & Levinson, E. M. (1988). A review of selected vocational interest inventories for use by school psychologists. *School Psychology Review, 17*(4), 673-692.

Streiner, D. L. (1986). Differences in MMPI profiles with the norms of Colligan et al. *Journal of Consulting and Clinical Psychology, 54*, 843-845.

Super, D. E. (1957). *The psychology of careers*. New York: Harper & Row.

Super, D., & Crites, J. O. (1962). *Appraising vocational fitness*. New York: Harper & Row.

Super, D. E., & Thompson, A. (1979). A six-scale, two factor measure of adolescent career or vocational maturity. *Vocational Guidance Quarterly, 28*(1), 6-15.

Super, D. E., Thompson, A. S., Lindeman, R. H., Jordan, J. P., & Myers, R. A. (1981). *The Career Development Inventory*. Palo Alto, CA: Consulting Psychologists.

Tenopyr, M. L. (1989). A review of the Kuder Occupational Interest Survey, Revised (Form DD). In J. C. Conoley & J. J. Kramer (Eds.), *The tenth mental measurements yearbook*. Lincoln: The University of Nebraska Press.

Thomas, L. E., Morrill, W. H., & Miller, C. D. (1970). Educational interests and achievement. *Vocational Guidance Quarterly, 18,* 199-202.

Thomas, R. G. (1985). A review of the Jackson Vocational Interest Survey. In J. V. Mitchell, Jr. (Ed.), *The ninth mental measurements yearbook*. Lincoln: The University of Nebraska Press.

Thorndike, R. L., Hagen, E. P., & Sattler, J. M. (1986). *Guide for administering and scoring the Stanford-Binet Intelligence Scale: Fourth Edition*. Chicago: Riverside.

Tiegs, E. W., & Clark, W. W. (1970). *California Achievement Test*. Monterey, CA: Author.

Timmerman, W. (1975). Using a sentence completion technique to predict the employment satisfactoriness of persons with disabilities. *Dissertation Abstracts International, 35*, 5836.

Touchton, J. G., & Magoon, T. M. (1977). Occupational daydreams as predictors of vocational plans for college women. *Journal of Vocational Behavior, 10*, 156-166.

Train-Ease Corporation. (1982). *System for Assessment and Group Evaluation*. New York: Author.

Turner, R. G., & Horn, J. M. (1975). Personality correlates of Holland's occupational types: A cross cultural study. *Journal of Vocational Behavior, 6*, 379-389.

Tseng, M. S., & Rhodes, C. I. (1993). Correlates of the perception of occupational prestige. *Journal of Counseling Psychology, 20*(6), 522-527.

Tzeng, O. C. S. (1985). A review of the Strong-Campbell Interest Inventory. In D. J. Keyser & R. C. Sweetland (Eds.), *Test critiques*. Kansas City: Test Corporation of America.

United States Department of Defense. (1984). *Test manual for the Armed Services Vocational Aptitude Battery*. North Chicago, IL: United States Military Entrance Processing Command.

United States Department of Labor. (1979). *Guide for occupational exploration*. Washington, DC: Government Printing Office.

United States Department of Labor. (1983). *Manual for the General Aptitude Test Battery, Section I: Administration and Scoring (Forms C and D)*. Salt Lake City, UT: Utah Department of Employment Security.

United States Employment Service Office. (1982). *USES Nonreading Aptitude Test Battery*. Washington, DC: Government Printing Office.

United States Employment Service Office. (1983). *General Aptitude Test Battery*. Washington, DC: Government Printing Office.

Vocational Research Institute. (1973a). *Jewish Employment Vocational Service Work Sample System*. Philadelphia, PA: Vocational Research Institute, Jewish Employment and Vocational Service.

Vocational Research Institute. (1973b). *Vocational Information and Evaluation Work Samples*. Philadelphia, PA: Vocational Research Institute, Jewish Employment and Vocational Service.

Vocational Research Institute. (1979). *Vocational Interest Temperament and Aptitude System*. Philadelphia, PA: Vocational Research Institute, Jewish Employment and Vocational Service.

Warren, S. A., & Gardner, D. C. (1981). Correlates of class rank of high school handicapped students in mainstream vocational education programs. *Adolescence, 16*(62), 335-344.

Watkins, N. W. (1980). Intellectual and special aptitudes of tenth grade educable mentally retarded students. *Education and Training of the Mentally Retarded, 15*, 139-142.

Webster, R. E. (1974). Predictive applicability of the WAIS with psychiatric patients in a vocational rehabilitation setting. *Journal of Community Psychology, 2*, 141-144.

Webster, R. E. (1979). Utility of the WAIS in predicting vocational success of psychiatric patients. *Journal of Clinical Psychology, 35*(1), 111-116.

Wechsler, D. (1958). *The measurement and appraisal of adult intelligence*. Baltimore, MD: Williams & Wilkins.

Wechsler, D. (1974). *Manual for the Wechsler Intelligence Scale for Children - Revised*. San Antonio, TX: The Psychological Corporation.

Wechsler, D. (1981). *Manual for the Wechsler Adult Intelligence Scale - Revised.* San Antonio, TX: The Psychological Corporation.

Wechsler, D. (1989). *Manual for the Wechsler Preschool and Primary Scale of Intelligence - Revised.* San Antonio, TX: The Psychological Corporation.

Wechsler, D. (1992). *Manual for the Wechsler Intelligence Scale for Children - Third Edition.* San Antonio, TX: The Psychological Corporation.

Westbrook, B. W. (1985). A review of the Strong-Campbell Interest Inventory. In J. V. Mitchell, Jr. (Ed.), *The ninth mental measurements yearbook.* Lincoln: The University of Nebraska Press.

Westbrook, B. W., Rogers, B., & Covington, J. E. (1980). Test review: The Harrington-O'Shea System for Career Decision Making. *Measurement and Evaluation in Guidance, 13,* 185-188.

Wiggins, J. D., & Westlander, D. L. (1977). Expressed vocational choices and later employment compared with Vocational Preference Inventory and Kuder Preference Record-Vocational scores. *Journal of Vocational Behavior, 11,* 158-165.

Williams, J. A., & Williams, J. D. (1988). A review of the Kuder General Interest Survey, Form E. In J. T. Kapes & M. M. Mastie (Eds.), *A counselor's guide to career assessment instruments.* Alexandria, VA: National Vocational Development Association.

Willis, C. G. (1978). A review of the Harrington-O'Shea Career Decision Making System. In O. K. Buros (Ed.), *The eighth mental measurements yearbook.* Highland Park, NJ: The Gryphon Press.

Willis, C. G. (1983). A review of the Harrington-O'Shea Career Decision Making System. In J. T. Kapes & M. M. Mastie (Eds.), *A counselor's guide to career guidance instruments.* Falls Church, VA: National Vocational Guidance Association.

Wirtenberg, J. T. (1979). *The impact of a sex desegregated practical arts course on maximization of occupational potential in seventh grade girls.* Unpublished doctoral dissertation, University of California at Los Angeles.

Wolf, J. C. (1983). Tests of general educational development as a predictor of 2-year college academic performance. *Measurement and Evaluation in Guidance, 16*(1), 4-12.

Wolfensberger, W. (1967). Vocational preparation and occupation. In A. Baumeister (Ed.), *Mental retardation: Appraisal, education and rehabilitation.* Chicago: Aldine.

Woodcock, R. W. (1987). *Woodcock Reading Mastery Test - Revised.* Circle Pines, MN: American Guidance Service.

Woodcock, R. W., & Johnson, M. B. (1989). *Woodcock-Johnson Psycho-Educational Battery — Revised.* Allen, TX: DLM.

Zurawell, J. M., & Das, J. P. (1982). Cognitive performance and success in automotives training. *Mental Retardation Bulletin, 10*(2,3), 61-68.

Zytowski, D. G. (1983). A review of the Wide Range Interest Opinion Test. In J. T. Kapes & M. M. Mastie (Eds.), *A counselor's guide to vocational guidance instruments.* Falls Church, VA: National Vocational Guidance Association.

6 PROGRAM DEVELOPMENT: PRACTICAL AND LOGISTICAL CONSIDERATIONS

This chapter includes a discussion of practical and logistical factors that need to be considered when establishing and implementing transdisciplinary school-based vocational assessment programs. Not all assessment programs are, can be, or should be the same. Certainly, the nature and type of assessment program established in a particular locality will depend upon such factors as the available resources and the characteristics and expertise of available personnel. It will also depend upon the population targeted for services, the nature and type of vocational and postsecondary training and placement options available in the locality, and the nature of auxiliary services available in the community. This chapter will address these issues, focusing specifically upon the steps involved in assessment program development and implementation, and the various roles school personnel, parents, and community agencies can assume in the vocational assessment process. The chapter will also address considerations in the assessment of special populations.

STEPS IN PROGRAM DEVELOPMENT AND IMPLEMENTATION

The steps involved in planning and implementing transdisciplinary school-based vocational assessment programs fall within three distinct phases: Planning and Development, Implementation, and Evaluation and Improvement. Table 6-1 summarizes the program development process.

Phase 1 - Planning and Development

This phase of program development involves the following steps: developing a task force, conducting a needs assessment, developing an

Table 6-1.
Steps Involved in Program Development

Phase 1—Planning and Development

1. Develop a Task Force
2. Conduct a Needs Assessment
3. Develop a Program Model and Establish Objectives
4. Develop Local Interagency Agreements/Action Plans
5. Identify Funding Requirements and Sources

Phase 2—Implementation

1. Hire a Vocational Assessment Program Coordinator
2. Select Vocational Assessment Site(s)
3. Develop a Procedure Manual
4. Select/Purchase Materials and Equipment
5. Train Personnel
6. Conduct Inservice Workshops with School Staff/Community
7. Pilot-Test the Assessment Program
8. Revise and Implement the Program

Phase 3—Evaluation

1. Identify Aspects of Program in Need of Evaluation
2. Identify Standards for Evaluation
3. Hire/Identify a Program Evaluator
4. Conduct Evaluation
5. Plan and Implement Program Improvements

assessment program model and establishing objectives, developing local interagency agreements and action plans, and identifying funding requirements and sources.

Developing a Task Force

The purpose of the task force is to take responsibility for all initial steps in program planning. This task force should adequately represent all school and community agency personnel who are in some way likely to be involved in or affected by the assessment program. As such, this task force should include school administrators drawn from regular, special, and vocational education; teachers (regular, special education, and vocational education); school psychologists and counselors; parents; community agency personnel (e.g., vocational rehabilitation, community mental health, employment agencies); and representatives from local employers. A school administrator, with authority to commit both personnel and finances to the program, should chair this task force.

Conduct a Needs Assessment

According to a report by the National Association of State Boards of Education (NASBE, 1979), a needs assessment is defined as

> . . . a process for identifying and examining the purposes against which needs are determined; getting these purposes modified if they are found to be improper or flawed; identifying the things that are requisite and useful for serving the validated purposes; assessing the extent that the identified needs are met or unmet; rating the importance of these met and unmet needs; and aiding the audience for the needs assessment to apply the findings in formulating goals, choosing procedures, and assessing progress. (p. 5)

One primary responsibility of the task force will be to conduct a needs assessment to determine what resources exist in the school and community that might facilitate program development, and what needs exist that must be addressed prior to program development. In so doing, potential obstacles to program development and implementation that can be addressed early in the planning process will be identified, as well as needs that the assessment program itself may be structured to address. The purpose of the needs assessment is to determine the adequacy of existing school, employment, and adult service programs. Data can be gathered using a variety of techniques, including survey questionnaires, interviews, observations, and accreditation reports. School programs should be evaluated to determine the extent to which there is a relationship between educational/vocational programs and employment opportunities in the local community, the number of students who have been successfully placed in jobs and residential facilities following graduation, the functional nature of the educational program (i.e., Does the educational program provide students with those skills they need in order to acquire and maintain employment, and to function independently and productively in the community?), and the extent to which students have access to community-based vocational training. Employment programs should be evaluated to determine the number of individuals successfully placed in vocational settings, the retention rate of placed clients, wages earned by employees, and the nature and type of follow-along services provided. Adult service programs should be evaluated to determine the type of vocational assessment and postsecondary training services provided and the availability of supported and sheltered employment opportunities. The quality of community living arrangements, transportation, recreational and leisure programs, and medical and psychological services available in the local area should also be evaluated. Similarly, the nature and type of employment options available in the community should also be assessed.

Table 6-2 summarizes information that should be obtained in the needs assessment. Based upon the needs assessment data gathered, the task force should recommend improvements in school and community services and begin plans for assessment program development. Timelines should be established for the initiation of improvements, and staff and agency responsibilities should be specified.

Develop an Assessment Program Model and Objectives

What are the purposes of the assessment program? Is the program designed to increase the frequency of appropriate placements of students with disabilities in vocational training programs? Is it to assist students in making realistic and informed decisions about what to do after they finish high school? Is it to facilitate successful job placements? Clearly, measureable objectives must be established prior to the development of the assessment program model, because the model is likely to be influenced by these purposes and objectives. Purposes and goals of assessment may vary depending upon several factors. Some common goals are to (Thomas & Coleman, 1988):

1. provide a clear picture of a student's abilities so that a total career development program for the student can be initiated;

2. recommend appropriate prevocational or remediation training;

3. recommend appropriate placement in vocational education programs and suggest useful teaching techniques and needed support services;

4. suggest appropriate job placement;

5. identify realistic obtainable skills; or

6. provide the student with vocational information and feedback concerning abilities so that a step-by-step transitional plan can be initiated.

The development of a program model should be based upon some underlying philosophy drawn from career and vocational development theory (see Chapter 2). The development of a program model involves a variety of decisions. Decisions such as the age at which to begin formal assessment and vocational planning, the numbers and types of students to receive services, the format and components of the assessment program to be developed for students, the professionals to be involved in the assessment program, and the roles and qualifications of these professionals must be made by the task force and be incorporated into the assessment program model. Timelines for implementation of various stages of the model should also be specified.

Table 6-2.
Needs Assessment: What to Assess

School Programs

1. Is there a relationship between vocational training opportunities and local employment opportunities?
2. Is the educational program "functional" in nature?
3. How many students have been successfully placed in jobs and residential facilities following graduation?
4. To what extent are students provided access to community-based vocational training?
5. Are vocational education curricula modified to meet the needs of special students?
6. Do students receive formal transitional planning; are Individual Transition Plans developed for students?
7. Are parents and students actively involved in vocational planning?
8. What professionals are involved in vocational planning; what are their roles; how well have they been trained?

Employment Programs

1. What are the program's eligibility requirements?
2. What population(s) is served?
3. What specific services are provided?
4. What is the program's placement rate?
5. What is the program's definition of "successful" placement?
6. What wages do placed clients earn?
7. What is the average salary earned?
8. What is the average length of employment?
9. What type of ongoing support and follow-up services are provided?

Adult Service Programs

1. What are the program's eligibility requirements?
2. What population is served?
3. What type of assessment and training services are provided; how adequate are these services?
4. Are supported and sheltered employment services provided; how adequate are these services?

Other Community Services

1. What community living arrangements are available; how adequate are they?
2. What type of transportation is available?
3. What recreational and leisure programs exist?
4. What medical and psychological services are available; how adequate are they?

Develop Local Interagency Agreements and Action Plans

The task force should take responsibility for initiating the development of interagency agreements that have the purpose of further defining the various school and community agency roles in the assessment program. Because many states have developed similar interagency agreements at the state level, these should be reviewed and considered when developing local agreements. According to Wehman, Moon, Everson, Wood, and Barcus (1988), the task force should identify and verify participation of key agencies and organizations, establish flow patterns of targeted students across local agencies and organizations following assessment (i.e., when a particular student is likely to be serviced by a particular agency and the nature of the services likely to be provided), and identify the means by which services will be evaluated.

Identify Funding Requirements and Sources

Based upon the needs assessment conducted, the task force should estimate the funding necessary to implement the program model developed. In estimating the funding necessary to implement the program model, one must consider whatever additional personnel the program may require, construction costs associated with an assessment center site (either the building of a new site or modification of an existing site), personnel training costs, purchase of assessment materials, maintenance and upgrading of assessment materials, inservice workshops for staff, hiring of consultants, and purchase of additional equipment and materials (i.e., furniture, paper, etc.).

Phase 2 - Implementation

This phase of program development involves the following steps: hiring a vocational assessment program coordinator, selecting a vocational assessment site(s), developing a vocational assessment procedures manual, selecting/purchasing assessment materials, training personnel, conducting inservice workshops with school staff and the community, and pilot-testing the assessment program prior to full program implementation.

Hire (or Appoint) a Vocational Assessment Program Coordinator

At some point, the task force must relinquish primary responsibility for program development and identify an individual to take over most program development responsibilities. This can be done earlier than is listed here (i.e., it can be done in the initial planning stages, after which time the coordinator would assume responsibility for all the remaining tasks). Regardless, once the program coordinator is appointed, (s)he would report to the task force on a regular basis relative to program development progress and enlist the help and support of task force members whenever necessary. Ideally, the individual appointed as the vocational assessment program coordinator should have experience in vocational assessment, special education, and vocational education, and prior administrative experience in the schools.

Select a Vocational Assessment Site(s)

A number of factors must be considered when selecting a vocational assessment site(s). Obviously, the program model developed will in some way dictate the nature of the site. That is, if the model is one that employs transportable assessment equipment to service a number of school districts in a decentralized cooperative program, several sites may need to be identified. However, if the model is to service only one district, or, if in a cooperative program, a centralized assessment center is to be developed, one large, centrally located site may need to be identified. Factors such as the size of the district(s) being served by the program or the number of students to be served at a given time will influence the size of the assessment center. Several other factors will influence the selection of a site, including whether the site is structurally accessible to and appropriate for individuals with various disabilities (for example, can it accommodate wheelchairs for students with physical disabilities? is it relatively free of distractions to accommodate students with attention and learning problems?); whether adequate restroom, lunch, and fire protection facilities are available; the adequacy of the lighting, heating, and ventilation; availability of office space for assessment personnel; the availability of storage areas, electrical outlets, and running water; accessibility to vocational education programs; noise level; the availability of telephone service; and whether the site can be securely locked. Generally, no less than 60 square feet of floor space per student should be available, and ideally 100 square feet should be allocated per person (Thomas & Coleman, 1988). A checklist of factors to be considered when selecting a vocational assessment site is provided in Table 6-3.

Develop a Vocational Assessment Procedures Manual

Developing a vocational assessment procedures manual assists in working out all the nitty-gritty details and nuts-and-bolts issues that need to be addressed when implementing a vocational assessment program. That is, it requires an elaboration on such mundane issues as who will fill out

Table 6-3.
Checklist of Factors Influencing Site Selection

Directions: Please review criteria listed. Add any additional criteria not listed which you consider to be important. Then, rate each criterion as to your perception of its *importance* (1–3, 1 of little importance, 2 of moderate importance, 3 of great importance). Then, for each site visited, list name and location of site, and rate each site according to the criteria listed (1—site does not meet criteria, 2—site does not meet criteria, but can be modified to meet criteria, 3—site meets criteria)

	Importance Rating	Site #1	Site #2	Site #3	Site #4
Structurally accessible to the handicapped					
Availability of adequate fire protection equipment and emergency exits					
Availability of restroom facilities					
Availability of lunch facilities					
Adequate ventilation, illumination, and heating					
Minimum of 500 square feet of space					
Availability of nearby storage area					
Room with capability of being locked and secured					
Availability of running water					
Availability of electrical outlets					
Availability of windows with blinds					
Accessibility to industrial arts and vocational education programs and equipment					
Availability of audio/video equipment					
Centrality of location to consortium staff and students to be served					
Aesthetic qualities					
Availability of telephone service					
Availability of office for center staff					

Criteria

Site #1 Name _____ Address _____

Site #2 Name _____ Address _____

Site #3 Name _____ Address _____

Site #4 Name _____ Address _____

Rated by: _____

School Division: _____

what form and when, who will administer what test and when, etc. The manual should clearly describe which professionals are involved in the program, the various roles involved personnel will assume in the program, timelines associated with assessment, the nature of the assessment (what instrumentation will be used), how results will be communicated and used, and so on.

Select/Purchase Vocational Assessment Instruments

The selection of assessment instruments will depend upon several factors including the nature of the program model developed, the financial resources available, the characteristics of the students to be assessed (e.g., age, nature of disability), and the background and training of involved personnel. It will also depend upon the psychometric characteristics of the instruments being considered for use. Factors to be considered when selecting assessment instruments were discussed in chapter 3. Readers are referred to Table 3-6 for an outline that can be used when evaluating assessment instruments.

Train Involved School and Community Agency Personnel

Because the role of several professionals involved in the assessment program may be altered or changed, these professionals must be trained prior to program implementation. Training will be more extensive and involved for some personnel than it will be for others. For example, if a certified and trained vocational evaluator is not employed, an existing professional may need to be trained as a "vocational specialist." In this case, training (which may be extensive and involve several weeks or more) may be necessary in the administration, interpretation, and use of vocationally specific assessment instruments (i.e., work samples, interest inventories, aptitude batteries, situational assessment techniques) and in the proper communication of assessment results. In contrast, an involved school psychologist, who is simply going to expand his or her use and interpretation of traditional psychoeducational measures, may only need to be trained in the vocational interpretation and use of intelligence, achievement, and personality assessment data, and in expanding his or her interviewing and observational assessment strategies so as to be able to gather more vocationally specific information. Because professionals will be working as a transdisciplinary team, team-building activities may need to be a part of training as well.

Conduct Inservice Workshops for School Staff and Community

Because the assessment program is likely to, in some small way, influence many people in the school and community, inservice workshops should be conducted for both the school staff and the community. All need to understand how and why the program was developed, what the goals and objectives of the program are, how the program will be operated, how other school staff and community members might utilize (or be affected by) the program, and how the program will be evaluated. It is important that the school staff and community have an opportunity to share feelings and reactions, and to eventually provide input relative to program modification and improvement.

Pilot-Test the Assessment Program

Prior to program implementation on a districtwide basis, the program should be implemented on a smaller scale to identify potential problems. That is, a group of students in one school could initially be targeted for assessment services. Following the implementation of the assessment model in that school, assessment personnel can formatively evaluate the program, make modifications and changes, and then implement the slightly revised program with a different group of students in a different location. Following this pilot testing, the program can again be modified and revised. It is important to provide an opportunity for all involved in the assessment process (e.g., teachers, administrators, support personnel, parents, students) to contribute feedback on the strengths and weaknesses of the program. The program should be revised and re-implemented on the basis of such feedback. Following this pilot testing–feedback–program revision–pilot-testing process, the program can be implemented on a districtwide basis.

Phase 3 - Program Evaluation

At some point in time after the program has been operational, it is important to evaluate the extent to which it has been successful at accomplishing its intended objectives. Because resources and personnel change over time, program evaluation should continue on a regular basis. The steps involved in program evaluation are: identifying aspects of the program in need of evaluation, identifying standards for program evaluation, hiring or identifying a program evaluator, and planning and implementing program improvements.

Identify Aspects of the Program in Need of Evaluation

Usually, the process of identifying aspects of the program in need of evaluation is simply a matter of restating program objectives. That is, for the most part, an evaluation of the program is designed to determine whether or not the program has accomplished its stated objectives. Hence, the aspects of the program in need of evaluation are those that are specifically related to program objectives. For example, if "appropriate placement of students in vocational training programs" was a major goal of the assessment program, the number of students placed and the adequacy or success of these placements would be aspects of the program in need of evaluation. Program evaluation should also evaluate the vocational assessment *process* as well as the outcome of the assessment.

Identify Preliminary Standards for Program Evaluation

In some cases, assessment personnel may wish to have their program conform to certain standards necessary for accreditation or certification — for example, certification as a vocational evaluation center by the Commission on Accreditation of Rehabilitation Facilities (CARF). In such cases, these standards must be incorporated into the evaluation schema. Regardless, assessment personnel will need to operationalize their program objectives and identify standards by which "success" or "failure" can be determined. For example, if an objective of the assessment program was to facilitate successful job placement of students following graduation from school, assessment personnel would need to determine what "successful" meant (this could be measured by supervisory evaluations, or length of time on the job, etc.), and what percentage of successfully placed "assessed" students would be considered a "success" (e.g., is a 60% successful placement rate adequate or inadequate?).

Hire a Program Evaluator/Conduct an Evaluation

Program evaluation is a highly specialized, difficult, and time-consuming function. Although it is possible to utilize "internal evaluators" (existing school personnel) to conduct a program evaluation, this is not always possible and has several drawbacks. Frequently, existing personnel have not had the training or experience necessary to conduct a program evaluation and, if trained and experienced, may not have the time. Because existing school personnel have much invested in the program, it is also difficult for them to be objective when evaluating the program. For these reasons, the hiring of an outside consultant who could take responsibility for all aspects of program evaluation should be considered. Such a consultant could also assist school personnel in identifying aspects of the program in need of evaluation and standards to be used in assessing program success (the prior two steps). Once the program has been evaluated, a report summarizing this evaluation and including recommendations for program modification and improvement may be produced and disseminated.

Plan and Implement Program Improvements

Following completion of the program evaluation, recommendations for program changes should be reviewed, and a plan should be developed to implement those changes believed to be necessary to accomplish program objectives. In some cases, a change in program objectives may be considered by school personnel as a result of the completed program evaluation.

Table 6-4 provides a checklist of issues to be addressed when establishing vocational assessment services.

Table 6-4.

Checklist: Establishing Vocational Assessment Services

Yes	No	
___	___	1. Is there an area within the facility designated exclusively for providing vocational evaluation services?
___	___	2. Is the physical size of the evaluation unit adequate to handle the number of students assigned to evaluation? (Average 100 sq. ft. per student.)
___	___	3. Is a private office available for the evaluator to speak confidentially to students or to consultants?
___	___	4. Is the evaluator's desk arranged so that s/he can readily observe students at the various work stations?
___	___	5. Is the area assigned for use in evaluation free from architectural barriers?
___	___	6. Is there sufficient lighting in the vocational evaluation area?
___	___	7. Is a soundproof or quiet testing room available if psychological tests are administered?
___	___	8. Are the students' case records and data sheets used by the evaluator kept in a secure place when not in use?
___	___	9. Are psychological tests, manuals, scoring keys, and related materials stored under lock and key?
___	___	10. Are the objectives and goals of the vocational evaluation program stated in writing?
___	___	11. Does the facility have a flow chart or plan of services that clearly specifies service components, and demonstrates how, and in what sequence, vocational evaluation services are performed?
___	___	12. Have criteria for accepting students into the evaluation program been established based on the facility limitations and assets?
___	___	13. Is there evidence that only those clients who are within the capabilities of the program are accepted into vocational evaluation?
___	___	14. Is access to student records limited to professional staff providing direct services to the student?
___	___	15. Is there evidence from the case file that the coordination and management of each student's program is conducted in a systematic and comprehensive manner?
___	___	16. Is there evidence that the overall vocational evaluation program is reviewed periodically so as to incorporate new strategies?
___	___	17. Are adequate funds available to the evaluation unit for purchasing appropriate psychological tests or for the development and construction of work or job samples?

(continued)

Table 6-4.
(Continued)

Yes	No	
____	____	18. If the facility indicates the availability of evaluation services for the following listed handicapping conditions, is there any evidence of special psychological testing or multiple strategies for evaluating:
____	____	A. Disadvantaged
____	____	B. Visually Impaired
____	____	C. Hearing Impaired
____	____	D. Mentally Retarded
____	____	E. Learning Disabled
____	____	F. Emotionally Disturbed
____	____	G. Orthopedically Handicapped
____	____	19. Is there at least one full-time vocational evaluator in the program?
____	____	20. Does the evaluator have responsibilities other than vocational evaluation, e.g., placement, administration, workshop supervision, etc.?
____	____	21. Is there at least one full-time vocational evaluator for every six students in evaluation? (This is not a standard figure, but is relative to the student population and the technique of evaluation emphasized.)
____	____	22. Are evaluator aides used to perform the more routine activities in vocational evaluation?
____	____	23. If there is more than one evaluator (full- or part-time), is there a supervisor in charge of the vocational evaluation program?
____	____	24. Does the evaluation staff meet the standards as recommended by the state agency?
____	____	25. Has the evaluator received formal, academic training in evaluation?
____	____	26. Is there an organized, inservice training program for staff?
____	____	27. Have job descriptions for all staff in vocational evaluation been prepared?
____	____	28. Is there a structured formal system within the facility for rating the effectiveness and performance of the vocational evaluation staff?
____	____	29. Is adequate time provided for vocational evaluators to review current literature and research in vocational evaluation?
____	____	30. Are vocational evaluation staff free and encouraged to participate in local or regional conferences related to vocational evaluation?
____	____	31. Do the evaluators belong to the Vocational Evaluation and Work Adjustment Association?
____	____	32. Are the staff of the vocational evaluation unit familiar with the code of ethics regarding testing and confidentiality of information?

ROLES FOR SCHOOL PERSONNEL

At the outset, it is important to note that the various roles assumed by school and community-based professionals in transdisciplinary vocational assessment programs will vary considerably from one locality to the next. Factors such as expertise and skills, interest, or time will influence whether or not a given professional is involved in the assessment process and, if involved, which role that professional will assume in the process. The following discussion is not meant to be exhaustive, and the roles outlined are not "written in stone." Instead, they are meant to be "food for thought" for both those professionals in charge of developing and implementing transdisciplinary vocational assessment programs in the schools, and for those professionals who may find themselves involved in these programs. The following sections describe the kind of role various school-based professionals, including administrators, teachers, counselors, vocational evaluators/specialists, and school psychologists, may assume. This section will also discuss the important roles parents and students may assume in the vocational assessment process.

Roles for the School Principal

As the head of operations within a school, the school principal has tremendous influence over all programs that operate in the school building. Therefore, the principal can influence the roles other professionals such as counselors, psychologists, and teachers assume in the assessment and planning process. Without the school principal's support, it is unlikely that other school personnel will be given the time or resources necessary to function effectively within an assessment program. Some roles the school principal may assume in the vocational assessment and planning process include:

— providing adequate facilities, clerical assistance, and funding for materials and other resources necessary for effective assessment program implementation;

— providing leadership and, most important, support for the establishment and implementation of the assessment program;

— assisting in developing an assessment program model and in defining the roles and responsibilities of various professionals functioning within the program;

— assisting in program implementation by overseeing and evaluating the roles performed by vocational assessment team members within their buildings; and

— promoting and helping to plan inservice workshops for staff.

Roles for Special Education and Vocational Education Supervisors

The roles of the special education and vocational education supervisors are similar to, and in many ways parallel, the role assumed by the principal. Special education and vocational education supervisors must work closely with the principal to encourage teacher support for and involvement in the vocational assessment and planning process, and must attend to the many administrative chores that such support and involvement entails. The following are among the many roles these supervisors might assume:

— ensuring that adequate facilities and funding for materials and other resources necessary for effective assessment program implementation are available to teachers;

— providing leadership and, most important, support for teachers involved in the establishment and implementation of the assessment program;

— assisting in developing an assessment program model and in defining the roles and responsibilities of special education and vocational education teachers functioning within the program;

— assisting in program implementation by overseeing and evaluating the roles performed by special education and vocational education teachers in the assessment process; and

— promoting and helping to plan inservice workshops for teachers.

Roles for the Classroom Teacher

Of all the professionals involved in the vocational assessment and planning process, the classroom teacher probably spends the most time in direct, face-to-face contact with the student. As such, the teacher is a valuable source of information on any student being assessed. Certainly, the type of information a particular teacher is able to supply and the role he or she will assume in the vocational assessment and planning process will vary somewhat depending upon his or her training (regular education, special education, or vocational education). A sampling of the kind of information each of these teachers can supply, and the role they might assume in the assessment and planning process follows:

Regular Classroom Teacher

— assisting in vocational assessment data gathering by conducting student and/or parent interviews, administering standardized or teacher-made tests to assess academic skills, providing information about a student's social/interpersonal skills and work habits via completion of behavior rating scales and checklists, and supplying student work samples;

— developing classroom activities that promote self-awareness, decision making, and awareness of the requirements and demands of various occupations via the use of role playing, dramatization and skits, autobiographies, self-appraisal rating activities, field trips, guest speakers, and work simulations; and

— integrating instruction of vocationally relevant academic skills into regular classroom instruction.

Vocational Education Teacher

—assisting in vocational assessment data gathering by administering teacher-made work samples or tests to assess vocationally specific skills, providing information about a student's social/interpersonal skills and work habits via completion of behavior rating scales and checklists, and by providing information about a student's overall vocational readiness;

—developing classroom activities that promote self-awareness, decision making, and awareness of the requirements and demands of occupations pertinent to the vocational training the student is receiving via field trips, guest speakers, and work simulations;

—integrating instruction of academic skills into vocational training;

—providing the vocational assessment team with information about the specific academic and vocational skills and competencies needed for successful functioning in specific occupations;

—assisting in the development and use of locally developed work samples and of situational assessment techniques to assess a student's aptitude and interest in a particular vocational area and to facilitate a student's vocational exploration; and

—acting as a liaison between the school and local employers in their specific training area.

Special Education Teacher

—assisting in vocational assessment data gathering by conducting student and/or parent interviews, administering standardized or teacher-made tests to assess academic skills, providing information about a student's social/interpersonal skills and work habits via completion of behavior rating scales and checklists, and supplying student work samples;

—developing classroom activities that promote self-awareness, decision making, and awareness of the requirements and demands of various occupations via the use of role playing, dramatization and skits, autobiographies, self-appraisal rating activities, field trips, guest speakers, and work simulations;

—integrating instruction of vocationally relevant academic skills into special education instruction; and

—providing information about a student's special learning needs, and instructional techniques effective in accommodating these special needs.

Roles for Vocational Evaluators/Specialists

Increasingly, schools are employing well-trained vocational evaluators to assist in developing and implementing school-based assessment programs. Vocational evaluators are trained in a variety of assessment techniques and strategies, including job analysis, use of work sampling and situational assessment techniques, interviewing, and the use of paper-and-pencil tests. They also receive training in psychometrics, the use of occupational information, report writing, and vocational planning. Not all schools employ such well-trained vocational evaluators, however. In some instances existing school personnel (such as teachers or counselors) are trained to function as vocational specialists within school-based programs. In other instances, individuals with backgrounds in vocational rehabilitation or rehabilitation counseling are employed within the schools to function as vocational evaluators/specialists. Although it is preferable to employ a trained vocational evaluator to perform vocationally specific assessment functions in the schools, it is clear that professionals currently performing these duties in the schools have a wide variety of backgrounds. In addition to performing evaluation/assessment functions, vocational specialists are often involved in job placement activities, and on-the-job training and supervision. The following are some of the roles the vocational evaluator/specialist may perform:

— assisting in the gathering of assessment data by administering vocationally specific assessment instruments designed to assess vocational interests, vocational aptitudes, and other work-related skills, by interviewing students, and by observing students in work-related situations;

— assisting in the development and use of situationally specific assessment strategies and work samples;

— participating in the development of vocational objectives via participation on Individual Education Planning teams and Individual Transition Planning teams;

— consulting with regular, special, and vocational education teachers regarding the vocational needs of students; and

— assisting in the transitioning of students from the school to the community and workplace, and in the vocational placement and on-the-job training of students.

School Psychologist Involvement in Vocational Activities: An Historical Perspective

In recent years, much has been written relative to the school psychologist's involvement in the vocational programming of students with disabilities, particularly in regard to the provision of vocational assessment services

(Capps, Levinson, & Hohenshil, 1985; Heinlein, Nelson, & Hohenshil, 1985; Hohenshil, 1982; Hohenshil, Anderson, & Salwan, 1982; Hohenshil, Levinson, & Buckland-Heer, 1985; Levinson, 1984; Levinson & Capps, 1985; Levinson & Shepard, 1982; Shepard & Levinson, 1985). That two major publications of the National Association of School Psychologists (*Best Practices in School Psychology*, Thomas & Grimes, 1985, and *Children's Needs: Psychological Perspectives*, Thomas & Grimes, 1987) each include a chapter relevant to the topic of vocational programming (Hohenshil, Levinson, & Buckland-Heer, 1985; Levinson, 1987a; respectively), attests to the significance of the topic for the profession of school psychology.

Historically, psychologists have always been interested in the relationship between psychology and work, and several eminent psychologists have written extensively about this relationship. Freud (1930/1962) considered love and work to be the two major areas of human endeavor, and proposed that an individual's self-worth was intimately related to work. Erikson (1968) proposed that work contributed to one's identity and believed that it was a particularly important contributor to development during adolescence. Bruner (1974) believed that neuroses among young people were more likely to involve choices about work and preparation for work than they were to involve sex. Jung (1960) contended that an individual in his or her natural state would not work, and that work was enculturated through civilization.

Despite psychology's longstanding interest in work, the school psychologist's involvement in vocational aspects of practice is a rather recent phenomenon. As Hohenshil (1984), who is widely considered to be the father of vocational school psychology, has noted, a 1973 computer search of the literature failed to identify a single article specifically dealing with roles for school psychologists in vocational programming. Judging from the paucity of the literature, Hummel and Hohenshil (1974) concluded that the career development of public school students was an area of human endeavor that had escaped the attention of school psychologists. However, since that time, there has been an upsurge of interest in vocational school psychology.

Largely due to the work of Hohenshil and his colleagues, the mid-1970s witnessed an increase in the number of programs presented at state and national conferences on the topic and an increase in the number of published articles and journals devoted to vocational school psychology. In 1977, the President of the National Association of School Psychologists appointed a National Commission to study the school psychologist's role in Career and Vocational Education. The ensuing report recommended that school psychology should expand its services in vocational and career education programs, and that a specialty area in vocational school psychology should be established to expand psychological services to adolescents and adults, and to provide training to school psychologists who wished to upgrade their skills in the vocational aspects of practice. Following through on this recommendation, the National Association of School Psychologists Delegate Assembly finally recognized vocational school psychology as the first (and currently only) *official* specialty area in the profession and established the National Committee on Vocational School Psychology. This committee now functions as a NASP special interest group that has been active in sponsoring cost-free workshops on vocational assessment and programming at school psychology conferences and in providing school psychologists with reference materials relative to vocational practice in the schools.

The National Association of School Psychologists (NASP) has provided considerable support for vocational school psychology since its inception and, in fact, incorporates both vocational assessment and intervention practices into its *Professional Conduct Manual* (National Association of School Psychologists, 1985). In its description of Standards for the Provision of School Psychological Services, NASP (1985) states:

> Psychological and psychoeducational assessments include consideration, as appropriate in the areas of . . . vocational development, aptitude, and interests. (p. 31)

In reference to intervention strategies, the standards state:

> School psychologists facilitate delivery of services by assisting those who play major roles in the educational system (i.e., parents, school personnel, community service agencies). Such interventions consist of, but are not limited to: . . . vocational development. . . . (p. 31)

If school psychologists are going to practice their profession in a manner consistent with their professional standards, they *should* be involved in vocational assessment and programming in the schools. Similarly, the Vocational Evaluation and Work Adjustment Association's (VEWAA, 1975) definition of vocational assessment actually incoporates a psychological component. Thus, if this definition is used as a conceptual basis by those developing school-based vocational assessment programs, involvement of the school psychologist (the only school-based professional capable of providing a "psychological component") becomes a necessity.

It is a well-accepted notion that intelligence test data, academic achievement test data, personality assessment data, and adaptive behavior data (which are typically gathered as part of a comprehensive school psychological evaluation) all have relevance for vocational programming. For example, intelligence test data can be used to assist in determining the degree to which an individual may attain success in a given vocational training program. Recent research by Heinlein (1987), which indicated that the factor structure of the Wechsler Scale is similar to the factor structure of some aptitude tests, supports such use of intelligence test data. Likewise, research has indicated that some personality assessment data can be used to predict both job satisfaction and job performance (Holland, 1985a).

Despite such a rationale for the school psychologist's involvement in the vocational assessment process, one might still question whether school psychologists, and those who influence the role of school psychologists (i.e., principals, supervisors), are supportive of school psychologists being involved in vocational practices. Previous research has provided some tentative answers to this question. In a survey of school superintendents, school psychologists, and school psychology trainers in Virginia, Murray (1975) found that administering, scoring, and interpreting vocational interest surveys for individual child study and making recommendations for placement of children in vocational classes were both activities in which school psychologists should be involved. Pfeffer (1978), in a survey of individuals in leadership positions with NASP, found that a majority of the respondents viewed career counseling and development as an area in which school psychologists should participate.

Despite this early support for the school psychologist's involvement in vocational activities, more recent data indicate that school psychologists are interested in, but not heavily involved in, vocational aspects of practice. Shepard and Hohenshil (1983) surveyed 218 practicing school psychologists and found that 75% of the respondents applied 3% or less of their time to vocational responsibilities, and that 91% felt unprepared to provide effective vocational services. However, these same respondents attached great importance to these activities, despite their noninvolvement (significant differences were found between ratings of importance and involvement). Levinson (1988), in a study of Pennsylvania school psychologists, found that to some degree 34% had performed vocational assessment, 39% had performed vocational counseling, 41% had consulted with vocational instructors, and that 13% had performed vocational program or curriculum development activities in their practice.

What are the reasons for the school psychologist's limited involvement in vocational activities? Studies conducted by Shepard and Hohenshil (1983), and by Levinson (1988, 1990b), provide some tentative answers to this question. Clearly, most school psychologists have had limited training in vocational assessment and programming (despite NASP-sponsored activities) and hence are reluctant to involve themselves in this aspect of practice, which is rarely included in school psychologist training programs. School psychologists likely to have had some training in this area are those who have previously been trained as guidance counselors, or who have purposefully sought out training via professional development seminars or workshops (Levinson, 1988). Second, role restrictions and time constraints typically associated with school psychologist roles often discourage or prevent school psychologists from becoming involved in activities outside of those that would be considered part of "traditional" service delivery (i.e, testing of students for possible placement in a special education program). Functioning in nontraditional ways sometimes elicits resistance. Third, despite the assumption that traditional school psychological assessment data have a great deal of vocational relevance, there is only limited empirical evidence at the present time to support vocational interpretation of this data. Consequently, translating traditional school psychological asssessment data into specific vocational recommendations is not easily done. Last, many existing vocational assessment instruments are time consuming to administer and lack acceptable psychometric characteristics. For these reasons, school psychologists shy away from learning and using these instruments.

It is clear that, given the traditional school psychologist practitioner role, if school psychologists are to become involved in vocational endeavors it will most likely be via the assessment role. School psychologists must be provided with a means by which to gather vocationally relevant data in a time- and cost-efficient fashion using methodology with a strong empirical and theoretical basis and acceptable psychometric characteristics. The methodology used must be easily integrated into traditional school psychological theory and practice so as not to elicit resistance from other personnel and must yield data that are easily and justifiably translated into vocational recommendations. For these reasons, this author has advocated use of the Self-Directed Search (SDS; Holland, 1985b) by school psychologists at the secondary school level (Levinson, 1990b).

When used as part of a comprehensive psychoeducational evaluation at a secondary school level, the SDS can provide vocationally specific information to assist school psychologists in vocational planning and recommendation generation. SDS data can be integrated with other psychoeducational assessment data in generating these recommendations. For example, intelligence and academic achievement test data can assist in determining the likelihood that a student would be successful in pursuing a career that requires postsecondary education. These data might also be helpful in determining the level within a given occupational area to which a student might successfully aspire. Using the SDS, school psychologists can identify occupational areas consistent with a particular student's personality and, by comparing the results to (a) vocational training programs available, (b) local jobs available, and (c) college majors, generate vocationally specific recommendations. Data from the SDS and other instruments can be used to confirm data generated from both sources, thereby increasing the reliability and validity of the overall evaluation. For example, it would be expected that realistic types would demonstrate superior perceptual organization skills when compared to verbal comprehension skills. The opposite would be expected of social types. Based upon the results of the SDS, and use of references such as the *Dictionary of Holland Occupational*

Codes (Gottfredson et.al, 1982), the *Dictionary of Occupational Titles* (Department of Labor, 1977), and the *Occupational Outlook Handbook*, psychologists can recommend activities designed to facilitate occupational awareness and exploration.

The reader should note that the description above is simply one example of how school psychologists might supplement their traditional psychoeducational assessment batteries via use of a vocationally specific instrument, and how this vocationally specific data might be integrated with other psychoeducational data to generate vocational interpretations and recommendations. Although this author has advocated use of the Self-Directed Search for the reasons cited previously, other instruments could be chosen by school psychologists to accomplish the same purpose. For a case study example illustrating the inclusion of a vocational component in a school psychological evaluation (using vocationally specific instruments other than the Self-Directed Search), readers are referred to Levinson (1987b).

It is likely that school psychologists will become increasingly involved in vocational programming as a result of their extensive involvement in the assessment and programming of students with disabilities. Although the specific role that school psychologists will play in the process is as yet undefined, it is clear that the skills possessed by school psychologists are critical to the development and implementation of successful vocational plans. The remainder of this section will discuss the various roles school psychologists may assume in vocational programming.

Roles for School Psychologists

Currently, a variety of professionals may assume major responsibility for the development and implementation of vocational programs. Although no agreement currently exists as to who should assume this major responsibility, a number of "vocational specialist" or "transition specialist" training programs for professionals with such titles as job coach, individual living specialist, supported employment specialist, rehabilitation counselor, and special education teacher do exist. The competencies acquired in these programs clearly overlap with the knowledge and skills possessed by school psychologists. In their study of the competencies taught in 13 university transition specialist training programs across the country, Baker, Geiger, and deFur (1988) found that general knowledge of learning theory (particularly behavioral theory) and assessment were areas in which an extensive amount of training was concentrated. Studies by both Baker, Geiger, and deFur (1988) and by Marinelli, Tunic, and LeConte (1988) agree that adolescent psychology is a frequently omitted but important area in the training of such specialists. Clearly, the school psychologist's expertise in assessment, learning and behavior theory, and adolescent psychology may be most critical to his or her involvement in vocational programming.

From an assessment perspective, school psychologists have much to contribute to vocational planning. As mentioned previously, particularly important in vocational planning will be an evaluation of intelligence, achievement, personality, interpersonal and social skills, independent living skills, and vocational skills (e.g., interests, aptitudes, work habits). Although the first four areas listed are routinely included in comprehensive school psychological evaluations, the remaining areas are not. School psychologists working at the secondary school level may need to alter their assessment strategies somewhat in order to emphasize these additional areas. For example, school psychologists might choose to incorporate measures of vocational interests, aptitudes and social skills (via interviews, observations, and paper-and-pencil tests) into their assessments. Of course, this will depend on the roles of other professionals on the transdisciplinary team. A number of time- and cost-efficient procedures for gathering this information are available to school psychologists and are discussed elsewhere in this book. Although this author has advocated use of the SDS for the reasons cited previously, many vocationally specific instruments exist that can easily be incorporated into a school psychologist's psychoeducational battery. School psychologists can also incorporate an evaluation of functional living skills into their assessments. An instrument such as the Social and Prevocational Information Battery (Halpern, Raffeld, Irvin, & Link, 1975), for example, would provide school psychologists with functional skills assessment data that could be utilized in vocational programming.

School psychologists' knowledge of learning and behavior theory and of adolescent psychology may allow them to serve as effective consultants to teachers (regular, special education, vocational education), rehabilitation counselors, job coaches, and employers relative to the conditions under which optimum learning and performance might be facilitated. Because a large amount of vocational training may occur outside of the school in job, community, or residential settings, school psychologists will have to prepare themselves to provide consultative services in settings other than the office or classroom. As a consultant, the school psychologist may also function as a liaison among parents, the transdisciplinary team, community service agencies, and employers or, in some cases, actually initiate the development of vocational programming. School psychologists who plan to function as behavioral consultants in order to assist in implementation of training programs are referred to Kratochwill's (1990) chapter on behavioral consultation.

Other roles for school psychologists in the vocational assessment and planning process encompass the areas of direct intervention, inservice, and research. From a direct intervention perspective, the school psychologist may assist by initiating the development of social skills training programs, designed to facilitate acquisition of those social skills necessary for successful vocational placement. Such programs might be most effective when implemented within residential, community, or employment settings. Readers are referred to Gresham (1990), who discusses social skills training. Similarly, school psychologists will probably find themselves working directly with parents of students with disabilities as a function of their role on the transdisciplinary team and are referred to Murray's (1990) chapter on counseling parents of students with disabilities. School psychologists might conduct inservice workshops on the use of assessment data in vocational programming with those involved in vocational assessment and programming, and on basic issues in adolescent psychology or learning for those professionals involved in direct training of skills necessary for successful vocational functioning. Finally, a need exists to evaluate the effectiveness of the various programs designed to facilitate acquisition of the skills necessary for successful vocational functioning. The degree to which local school and community-based services are successful in facilitating the transition of students from school to work and community must be evaluated as well. Although school psychologists are adequately trained to conduct such research, they are infrequently involved in research in the schools (Levinson, 1990). School psychologists interested in evaluating the effectiveness of vocational programming are referred to chapters by Keith (1990) on conducting school-based research and by McConnell (1990) on evaluating educational programs.

Last, the development and implementation of vocational assessment programs involve the selection, use, and interpretation of vocational tests. In the past, those professionals entrusted with these responsibilities have historically had limited training in psychology and have often been ill prepared to deal with the psychometric and measurement issues that development and implementation of an assessment program require. In contrast, school psychologists are well trained in assessment methodology and knowledgeable about psychometric and measurement issues. Consequently, involvement of school psychologists in the establishment and implementation of vocational assessment programs can reduce the risk of inapropriate selection, use, and interpretation of assessment instruments and can increase the validity of the overall assessment process.

In summary, research has indicated that school psychologists are interested but relatively uninvolved in vocational assessment activities at the present time. Factors such as lack of training in the administration and use of vocational instruments, the time and cost associated with vocational involvement, lack of familiarity with vocational development theory, and the psychometric inadequacy of many vocational assessment instruments have hindered school psychologist involvement in vocational activities. This author has argued that the SDS is an instrument that both overcomes many of these obstacles and can be used by school psychologists to generate vocationally specific recommendations in a theoretically sound and time-efficient manner. Although the specific instruments selected to comprise a vocational component of a psychoeducational assessment must be based upon the individual characteristics of the referred student, the SDS has wide applicability. Nevertheless, the school psychologist can contribute to the transdisciplinary vocational assessment and planning process in a number of ways, including:

— considering the vocational implications of the assessment data typically gathered as part of psychoeducational assessments (i.e., interpreting intelligence test data, academic achievement test data, personality assessment data, and adaptive behavior data from a vocational perspective);

— gathering vocationally specific assessment information when conducting their psychoeducational assessments, by expanding their interviewing and observational procedures to include consideration of vocational development, and by incorporating the use of vocationally specific assessment instruments (like interest inventories or aptitude measures) in these assessments;

— using their knowledge of assessment methodology, measurement theory, and psychometrics to assist other transdisciplinary vocational assessment team members in selecting appropriate assessment instruments, and in properly interpreting the results of these instruments;

— using their consultation skills and knowledge of disabilities, learning/behavior theory, and adolescent psychology to assist other professionals in developing and implementing appropriate vocational training objectives; and

— using their knowledge of research and statistics to assist other team members in developing and implementing procedures to assess the overall effectiveness of the transdisciplinary assessment program being implemented.

Roles for Counselors

Although school psychologists and school counselors have somewhat overlapping roles (particularly in regard to the provision of counseling services to students), there are significant differences between these two professionals, both in background and training and in common day-to-day activities. Whereas school psychologists work most frequently (though not exclusively) with students who have disabilities, school counselors work most frequently with students who do not have disabilities. In contrast to school psychologists, who get little formal training in vocational development theory and vocational assessment, school counselors are generally extremely knowledgeable in these areas. As such, school counselors are often involved in areas such as vocational/career assessment, career counseling, or establishing career information centers in schools.

School counselors can assume numerous roles in the vocational assessment and planning process. Drawing upon the work of Smith (1983) and others, the following are some of the roles school counselors can assume:

— assisting in vocational assessment data gathering, by reviewing student cumulative folders, conducting individual and group career assessments, and by gathering information from home and school by interviewing students and teachers;

— providing parents, students, teachers, and other team members with information about postsecondary educational opportunities, vocational training opportunities, and jobs available in the local area, and with the requirements for entry, application procedures, and demands associated with each of these;

— providing teachers with vocational/career assessment and guidance information that can be incorporated into regular educational curricula;

— identifying and updating local, state, and national occupational information (i.e., labor market trends, availability of jobs) so as to facilitate informed vocational decision making;

— functioning as a liaison between the school and local employers;

— assisting in the development and operation of a job placement service;

— assisting in informing the public of the vocational assessment and planning services available in the school district; and

— assisting in conducting follow-up studies of graduates to assess the overall effectiveness of the vocational assessment, planning, and placement process.

Roles for Community Agency Personnel

As previously stated, representatives from community agencies should be involved in the planning and implementation of transdisciplinary school-based vocational assessment programs, via participation on task forces and advisory committees. Personnel from Vocational Rehabilitation can assist in identifying (and in some cases providing) funding for assessment and job placement services, providing direct vocational evaluation services, identifying and facilitating placement of students in community jobs, providing follow-along and follow-up services for students placed in such jobs, and providing inservice workshops designed to educate parents, school personnel, and others in the community relative to the services provided by their agency. Representatives from Mental Health/Mental Retardation Services can provide information to school personnel, parents, and students about eligibility for medical and social security benefits and the application process necessary to attain those benefits, supportive counseling and advocacy services, and inservice workshops and community education programs designed to increase public awareness of their services. In some states, mental health agencies provide job coach, club house, and other work-related activities for mentally retarded individuals. Local employers can provide input on local business needs and job market trends, identify and provide access to job training sites (which can be used for assessment or job training), provide input on curriculum needs, and function as guest speakers in classes or arrange visitation to work sites (which can be used to facilitate vocational exploration). State and local employment agencies are often good sources of information on labor market trends and local needs.

Roles for Students

Who knows a student's interests better than the student? Clearly, students have much to contribute to the vocational assessment and planning process. Although student involvement will depend upon several factors including the student's intelligence and maturity, students should participate, to the maximum extent possible, in any decisions regarding their educational or vocational future. The following are some of the ways students can participate in the vocational assessment and planning process:

—assisting in assessment by providing assessment personnel with information about their interests, goals, and perceived abilities and strengths via interviews and other self-reporting procedures;

—assisting in program evaluation by providing assessment personnel with feedback relative to the adequacy of their assessment, vocational training, and work-related experiences;

—serving on advisory councils and assisting with program modifications and improvement.

Working with Parents

Any effort at improving the school to work transition of students that fails to incorporate parental involvement as a major component of the process will have limited success. . . . A mutual trust relationship between parents and professionals needs to be nourished. Even though there is a trend toward recognizing parents as partners in their child's education-vocational process, the relationship may be fragile and too easily characterized by residual feelings from the past. (Pennsylvania Transition from School to Work, 1986; p. 83)

Parents of adolescents often face difficulty when the time comes for their children to make personal and vocational decisions regarding their future. Childrens' decisions regarding living arrangements, higher education, vocational pursuits, and marriage often cause parents to wonder if they have done their best in raising children who will become responsible, satisfied, and productive adults (Levinson & McKee, 1991).

For a variety of reasons, the parents of individuals with disabilities face even greater challenges when this time is reached. Many parents continue to feel guilt and personal responsibility in regard to their child's disability and this may result in them having difficulty in "letting go" when the time comes. The parents of individuals with disabilities are also faced with the knowledge that, in the past, the vocational and life-style options for individuals with disabilities have been quite limited (Levinson & McKee, 1991). As a consequence, they experience anxiety as they worry about what the future will be like for their children.

Research involving the impact of parental participation has indeed shown that the role of the family in the vocational planning process is critical. Yet, as Ott (1991) has suggested, family involvement in the school in any form has only rarely matched the enthusiastic rhetoric advocating it, or the considerable body of research supporting it.

In studying individuals with moderate and severe disabilities, Schalock and Lilley (1986) found that students whose families were moderately to highly involved in their programming were more successful on employment outcome measures than were students whose families had low involvement. Further findings indicated that those who had high family involvement received higher wages and worked more hours/weeks than did those with low family involvement. Shalock and Lilley (1986) reported that family involvement is repeatedly shown to be related to successful living as well as employment. Hasazi, Gordon, and Roe (1985), in studying educable and trainable mentally retarded individuals, found that 61% found employment through a self–family–friend network. In a similar study, Hasazi et al. (1985) found that among all postschool individuals with disabilities, 84% had found work through the self–family–friend network. The value of active family involvement in achieving successful vocational functioning appears to be well documented.

Unfortunately, there is some indication that as the child grows older, the family becomes less involved in the educational planning process. Johnson, Bruininks, and Thurlow (1987) cite a 1982 study by Lynch and Stein which found that parents of older students participated in Individual Education Planning conferences significantly less often than did parents of younger children. Benz and Halpern (1987) reported on the results of question-naires sent to administrators, teachers, and parents in the state of Oregon and found that 36% of the responding teachers indicated that they were dissatisfied or very dissatisfied with parental support received and that 44% indicated that they would like more communication and parent in-volvement in classroom activities. Over half of the parents indicated contact with their child's teacher once per term or less. Relatedly, one third of the parents indicated that they had no idea what their children would be doing in terms of employment either 1 year or 10 years following high school, and one quarter of them had no idea where their children would be living 1 or 10 years postschool. In a survey of special education administrators in New Hampshire, only 11% of the reporting districts indicated that parents were routinely invited to attend team meetings, whereas 52% reported that parents were either seldom or never invited to attend these team meetings (Ott, 1991). Even when parents are invited and do participate in educational and vocational planning in the schools, they usually occupy a very passive, rather than active, role (Ott, 1991).

Barriers to Active Parent Involvement

In a survey of the literature, Ott (1991) identified three common bar-riers to effective school–family collaborative planning: adherence to an "expert" model of consultation/problem solving, competitive relationships between parents and school personnel, and logistical and cost considerations.

Adherence to an "expert" model. Educators sometimes communicate the message that decision making is solely their responsibility and that parents have little say in decisions that are to be made. Clearly, when someone is made to feel less knowledgeable, less powerful, and less important than another, he or she will frequently assume a more passive and withdrawn position. If parents are made to feel unneccesary or unimportant, they will frequently act accordingly. Unfortunately, school personnel are often more comfortable with passive, uninvolved parents than they are with in-volved, assertive parents. Hence, school personnel sometimes behave in subtle (and not so subtle) ways to encourage such passivity.

Competition between home and school. The expert stance taken by educators frequently elicits a defensive posture on the part of parents. Parents sometimes feel responsible for the school difficulties their children may be experiencing and react with defensiveness. Sometimes parents feel that expert educators are usurping their role as parents by taking responsibility for making important decisions. These feelings sometimes elicit resent-ment, hostility, and anger. When educators assume an expert stance, and parents feel as if they have less freedom of choice, a natural competition between parent and professional may develop.

Logistical and cost considerations. It is inconvenient and costly, from both a time and money perspective, to involve parents in educational and vocational planning. Parents work and must frequently rearrange their schedules and sometimes sacrifice pay to meet with school personnel. Sometimes their schedules prohibit meeting with school personnel during the work day. School personnel often find it difficult and frustrating to contact and schedule parents for daytime meetings and are frequently unwilling or unable to arrange such meetings outside of the school day. All of these factors lead both parents and school personnel to be comfortable with parental noninvolvement. Simply put, there are often too many costs associated with parental involvement for both parents and professionals alike.

Relatedly, Murray (1990), drawing on the work of Brynelsen (1984), has identified obstacles faced by both parents and professionals when attempting to create a good, collaborative working relationship. The following are among the many obstacles faced by parents when working with professionals (Murray, 1990): lack of confidence in themselves as parents, negative past experiences with professionals, problems in balancing the demands of their children with their other family needs, under- or overestimating their child's potential, under- or overestimating the contributions professionals can make, and coping with the pressures and demands placed upon them by professionals. The following are among the obstacles faced by professionals when working with parents: no preparation in working with parents, anxiety or resistance to the prospect of parent involvement, a tendency to adopt an authoritarian approach with parents, uncertainty about admitting limitations in knowledge or skills, expecting too much or too little from parents, not taking parent concerns seriously, withholding or refusing access to information, using professional jargon, and emphasizing weaknesses rather than strengths in the child.

Overcoming Barriers to Parental Involvement

As Ott (1991) suggests, professionals should be *trained* to work with parents. As such, training conducted with staff during the initial planning stages of vocational assessment programs should include a training module on working with parents. Professionals should be trained to:

1. provide parents with recognition for their strengths and their successes, and reinforce them for their involvement in the vocational planning process;

2. encourage parents to believe that they are experts too, and to believe that they have knowledge about their children that school personnel

do not have. Professionals should explain to parents that this knowledge is critical to effective vocational planning;

3. show respect, support, encouragement, and understanding to parents, and refrain from patronizing them. Professionals should be trained to listen carefully to parent opinions and to demonstrate that these opinions and ideas are important by incorporating them into vocational plans;

4. present information to parents in language they can easily understand.

Involving Parents in Vocational Assessment and Programming

The involvement of the parent in the vocational assessment and planning process must begin early in the child's life. It is highly unlikely that a parent who has not been involved in the child's educational planning prior to adolescence will suddenly become involved when the time for vocational planning arrives. It is important that vocational awareness on the part of the parent begin early in the child's academic career and be ongoing throughout the child's life (Levinson & McKee, 1991). Ideally, students should be involved in career development activities from early elementary school onward, and parents should be aware of and involved in these activities. Parents of students with disabilities should be involved in Individual Education Plan development from the time their child is initially placed in a special education program and, as part of such involvement, should assist in developing specific vocational objectives for their children. Just as the role of various professionals will vary from one locality to the next, the specific role parents play in the transdisciplinary vocational assessment and planning process will also vary. There are many ways to involve parents in the process, not all of which are feasible in every locality. The following is a listing of some of the ways parents may be involved in the assessment process:

—contributing to the transdisciplinary vocational assessment process by providing the transdisciplinary vocational assessment team with information about their child's interests, skills, work habits, and personality characteristics, via interviews and the completion of rating scales and checklists;

—assisting in developing educational and vocational objectives for their child by participating in the development of their child's Individual Education Plan;

—assisting in developing objectives in the areas of employment, residential living, and community functioning, by participating as a member of their child's Individual Transition Planning Team;

—serving on local, state, and federal Advisory Councils; and

—joining Advocacy Groups for individuals with disabilities and participating in various special education, adult services, and family organizations.

In particular, parental participation in advisory, advocacy, and support groups has numerous advantages for both parents and school personnel. These groups allow parents to provide support to one another and, most important, provide a forum for open communication and discussion between parents and school personnel. By jointly serving on such groups, school personnel can come to a better understanding of the stresses and difficulties parents may be facing and, as a result, develop increased sensitivity to parents. Conversely, parents can gain a better understanding of the bureaucratic, political, and organizational factors that influence educational and vocational services in the school and community. Perhaps most important, these groups place parents and professionals on the same "team," working toward the same goals. To that end, they provide a "training ground" for parents and professionals to learn how best to work together.

Roles for Professionals When Working with Parents

Fine (1991) has developed a collaborative model of parent involvement that incorporates four major objectives: (1) to include parents in all decision making regarding their children, (2) to educate parents for participation in the decision-making process regarding their children, (3) to assist parents therapeutically as needed so that they will be better able to cope with the specific issues that may need to be addressed regarding their children, and (4) to empower and enable parents to work actively on behalf of their children. Based upon this collaborative decision-making model, there are several roles that a professional may assume when working with parents in the vocational assessment and planning process. These roles can be conceptualized as advocate, expert, and therapist (Fine, 1991; Levinson & McKee, 1991).

Advocate

The vocational assessment and planning process is complex and often confusing to parents. Many different professionals and agencies are often involved and assume different roles in the process. The fact that different agencies often utilize different criteria to determine eligibility for services, and that different professionals often disagree as to what is best for a child, simply complicates matters. As an advocate for the parents and their child, it is the professional's responsibility to sort through this confusion, to identify all services to which the child is entitled, and to attempt to resolve disagreements professionals may have about programming. As an advocate, the professional should attempt to organize all information and present this information in a coherent, organized, and easily understood fashion. In the role of advocate, the professional may act as a liaison between the parent and other involved agencies and professionals.

Expert

As stated earlier, assuming an expert stance with parents can discourage active parental involvement and encourage the development of competition between school personnel and parents. However, there is a difference between being an expert and assuming an expert stance. The former implies one's ability to bring expertise to bear on a problem. The latter implies an unequal manner of interacting with others (that is, "I am an expert and you are not . . . therefore things will be done my way"). It *is* important for professionals to utilize and share their expertise with parents when working with them. However, in doing so, parents must be treated as equals and as team members who possess expertise of their own.

The role of expert requires that the professional assume both an educational and problem-solving perspective when working with parents. As an expert, the professional must educate parents about the kinds of decisions they and their children must make, the time when such decisions must be made, and the type of information to be considered when making informed, realistic vocational decisions. The types of decisions to be made will vary but will include such things as what vocational training program the child should enroll in, what type of job placement service should be initiated, what type of job should be sought, or what on-the-job assistance or modifications will be necessary. The type of information the professional, as an expert, must ensure is available to the parent is two-fold: (1) information about the child (i.e., his or her abilities, interests, values, or personality characteristics), and (2) information about the world of work (i.e., the rewards, requirements, and demands of different training programs and jobs). More specifically, parents may need to be provided with the following information:

— current graduation requirements, and requirements that exist for placement in specific vocational training programs;

— requirements that exist for entry into specific jobs, and what expectations employers have for employees in these jobs;

— the types of services other community, state, and federal agencies provide, which of these services their child will need, and how these services can be accessed;

— the role of and services provided by school personnel with whom the parent will have contact;

— the rights and responsibilities they have as parents under the law; and

— the nature of the various educational, vocational, and residential options that exist in the community.

Although it is the professional's responsibility as an expert to ensure that this information is available to the parents, the professional should encourage the parents to gather as much of this information as they can on their own. Once this information is available, the parent(s) and professional(s) can jointly assume responsibility for initiating a collaborative problem-solving perspective for making the necessary vocational decisions.

Therapist

Professionals must be aware that many parents experience anxiety and fear when making decisions about their children's future. Some fear the "empty nest syndrome" and discourage their children from making vocational decisions. Parents of individuals with disabilities often experience guilt about their child's disability. Some never accept the fact that their child has a disability and continue to expect their child to "grow out of it" and eventually to become "normal." All of these feelings and emotions can present obstacles to parental involvement, and objective and realistic decision making. In the role of therapist, the professional must identify, address, and resolve those feelings and emotions that may inhibit parental involvement and/or realistic vocational decision making. In some cases, a transdisciplinary team member such as the school psychologist or school counselor may need to involve the parent in counseling to address such feelings and issues.

CONSIDERATIONS IN THE ASSESSMENT OF STUDENTS WITH DISABILITIES

The following section discusses some general characteristics of students with disabilities who are likely to receive vocational assessment services in the schools, and the special considerations that must be made for these students in the assessment process. This section will discuss students who are mentally retarded, learning disabled, emotionally disturbed, hearing impaired, visually impaired, and physically disabled. The purpose of this section is *not* to discuss in detail the means by which these students are assessed and identified in the public schools. Clearly, entire books have been devoted to this topic alone. Rather, the purpose of this section is to review briefly the general characteristics of these students and to discuss how these characteristics may influence the vocational assessment process. Given the special characteristics that these students possess, traditional vocational assessment methods and techniques sometimes need to be altered, and different areas of assessment emphasized.

Mentally Retarded Students

Mental retardation is a condition characterized by significantly below average intelligence and deficits in adaptive behavior. Relatedly, mentally retarded students often possess a limited attention span, and weak academic, social, and expressive language skills. These students demonstrate a subaverage rate of learning and tend to have great difficulty generalizing skills learned in one setting to another similar setting. This difficulty in "transfer" of skills often necessitates that skills training take place in realistic settings. For example, it is frequently beneficial to conduct job training in the actual setting in which the mentally retarded student is to perform the job (rather than conducting training in a classroom, and hoping the skills learned in that setting will "transfer" to the work setting in which the student is eventually placed). Hence, with mentally retarded students, the usual process of providing skills training in a vocational program, and then identifying and placing the student in a job, may need to be reversed. Identifying and placing a mentally retarded student in a job first and then training the student to perform the job (via assistance from a job coach) is often a more productive strategy. This is particularly true with more severely retarded students.

Mentally retarded students can be classified in several different ways. Figure 6-1 lists the various labels used to describe different ranges or levels of retardation and lists some characteristics associated with each of these levels or ranges. Given that there exists a continuum of retardation, one must remember that not all mentally retarded students are the same. The mentally retarded are a heterogeneous population.

The unique characteristics of the mentally retarded student require that special considerations be made in the vocational assessment process. First, the mentally retarded student's intellectual deficits, limited attention span, and weak academic and language skills present serious difficulties in the use of traditional, paper-and-pencil, psychometric tests. Mentally retarded students are likely to have difficulty understanding the language used by the examiner in administering the tests and will have difficulty comprehending any portions of the test that require reading. As a result, the tests may not measure traits they were intended to measure (interests or aptitudes, for example), but may simply measure the student's inability to comprehend and understand written and oral language. For these reasons,

Figure 6-1.
Classification and Characteristics of Mental Retardation
(Adapted from U.S. Department of Health, Education and Welfare, 1969 and Slavin, 1988)

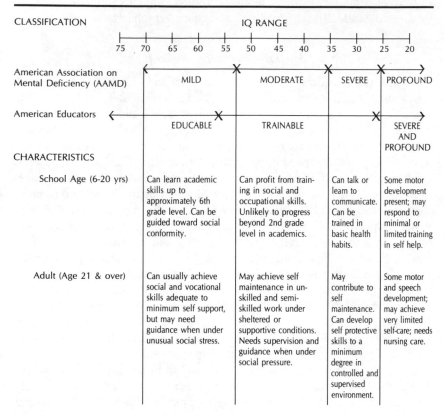

paper-and-pencil tests that eliminate or significantly reduce any reading and language requirements are preferred. For example, picture-based (nonreading) interest inventories are more desirable instruments to use with the mentally retarded than are interest inventories that require reading. Relatedly, administering standardized tests in several sessions can help to overcome the limited attention span these students demonstrate. One can also modify and simplify the instructions of the standardized test, but this is likely to invalidate the score yielded by the test and is not highly recommended.

Botterbusch (1976) has offered several useful suggestions on how assessment techniques, especially tests, can be modified for mentally retarded students. Among these suggestions are:

Simplification of Instructions—Vocational assessors can review instructions prior to the administration of a test and change any words that may be difficult for the mentally retarded student to understand. Complex sentences can be simplified, and additional instructions, visual aids, or demonstrations can be added.

Use of Pre-Trials—Assessors can orient mentally retarded individuals to tests prior to the administration of these tests. "Mock tests," whose purpose is to familiarize the student with instructions and procedures, can be used. Although such a mock test should contain items that are similar (in content, format, and difficulty) to those on the test, they should not be identical.

Repeating Instructions to Administrator—Test administrators can ask the student to repeat test instructions to determine how well these instructions were understood. Because retarded individuals have difficulty remembering complex instructions, these instructions can be broken down into segments, and each segment can be repeated back sequentially.

Color Coding—Some paper-and-pencil and performance tests can be color-coded for greater understanding. For example, instead of having to explain the difference between right and left, test administrators may simply color-code each side differently and refer to the "white" side and the "black" side.

Marking Answers in Test Book—Poor motor skills sometimes lengthen the time required for mentally retarded students to mark answers, and this often detracts from their performance. Test administrators can mark answers themselves, thereby eliminating this burden.

Low Literate and Nonverbal Test Forms—Because retarded persons do not read at the levels required for the successful administration of certain tests, nonreading, pictorially based instruments or low reading requirement instruments can be used.

It should be noted that use of assessment modifications may invalidate the norms associated with many tests, because these tests were not standardized using such modified administration procedures. Consequently, use of such norms following implementation of these administration modifications is often inappropriate.

The use of standardized, norm-referenced tests with mentally retarded individuals is often problematic for reasons other than those cited above. As discussed briefly in chapter 3, the background experiences of mentally retarded students are significantly different than are the background experiences of students often included in a test's standardization sample.

As a result, such tests may offer unfair comparisons when used with a mentally retarded student. For example, interest inventories are generally standardized on samples of students without disabilities who have had a "normal" range of life experiences. The development of interests is somewhat dependent upon the range and breadth of experiences one has had. Because mentally retarded students have had a much more limited range of experiences than have the students typically included in the standardization sample of many interest inventories, they often do not demonstrate distinct patterns of interest on these tests. That is, their low scores are often reflective of the limited experiences they have had in comparison to those of students included in the standardization sample of the test, rather than lack of interest, per se. For this reason, it is helpful to choose standardized tests that have been specifically standardized on mentally retarded populations.

Given the characteristics of mentally retarded students and the problems with traditional, standardized, paper-and-pencil tests cited above, it is helpful to emphasize the use of observations, interviews, and rating scales/checklists (in lieu of standardized, norm-referenced, paper-and-pencil tests) in the vocational assessment of this population. For example, rather than using the student as an informant in the assessment of interests (which is what interest inventories essentially do), significant others (parents, teachers, etc.) can be used as informants. One can assess interests (and other traits) of mentally retarded students more easily and perhaps more validly by having parents and teachers fill out checklists and rating scales designed to measure interests (and other traits) than by having the student complete an interest inventory. Observations made of the student by different professionals in different settings can also assist in gathering vocational assessment information on mentally retarded students without the use of standardized paper-and-pencil tests.

The difficulties associated with using traditional paper-and-pencil tests with the mentally retarded, and the retarded person's limited breadth and range of life experiences and difficulty in generalizing skills learned in one setting to another setting, argue in favor of using a more experientially based assessment process that incorporates both an exploration (or exposure) and training component, and in which assessment and training are both conducted in the setting in which the student is to use the skills being taught. Several approaches of this type, variously labeled *community-referenced assessment* and *functional assessment*, are described in the next chapter. Professionals who are extensively involved in the vocational assessment of the retarded are encouraged to become familiar with these assessment approaches. It is important to emphasize that, depending upon the nature and severity of a student's retardation, a vastly different method of vocational assessment than is emphasized in this book or frequently present in school settings may be necessary. Also, one must not underestimate the mentally retarded student's work capabilities, and limit his or her vocational or job placement options. It is clear that many mentally retarded students can be successfully trained to function in a variety of competitive employment situations.

Learning Disabled Students

Learning disabled students are students who generally possess average to above-average intelligence, but who demonstrate significantly below-average achievement in specific academic areas. By definition, this poor academic achievement is not the result of mental retardation, emotional disturbance, environmental/cultural/economic disadvantage, or physical disabilities such as blindness or deafness. It is believed to be the result of a deficit in a "basic psychological process involved in understanding and using language" (P.L. 94-142). Unfortunately, the identification of learning disabled children has been plagued by several problems, the most basic of which is the lack of universal agreement over the condition's definition. Several different definitions of "learning disability" have been proposed. However, all of these definitions have one universal flaw: They use terms that are vague and unclear, and incorporate concepts and traits that are difficult to operationalize and almost impossible to measure. For example, what is a "significant" discrepancy? How significant must a discrepancy be for a student to qualify as learning disabled? How do we validly measure a "psychological process"? How can we rule out "environmental influences" as a potential cause of a learning difficulty? These and other definitional problems have led to identification difficulties. Because different professionals operate with a somewhat different definition of the term, and are attempting to measure constructs that may not lend themselves to reliable and valid measurement, professionals often disagree as to who is and who is not learning disabled. As Ysseldyke and his associates have demonstrated, students who have been identified and placed in programs for learning disabled students in the schools are a rather heterogeneous group who may be indistinguishable from low-achieving students who have not been identified and placed in such programs. As a result, Algozzine and Ysseldyke (1983) have argued that there is no defensible system for classifying children as learning disabled.

For the reasons cited above, it is difficult to identify uniform characteristics of this group of students. However, most do possess at least average intelligence and demonstrate below-average academic skills. These students sometimes demonstrate social and interpersonal skills deficits, short attention spans, and hyperactivity. Several studies have suggested that learning disabled students demonstrate a slower rate of career maturity than do non-learning disabled students (Bingham, 1975, 1978, 1980; Kendall, 1980, 1981), are employed in lower level jobs than are their non-learning disabled counterparts (Weller & Buchanan, 1983; White, Schumaker, Warner, Alley, & Dreshler, 1980), and are less satisfied with their jobs than are their non-learning disabled peers (Weller & Buchanan, 1983). Several studies reviewed by Biller (1987) have suggested that learning disabilities have a negative impact on educational attainment and that this subsequently influences the learning disabled student's occupational outcomes.

Modifications in the vocational assessment program of learning disabled students must be guided by the specific nature of the individual student's disability. Because disabilities will vary from one student to another, a necessary and appropriate modification for one student may be unnecessary and inappropriate for another student. Because many learning disabled students have limited reading skills, the use of nonreading interest inventories with these students may be necessary. Regardless, it is important to ensure that there is a match between the learning disabled student's reading level and the reading requirements posed by any test utilized in the assessment process. Because these students often demonstrate poor social and interpersonal skills, it is particularly important to assess occupational social skills in the vocational assessment process. There must also be an attempt to pinpoint the student's specific academic and related deficits to determine the implications of these for vocational training and placement. When administering assessment instruments, the assessor needs to be concerned about the learning disabled student's potential attention difficulties and hyperactivity. Conducting the assessment over several sessions, taking frequent breaks, and reducing or eliminating distractions in the assessment environment will all assist in the assessment of the learning disabled student. Because these students demonstrate delays in career development and maturity, and often demonstrate social skills deficits that could have a negative impact on employability, assessment of these two areas is a particularly important component of the overall vocational assessment of learning disabled students.

A condition that has recently received considerable study and has frequently been subsumed under the category of "learning disability" is "attention deficit disorder." Currently termed Attention Deficit Hyperactivity Disorder (ADHD), this condition is distinguished by the characteristics listed below. According to the *Diagnostic and Statistical Manual* (DSM III; American Psychiatric Association, 1987), at least eight of these characteristics must be displayed for 6 months or more before the age of 7, in order for a diagnosis to be made:

1. fidgets, squirms, or seems restless;
2. has difficulty remaining seated;
3. is easily distracted;

 4. has difficulty awaiting turn;
 5. blurts out answers;
 6. has difficulty following instructions;
 7. has difficulty sustaining attention;
 8. shifts from one uncompleted task to another;
 9. has difficulty playing quietly;
10. talks excessively;
11. interrupts or intrudes on others;
12. does not seem to listen;
13. often loses things necessary for tasks;
14. frequently engages in dangerous acts.

P.L. 101-476, the Individuals with Disabilities Education Act (passed in October, 1990), provides for the establishment of a center on attention deficit disorder. Specifically, the legislation states the following:

[Congress] directed the secretary to fund one or more centers designed "to organize, synthesize, and disseminate current knowledge relating to children with attention deficit disorder; information such as assessment techniques, instruments, and strategies for identification, location, evaluation, and measurement of progress; competencies needed by professionals providing special education and related services; conditions needed for effective professional practice; developmental and learning characteristics; instructional techniques, strategies, and activities." (as cited in Ysseldyke, Algozzine, & Thurlow, 1992, p. 57)

Despite the widespread attention ADHD is currently receiving, diagnosis of the condition is plagued by many of the same definitional and methodological difficulties discussed previously. Relatedly, it is likely that many students *without* disabilities will demonstrate the characteristics listed above. In fact, many of the characteristics of ADHD as listed above are developmentally appropriate characteristics for young children. As Ysseldyke, Algozzine, and Thurlow (1992) have stated, "one could argue that professionals should be concerned when a child *does not* demonstrate these characteristics before the age of seven" (p. 108). As is true with "learning disabilities" in general, additional research needs to be conducted on ADHD before students possessing the disability can be validly identified and appropriately served.

Visually Impaired Students

Visually impaired students are those students who possess a visual impairment which, even with correction, adversely affects their educational performance. The term includes both partially sighted and blind students. A legally blind student is one who has a central vision acuity of 20/200 or less in the better eye after correction, whereas a partially sighted student is one who has visual acuity greater than 20/200 but not greater than 20/70 in the better eye with correction (Kirk, 1982).

As Kirk (1982) has suggested, the visually impaired often experience vocational aspirations and expectations that are different from those experienced by persons who are not visually impaired. Sinick (1979) has suggested that these lowered expectations are a function of feelings of inadequacy and a distorted self-image. Frequently, the visually impaired student does not learn important life skills due to a lack of community life experiences (such as part-time work). This has a detrimental impact on overall vocational functioning (Brolin & Gysbers, 1979; Scholl, 1973). Kirchner and Peterson (1979) have suggested that the visually impaired often suffer from poor labor market participation as a result of receiving discouragement from significant others in their lives (e.g., parents, teachers, counselors) who similarly hold low vocational expectations for them. Traditionally, guidance programs have sought to place visually impaired students in low-level and stereotypical occupations (Sinick, 1979; White, Reardon, Barker, & Carlson, 1979).

Clearly, many traditionally used assessment devices require vision and are inappropriate for use with visually impaired students without some modification. For example, the performance scale on the Wechsler Intelligence Scale for Children - Revised (WISC-R; Wechsler, 1974) is inappropriate for use with these students. Although the verbal scale of the Wechsler Intelligence Scale (the WISC-R's predecessor) has been shown to possess adequate reliability for blind children (Tillman, 1973), much less is known about the psychometric characteristics of the WISC-R verbal scale for this population (Sattler, 1988). The same may be said of the WISC-III. However, for reasons having to do with acculturation and test norms discussed previously, even use of the verbal scale on the WISC-III is somewhat problematic. Regardless, professionals must be concerned with the psychometric properties of the instruments they use with this population (i.e., they must ensure that the tests are reliable and valid for visually impaired students; preferably, instruments that have been standardized on this population, or have included visually impaired students in the test's standardization, should be employed). Tests must be selected so as to ensure that the student's disability doesn't overly influence the score yielded by the test. Unfortunately, most standardized tests for use with visually impaired students are out-of-date and technically inadequate (Bradley-Johnson & Harris, 1990). Some tests recommended for use with visually impaired students by Bradley-Johnson and Harris (1990) include the WAIS-R (Wechsler, 1981), the Blind Learning Aptitude Scale (Newland, 1969), the Detroit

Test of Learning Aptitude (Hammill, 1985), the Stanford Achievement Test (Gardner, Rudman, Karlsen, & Merwin, 1982), and the Test of Academic Skills (Gardner, Callis, Merwin, & Rudman, 1983).

Considering the special needs of visually impaired students, three areas of assessment need to be given special consideration: vision utilization skills, mobility skills, and daily living skills (Scott, 1982). The assessment should initially determine the student's functional vision capacity with maximum aid then, based upon such maximum aid, determine the student's ability to move about the environment adequately (e.g., school, worksite, residence). Additionally, the assessment should address the student's independent living skills, especially the student's dress and grooming, because many blind and visually impaired students do not pay as much attention to their appearance as sighted persons do. Assessments should take place in rooms free of distractions (even subtle auditory distractions can interfere with the concentration and test performance of visually impaired students) that are well lit (it is best if the source of light comes from the side of the better eye). Special materials such as enlarged print, braille materials (such as a braille writer), magnifiers, and bookstands may also need to be employed to assess visually impaired students adequately (Bradley-Johnson & Harris, 1990).

Hearing Impaired Students

According to definitions used for educational placements, students whose hearing loss in their better ear exceeds 70 db are classified as deaf, whereas those whose hearing loss ranges from 35 to 70 db in their better ear are classified as hearing impaired or hard of hearing (Vess & Douglas, 1990). Deaf and hearing impaired individuals have been traditionally "forced" to work in low socioeconomic jobs that are menial, low paying, and have little relationship to the training they received, apparently because both they and others (employers, counselors, parents) underestimate their true vocational potential (Blevins, 1982; Scorzelli & Scorzelli, 1982). Data indicate that many deaf workers have historically been employed in printing, bakery, dry cleaning, tailoring, and shoemaking occupations (Blevins, 1982; Scorzelli & Scorzelli, 1982). Blevins's (1982) review of the literature indicated that (a) many professionals were unfamiliar with the needs of deaf and hearing impaired individuals, (b) that there existed a paucity of psychometric instruments appropriate for use with this population, and (c) that a prevailing attitude existed that the evaluation, training, and vocational preparation of deaf and hearing impaired individuals does not differ from those of other minority groups. Blevins concluded that the vocational assessment and planning process with this population has been fraught with difficulties and may be at least partially responsible for the frequent placement of these individuals in low-level jobs.

Because of their hearing impairment, these students often do not develop language, communication, social, and academic skills at the same rate as do their non–hearing impaired counterparts. However, hearing impaired and deaf students enter postsecondary education at about the same rate as hearing students and 65% of the graduates of Gallaudet College attend graduate schools with hearing students (Moores, 1987). Based upon this, Vess and Douglas (1990) have concluded that the extent of the gap between the academic achievement of hearing and hearing impaired students is unclear. Vocational development of these students also lags in comparison to that of the non–hearing impaired. As Blevins (1982) has suggested, deaf and hearing impaired students frequently lose jobs because they have problems with interpersonal relationships, not because they lack specific work skills. Of particular concern in the assessment of these students is the following: the severity and implications of the student's hearing loss; the student's current level of language, communicative, and academic functioning; and the degree to which the student has acquired the occupational social skills necessary for successful employment.

There are few psychological tests that have been specifically normed on the deaf and hearing impaired population. Use of traditional, pencil-and-paper tests with this population is plagued by many of the same problems that were cited for other disability populations elsewhere in this section and throughout this book. Thus, the assessment of deaf and hearing impaired students should frequently employ interviews, observations, use of rating scales and checklists, sociometrics, work samples, and situational assessment techniques in addition to whatever norm-referenced instruments are employed.

Scorzelli and Scorzelli (1982) have listed several intelligence, aptitude, and interest tests they suggest are appropriate for use with the deaf. Although they acknowledge that many of these tests lack specific norms for this population, they advocate use of these tests with such modifications as administration in sign language, or the use of pantomine, or imitation. However, such modification in administration procedure may only further serve to invalidate the score yielded by the test. Scorzelli and Scorzelli (1982) also cite several tests that *do* possess norms for the deaf and hearing impaired population and could be considered for use. Among these are the Wechsler Intelligence Scale for Children - Revised (WISC-R; Wechsler, 1974) and the Wechsler Adult Intelligence Scale - Revised (WAIS-R; Wechsler, 1981) (both of which included hearing impaired students in the standardization samples), and the Geist Picture Interest Inventory—Revised (Geist, 1964). As Sattler (1988) has indicated, the performance scale of the WISC-R has been shown to be a reliable and valid measure of intelligence for deaf children. The verbal scale and other verbal subtests are inappropriate for measuring the intelligence of deaf children (Sattler, 1988). However, the verbal scale can be used as a measure of language delay (Vess & Douglas, 1990), and when compared to the Performance IQ, the Verbal IQ can provide an estimate of the degree to which the student has mastered verbal concepts (Sattler, 1988).

Vess and Douglas (1990) have cited several resources that are available to assist professionals in selecting assessment instruments for use with the hearing impaired: *Assessment of Hearing-Impaired People* (Zieziula, 1982), and *Mental Health Assessment of Deaf Clients: A Practical Manual* (Elliott, Glass, & Evans, 1987). They have also offered several excellent suggestions for professionals when selecting and administering norm-referenced instruments to hard of hearing and deaf children. Among these suggestions are:

1. The standardized administrative guidelines of the test should be adhered to strictly. Any deviations or accommodations that have been made (which may then influence test scores) should be mentioned in the assessment report.

2. A certified interpreter for the deaf should be used when the student's primary language is sign. Certified interpreters can be located through the registry for Interpreters for the Deaf.

3. Verbal tests of intelligence should only be used as measures of language development, not as measures of intelligence.

4. Recognize that tests that are invalid with hearing children are invalid for hearing impaired children, even if the communication problems inherent in testing hearing impaired children are eliminated. Vess and Douglas (1990) note that nonverbal tests such as the Leiter (Arthur, 1950) and Hiskey-Nebraska (Hiskey, 1966) (which are popular and frequently used with the hearing impaired population) possess outdated and questionable norms and are in need of revision.

5. Schedule several short evaluation sessions rather than one lengthy evaluation session.

Emotionally Disturbed Students

Among students with disabilities, emotionally disturbed students may be at a particular disadvantage in regard to securing and maintaining long-term employment. It has been said that individuals lose their jobs not because of technical incompetence, but because of skill deficiencies within the affective and social domain (Hooper, 1980). Because emotionally disturbed students by definition lack "an ability to build or maintain interpersonal relationships," display "inappropriate types of behaviors or feelings under normal circumstances," and display "a generally pervasive mood of unhappiness or depression" (Education for All Handicapped Children Act of 1975, p. 42478), their chance of maintaining employment once it is secured is greatly diminished. The stigma associated with the label "seriously emotionally disturbed" may in and of itself be as much of a disability as the condition to which the label applies. Regardless of the healthy adjustment an emotionally disturbed student may have made as a result of treatment, potential employers may think twice about employing a student who has been so labeled.

Just as the identification of learning disabled students has been plagued by definitional and measurement problems, so too has the identification of emotionally disturbed students. However as Hollingsworth (1982) has suggested, emotionally disturbed students are students who demonstrate behavioral disorders (such as conduct problems, overaggressiveness, or emotional outbursts) and/or emotional disorders (such as excessive anxiety). Behaviors that frequently characterize emotionally disturbed students include: noninvolvement or withdrawal, hyperactivity, emotional outbursts, excessive aggressiveness, low frustration tolerance, temper tantrums, and unpredictability (Tellefsen, 1982). As Tellefsen (1982) has noted, it is the frequency, intensity, and duration of these behaviors that sets the emotionally disturbed student apart from his or her peers.

Previous research has indicated that emotionally disturbed students demonstrate delayed vocational development and lower vocational aspirations than do their non–emotionally disturbed peers (Goldberg, 1981; Plata, 1981). However, vocational assessment and planning should not take priority over the emotional and behavioral interventions that are needed to address this population's primary social and emotional needs. As Hollingsworth (1982) has suggested, vocational interventions in the purest sense are likely to have little impact with this group because the emotionally disturbed student's primary needs are psychotherapeutic (emotional and behavioral). As Woodbury and Pate (1977), Beley and Felker (1981), and Bordin (1968) have suggested, therapy designed to treat this student's emotional, social, and/or behavioral problems should precede any vocational/career intervention. At best, vocational assessment and intervention can occur simultaneously with the social/personal counseling and behavioral interventions these students often require. Levinson (1985) has described a model that can be used by professionals developing such a program and has described the development of a school-based program based upon such a model, which incorporates a behavioral incentive system, academic training, vocational training, work adjustment, and counseling (Levinson, 1984).

When assessing emotionally disturbed students, the examiner must ensure that the test situation is nonthreatening and the student feels as comfortable as possible. The examiner should possess behavior management skills which, during the assessment, can be used to reduce or eliminate undesired behavior. Given the emotionally disturbed student's special needs, assessments of work attitudes and work habits and of occupational social and interpersonal skills are particularly important components of any comprehensive vocational assessment. A major focus of the assessment should be to determine the extent to which the student's social, emotional, and/or behavioral difficulties present a threat to successful acquisition and maintenance of employment. Relatedly, the assessment should determine what special services the student may need in order to secure and maintain a job.

Physically Impaired Students

This disability is probably the most diverse and varied of those discussed in this section. These students are variously referred to as physically handicapped, physically impaired, motorically impaired, and orthopedically handicapped. Frequently, these students will be classified as multiply handicapped, as well, because motor impairments rarely occur in isolation from other disabilities (Christensen, 1990). Concurrent language and communication problems, sensory difficulties, convulsive disorders, and cognitive deficits are frequently present in students with physical disabilities.

Because of the variability inherent in this population, and in the interest of space, a listing of the characteristics of all physical disabilities will not be provided here. However, Bettmann (1978) defines the orthopedically handicapped as comprising "all anatomical and functional abnormalities of the musculoskeletal system, either manifest at birth, or developing during the growth period (ages 1 to 18), or during the active vocational life (ages 19 to 70)" (p. 503). Typically, this population will include those with rheumatoid arthritis, cerebral palsy, muscular dystrophy, spinal cord injuries, and spina bifida.

As Sheldon and DuBose (1982) have indicated, the effects of an orthopedic disability on vocational assessment and planning will be dependent on the nature, severity, and location of the disability. Some conditions are degenerative. Hence, an initial step in the assessment of such students would be to determine the nature and severity of the disability and to project the likely vocational implications of such disability.

In addition to an assessment of intelligence, academic achievement, personality characteristics, and so on, that should be commonly included in any comprehensive vocational assessment, certain areas should be given special consideration in the assessment of physically impaired students. Certainly, the student's physical capacities and tolerances need to be assessed, and the implications of these capacities and tolerances for vocational training and eventual job functioning must be identified. Additionally, the student's bowel and bladder continence, communication skills, mobility, sexuality, independent living skills, and ability to adapt and adjust to the disability should also be given special consideration (Gans, 1982).

As has been mentioned with other disabled populations, the selection of assessment instruments with physically disabled students is problematic. Many power and timed standardized tests penalize physically impaired students for slow or awkward responding, or excessive delay between the presentation of a test item and the student's response. As Christensen (1990) has concluded, in either of these cases, responding is compromised, and the test ends up assessing the student's disability rather than the trait the test is designed to assess. Christensen (1990) offers several suggestions regarding test selection and use with physically impaired students:

1. Determine the degree of motor loading of tests being considered for use, and select only those tests that do not make excessive motor demands.

2. Consider "testing of limits" with physically impaired students when using standardized tests. That is, administer the test in a standardized fashion at first (including adherence to all timing requirements). Then, after the test has been administered, readminister timed portions of the test without adhering to timing requirements. Compare the student's performance on the two administrations (recognize, however, that a practice effect may slightly inflate performance on the second administration) to assess the range of task performance to be expected of the student under varying degrees of time constraints.

3. Use tests that include teaching items, to ensure that the student understands the task before testing begins.

4. Consider use of adaptive devices with physically impaired students when testing them (to assess maximum performance/skill), and do not impose penalties for their use. (Christensen suggests, for example, that if a student uses a particular device to assist in zipping a zipper, only the ability to zip the zipper should be measured, and the student should not be penalized in any way for the means or method by which the zipping was accomplished, unless the test prescribes otherwise.)

5. Consider consulting with an occupational or physical therapist when planning the assessment of a physically impaired student so as to determine the optimum structuring of the test environment and optimum positioning of the student in the environment so as to elicit a maximum level of performance. Similarly, a speech/language therapist could be utilized to

assist in planning the assessment of students whose speech and language skills are impaired.

6. Consider the use of tests that minimize the amount and degree of responding necessary and consider modifying the response format. For example, use tests that require a simple yes/no response (which can be communicated via a nod, blink, etc.) or multiple choice. Modify the response format to compensate for the student's disability. For example, pointing, nodding, eye blinking, or eye pointing can be used in place of a verbal response.

7. Consider modifying the test procedure to improve the student's chances of responding to a task (for example, tape the answer sheet to the desk, and use oversized pencils to assist a student in responding).

8. Use adaptive equipment (e.g., communication board, voice synthesizer) to assist the student during testing.

Among the various tests Christensen (1990) recommends be considered for use with physically disabled children are the following:

Cognitive Assessment:

Test of Nonverbal Intelligence (Brown, Sherbenou, & Dallor, 1982)

Kaufman Assessment Battery for Children (Kaufman & Kaufman, 1983)

Detroit Test of Learning Aptitude-2 (Hammill, 1985)

Academic Assessment:

Peabody Individual Achievement Test (Dunn & Markwardt, 1970) (Although Christensen recommends this original instrument, readers should note that a revised form of the test is now available and should be considered for use in lieu of the original test.)

Peabody Picture Vocabulary Test (Dunn, 1981)

Brigance Diagnostic Inventory of Essential Skills (Brigance, 1981)

Clinical Evaluation of Language Functions, Diagnostic Battery (Semal & Wiig, 1980)

Adaptive Behavior:

Vineland Adaptive Behavior Scales—Expanded Form (Sparrow, Balla, & Cicchetti, 1984)

SUMMARY

This chapter has discussed the practical and logistical factors that must be considered when developing and implementing school-based vocational assessment programs. Steps involved in program development and implementation, and the roles that school and community personnel may assume in the assessment process, were discussed. Because vocational assessment programs will be developed with local needs and resources in mind, the particular assessment model developed and the roles that various professionals will assume in the assessment program will necessarily vary from one locality to the next. What should not vary, however, is the extent to which parents are involved in the vocational assessment and planning process. Although parents should be involved in the assessment process to the maximum extent possible, research has suggested that they are frequently uninvolved. This chapter has discussed some of the barriers that have traditionally inhibited parental involvement and has discussed some of the methods by which school personnel may enlist parental cooperation and participation. Last, this chapter has included a discussion of adaptations that may need to be made in the assessment process for students with varying disabilities.

REFERENCES

Algozzine, B., & Ysseldyke, J. E. (1983). Learning disabilities as a subset of school failure: The oversophistication of a concept. *Exceptional Children, 50,* 242-246.

American Psychiatric Association. (1987). *Diagnostic and statistical manual of mental disorders* (3rd ed., rev.). Washington, DC: Author.

Arthur, G. (1950). *The Arthur adaptation of the Leiter International Performance Scale.* Chicago: C. H. Stoelting.

Baker, B. C., Geiger, W. L., & deFur, S. (1988, November). *Competencies for transition personnel.* Paper presented at the Mid-East Regional Conference of the Career Development Division of the Council for Exceptional Children, White Sulphur Springs, WV.

Beley, W., & Felker, S. (1981). Comprehensive vocational evaluation for clients with psychiatric impairments. *Rehabilitation Literature, 42*(7), 194-201.

Benz, M. R., & Halpern, A. S. (1987). Transition services for secondary students with mild disabilities: A statewide perspective. *Exceptional Children, 53*(6), 507-514.

Bettmann, E. H. (1978). Orthopedic disorders. In R. M. Goldenson (Ed.), *Disability and rehabilitation handbook.* New York: McGraw-Hill.

Biller, E. F. (1987). *Career decision making for adolescents and young adults with learning disabilities: Theory, research and practice.* Springfield, IL: Charles C. Thomas.

Bingham, G. (1975). Career attitudes and self-esteem among boys with and without specific learning disabilities. *Dissertation Abstracts International 36*, 02A-75347. (University Microfilms No. 75-17, 340)

Bingham, G. (1978). Career attitudes among boys with and without specific learning disabilities. *Exceptional Children, 44*, 341-342.

Bingham, G. (1980). Career maturity of learning disabled adolescents. *Psychology in the Schools, 17*, 135-139.

Blevins, B. (1982). Vocational assessment procedures for the deaf and hard of hearing. In T. H. Hohenshil, W. T. Anderson, & J. F. Salwan (Eds.), *Secondary school psychological services: Focus on vocational assessment procedures for handicapped students.* Blacksburg, VA: Virginia Polytechnic Institute and State University. (ERIC Document Reproduction Service No. 229704)

Bordin, E. S. (1968). *Psychological counseling* (2nd ed.). New York: Appleton-Century-Crofts.

Botterbusch, K. (1976). *A comparison of seven vocational evaluation systems.* Menomonie, WI: Materials Development Center, Stout Vocational Rehabilitation Institute, University of Wisconsin - Stout.

Bradley-Johnson, S., & Harris, S. (1990). Best practices in working with students with a visual handicap. In A. Thomas & J. Grimes (Eds.), *Best practices in school psychology II.* Washington, DC: National Association of School Psychologists.

Brigance, A. (1981). *Brigance Diagnostic Inventory of Essential Skills.* North Bellerica, MA: Curriculum Associates.

Brolin, D. E., & Gysbers, N. C. (1979). Career education for persons with handicaps. *The Personnel and Guidance Journal, 58*, 258-262.

Brown, L., Sherbenou, R., & Dallor, S. (1982). *Test of nonverbal intelligence.* Austin, TX: Pro-Ed.

Bruner, J. (1974). Continuity of learning. *The School Psychology Digest, 3*, 20-25.

Brynelsen, D. (1984). *Working together: A handbook for parents and professionals.* (British Columbians for Mentally Handicapped People, Vancouver). Toronto: National Institute on Mental Retardation.

Capps, C. F., Levinson, E. M., & Hohenshil, T. H. (1985). Vocational aspects of psychological assessment: Part 3.*The Communique, 13*(5), 5-6.

Christensen, B. (1990) Best practices in working with children with motor impairments. In A. Thomas & J. Grimes (Eds.), *Best practices in school psychology II.* Washington, DC: National Association of School Psychologists.

Dunn, L. M. (1981). *Peabody Picture Vocabulary Test, revised.* Circle Pines, MN: American Guidance Service.

Dunn, L. M., & Markwardt, F. (1970). *Peabody Individual Achievement Test.* Circle Pines, MN: American Guidance Service.

Education for All Handicapped Children Act of 1975, 100-121, 45 U.S.C. 1401 (1977).

Elliott, H., Glass, L., & Evans, J. (Eds.). (1987). *Mental health assessment of deaf clients: A practical manual.* Boston, MA: Little, Brown.

Erickson, E. H. (1968). *Identity: Youth and crisis.* New York: W. W. Norton.

Fine, M. J. (Ed.). (1991). *Collaboration with parents of exceptional children.* Brandon, VT: Clinical Psychology Publishing.

Freud, S. (1962). *Civilization and its discontents.* In J. Strachey (Editor and Translator). New York: W.W. Norton. (Original work published in 1930)

Gans, B. (1982). The physically impaired and multihandicapped. In T. F. Harrington (Ed.), *Handbook of career planning for special needs students.* Rockville, MD: Aspen.

Gardner, E. F., Callis, R., Merwin, J. C., & Rudman, H. C. (1983). *Test of Academic Skills* (2nd ed.). San Antonio, TX: The Psychological Corporation.

Gardner, E. F., Rudman, H. C., Karlsen, B., & Merwin, J. C. (1982). *Stanford Achievement Test* (7th ed.). San Antonio, TX: The Psychological Corporation.

Geist, H. (1964). *The Geist Picture Interest Inventory.* Beverly Hills, CA: Stanford University Press.

Goldberg, R. T. (1981). Toward an understanding of the rehabilitation of the disabled adolescent. *Rehabilitation Literature, 42*(3), 66-74.

Gottfredson, G. D. (1977). Career stability and redirection in adulthood. *Journal of Applied Psychology, 62,* 436-445.

Gottfredson, G. D. (1981, August). *Why don't interests predict job satisfaction better than they do?* Paper presented at American Psychological Association Convention, Los Angeles, CA.

Gottfredson, G. D., Holland, J. L., & Ogawa, D. K. (1982). *Dictionary of Holland Occupational Codes.* Palo Alto: Consulting Psychologists Press.

Gresham, F. (1990). Best practices in social skills training. In A. Thomas & J. Grimes (Eds.), *Best practices in school psychology II.* Washington, DC: National Association of School Psychologists.

Halpern, A. S., Raffeld, P., Irvin, L. K., & Link, R. (1975). *Social and prevocational information battery.* Monterey, CA: CTB/McGraw-Hill.

Hammill, D. D. (1985). *Detroit Test of Learning Aptitude-2.* Austin, TX: Pro-Ed.

Hasazi, S. B., Gordon, L. R., & Roe, C. A. (1985). Factors associated with the employment status of handicapped youth exiting high school from 1979 to 1983. *Exceptional Children, 51*(6), 455-469.

Heinlein, W. E. (1987). *Clinical utility of the Wechsler scales in psychological evaluations to estimate vocational aptitude.* Unpublished doctoral dissertation, Virginia Polytechnic Institute and State University, Blacksburg, VA.

Heinlein, W. E., Nelson, M. D., & Hohenshil, T. H. (1985). Vocational aspects of psychological assessment: Part II. *The Communique, 13*(4).

Hiskey, M. (1966). *Hiskey-Nebraska Test of Learning Aptitude.* Lincoln, NE: Marshall S. Hiskey.

Hohenshil, T. H. (1982). School psychology + vocational counseling = vocational school psychology. *The Personnel and Guidance Journal, 61*(1), 11-14.

Hohenshil, T. H. (1984). The vocational aspects of school psychology: 1974-1984. *School Psychology Review, 13*(4) 503-509.

Hohenshil, T. H., Anderson, W. T., & Salwan, J. F. (1982). *Secondary school psychological services: Focus on vocational assessment procedures for handicapped students*. Blacksburg, VA: Virginia Polytechnic Institute and State University.

Hohenshil, T. H., Levinson, E. M., & Buckland-Heer, K. (1985). Best practices in vocational assessment for handicapped students. In J. Grimes & A. Thomas (Eds.), *Best practices in school psychology*. Washington, DC: National Association of School Psychologists.

Holland, J. (1985a). *A theory of vocational personalities and work environments*. Englewood Cliffs, NJ: Prentice-Hall.

Holland, J. L. (1985b). *The Self-Directed Search professional manual — 1985 edition*. Odessa, FL: Psychological Assessment Resources.

Hollingsworth, D. K. (1982). The mentally troubled. In T. F. Harrington (Ed.), *Handbook of career planning for special needs students*. Rockville, MD: Aspen.

Hooper, P. G. (1980). Guidance and counseling: Potential impact on youth unemployment. *Journal of Career Education*, *6*, 270-287.

Hummel, D. L., & Hohenshil, T. H. (1974). The psychological foundations of career education: Potential roles for the school psychologist. *School Psychology Digest*, *3*(3), 4-10.

Johnson, D. R., Bruininks, R. H., & Thurlow, M. L. (1987). Meeting the challenge of transition service planning through improved interagency cooperation. *Exceptional Children*, *53*(6), 522-530.

Jung, C. (1960). *The collected works of C. G. Jung*. New York: Bollinger Foundation, Princeton University Press.

Kaufman, A. S., & Kaufman, N. L. (1983). *K-ABC: Kaufman Assessment Battery for Children*. Circle Pines, MN: American Guidance Service.

Keith, T. (1990). Best practices in conducting school based research. In A. Thomas & J. Grimes (Eds.), *Best practices in school psychology II*. Washington, DC: National Association of School Psychologists.

Kendall, W. S. (1980). *Affective and career education for the learning disabled adolescent*. Prairie View, TX: Prairie View A & M University. (ERIC Document Reproduction Service No. ED 188772)

Kendall, W. S. (1981). Affective and career education for the learning disabled adolescent. *Learning Disability Quarterly*, *4*, 69-75.

Kirchner, C., & Peterson, R. (1979). Employment: Selected characteristics. *Journal of Visual Impairment and Blindness*, *73*, 239-242.

Kirk, D. (1982). Vocational assessment of visually impaired secondary students. In T. H. Hohenshil, W. T. Anderson, & J. F. Salwan (Eds.), *Secondary school psychological services: Focus on vocational assessment procedures for handicapped students*. Blacksburg, VA: Virginia Polytechnic Institute and State University. (ERIC Document Reproduction Service No. 215245)

Kratochwill, T. (1990). Best practices in behavior consultation. In A. Thomas & J. Grimes (Eds.), *Best practices in school psychology II*. Washington, DC: National Association of School Psychologists.

Levinson, E. M. (1984a). A vocationally oriented secondary school program for the emotionally disturbed. *Vocational Guidance Quarterly, 33*(1), 76-81.

Levinson, E. M. (1984b). Vocational/career assessment in secondary school psychological evaluations: Rationale, definition, and purpose. *Psychology in the Schools, 21*(1), 112-117.

Levinson, E. M. (1985). Vocational and career-oriented secondary school programs for the emotionally disturbed. *The School Counselor, 33*(2), 100-106.

Levinson, E. M. (1987a). Children and vocational development. In A. Thomas & J. Grimes (Eds.), *Children's needs: Psychological perspectives*. Washington, DC: National Association of School Psychologists.

Levinson, E. M. (1987b). Incorporating a vocational component into a school psychological evaluation: A case example. *Psychology in the Schools, 24*(3), 254-264.

Levinson, E. M. (1988). Correlates of vocational practice among school psychologists. *Psychology in the Schools, 25*(3), 297-305.

Levinson, E. M. (1990a). Actual/desired role functioning, perceived control over role functioning, and job satisfaction among school psychologists. *Psychology in the Schools, 27*(1), 64-74.

Levinson, E. M. (1990b). Vocational assessment involvement and use of the Self-Directed Search by school psychologists. *Psychology in the Schools, 28*(3), 217-227.

Levinson, E. M., & Capps, C. F. (1985). Vocational assessment and special education triennial reevaluations at the secondary school level. *Psychology in the Schools, 22*(3), 283-292.

Levinson, E. M., & McKee, L. M. (1991). The exceptional child grows up: Transitions. In M. Fine (Ed.), *Collaboration with parents of exceptional children*. Brandon, VT: Clinical Psychology Publishing.

Levinson, E. M., & Shepard, J. W. (1982). Integrating vocational assessment data into school psychological evaluations. In T. H. Hohenshil, W. T. Anderson, & J. F. Salwan (Eds.), *Secondary school psychological services: Focus on vocational assessment services for handicapped students*. Blacksburg, VA: Virginia Polytechnic Institute and State University. (ERIC Reproduction Service No. 229704)

Marinelli, R. P., Tunic, R. H., & LeConte, P. (1988, November). *Vocational evaluation education: Regional programs*. Paper presented at the Mid-East Regional Conference of the Career Development Division of the Council for Exceptional Children, White Sulphur Springs, WV.

McConnell, S. R. (1990). Best practices in evaluating educational programs. In A. Thomas & J. Grimes (Eds.), *Best practices in school psychology II*. Washington, DC: National Association of School Psychologists.

Moores, D. (1987). *Educating the deaf: Psychology, principles, and practices* (3rd ed.). Boston, MA: Houghton Mifflin.

Murray, J. (1990). Best practices in counseling parents of handicapped children. In A. Thomas & J. Grimes (Eds.), *Best practices in school psychology II*. Washington, DC: National Association of School Psychologists.

Murray, P. (1975). *An analysis of the role of the school psychologist in the Commonwealth of Virginia*. Unpublished doctoral dissertation, Virginia Polytechnic Institute and State University.

National Association of School Psychologists. (1985). *Professional conduct manual*. Kent, OH: National Association of School Psychologists.

National Association of State Boards of Education. (1979). *Vocational education of handicapped youth: State of the art*. Washington, DC: Author.

Newland, T. E. (1969). *Blind Learning Aptitude Test*. Champaign, IL: Ernest Newland.

Ott, C. (1991). *Family involvement on the intervention assistance team: An untapped resource for building home-school partnerships*. Paper presented at the Annual Conference of the National Association of School Psychologists, Dallas, TX.

Pennsylvania Departments of Education & Labor and Industry. (1986). *Pennsylvania Transition from School to the Workplace* (pp. 3,7,83). Harrisburg, PA: Author.

Pfeffer, R. (1978). *Proposed functions for school psychologists in career education*. Unpublished doctoral dissertation, Virginia Polytechnic Institute and State University.

Plata, M. (1981). Occupational aspirations of normal and emotionally disturbed adolescents: A comparative study. *Vocational Guidance Quarterly, 30*, 130–138.

Sattler, J. (1988). *Assessment of children* (3rd ed.). San Diego, CA: Author.

Schalock, R. L., & Lilley, M. A. (1986). Placement from community-based mental retardation programs: How well do clients do after 8 to 10 years? *American Journal of Mental Deficiency, 90*(6), 669–676.

Scholl, G. (1973). Understanding and meeting developmental needs. In B. Lowenfield (Ed.), *The visually handicapped child in school*. New York: John Day.

Scorzelli, J., & Scorzelli, M. R. (1982). Deafness. In T. F. Harrington (Ed.), *Handbook of career planning for special needs students*. Rockville, MD: Aspen.

Scott, R. (1982). The visually impaired. In T. F. Harrington (Ed.), *Handbook of career planning for special needs students*. Rockville, MD: Aspen.

Semal, E., & Wiig, E. (1980). *Clinical evaluation of language functions*. Columbus, OH: Merrill.

Sheldon, K. L., & DuBose, L. (1982). Vocational assessment of the orthopedically handicapped. In T. H. Hohenshil, W. T. Anderson, & J. F. Salwan (Eds.), *Secondary school psychological services: Focus on vocational assessment procedures for handicapped students*. Blacksburg, VA: Virginia Polytechnic Institute and State University. (ERIC Document Reproduction Service No. 229704)

Shepard, J. W., & Hohenshil, T. H. (1983). National survey of career development functions of practicing school psychologists. *Psychology in the Schools, 20*(4), 445–449.

Shepard, J. W., & Levinson, E. M. (1985). Vocational assessment for school psychologists at the secondary level. *Journal of Psychoeducational Assessment, 3*(3), 257-266.

Sinick, D. (1979). Career counseling with handicapped persons. *The Personnel and Guidance Journal, 58*, 252-257.

Slavin, R. E. (1988). *Educational psychology: Theory into practice.* Englewood Cliffs, NJ: Prentice-Hall.

Smith, R. L. (1983). *The vocational counselor and guidance team* (5th ed.). Commerce, TX: Occupational Curriculum Laboratory, East Texas State University.

Sparrow, S. S., Balla, D. A., & Cicchetti, D. V. (1984). *Vineland Adaptive Behavior Scales.* Circle Pines, MN: American Guidance Service.

Tellefsen, D. J. (1982). Comprehensive vocational/career assessment of emotionally disturbed adolescents and adults. In T. H. Hohenshil, W. T. Anderson, & J. F. Salwan (Eds.), *Secondary school psychological services: Focus on vocational assessment procedures for handicapped students.* Blacksburg, VA: Virginia Polytechnic Institute and State University. (ERIC Document Reproduction Service No. 229704)

Thomas, S., & Coleman, N. (1988). *Vocational assessment training manual.* Raleigh, NC: Department of Vocational Education, North Carolina Department of Public Instruction.

Thomas, A., & Grimes, J. (1985). *Best practices in school psychology.* Kent, OH: National Association of School Psychologists.

Thomas, A., & Grimes, J. (1987). *Children's needs: Psychological perspectives.* Washington, DC: National Association of School Psychologists.

Tillman, M. H. (1973). Intelligence scales for the blind: A review with implications for research. *Journal of School Psychology, 11*, 80-87.

U.S. Department of Health, Education and Welfare. (1969). *The problem of mental retardation.* Washington, DC: Government Printing Office.

U.S. Department of Labor. (1977). *Dictionary of occupational titles.* Washington, DC: Government Printing Office.

Vess, S. M., & Douglas, L. S. (1990). Best practices in working with students with a hearing loss. In A. Thomas & J. Grimes (Eds.), *Best practices in school psychology II.* Washington, DC: National Association of School Psychologists.

Vocational Evaluation and Work Adjustment Association. (1975). Vocational evaluation project final report [Special Edition]. *Vocational Evaluation and Work Adjustment Bulletin, 8.*

Wechsler, D. (1974). *Manual for the Wechsler Intelligence Scale for Children - Revised.* San Antonio, TX: The Psychological Corporation.

Wechsler, D. (1981). *Manual for the Wechsler Adult Intelligence Scale - Revised.* San Antonio, TX: The Psychological Corporation.

Wehman, P., Moon, M. S., Everson, J. M., Wood, W., & Barcus, J. M. (1988). *Transition from school to work: New challenges for youth with severe disabilities.* Baltimore, MD: Paul H. Brookes.

White, P., Reardon, R., Barker, S., & Carlson, A. (1979). Increasing career center accessibility for the blind. *The Personnel and Guidance Journal, 58*, 292-295.

White, J., Schumaker, J., Warner, M., Alley, G., & Deshler, D. (1980). *The current status of young adults identified as learning disabled during their school career*. (Research Paper #21). Lawrence, KS: University of Kansas, Institute for Research in Learning Disabilities.

Weller, C., & Buchanan, M. (1983). *Career assessment inventories for the learning disabled*. Novato, CA: Academic Therapy.

Woodbury, R., & Pate, D. H. (1977). Vocational and personality dimensions of adjudicated delinquents. *Measurement and Evaluation for Guidance, 10*, 106-112.

Ysseldyke, J. E., Algozzine, B., & Thurlow, M. L. (1992). *Critical issues in special education* (2nd ed.). Princeton, NJ: Houghton Mifflin.

Zieziula, F. R. (Ed.). (1982). *Assessment of hearing impaired people*. Washington, DC: Gallaudet College Press.

7 PROGRAM MODELS AND METHODS

This chapter includes a description of several different vocational assessment program models that can be adapted for use in school settings. Included are a discussion of the transdisciplinary school-based vocational assessment model advocated by this writer, a traditional vocational rehabilitation center vocational evaluation model, and school-based programs/models that have been developed in Virginia, Texas, North Carolina, Tennessee, and Pennsylvania. Although each of these programs/models is relatively unique (because each was developed to accommodate local needs and resources), they all share common elements. Whereas the models presented here are adequate in accommodating and serving most students in the schools, these "traditional" assessment programs are in most cases inadequate in serving students with severe disabilities. As alluded to in the previous chapter, reliance on traditional assessment procedures (such as paper-and-pencil psychometric tests) is inappropriate for many students with physical and mental disabilities, especially those with severe disabilities. Hence, this chapter also includes a discussion of community-referenced vocational assessment, an assessment method better suited to meet the needs of students with severe disabilities. Relatedly, this chapter includes a discussion of curriculum-based vocational assessment procedures, an approach that can also be adopted for use with these and other students.

TRANSDISCIPLINARY SCHOOL-BASED ASSSESSMENT

As stated in Chapter 1, transdisciplinary school-based vocational assessment (TVA) is defined as follows:

A comprehensive assessment conducted within a school setting whose purpose is to facilitate educational and vocational planning in order to allow a student to make a successful adjustment to work and community living. The assessment is conducted by educational, community agency, and state agency personnel, in cooperation and consultation with the student's parents, and incorporates an assessment of the student's psychological, social, educational/academic, physical/medical, and vocational functioning.

As stated previously, the term *transdisciplinary* is used instead of *multidisciplinary* in order to depict the need to involve professionals "across disciplines" in the vocational assessment process. Traditionally, the term *multidisciplinary* has been used in education to depict the need to involve educators from different fields *within* education in a particular process. For example, multidisciplinary teams responsible for identifying students with disabilities are composed of school psychologists, teachers, guidance counselors, school nurses, and school administrators, all of whom are educational personnel based in schools. These multidisciplinary teams do not typically include professionals from outside of the schools (they include professionals from multiple disciplines *within* schools).

Figure 1-1 (p. 23) depicts the transdisciplinary school-based vocational assessment program model. The model is one that involves both school and community-based professionals in the planning and development of school-based assessment programs, and in the gathering and use of assessment data. Four phases are included in the TVA model. Phase 1 involves planning, organizing, and implementing the assessment program. Both community agency and school personnel are involved in this planning. The principles discussed in the previous chapter should form the basis for Phase 1 implementation.

Phase 2 involves conducting an initial level 1 vocational assessment. This assessment yields data that are used to establish educational and vocational objectives to be included in the student's Individual Education Plans and Individual Transition Plans. These data are used for tentative identification of viable vocational training options for students, options which can form the basis for further vocational exploration. Data are also used to identify residential living options for the student, curricula modifications that might be necessary in order for the student to achieve success in vocational training, school-based support services the student may require, and community agency services the student may currently or eventually need in order to make a successful transition from school to work and community living.

Phase 3 consists of specific vocational training (which may occur in a variety of settings). Should additional problems or questions arise about the appropriateness of this training, a level 2 vocational assessment may be conducted. Following this assessment, a revised educational/vocational plan can be developed for the student, and modifications in training can be initiated. Phase 4 follows this training and involves placement in a job, a postsecondary institution, and/or a residential living facility. To facilitate successful transition from school to work and community living, follow up and ongoing support (if necessary) are provided as part of this phase.

Clearly, the extent to which all of the school and community-based professionals listed in Figure 1-1 will actually be involved in the TVA process will depend upon local resources. Thus, the reader should recognize that Figure 1-1 depicts the range of professionals who might actually be involved in the TVA process under ideal conditions. In reality, the implementation of this transdisciplinary model in various locales will differ both in terms of the actual professionals involved and in terms of the roles and responsibilities of these professionals (because of practical and logistical issues; see Chapter 6). Table 1-3 (p. 24) depicts the type of information that ideally should be included in the TVA. Information should be collected on the student's psychological, social, educational/academic, physical/medical, and vocational functioning. Again, practical and logistical issues may influence the extent to which all of this information can be gathered and used by the transdisciplinary assessment team.

A VIRGINIA SPECIAL EDUCATION CONSORTIUM MODEL

The school-based vocational assessment model developed by this author, in consultation with administrators and staff of a Virginia Special Education Consortium (VSEC), provided the generic roots for the transdisciplinary school-based vocational assessment program model just discussed. Although relatively unique, the VSEC assessment program was based upon a two-phase model advocated by the Virginia Department of Education (VDE) and was initially funded by VDE. Similar assessment programs in other localities around the state of Virginia were also based upon such a two-phase model and also received state funding. The following discussion incorporates information on the background of the VSEC, identification of the need for vocational assessment services, initial program planning, the assessment program model, and issues in program development and implementation. This model is presented in some detail in order to illustrate some of the practical and theoretical considerations that must be addressed when developing and implementing a school-based vocational assessment program. In no way, however, should this model be conceptualized as an ideal case study in program development and implementation. Although possessing numerous strengths, it has several limitations as well. A discussion of the program's strenths and weaknesses will follow presentation of the model.

VSEC Background

The VSEC was a regional program that provided special education and related services (e.g., psychological services, itinerant vision services, physical and occupational therapy services) to seven primarily rural public school divisions in southside Virginia. Each district served approximately 2,500–3,500 students. Travel from one end of the consortium to the other could take well over 1 hour. The VSEC operated classes at both the elementary and secondary school levels for students with emotional, learning, and physical disabilities. Classes were held in a centrally located district, so as to minimize transportation time and cost. The school superintendents of each of the seven school districts formed the VSEC administrative council. One superintendent functioned as chief operating officer of VSEC for a term of 2 years, after which another superintendent would assume control on a pre-established and rotating basis. The VSEC employed a consortium director (who reported to the superintendent in charge), a psychologist (who reported to the consortium director), teachers for each of the classes operated (who were jointly evaluated by the consortium director and special education administrator of the district in which the classes were being held), and clerical personnel. Special education directors for each of the school divisions formed an advisory council, which was chaired by the consortium director and which met on a monthly basis. This group would make recommendations regarding programming that would then go to the superintendent's council for formal approval. Partial funding assistance for the VSEC was provided by VDE.

Identification of Need

Innocently enough, the seeds of program development were planted as a result of a Friday afternoon discussion between this author, then a psychologist with the consortium, and the consortium director. In his usual divergent, semidepressive, and unfocused style, this author wondered aloud what benefit, if any, consortium services for the students with disabilities were having. Aware of the unemployment and underemployment rates that characterized individuals with disabilities nationally (see chapter 1), this author reasoned that the students being provided with special education services in the seven counties served by the VSEC were, for the most part, not going to college (because of academic and cognitive limitations) and were having a difficult time getting jobs (because they were not being trained in how to get and keep jobs, and because they were not receiving any specific vocational training). In *his* usual focused, task-oriented, and optimistic manner, the consortium director recommended that a survey be initiated to determine what "graduates" of special education programs in the seven-county area were doing once they finished school, and that a needs assessment be conducted, if necessary, to determine why whatever was happening was happening!

This survey was completed and indicated that a large percentage of students who had "graduated" from special education programs did not go to college, were not employed, and were continuing to live at home. A subsequent needs assessment suggested that (a) students were not being provided with a functional curriculum that taught them job acquisition and job maintenance skills as part of their special education programs and (b) that students were being placed in vocational education programs on a random and inconsistent basis. That is, some districts were ensuring that most if not all of their special education students were afforded some type of vocational training. Other districts were almost totally excluding special education students from vocational education. However, even in districts where students were being placed into vocational education classes, decisions were being made on the basis of inadequate data, or no data at all. For example, in one district, the special education director scheduled special education students for their vocational classes after their "academic" schedule had been prepared. He would do this by comparing the free periods the student had in his or her schedule with openings in whatever vocational classes were scheduled for those periods. Clearly, this haphazard and inconsistent method of making vocational placement decisions resulted in the enactment of a large number of inappropriate placements. That is, students were often being placed into classes in which they were not interested and for which they were unprepared and poorly suited. As a consequence, some students dropped out of school, some instructors asked that certain students be removed from their classes, and some students simply didn't progress at an acceptable rate within the program. Thus, the problem in the districts served by VSEC was not lack of access to vocational education (although this did occur in several districts), but rather the lack of available and appropriate assessment data upon which to make informed decisions about vocational placement. A decision was made to pursue the development of a vocational assessment program to provide school personnel with the information they needed to make better choices about vocational training for the special education students being served by the consortium.

Initial Program Planning

The Virginia Department of Education was initially contacted for assistance in developing a vocational assessment program. At that time, VDE supported the establishment of regionally based vocational assessment programs, and offered regional inservice workshops to school personnel interested in establishing such programs. VDE was also willing to fund the establishment of programs and sent out annual Requests For Proposals (RFPs) to school districts interested in preparing a grant to fund the development of a school-based vocational assessment program. Then, the VDE gave priority to assessment program models that were to be cooperatively established and jointly operated by several school districts (given the limited funds available and the expense associated with establishing comprehensive assessment programs).

Following consultation with the special education directors in the seven counties, approval was given by the superintendents and consortium director for this author (working as the consortium psychologist) to attend a week-long VDE-sponsored workshop on developing and implementing school-based vocational assessment programs. This workshop was jointly conducted by VDE personnel and faculty from the University of Wisconsin-Stout and included consideration of such topics as issues in program development; models of vocational assessment; selecting, using, and interpreting assessment instruments; roles of school personnel; and grant writing. Participants in the workshop were encouraged to go back to their school districts, develop a vocational assessment program model that would adequately serve students with disabilities in their districts and accommodate local resources, and develop a grant proposal to fund costs associated with the development and implementation of the model. This author, in consultation with the consortium director and with the approval of the superintendents, developed a program model and submitted a grant. The grant was funded, and approximately $60,000 was awarded to the VSEC for implementation of the program.

Program Model

Recognizing the comprehensive and expansive nature of vocational assessment, the VSEC developed a two-phase multidisciplinary vocational assessment program model based upon the Vocational Evaluation and Work Adjustment Association's (VEWAA, 1975) definition of vocational assessment mentioned in Chapter 1:

> A comprehensive process that systematically uses work, real or simulated, as the focal point of vocational assessment and exploration, the purpose of which is to assist individuals in vocational development. Vocational evaluation incorporates medical, psychological, social, vocational, and economic data in the attainment of the goals of the evaluation process. (p. 86)

In accordance with the provisions associated with the VDE grant, and consistent with the major population served by the VSEC, the program model was initially designed to service only students with disabilities. However, the model was also designed to be capable of servicing students without disabilities in the seven districts served by the VSEC, should vocational assessment services eventually be expanded to include this population. Because much of the information to be gathered as part of the vocational assessment process was currently being gathered by school personnel within a student's triennial reevaluation process, the model developed was designed to integrate the vocational assessment and special education reevaluation processes.

Federal regulations governing implementation of Public Law 94-142, the Education for All Handicapped Children Act (Department of Health, Education and Welfare, 1977), require that handicapped students receiving special education services be reevaluated for such services once every 3 years, or more frequently if conditions warrant. Such an evaluation must include a number of assessment components and is usually a multidisciplinary endeavor involving a variety of school personnel including regular and special education teachers, school psychologists, school nurses, guidance counselors, school social workers/visiting teachers, and administrators. Purposes of the reevaluation include determining the student's continuing eligibility for special education services, assessing student progress, identifying unmet areas of need, and generating information relevant to the student's future educational programming.

Given that components of a comprehensive vocational assessment (e.g., psychological assessment, medical assessment) were already being administered to all students with disabilities in each of the seven school districts as part of the special education triennial reevaluations, it seemed only appropriate for vocational assessment to be interfaced with this reevaluation process at intermediate and secondary school levels.

As Levinson and Capps (1985) have noted, integrating these two processes has several advantages. First, it provides for a rather time- and cost-efficient assessment process. Rather than having the same school personnel gather the same information at two different points in time for two different purposes, the interfacing of the vocational assessment and special education triennial reevaluation processes reduces redundant information gathering and conserves personnel time (resulting in cost savings). Second, the special education reevaluation process provides a framework for the multidisciplinary cooperation that must exist in a comprehensive vocational assessment program. Given the VEWAA definition of vocational assessment, the vocational assessment process must be one that involves a variety of school personnel. Many of these professionals are the same professionals who are already functioning as a multidisciplinary team involved in completing special education reevaluations. Much of the data gathered by these professionals is the same data that must be gathered as part of a comprehensive vocational assessment. With personnel training and slight modifications in their data-gathering and assessment strategies, these same professionals can be trained to gather additional information relevant to vocational programming, can learn about the vocational relevance of the information they typically gather, and can be trained to use this information to facilitate the vocational planning process. Third, integrating the vocational assessment and special education reevaluation processes ensures a holistic and comprehensive assessment of the student. That is, vocational assessment will not be completed in isolation, but will be combined with psychological, educational, social, medical, and other data to provide a complete picture of the student. An assessment that focused only upon the student's vocational functioning (and ignored other aspects of the student's functioning) would be very narrow in scope and prone to error. Combining the two processes ensures comprehensiveness, and ensures the development of a vocational plan based upon all aspects of the student's functioning. Last, integrating the vocational assessment and special education triennial reevaluation processes ensures the involvement of the school psychologist in the vocational assessment process. Advantages of involving school psychologists in the vocational assessment process have been discussed previously. (See chapter 6.)

The VSEC's vocational assessment and programming continuum and its interfacing of the two processes are described in Figures 7-1 and 7-2, respectively. A Phase I vocational assessment (depicted in Figure 7-3) was conducted at the time of a student's triennial special education reevaluation (or initial special education evaluation used to identify the student as having a disability) in either the 6th, 7th, or 8th grades and was completed by school personnel from the student's home school division. All special education students who were identified prior to their 9th grade year were thus guaranteed to be provided with a Phase I vocational asssessment.

A "vocational specialist" was a member of the multidisciplinary team conducting the evaluation and was responsible for collecting information relative to a student's vocational interests, vocational aptitudes, work attitudes, and general educational development (in reasoning, math, and language). The vocational specialist was a school professional (e.g., psychologist, counselor, teacher) who had volunteered for or who had been nominated to be trained in administering and interpreting the System for Assessment and Group Evaluation (SAGE; Train-Ease Corporation, 1982), a vocationally specific assessment battery. SAGE is a portable assessment unit that provides measures of vocational interests, vocational aptitudes, work attitudes, and general educational development. Four students can be simultaneously evaluated by one professional in approximately 4 hours

Figure 7-1.

VSEC Vocational Assessment and Programming Continuum

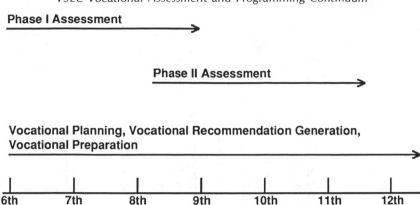

Phase I Assessment

Phase II Assessment

Vocational Planning, Vocational Recommendation Generation, Vocational Preparation

| 6th | 7th | 8th | 9th | 10th | 11th | 12th |

with SAGE. The unit was scheduled into each of the seven school divisions each year for a minimum of a 2-week period to allow for the assessment of all 6th- through 8th-grade students who were due to have their triennial reevaluation completed sometime during that academic year. Other team members, in addition to conducting their usual assessments, were trained to expand their assessment methods and were involved in gathering vocationally relevant data as well. For example, as part of their responsibility in completing a social/family history, the school social worker collected information regarding the vocational aspirations and expectations parents had for their children and the degree to which these expectations and aspirations were realistically attainable. They also gathered information about student interests via parent interviews. Similarly, special education teachers and school psychologists were also involved in interviewing students and gathering similar information. Guidance counselors sometimes conducted

Figure 7-2.

Interfacing of Vocational Assessment with Special Education Triennial Re-Evaluation

Student's Triennial Special Education Re-evaluation	Phase I Assessment	Phase II Assessment
6th Grade	6th Grade	9th Grade - or when needed
7th Grade	6th 7th Grade	10th Grade - or when needed
8th Grade	7th - 8th Grade	11th Grade - or when needed

Figure 7-3.
Phase I Vocational Assessment
(Completed in student's home school division and interfaced with special education triennial re-evaluation)

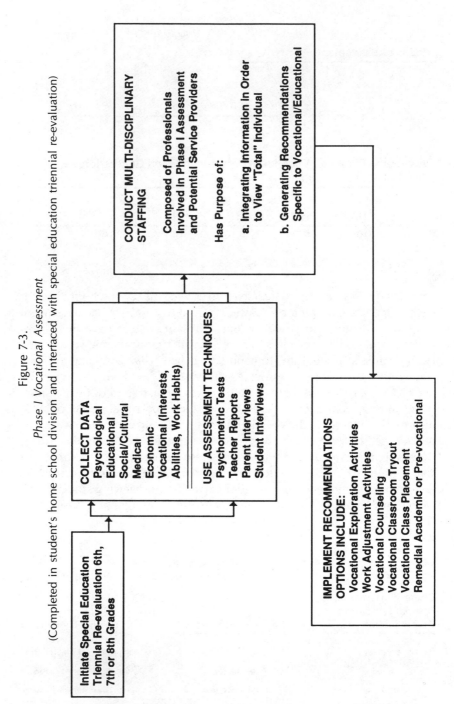

parent interviews and were responsible for reviewing and sharing information present in the student's cumulative folder. School psychologists sometimes expanded their assessment batteries to include measures of vocational interests, work habits, and career maturity. Following information gathering, a multidisciplinary staffing was held in which all information was shared and integrated, and recommendations were made relative to educational and vocational placements and remediation needs.

A Phase II assessment was initiated during the 9th, 10th, or 11th grades upon referral only and was conducted at a regional vocational assessment center. This center was staffed by two full-time vocational evaluators. Students were bused to the center from their home districts each day and remained there for the entire school day. The assessment was conducted over a 4½-day period. Figure 7-4 depicts the Phase II assessment process.

For the majority of students with disabilities in the consortium area, a Phase I assessment was sufficient in providing the information necessary for successful vocational planning. The Phase II assessment was designed for students who needed additional evaluation, or who might have needed an assessment composed of more work-oriented, experientially based assessment devices. Although it was deemed desirable for this Phase II assessment to be interfaced with the special education reevaluation process (for the reasons cited previously), it was recognized that the time at which a student might need and be referred for an assessment might not correspond to the reevaluation anniversary date. Consequently, interfacing of the two processes was encouraged but not required at the Phase II assessment level. Upon referral for a Phase II assessment, all Phase I assessment data were collected, and an initial interview with the student was conducted by a vocational evaluator. Based upon the referral question(s) and information from both the interview and the Phase I assessment, an individualized vocational evaluation plan, designed to answer the referral question(s) posed, was developed for the student by the evaluator. The assessment, conducted over a 4½-day period, utilized work samples, situational assessment, work behavior observation, and, to a lesser extent, psychometric testing. Following the assessment, all information was synthesized, and the student was apprised of the results of the assessment via an exit interview. A vocational evaluation report was written summarizing the assessment results (including recommendations) and was shared with other professionals via a multidisciplinary staffing.

Considerations in Program/Model Development

The above-described model was developed in consultation with the special education directors, vocational education directors, and superintendents of the seven districts served by VSEC. In the course of

Figure 7-4.
Phase II Vocational Assessment
(Completed at comprehensive vocational assessment center, and interfaced with special education triennial re-evaluation, if possible)

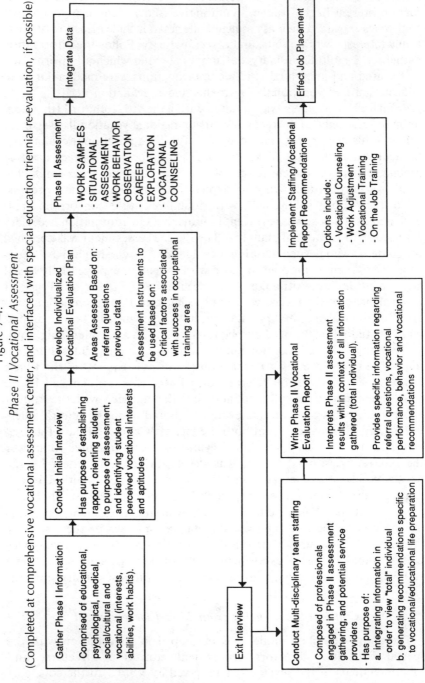

developing the program model, several issues were raised that would influence the model developed and, hence, needed to be addressed prior to development of the model. These issues included whether to develop a regional center–based or local district–based Phase I assessment program, personnel time and cost considerations, demographic characteristics of the VSEC, and the age at which to initiate assessment services.

Regional Center–Based vs. Local District–Based Phase I

In the course of developing the program model, superintendents and, to a lesser extent, special education directors demonstrated a preference for a regional center–based Phase I assessment program. It is this writer's opinion that this preference was motivated by a less than total commitment to providing students with vocational assessment and programming services. That is, the development of a local district–based assessment program would entail greater responsibility and commitment on the part of local district personnel. In such a program, local district personnel would need to oversee the operation of the program and would need to become knowledgeable about vocational assessment service delivery. In a sense, they would need to assume some "ownership" of the program. In contrast, the development of a regional-based center to conduct Phase I assessments would allow local school personnel to avoid almost all responsibilities associated with vocational assessment and programming, other than to identify and transport students and to receive some written report summarizing assessment results.

This writer, with the support of the consortium director, fought for the establishment of a local district–based Phase I assessment program. From a systemic perspective, it was believed that only this type of program would be effective in creating long-term changes in the vocational services being provided to students with disabilities served by VSEC. Only a district–based program would require local school personnel to assume responsibility for effecting change in the type of services being provided to students. A local district–based program would require extensive training of local personnel, thus increasing their knowledge of vocational assessment and programming of students with disabilities. Via such training, local experts in vocational assessment and programming would be developed in each of the districts and could serve as valuable consultants to other personnel. Allowing districts to send their students out of the district to a center for assessment, receiving only a report back, would do little in the way of developing local vocational assessment "experts" who could oversee the entire assessment and programming process and be available to assist other professionals in using assessment information in vocational planning. The development of a regional-based Phase I assessment center would simply entail the hiring of vocational "experts" who would not be a part of any of the school districts served by VSEC and who might have only limited contact with school personnel in these districts. Despite some resistance, special education directors and school superintendents were eventually convinced of the benefits of a local district–based Phase I program and were accepting of the development of a program model based upon this concept.

Personnel and Time Costs

Because the grant received by VSEC provided funding for only 1 year, and because the funds available for hiring new personnel were limited and finite, administrators raised concerns about the ongoing, postgrant funding requirements of the program. An argument based on this issue was partially used to convince administrators to support a district-based Phase I assessment program. That is, the costs associated with employing additional vocational evaluators to staff and operate a Phase I assessment program would be significantly greater over time than would be retraining existing personnel to conduct the Phase I assessments within their own districts. Although this argument encouraged support for a district–based Phase I program, it also raised concerns about the amount of personnel time that would need to be devoted to the program.

The development of a model that integrated the special education triennial reevaluation and vocational assessment processes assisted in allaying concerns over personnel time. However, the Phase I model developed did require that an existing member of the school staff be trained to function as a "vocational specialist" and assume major responsibility for the "vocationally specific" component of the overall assessment. Thus, the amount of time required of this staff member was of concern to administrators. Decisions regarding the model developed, the equipment selected for use in the Phase I program, and the means by which this equipment was to be scheduled into and used in each district were made so as to reduce personnel time and involvement. Essentially, districts were encouraged to identify a staff member who could be trained as a vocational specialist whose primary responsibility was other than teaching and whose schedule provided some degree of flexibility (most districts nominated professionals like guidance counselors, psychologists, or itinerant teachers who could block out periods of time to devote to this process). Based upon the model developed, the number of students to be provided with a Phase I assessment in each district each year (which was usually not more than 30–35), and the time associated with administration of the equipment selected for use in the Phase I program (SAGE and associated checklists and rating forms), it was estimated that approximately 2 to 3 weeks of this staff member's time would be associated with administration, scoring, interpreting, and integrating vocational assessment data each year. This estimate was in addition to the amount of time the staff member might already be spending on involvement in the special education reevaluation process (most identifed professionals were already involved in this process in some way). Superintendents were accepting of this commitment of staff time.

Demographic Characteristics

The demographic characteristics of the local area also influenced development of some aspects of the program model. VSEC districts were rural, sparsely populated, and spread out over a relatively large geographical area. The decision to develop a district-based Phase I assessment program was partially based upon the transportation costs (from both a time and financial perspective) associated with the operation of a regionally based Phase I assessment center. The costs associated with transporting assessment equipment from one district to another would be considerably less than would be transporting students to a center. However, equipment selected for use in the Phase I program would need to be portable. Given that this writer was to be primarily responsible for transporting the equipment, the only cost for transportability would be mileage allowance. However, this required that equipment selected for use and eventually purchased be capable of fitting into this writer's 1979 Ford Mustang (which had well over 100,000 miles on it!). The portability of the SAGE was a major factor influencing its selection for use in the Phase I assessment program.

Age to Begin Assessment

The age at which to initiate the assessment program was a major concern in program development. Although most districts were accepting of the ages/grades specified in the model previously described, other districts were not. To some extent, this decision was one that was made individually in each district. That is, while most districts initiated the Phase I assessment in the 6th, 7th, and 8th grades, some districts decided to initiate this assessment in the 7th, 8th, and 9th grades instead. These decisions were made on the basis of career development theory and local logistics, including the age or grade at which students in a particular district were eligible for placement in a vocational training program. Several other decisions needed to be made on a district by district basis as well, as described in the following section.

Issues in Program Implementation

Given that VSEC was composed of seven different school districts, each possessing some unique local characteristics, it would have been naive to think that the above-described model could be implemented in exactly the same manner in each district. Prior to program implementation, this writer consulted separately with personnel from each VSEC district to discuss implementation of the assessment model. These meetings provided an opportunity to identify and address any district-based concerns about the implementation of services and allowed for the development of a Phase I assessment implementation plan unique to that district. The slight modifications to the general assessment model that were made in each district had several benefits. First, they allowed for the development of an assessment program that better "fit" the district (i.e., made better use of local resources, worked around local concerns or problems, or was more consistent with local philosophy). Second, they enabled local school personnel to assume some ownership in the development of the program. That is, as the suggestions and recommendations of local school personnel were used to modify the existing model slightly, local personnel began to see the model as their own. With such ownership came greater commitment to the vocational assessment process; with greater commitment came a greater chance for successful implementation of services.

Several issues regarding program implementation were consistently raised and addressed in district meetings. These issues were the age at which to begin assessment, selection of instruments, personnel involvement and roles, site selection, and paper flow/timelines/logistics.

Age at which to begin assessment. Although this issue was addressed on a more general level when developing the original program model, concerns about the age at which to begin the Phase I assessment continually resurfaced in district meetings. For philosophical and programmatic reasons, several districts believed that grade 6 was too early to initiate a comprehensive vocational assessment for all special education students. In other cases, grade 6 was opposed by a district because 6th-grade students were housed in a different building than were 7th-, 8th-, and 9th-grade students. Hence, in these districts, including 6th-grade students in the assessment program presented logistical complications. Based upon these and other concerns, several districts shifted their Phase I assessment program from the 6th, 7th, and 8th grades to the 7th, 8th, and 9th grades. The Phase II assessment, which was based upon referral only, did not need to be altered as a result of such a change and, in most cases, was not modified.

Selection of instruments. To some extent, the selection of instruments was based upon the decisions previously described. That is, instrument selection was based upon the age of students to be assessed, the type of students to be assessed, and the demographic characteristics of the VSEC districts. Practical considerations such as ease of use, amount of training required, portability, cost, or administrative convenience were other factors considered. Psychometric characteristics were also assessed in the selection of instruments. VSEC personnel visited other vocational assessment programs to observe the use of instruments being considered for selection and solicited recommendations and evaluations from assessment personnel from other districts. VSEC personnel also contacted vendors of assessment equipment and invited them to demonstrate their equipment.

Personnel involvement and responsibilities. This issue generated considerable debate and required that an extensive amount of time be devoted to its discussion and resolution. First, a decision needed to be made about who would assume the role of "vocational specialist" and be responsible for the vocational component of the overall assessment. Generally, the special education director in each county surveyed several staff members about their interest in assuming this responsibility. After several candidates were identified, the special education director and superintendent considered the impact of selecting each of the candidates from a time and scheduling perspective, and eventually nominated a candidate for training.

Decisions also needed to be made about the roles of existing multidisciplinary team members in the vocational assessment data-gathering process. For example, who would interview a student's parents about vocational aspirations and postschool plans? Who would interview the student about his or her interests and perceived abilities? Would the psychologist be asked to incorporate a measure of career maturity or vocational interests into the assessment batteries? What role would the student's teacher assume in the process? Each district considered these and other personnel questions, and each district made different decisions about who would do what in the process. Decisions were made on the basis of such factors as personnel expertise, interest, or time availability. Although a student interview was a required component of the vocational assessment process, in some districts the student's teacher assumed major responsibility for conducting the interview, and in other districts, the psychologist assumed major responsibility for it. Once all decisions about personnel responsibilities were made, they were integrated into the district's Phase I implementation plan. Personnel training needs were then identified, and plans to initiate such training were made.

Site selection. Districts needed to decide where they would conduct their Phase I assessments. Site selection was based upon these and other criteria: Sites had to be strategically located to reduce transportation time and cost; had to be large enough to accommodate the SAGE equipment, one staff person, and four students at a time; had to have adequate ventilation, lighting, and furniture; and had to have a room that could be scheduled on a rather flexible basis.

Paper flow/timelines/logistics. A host of decisions needed to be made about who would complete what form, when the forms would be completed, and the order in which forms would flow from one staff member to another. Relatedly, decisions had to be made about when during the school year different parts of the Phase I assessment would be completed. These decisions were based upon the personnel responsibilities identified previously, and the work schedules of involved staff members. Individual forms were often modifed for use within a district.

Based upon the district modifications outlined above, each district developed a Phase I Assessment Implementation Plan. This plan identified the steps involved in the Phase I assessment and identified personnel responsibilities and paper flow. Implementation plans varied from one district to another. A diagram depicting the Phase I assessment plan developed by one VSEC district appears in Figure 7-5. The "basic" forms used in this and other districts are included in Appendix A. These forms included a referral form, a data collection/summation form, a student interview form, a parent interview form, a living skills checklist, and a Phase I vocational assessment report form. Additionally, a vocational education course information form was used to gather information about the requirements and demands of every vocational education class offered in the VSEC school districts, and a form was also used to evaluate the adequacy of potential vocational assessment center sites. The actual steps involved in the Phase I assessment, as determined by local personnel in one VSEC district, were as follows (NOTE: the term *vocational evaluator* is used to describe the staff member trained to function as a vocational specialist in the district):

1. The special education administrator identified all students with disabilities in grades 7, 8, and 9 who were due for their triennial special education reevaluation during the academic year and sent a parent interview form and a living skills checklist to the school social worker/visiting teacher.

2. The school social worker/visiting teacher completed the parent interview form and part of the living skills checklist during a home visit and returned these forms to the special education administrator.

3. For each student, the special education administrator completed a portion of the data collection/summation form (which provided background information gleaned from a review of the student's cumulative and confidential files) and sent this form and the living skills checklist to the student's special education teacher.

4. The special education administrator contacted the VSEC and scheduled the SAGE equipment for use in the district.

5. The special education teacher completed the remainder of the data collection/summation form, conducted a student interview, and completed the student interview form, work behavior and work skills checklist, and living skills checklist. These forms were then forwarded to the vocational evaluator.

6. The VSEC delivered the materials for administration of the SAGE interest inventory and assessment of work attitudes to the district.

7. The vocational evaluator scheduled and conducted a group administration of the interest inventory and assessment of work attitudes to all students who were to receive a Phase I assessment during the current academic year.

8. The VSEC delivered the remainder of the SAGE (aptitude battery and tests of general educational development) to the district.

9. The evaluator administered the remainder of the SAGE to all students who were to receive a Phase I assessment during the current academic year.

10. The vocational evaluator integrated all assessment information gathered from the forms received and from the finished assessment, and completed the Phase I vocational assessment report form.

11. The vocational evaluator presented the results of the vocational component of the overall assessment to other staff members as a member of the multidisciplinary team responsible for completing the student's special education triennial reevaluation.

12. Other multidisciplinary team members (e.g, psychologist, nurse, counselor, or teacher) presented the results of the assessments (some of which also included vocationally specific information about the student), all assessment information was integrated and synthesized, and broad recommendations regarding educational and vocational programming were made.

13. The student's teacher developed a skeletal IEP based upon assessment results and contacted the vocational evaluator to schedule an IEP conference.

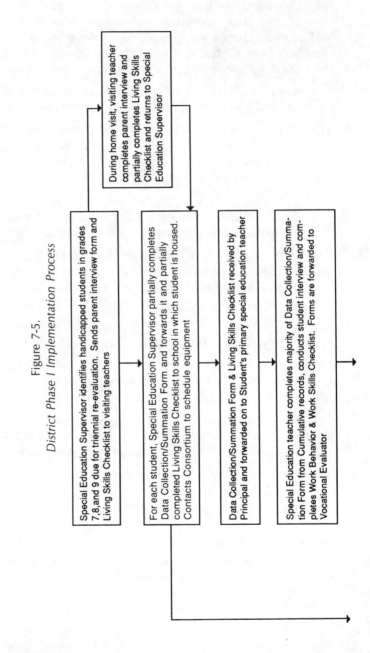

Figure 7-5.

District Phase I Implementation Process

During home visit, visiting teacher completes parent interview and partially completes Living Skills Checklist and returns to Special Education Supervisor

Special Education Supervisor identifies handicapped students in grades 7, 8, and 9 due for triennial re-evaluation. Sends parent interview form and Living Skills Checklist to visiting teachers

For each student, Special Education Supervisor partially completes Data Collection/Summation Form and forwards it and partially completed Living Skills Checklist to school in which student is housed. Contacts Consortium to schedule equipment

Data Collection/Summation Form & Living Skills Checklist received by Principal and forwarded on to Student's primary special education teacher

Special Education teacher completes majority of Data Collection/Summation Form from Cumulative records, conducts student interview and completes Work Behavior & Work Skills Checklist. Forms are forwarded to Vocational Evaluator

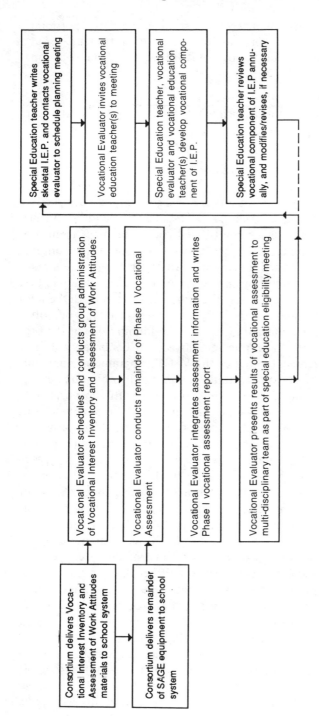

14. The vocational evaluator contacted the student's parents, appropriate vocational education teachers, and other selected staff members, and together these professionals wrote an IEP that included a vocational component.

15. The student's teacher reviewed the vocational component of the IEP annually and, in consultation with other staff members, modified and revised it.

Discussion

The detailed description of the preceding program was designed to exemplify the many theoretical and practical issues to be addressed when developing and implementing a school-based vocational assessment program. Although the program described above has numerous advantages and illustrates many of the actions that need to be taken by professionals when developing assessment programs, it is far from a case study in best practice. Clearly, when one compares the above description with the steps involved in developing and implementing assessment programs described in the preceding chapter, one can identify several limitations of the process described above. For example, employer and community agency involvement was extremely limited in the VSEC program development. No interagency agreements were formulated during the program planning phase, and no clear plan for providing students with the postschool services they might need to secure and maintain employment was developed. Although program objectives were implied (to improve the placements of students with disabilities in vocational training programs, and to facilitate acquisition and maintenance of employment), they were not formally agreed upon by districts and stated in writing. As such, no plan for program evaluation could be or ever was developed. Some of the assessment instruments used in the program lacked desirable psychometric characteristics (the SAGE, for example). Despite a clear elucidation of the strengths and weaknesses of the many instruments being considered for use in the program, some instruments were selected on the basis of cost and convenience factors rather than on the basis of their psychometric properties. Last, one could argue that the time at which the Phase I assessment was initiated (6th grade) was too early to obtain reliable and valid results. Although career development theory does suggest that students at these ages will be progressing through the interest and capacity substages of the growth stage (and, hence, an initial assessment of interests and aptitudes is appropriate at this time), one could also argue that many students with disabilities will demonstrate delayed career development and will not be at this developmental stage at this age/grade.

As will be discussed shortly, however, beginning assessment at the earliest developmentally feasible age has several advantages.

The program described above possessed numerous strengths. Integrating the vocational assessment and special education reevaluation processes served to conserve personnel time and to encourage a holistic assessment of the student. Vocational planning was embedded within the context of more general planning for the student. The expertise of existing personnel was used in an effective manner, and the program was modified to meet the unique needs of particular VSEC districts. Assessment was initiated early enough in a student's academic career so as to allow time for the development of skills necessary for successful functioning in vocational education classes. Frequently, vocational assessments are conducted so late in a student's academic career that, despite identifying an appropriate course of vocational training, there is not enough time to prepare the student for success in the vocational training program prior to the student's enrollment in the program or there is too little time to prepare the student for employment before the student graduates from school. By initiating the assessment in the 6th, 7th, and 8th grades, school personnel had 2 to 5 years to prepare a student for enrollment in a specific vocational training program, and 4 to 6 years to prepare the student for postschool functioning.

The program not only assessed a student's personal characteristics but also the demands and requirements of various vocational education classes. Thus, placement decisions were made on the basis of a "match" between the student and the educational/work environment, rather than on the basis of a student's characteristics alone. That is, factors such as the amount of reading required in a particular vocational education program, and the degree to which grades in the program were based upon projects or paper-and-pencil tests, were considered along with the student's strengths and weaknesses when making placement decisions. This too is consistent with the "person–environment fit" notion incorporated in many career development theories (discussed in chapter 2). The program described above also involved vocational education teachers in the vocational planning process. Traditionally, there has been little communication between special education and vocational education teachers. Special education teachers have assumed major responsibility for the educational planning of students with disabilities. In terms of integrating vocational objectives into a student's IEP, the lone involvement of a special education teacher is often insufficient. Vocational education teachers are generally more knowledgeable than are special education teachers about the skills necessary for success in vocational education classes and in jobs that emanate from training in specific areas. As such, they can function as valuable consultants to special education teachers when making vocational decisions and when developing vocational objectives for students.

A PENNSYLVANIA MODEL:
MIDWESTERN INTERMEDIATE UNIT IV

Midwestern Intermediate Unit IV (MIU) provides special education and related services to 27 school districts and 3 vocational schools in three largely suburban/rural counties in Pennsylvania. MIU is governed by a 13-member board. Board members are elected from each of the 27 districts' public school directors. The executive director of the intermediate unit is the administrative officer of the board. The superintendents from the 27 school districts serve in an advisory capacity to the executive director and meet regularly to exchange information on current educational issues and intermediate unit programs and services. Funding for the MIU is provided by state subsidies, local district contributions, and state and federal grants. MIU provides services for moderately, severely, and profoundly retarded students and students with mild disabilities. It also provides audiological testing, physical and occupational therapy services, preschool programming, psychiatric evaluation, psychological services, social worker services, speech and hearing services, and services for visually and hearing impaired students.

Initial planning for the vocational assessment program began in 1988, at which time an advisory committee consisting of 10 staff members from various disciplines within special education began the process of developing a program model. The MIU vocational assessment program model is depicted in Figure 7-6. Table 7-1 depicts the information-gathering process inherent in the MIU model. The model integrates the career education, career exploration, and vocational assessment processes and consists of three distinct phases. Conceptualizing vocational/career development as a lifelong process, Phase I is initiated in kindergarten and continues through the 6th grade. It consists of career awareness activities interspersed with some initial data-gathering activities. During grades 1–5, background and demographic information on a student are gathered, and the student is afforded an opportunity to participate in activities designed to facilitate increased knowledge of job families, acquisition of positive work attitudes and social skills, and the development of a positive self-concept. A comprehensive psychological/multidisciplinary team evaluation is completed during the 6th-grade school year for all students identified as having a disability. School personnel involved in this evaluation include regular and special education teachers, guidance personnel, regular and special education administrators, school psychologists, parents, school nurses, school social workers/home school visitors, and other professionals, depending upon the student's needs (i.e., psychiatrist, audiologist, speech therapist, physical/occupational therapist, physicians). Following the completion of this evaluation, a team staffing is conducted that includes the student's parents. Parents are provided with feedback on the results of the psychological/MDT evaluation and are provided with a projected timeline of vocational assessment/career exploration/vocational planning that is to take place within the next 5 years. Vocational/career education goals are identified and are included as an addendum to the student's IEP. All gathered information is summarized in a student's School-Vocational Program Plan (SVPP), which becomes a part of the student's permanent record for the remainder of his or her school career. In a fashion similar to the VSEC model just described, the MIU model integrates the vocational assessment and special education reevaluation processes. (Both are conducted simultaneously during the 6th and 9th grades.)

Phase II of the model encompasses grades 7–9. During this second phase, career exploration activities are initiated and are provided to students via guidance classes, industrial arts classes, home and family living classes, shop classes, and home economics classes. Formal vocational assessment is also initiated during this phase, and provides a basis for the exploration activities conducted. Interest inventories are administered in the 8th grade, and aptitude measures are administered in the 9th grade. A prevocational skills checklist, which measures self-help skills, social and interpersonal skills, and other work-related behaviors, is also administered to the student during this phase of assessment. During the 9th grade, students are again provided with a comprehensive psychological/multidisciplinary team re-evaluation. This evaluation may be expanded to include additional assessment of interests and aptitudes, if necessary. All assessment data are integrated, and a staffing, including parents, the school psychologist, the special education teacher, guidance personnel, and a representative from the vocational school targeted to serve the assessed student, is conducted. Because students can formally enter vocational education in either the 10th or 11th grades, one purpose of the staffing is to identify an appropriate vocational education program for the student and any educational provisions that may need to be made for the student within the program. Vocational objectives are further delineated, an individual transition plan is developed, and all information is integrated into the student's SVPP.

Phase III encompasses grades 10–12 and emphasizes postschool planning. As the student is provided with vocational services, checklists are completed by instructors to monitor the student's progress and to identify any areas of unmet need. These are incorporated into the student's SVPP. Should vocational placement decisions need to be reconsidered, or should additional assessment need to be initiated, services are provided by the Office of Vocational Rehabilitation or the Bureau of Vocational Services.

Figure 7-6.
Midwestern Intermediate Unit (Pennsylvania) Model

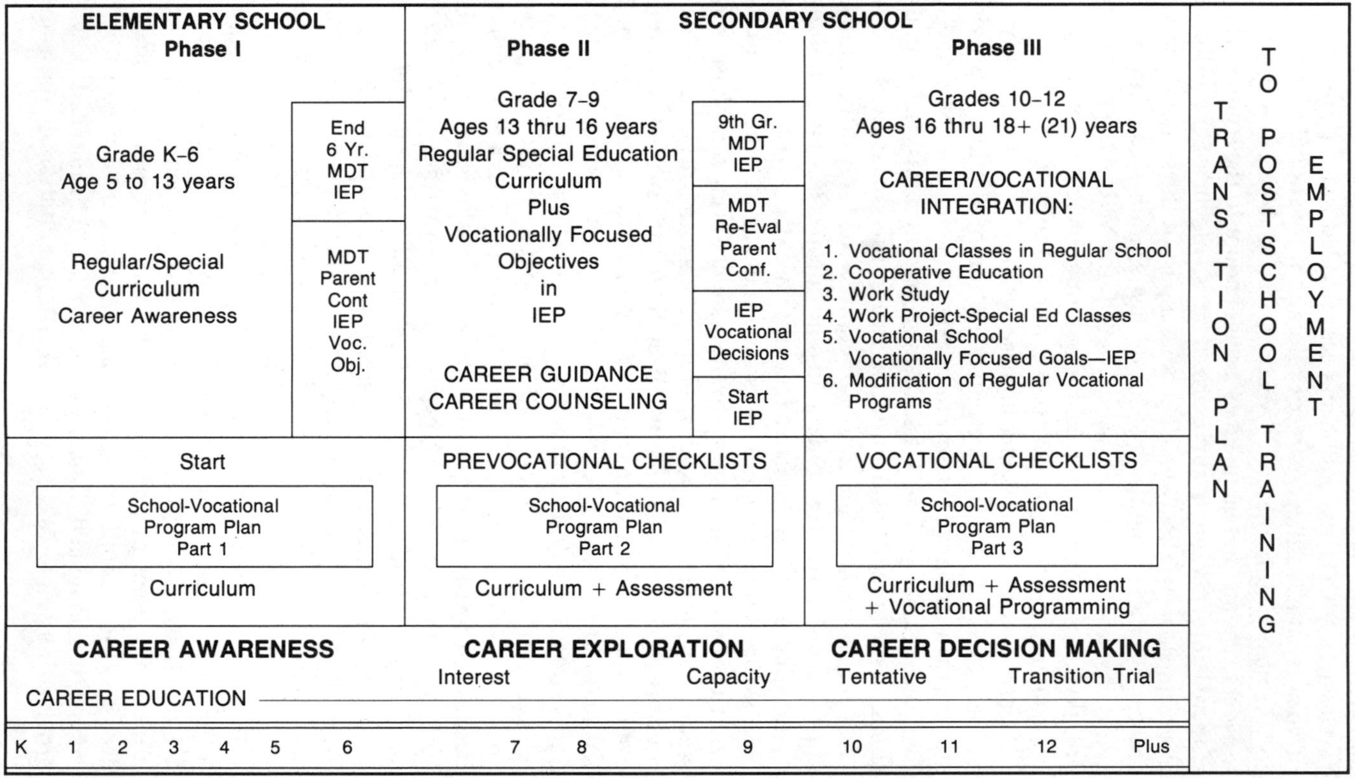

TO POST SCHOOL EMPLOYMENT
TRANSITION PLAN
TRAINING

ELEMENTARY SCHOOL
Phase I

Grade K-6
Age 5 to 13 years
Regular/Special
Curriculum
Career Awareness

End 6 Yr. MDT IEP

MDT Parent Cont IEP Voc. Obj.

Start
School-Vocational Program Plan Part 1
Curriculum

SECONDARY SCHOOL

Phase II

Grade 7-9
Ages 13 thru 16 years
Regular Special Education Curriculum Plus Vocationally Focused Objectives in IEP

CAREER GUIDANCE
CAREER COUNSELING

9th Gr. MDT IEP

MDT Re-Eval Parent Conf.

IEP Vocational Decisions

Start IEP

PREVOCATIONAL CHECKLISTS
School-Vocational Program Plan Part 2
Curriculum + Assessment

Phase III

Grades 10-12
Ages 16 thru 18+ (21) years

CAREER/VOCATIONAL INTEGRATION:

1. Vocational Classes in Regular School
2. Cooperative Education
3. Work Study
4. Work Project-Special Ed Classes
5. Vocational School
   Vocationally Focused Goals—IEP
6. Modification of Regular Vocational Programs

VOCATIONAL CHECKLISTS
School-Vocational Program Plan Part 3
Curriculum + Assessment + Vocational Programing

CAREER EDUCATION

CAREER AWARENESS

CAREER EXPLORATION
Interest   Capacity

CAREER DECISION MAKING
Tentative   Transition Trial

K	1	2	3	4	5	6	7	8	9	10	11	12	Plus

Table 7-1.
Midwestern Intermediate Unit (Pennsylvania) Instrumentation,
Timeline and Personnel Responsibilities

	INFORMATION	PERSONNEL	TIMELINE
Phase I	1. Demographic Information	Administrator Guidance Teacher Secretary	Begin when student first identified
	2. Medical Information	School Nurse Secretary	——
	3. Permanent Record: Attendance Report Card Grades Group Test Scores	Administrator Guidance Personnel Secretary	——
	4. Psychological/ MDT Data	School Psychologist Special Education Teacher	——
	5. Parent Checklist Conference Form	MDT Staff	6th Grade IEP
Phase II	1. Adaptibility Checklist	Teacher	Middle School Years
	2. Family Intake Information	Home-School Visitor Guidance Personnel Social Worker	——
	3. Parent Checklist	Parents/Guardians	——
	4. Prevocational Inventory (PACG)	Teacher	——
	5. Student Evaluation Form	Teacher	——
	6. Interest Inventory	School Psychologist Guidance Personnel	——
	7. Parent Checklist Conference Form	MDT Staff	8th/9th Grade IEP
	8. Initial Transition Plan (ITP)	IEP Team	8th/9th Grade IEP
	9. Student Interview Form	School Psychologist Guidance Personnel	8th/9th Grade
Phase III	1. Student Evaluation Form (RE-EVAL)	Teacher—Regular, Special, Vocational	9th to 10th Grade
	2. Vocational Assessment Results	School Psychologist Vocational Evaluator	8th to 10th Grade and Beyond
	3. Vocational Inventory (VACG)	Teacher—(R, S, V)	Every Year Beginning in 9th to 10th Grade
	4. Cooperative Competency Checklist	Teacher—(R, S, V)	——
	5. Work Behavior Work Skills Checklist	Teacher—(R, S, V)	——
	6. Living Skills Checklist (Low EMR, TMR, PMR)	Teacher—(R, S, V)	——
	7. Work Activity Assessment Profile	Teacher—(R, S, V)	——
	8. Community Assessment	Work-Study Vocational Teacher or Coordinator	10th Grade
	9. Student Work Experience Assessment	——	10th to 12th Grade
	10. Student Interview Form	School Psychologist Guidance Personnel	Every other year starting at 8th to 9th grade
	11. Transition Plan (ITP)	IEP/ITP Team	Every other year starting at 8th to 9th grade
	12. Parent Checklist Conference Form	Educational Staff	As needed

A TENNESSEE MODEL:
TENNESSEE DEPARTMENT OF EDUCATION

A three-level vocational assessment model similar to the MIU model just presented has been developed by the Tennessee Department of Education, Office of Special Education Programs, Division of Vocational Education (Tennessee Department of Education, 1987). In this model, a Level I and Level II assessment are provided to all secondary special education students. A Level III assessment is provided when additional information is needed to recommend vocational programming for the student. A Level I assessment consists of data traditionally gathered as part of a student's special education evaluation. A Level II assessment consists of interest and aptitude assessments. A Level III assessment (if needed) utilizes experientially based assessment techniques, including work samples and situational assessment techniques. This model is depicted in Figure 7-7.

Figure 7-7.
Tennessee Three-Level Vocational Assessment Process

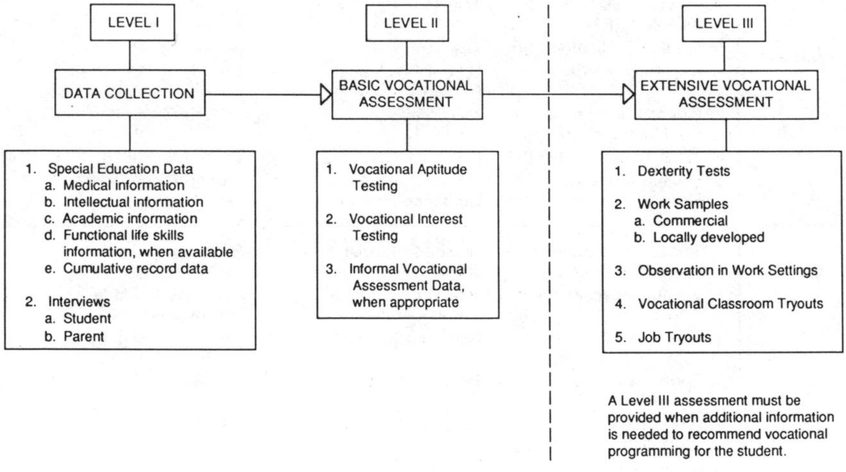

A NORTH CAROLINA MODEL:
NORTH CAROLINA DEPARTMENT OF PUBLIC INSTRUCTION

The North Carolina Department of Public Instruction has developed a vocational evaluation/assessment program model that incorporates the assessment of vocational interests, academic development, learning styles, vocational aptitudes, worker characteristics (work traits and employability skills), and special needs and includes a counseling component (Thomas & Coleman, 1988). The three phases consist of a prevocational evaluation (Phase I), a vocational assessment (Phase II), and a vocational evaluation (Phase III). Figure 7-8 depicts this three-phase model.

Phase I — Prevocational Evaluation

The prevocational evaluation is administered in the 8th grade or is provided to any student at any grade level who is suspected of having problems with activities of daily living, or job-related skills or behaviors (job-seeking or job-maintenance skills). The skills and behaviors assessed during the prevocational evaluation are those that should be attained prior to the initiation of any specific vocational training and are those skills that are universally necessary for successful acquisition and maintenance of employment. These skills include basic self-help and daily living skills (like grooming and hygiene), interpersonal skills, academic skills, job seeking skills, and work habits. This evaluation is to be conducted by classroom teachers, counselors, and other existing school personnel primarily using existing information on the student. A review of the student's cumulative file, observation of the student's current performance in school, and background information gleaned from parent and student interviews would all be a part of the prevocational evaluation. Administration of an interest inventory might also be a part of this Phase I assessment. Should significant problems be identified, a more comprehensive assessment by a vocational evaluator might be recommended. This evaluation would utilize a wide range of instruments and techniques designed to pinpoint specific problems and would last approximately 3 to 8 hours depending upon the student's needs. Results are used to plan remedial activities, develop vocational exploration activities, determine the need for career counseling, assist in career planning, and facilitate the development of vocational objectives to be included in the student's IEP.

Phase II — Vocational Assessment

This second phase of vocational assessment is administered to students in the 9th, 10th, and 11th grades, and to 12th-grade students who demonstrate vocational indecision. It is timed to be administered just prior to the student's enrollment in a vocational training program. The purpose of the assessment is to determine what curriculum needs and modifications should be made in the training program in order to optimize the student's chances for success in the program. The establishment of realistically attainable vocational objectives is another objective of the assessment.

Figure 7-8.
North Carolina Three-Phase Assessment/Evaluation Process

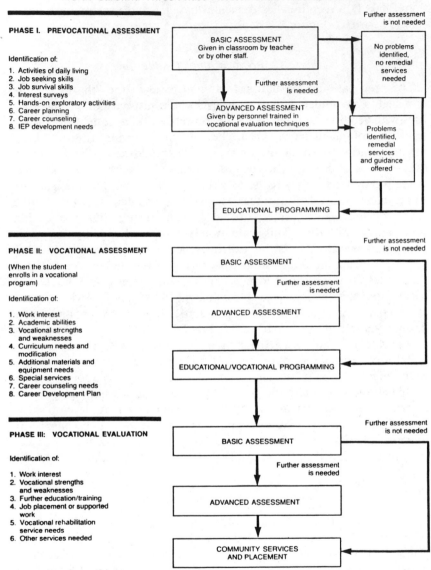

This assessment is designed to assess the student's achievement, intelligence, personality, interests, aptitudes, and work values using standardized tests and work samples. If a more comprehensive assessment is needed, students are referred to a vocational evaluator. This comprehensive assessment would involve an evaluation of the student's dexterity, aptitude, and achievement and would take between 3 and 20 hours, depending upon the student's needs.

Phase III — Vocational Evaluation

This final phase of assessment is administered to 11th- and 12th-grade students, depending upon need. When the previous phases have been inadequate in identifying and meeting a student's vocational needs, a Phase III evaluation is recommended. Because it is generally too late to focus the assessment on needs that can be adequately addressed with school-based services, and because most students recommended for this evaluation are already likely to have been provided with the school-based services available, the Phase III evaluation focuses on the postschool educational, vocational, and support services the student might need or profit from. That is, the goal of the Phase III evaluation is to identify appropriate job placements or supported work environments for the student, and to determine what community services the student might need in order to make a successful transition from school to work and community. Essentially, the same instruments used in the previous phase are utilized in this phase of the program, only with a different goal and focus. Again, a more comprehensive/advanced assessment can be provided to the student at this level, should the basic assessment be inadequate.

A TEXAS MODEL: TEXAS EDUCATION AGENCY

Texas has developed a three-level vocational assessment program model (Texas Education Agency, 1985). Vocational assessment is considered to be a continuous process that occurs throughout a student's participation in vocational programs. Although the model does not clearly specify when each phase of the model should be implemented with a particular student, it does offer guidelines as to when to conduct assessments. A student entering vocational programs during the 7th or 8th grades is recommended to have a basic vocational assessment during the first year of participation in the vocational education program. A student planning to enter a vocational program in high school is recommended to have a basic vocational assessment in the year prior to entry into the program. For those students who participate in vocational programs at the 7th- and 8th-grade levels but do not enroll in vocational programs until the 10th or 11th grade, it is recommended that an additional vocational assessment designed to update records be initiated during the year prior to entry into vocational education at the high school level. The Texas model does not specify the roles and responsibilities to be assumed by various school personnel and suggests that administrators from each district assign personnel vocational assessment responsibilities based upon their qualifications. The model suggests that vocational assessment may be the responsibility of a single person or be assigned to different personnel on either a part-time or full-time basis. The model suggests that the following areas be included in the assessment: basic skills (reading comprehension, spelling, grammar, functional math, measurement, money handling), sensory and motor skills (dexterity, coordination, strength, mobility, range of motion, visual acuity, auditory acuity), learning preferences (receptive and expressive), vocational skills and aptitudes (use of tools, materials, equipment, general potential for work), career awareness and interest (knowledge of jobs, expressed interest, observed interests, etc.), and behavior (worker characteristics and habits, job-seeking skills, job-keeping skills).

Basic Vocational Assessment (Level I)

Level I assessment is designed to provide a summary of all preexisting information on the student that is relevant to vocational programming and involves data collection and interpretation rather than additional testing. Cumulative and confidential records are reviewed to gather information on grades, attendance, academic achievement, discipline, and health. Confidential records maintained for students with disabilities who have already been placed in special education programs will provide information on intelligence, achievement, adaptive behavior, personality, and any instructional modifications or support services needed by the student. Interviews with parents, teachers, and the student are also a part of Level I assessment and are designed to gather the aforementioned information, in addition to the student's career aspirations and expectations, interests, work habits, and future plans.

Basic Vocational Assessment (Level II)

The Level II assessment involves the collection of vocational interest and vocational aptitude data. Tests and other assessment devices are used to determine the student's vocational interest, aptitudes and abilities, awareness of vocational options, and work-related behaviors.

Additional Vocational Assessment (Level III)

A Level III assessment is conducted when school personnel cannot identify long-range goals for students, or cannot place them in a vocational program based upon the information gathered from the first two levels of assessment. This additional assessment may utilize work samples and include a variety of observational and exploratory experiences in vocational education classes.

A REHABILITATION MODEL: THE HIRAM G. ANDREWS VOCATIONAL REHABILITATION CENTER, JOHNSTOWN, PA

Traditional vocational rehabilitation center evaluation procedures provided the generic roots from which school-based vocational assessment services developed. The Hiram G. Andrews Vocational Rehabilitation Center in Johnstown, PA, is a comprehensive vocational rehabilitation facility that offers vocational training in 36 areas ranging from semiskilled to technical levels, including 2-year college-level programming in accounting and drafting. The center is accredited by the Commission for Accreditation of Rehabilitation Facilities, the National Association of Trade and Technical Schools, and the Pennsylvania Department of Education. The types of disabilities served at the center include physical disabilities, emotional disturbance, mental retardation, learning disabilities, neurological impairment, blindness, deafness, and other educational and cultural disadvantages. The center works with local school districts in vocational programming and transitioning of students with disabilities by providing vocational evaluation services to secondary school students. The vocational evaluation program is supervised by a subdoctoral-level certified school psychologist who possesses certification as a vocational evaluator, 10 years of experience as a school psychologist, and 20 years of rehabilitation experience.

The vocational evaluation program is a 2-week, 3-track, multidisciplinary process that involves four vocational evaluators, a licensed clinical psychologist, a master's-level vocational guidance counselor, and three counseling assistants. Figure 7-9 and Table 7-2, respectively, illustrate the overall evaluation program and a typical schedule of 2-week evaluation activities for high school students served by the center. During intake, students are provided with an orientation to the center, and the purpose and nature of the evaluation are explained. Previously gathered background information (i.e., psychological, educational, medical) on the student is gathered, reviewed, and combined with a medical/physical assessment and reading assessment to plan an individual evaluation program for the student. Based on this assessment, the student is placed in one of three evaluation tracks: high verbal, low verbal, and individualized. Although the dimensions assessed in each of these tracks are similar, the methods used to conduct the assessment differ. Whereas the high verbal and low verbal tracks both utilize group-administered assessment procedures, the latter employs assessment techniques that require little reading

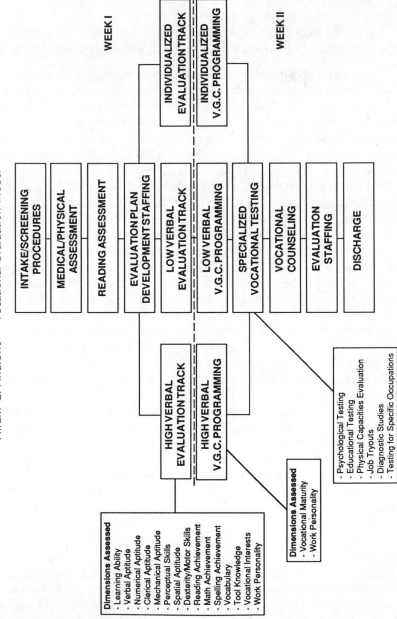

Figure 7-9.
Hiram G. Andrews — Vocational Evaluation Model

Table 7-2.
Hiram G. Andrews Individual Vocational Evaluation Schedule—High School Students

			Factors Evaluated

Week I

Tuesday	9:30	Intake	
	9:45	Evaluation Orientation Film	
	10:00	Gates MacGinitie Reading Survey	(Reading Achievement)
	11:00	Basic Skills in Arithmetic/C-CAT	(Arithmetic Achievement)
	11:30	Revised BETA	(Vocational Learning Aptitude)
	12:30	Lunch	
	1:00	Return Home	
Wednesday	9:30	Social & Prevocational Information Battery	(Formal assessment of Life Skills Development and Vocational Interest)
	11:00	Interest Inventory	
	12:30	Lunch	
	1:00	Return Home	
Thursday	9:30	Work Sampling	(Functional assessment of work behavior, interests, self-evaluative skills, verbal comprehension, clerical perception, motor coordination, and physical capacities)
		—Want Ads Comprehension	
		—Record Checking	
		—Filing	
	12:30	Lunch	
	1:00	Return Home	
Friday	9:30	Work Sampling	(Functional assessment of work behavior, interests, self-evaluative skills, verbal comprehension and usage, numerical reasoning, spatial reasoning, form perception skills, and physical capacities)
		—Message Taking	
		—Making Change	
		—Blueprint Reading	
	12:30	Lunch	
	1:00	Return Home	

Week II

Monday	9:30	Work Sampling	(Functional assessment of work behavior, interests, self-evaluative skills, spatial reasoning, clerical perception, manual dexterity, motor coordination and physical capacities)
		—Graphics Illustration	
		—Zip Coding	
		—Bottle Capping	
	12:30	Lunch	
	1:00	Return Home	
Tuesday	9:30	Work Sampling	(Functional assessment of work behavior, interests, self-evaluative skills, numerical skills, clerical skills, finger dexterity, motor coordination, and physical capacities)
		—Payroll Computation	
		—Mail Sorting	
		—Electronic Connector Assembly	
	12:30	Lunch	
	1:00	Return Home	
Wednesday	9:30	Vocational Guidance Center	(Functional assessment of vocational interest, career maturity, and job-seeking skills)
		—Self-Directed Search	
		—Interest Check List	
		—Job Application	
		—Career Maturity Inventory	
	12:30	Lunch	
	1:00	Return Home	

(continued)

Table 7-2.

(Continued)

			Factors Evaluated
		Week II (continued)	
Thursday	9:30	General Aptitude Test Battery	(Formal assessment of specific vocational aptitude)
	12:30	Lunch	
	1:00	Return Home	
Friday	9:30	Vocational Counseling —Individualized Supplemental Testing —Computerized Job-Ability Matching —Consults	(Developmentally appropriate Job-Ability Matching and Career Awareness Experiences)
	12:30	Lunch	
	1:00	Return Home	

and focus upon occupational alternatives more appropriate for those who possess limited verbal skills. Students whose special needs preclude the use of group-administered tests are provided with one-to-one assessment in the individualized evaluation track. The latter is particularly appropriate for severely impaired students, or students who are particularly disruptive, hyperactive, or inattentive. Assessment techniques used in the program include psychometric tests, work samples, situational assessments, and job tryouts.

Following completion of the assessment component of the program, students are afforded an opportunity to explore various occupations consistent with their assessment results in the center's vocational guidance center (VGC). Specialized testing of a student's interests, career maturity, and knowledge of job-seeking skills may also be completed while the student is exploring occupations in the VGC. Following exploration, students are provided with vocational counseling designed to assist them in using the assessment data in decision making. A multidisciplinary staffing is conducted to synthesize assessment results and to develop an Individualized Written Rehabilitation Plan (IWRP) for the client. The IWRP, similar in nature to an IEP, is a plan developed between a rehabilitation counselor and a client that designates services and techniques/methods that will be used to assist the client in formulating and achieving realistic vocational goals.

COMMUNITY-REFERENCED VOCATIONAL ASSESSMENT

As has been alluded to previously, the use of traditional paper-and-pencil, norm-referenced assessment procedures with many students with disabilities, especially those with more severe disabilities, is problematic for several reasons. Often, these instruments have not been standardized on students with disabilities and have not even included members of this population in the standardization sample. Because acculturation of the norm sample deviates significantly from that of the student being assessed, scores yielded by the test are invalid for the student. Also, the standardized method for administering these assessment instruments penalizes students because of their disability. Students with physical disabilities, for example, are often penalized on timed tasks for slow responses. In such cases, test scores are reflective of the physical disability rather than of the trait purported to be measured by the test. Hence, the score becomes an invalid measure of the trait assessed by the test. Unfortunately, many pencil-and-paper assessment instruments also lack acceptable psychometric properties (reliability, validity) for students with low incidence and severe disabilities. This too renders them unacceptable for use with these students. Because of these and other reasons, traditional psychometric instruments are often improperly interpreted by professionals when used with students who have severe disabilities and are of limited usefulness in vocational planning. Results of traditional vocational assessment instruments often yield little if any usable information for such students, do not adequately reflect the available employment options in the local community, and often result in restricting or limiting the vocational opportunities of students with severe disabilities.

For these reasons, a community-referenced vocational assessment model is advocated in lieu of a traditional vocational assessment model for students with severe disabilities (Rudrud, Ziarnik, Bernstein, & Ferrara, 1984). According to Rudrud et al. (1984), a community-referenced assessment system provides a proactive alternative to traditional vocational assessment (which relies heavily on standardized norm-referenced procedures) and is designed to answer the following key questions:

What local job opportunities exist into which students with severe disabilities could be successfully placed, following appropriate training?

Which of the available jobs does the student prefer?

Which tasks of the available/preferred job can the student competently perform, and, conversely, which of these tasks will the student need to be trained to perform?

How well is the student progressing toward acquiring the skills needed to perform the job competently?

There are several steps involved in implementing a community-referenced vocational assessment program. These include surveying employers to identify local job opportunities, screening all identified jobs, identifying the skills needed to perform each job, identifying which job(s) the student prefers, assessing the student's ability to perform the job, and training the student to perform the job.

Surveying Employers to Identify Job Opportunities

A variety of methods can be used to survey local employers in an attempt to generate a listing of available job opportunities for students with severe disabilities. Telephone or mail surveys can be utilized. Interviews can be conducted with local employers. Local business/industrial councils and organizations can be contacted, and a representative of the school system can request a meeting to present information about the employability of students with disabilities to potential employers. Leads on potential employment opportunities can also be identified through state vocational rehabilitation agencies, sheltered workshops, labor unions, employment offices, the local chamber of commerce, and through local advocacy and support groups for individuals with disabilities.

Screening All Identified Jobs

Not all of the jobs identified via employer surveys will prove to be appropriate for students with severe disabilities. Jobs should be screened on the basis of education, certification/licensure, and prior experience requirements. All characteristics of the identified jobs should be noted, including the cognitive and physical demands of the job, the tools and equipment used to perform the job, and the environmental conditions under which the job is performed. Obviously, the screening of jobs must take into consideration the characteristics and needs of the individual student, as well as the demands and requirements of the identified job. Although Rudrud (1981) and Rudrud et al. (1984) recommend that jobs that require a high school diploma or have additional educational requirements, require any specialized certification or licensure, or require any previous work experience be screened out, these screening guidelines may not always be appropriate. Professionals should define the characteristics of the disability group targeted for community-referenced vocational assessment services and should identify screening guidelines based upon the prevailing characteristics of this population. For example, if it is unlikely that most of the students targeted for these services will receive a high school diploma, then jobs that require such a diploma should be screened out. The screening guidelines to be established in a particular locality should depend upon the population of students targeted for community-referenced vocational assessment services and the prevailing characteristics of the majority of these students.

Identifying the Job Preferences of Students

For many of the reasons cited previously, the use of paper-and-pencil interest inventories will be inappropriate when identifying the job preferences of students with severe disabilities. Rudrud et al. (1984), in discussing the mentally retarded student, have indicated several problems that exist when attempting to assess job preferences of students with severe disabilities by using traditional interest inventories. These include low reading ability, unrealistic impressions of job requirements, limited life and job experiences, and limited knowledge about the nature of various jobs. Of particular importance are the limited life and work experiences these students frequently possess. It is inappropriate to assess students' preference for something they know little or nothing about. Clearly, it is important to acquaint a student with a particular job before assessing that student's interest in the job. The importance of doing this with students who have less severe disabilities is minimized because their normal life experience allows them to come into contact with, and learn about, many different jobs on their own.

A variety of techniques exist for assessing the job preferences of students with severe disabilities. Most of these techniques require locally developed procedures, and all expose the student to all available jobs before assessing the student's preference for any one of the jobs. Techniques that can be employed include slide/tape presentations, site visits, work/job tryouts, work samples, and situational assessment.

Slide/Tape Presentations

Following the identification of available job opportunities, professionals can construct a slide/tape presentation to demonstrate and explain the various functions of each identified job. This presentation should show the job being performed in a real-life work environment, should sample all major functions of the job, should show other students with disabilities performing the job (if possible), and should use language easily understood by students. Some assessment of the extent to which students have derived an adequate understanding of each job should be incorporated into this procedure. Following the slide/tape presentation and some assurance that students have derived an adequate understanding of the various jobs depicted, students can be asked to indicate their job preferences.

Site Visits

Students can take actual tours of work sites in which the identified jobs are being performed. While in such settings, a professional should explain what each job is and explain the major functions of each job. Explanations should be in language easily understood by the student. Students should have an opportunity to observe as many different job functions as possible and should have an opportunity to observe students similar to themselves performing the job. Following the tour, knowledge of different jobs and job preferences can be assessed.

Work/Job Tryouts

In addition to visiting work settings and observing the identified jobs being performed by others, students may be afforded an opportunity to perform aspects of the jobs themselves. In most cases, it may be necessary for a professional to provide some initial training. Hence, a student may observe the job being performed by another, attempt to perform aspects of the job by modeling the individual observed, be provided with feedback and some minimal training, be given an opportunity to practice the job again, and so on. This observation–modeling–feedback–practice–feedback process would not only allow professionals to assess a student's job preferences via observation and postobservation assessment, but would also allow for some assessment of the student's ability to learn the job (i.e., would allow for an assessment of aptitude or ability as well as interest or preference). However, given the limited amount of training that would be associated with such a procedure, the assessment of a student's ability to learn the task is likely to be unreliable.

Work Samples

Various work samples can be developed to replicate certain aspects of all identified jobs. Students can be trained to perform these locally developed work samples and, following their involvement with them, express their preferences. Again, a student's interests (and, to a lesser extent, abilities) can be assessed both during the student's involvement with the work sample (via observation and interview) and following involvement with all work samples.

Situational Assessment

Professionals can establish in-school situations that simulate various aspects of the identified jobs, or use/modify existing situations. For example, school cafeterias can be used to simulate a variety of food service jobs that may exist in the local community. School janitors or maintenance personnel can assist in establishing a means of assessing interest in custodial services or maintenance jobs. The school bookstore might provide a means of assessing interest in retail sales jobs. Vocational education classes/shops may provide a suitable location for establishing other simulations. Situational assessment techniques should be used in a fashion similar to that described for the other procedures discussed here. That is, students should be given an opportunity to explore all simulations prior to their preferences being assessed. It is important to ensure that all important aspects of identified jobs are in some way represented in the developed simulations. Prior to assessing preferences, it is important to ensure that students have derived an adequate understanding of each job as a result of participating in the simulation. In all cases, individuals working with the student at the job site need to be consulted regarding the student's learning style, temperament, frustration tolerance, and other issues that may have an impact on the assessment.

Identifying the Sequential Skills Necessary to Perform Each Job

Each identified job should be task-analyzed to determine the exact sequence of skills necessary to perform the job competently. This sequential listing of skills can be used to assess a student's ability to learn a job and to train the student to perform the job. Two broad methods of identifying job skills exist: descriptive validation and comparative validation (Schutz & Rusch, 1982). Descriptive validation involves the use of surveys or interviews that are designed to allow experts in the field to identify and describe the specific skills they believe are important in their jobs. Comparative validation involves the actual observation of workers performing their jobs, and the recording of the specific tasks performed. Moyer and Darwig (1978) have suggested several procedures for conducting task analysis, including observing an expert perform the job, performing the job yourself, working backward through a task, and brainstorming (having several people familiar with the task work together to generate a sequential listing of skills). Clearly, some combination of descriptive and comparative procedures should probably be used when conducting a task analysis.

Assessing the Student's Ability to Perform the Job

Once the sequential skills necessary to perform a given job and the student's preference for available jobs have both been identified, the student's ability to learn the skills associated with specific jobs can be assessed.

Ideally, the decision about which job a particular student should be trained to perform should be based upon both the student's preferences and ability to learn the skills associated with a job. Certainly, decisions should not be based upon preferences (interests) alone. The amount of time necessary for a student to learn a particular job should be considered. Curriculum-based assessment procedures, to be discussed in the next section, can be used to assess the amount of time a student may need in order to acquire necessary skills.

Ideally, students should be given an opportunity to learn some of the beginning skills associated with several of the jobs for which they have demonstrated a preference. The amount of time it takes the student to learn these skills can be combined with the number of skills to be learned (in order to qualify for entry-level employment) to *estimate* the amount of time that may be necessary to train the student for that job. Clearly, this is a rough estimate at best, given that the amount of time needed to learn each skill will vary. Any special problems that may be associated with training a student in a particular job may also be identified. As Rudrud et al. (1984) note, it is particularly important to incorporate whatever competitive standards exist in a job into the assessment process. That is, in order to be employable in a given position, an employee must often be able to complete a given task in a certain amount of time, or with a certain degree of accuracy. The degree to which a student can perform (or can be trained to perform) each task in accordance with these standards must be evaluated. Based upon the student's preferences, an estimate of the student's ability to learn the skills associated with a particular job, *and* the amount of time projected to train a student for that particular job, a final decision can be made about job training. Several techniques can be used to assess the student's ability to learn a particular job including work samples, situational assessment strategies, and work tryouts. Each of these procedures has been discussed elsewhere.

Training a Student to Perform the Job

Once the job the student is to be trained to perform has been identified, training can be initiated. Training will require use of specific behavioral principles and should be taught in sequence. The teaching process should involve several steps including establishing criteria for successful performance of the task, breaking the task down into its component parts (task analysis), assessing the student's current level of performance on the first component of the task, teaching the first component of the task, assessing student performance, reteaching (and reassessing) until mastery, and so on. Given the difficulty many students with severe cognitive disabilities have generalizing skills, this training should occur in the setting in which the job is to be performed. Often, job coaches can be used to conduct this training and can complete aspects of the job the student is unable to perform. This guarantees to the employer that a particular job will be performed competently from the beginning of training and, as such, reduces employer resistance to training and placement.

CURRICULUM-BASED ASSESSMENT

Curriculum-Based Assessment (CBA) can be defined as a system for determining the instructional needs of a student based upon the student's ongoing performance within existing course content in order to deliver instruction as effectively and efficiently as possible (Gickling, Shane, & Croskery, 1989). CBA uses a curriculum's scope and sequence to assess the student's instructional needs and progress. The curriculum's scope and sequence usually consist of a list of important concepts, skills or procedures taught within the curriculum, along with a specification of the sequence and the grade level in which these are to be taught.

CBA can be used to determine (a) the extent to which a student possesses the entry-level skills necessary for success in a given vocational program; (b) the time frame necessary for a student, with training and assistance, to develop the entry-level skills necessary for success in a given vocational training program; (c) the effectiveness of any support or assistance provided to a student; (d) the appropriate entry-level point for instruction within a curriculum for a particular student; and (e) the length of time necessary for a student to acquire the skills necessary for entry-level employment in a given area. CBA can also assist in determining the reasons why a student may be having difficulty learning specific skills.

As an example of how CBA may be used for several of the aforementioned purposes, assume that Table 7-3 lists the specific math skills necessary for success in a beginning automotive servicing training program (Table 7-3). Further assume that we are concerned with whether an 8th-grade learning disabled student will be able to acquire most of the prerequisite math skills necessary for success in the automotive servicing program within the next 2 years (assume students enter the program in 10th grade). Using test items that were developed and keyed directly to each math competency, the teacher (or other professional) would:

1. Determine which math competencies the student had already mastered and where in the curriculum instruction should be initiated.
2. Begin instruction of math competencies.
3. Determine the length of time necessary for the student to acquire each competency.

Table 7-3.
Sample Vocational Math Competencies

Specific math skills to be learned in order to perform occupational tasks at satisfactory levels.

Vocational Math Competencies

Identify, read, write whole numbers

Perform addition, subtraction—whole numbers

Perform multiplication, division—whole numbers

Express fractions in lowest terms

Express fractions as equivalents

Change whole numbers to fractions

Change fractions to whole numbers

Perform addition, subtraction using fractions

Peform multiplication using fractions

Identify, read, write, decimal numbers

Round off decimal numbers

Identify place value of decimals

Perform addition, subtraction of decimal numbers

Perform division, multiplication of decimal numbers

Use the table of decimal equivalents

Perform simple percentages

Measure using English linear measurements

Identify and read temperature scale

Read a volt meter

Read an amp meter

Identify and read volume measurements

Measure time, speed

Perform money calculations

Read a bar and circle graph

Perform basic key functions using a calculator

Measure and construct angles with a protractor

Measure and identify pipe sizes

4. Determine the "average learning time" necessary for competency acquisition. (For example, if the student required 2 weeks to acquire one competency and 4 weeks to acquire another competency, 3 weeks would be an estimate of the amount of time the student would need to master each competency; thus 3 weeks would be the student's "average learning time." Because competencies vary in difficulty level, an estimate of average learning time should be based on the acquisition of many competencies over a period of months and should only be considered an estimate.)

5. Multiply "average learning time" by number of competencies to be learned to determine total length of time necessary for the student to acquire all entry-level competencies (interpret this as an *estimate*).

6. Compare amount of time needed by the student to acquire all competencies with the amount of time available for instruction prior to enrollment in the program (2 years) to estimate the student's readiness for the program at enrollment time.

The same steps outlined above could be used to estimate the length of time necessary for a student to acquire all of the vocational competencies needed for entry-level employment in an occupational area. Because many students will be provided with special instruction or some type of remedial or support service designed to assist them in learning, CBA is often used to assess the effectiveness of these services, or to determine which type of service might be most effective for a particular student. The same steps as outlined above would be used to do this. For example, assume two different support services were being considered for a particular student. The student could be instructed in a traditional fashion with no support service for a period of time. This could be followed by instruction with support service #1 for a period of time, and with instruction with support service #2 for a period of time. Average time required for competency acquisition using each of these procedures could be determined and could be compared to assess the differential effectiveness of the services.

CBA procedures can also be used to develop local norms for comparison purposes. For example, the amount of time required of "average" 10th-grade students to acquire vocational competencies in a particular vocational class can be determined. Should a learning disabled student be "mainstreamed" into this class, CBA can be used to determine if the student will be able to progress in the program (with or without support services) at about the same rate as other students in the class. These data can be used by the TVA team in determining the appropriateness of (a) placement in the regular vocational class without assistance or modification, (b) placement in a regular class with assistance or modification, or (c) placement in a special vocational class.

Although CBA possesses numerous advantages and is extremely popular at the current time, the research base underlying CBA is still in the developmental stage (Rosenfield & Kuralt, 1990). Thus, CBA should be used cautiously and should be combined with data generated from other sources and techniques when used for decision-making purposes. For more information on CBA models and procedures, readers are referred to Idol, Nevin, and Paolucci-Whitcomb (1986) and Tucker (1985).

SUMMARY

This chapter has described several school-based vocational assessment program models that have been developed for use in various states, including the Virginia Special Education Consortium model developed by this author. Although the models discussed in this chapter share several characteristics, each is unique in that it was developed to accommodate local concerns and resources. Because the models described were primarily developed to service students with mild disabilities and are not fully applicable to students with more severe disabilities, this chapter also included a discussion of community-referenced vocational assessment and curriculum-based assessment procedures. In particular, community-referenced vocational assessment procedures should be considered for use with students who have severe cognitive disabilities. When developing a vocational assessment program model, professionals must consider both the resources and characteristics of the locality in which the program will operate, and the students the program will serve. It is hoped that the models described in this chapter will serve as a starting point for those professionals who are beginning to develop assessment program models in their local school districts.

REFERENCES

Department of Health, Education and Welfare. (1977). Education of handicapped children. *Federal Register, 42*(163), 42474-42518.

Gickling, E. E., Shane, R. L., & Croskery, K. M. (1989). Assuring math success for low-achieving high school students through curriculum-based assessment. *School Psychology Review, 18*, 344-355.

Idol, L., Nevin, A., & Paolucci-Whitcomb, P. (1986). *Models of curriculum-based assessment*. Rockville, MD: Aspen.

Levinson, E. M., & Capps, C. F. (1985). Vocational assessment and special education triennial reevaluations at the secondary school level. *Psychology in the Schools, 22*(3), 283-292.

Moyer, J. R., & Darwig, J. C. (1978). Practical task analysis for special educators. *Teaching Exceptional Children, 11*, 16-18.

Rosenfield, S., & Kuralt, S. K. (1990). Best practices in curriculum-based assessment. In A. Thomas & J. Grimes (Eds.), *Best practices in school psychology II*. Washington, DC: National Association of School Psychologists.

Rudrud, E. (1981). Job openings and client placements: Over and under-met needs. *Vocational Evaluation and Work Adjustment Bulletin, 14*, 80-82.

Rudrud, E., Ziarnik, J., Bernstein, G., & Ferrara, J. (1984). *Proactive vocational habilitation*. Baltimore, MD: Paul H. Brookes.

Schutz, R. P., & Rusch, F. R. (1982). Competitive employment: Toward employment for mentally retarded persons. In K. P. Lynch, W. E. Kiernan, & J. A. Stark (Eds.), *Prevocational and vocational education for special needs: A blueprint for the 1980s*. Baltimore, MD: Paul H. Brookes.

Tennessee Department of Education. (1987). *Vocational assessment information*. Nashville: Author.

Texas Education Agency. (1985). *Serving special needs students in vocational education*. Austin, TX: Author.

Thomas, S. W., & Coleman, N. (1988). *Vocational assessment training manual*. Raleigh, NC: Division of Vocational Education, North Carolina Department of Public Instruction.

Train-Ease Corporation. (1982). *System for Assessment and Group Evaluation*. Pleasantville, NY: Author.

Tucker, J. (Ed.). (1985). Curriculum-based assessment [Special Issue]. *Exceptional Children, 52*(3).

Vocational Evaluation and Work Adjustment Association. (1975). Vocational evaluation project final report [Special Edition]. *Vocational Evaluation and Work Adjustment Bulletin, 8*.

8 VOCATIONAL PLANNING, PROGRAMMING, AND SERVICES

Vocational assessment data are designed to be used by school-based professionals to assist in vocational planning. As such, professionals who are involved in the vocational assessment process should have an understanding of the various uses of vocational assessment data and of the types of programs and services that may be recommended and enacted based upon the results of the completed assessment. To this end, this chapter discusses the use of assessment data in vocational planning and includes a discussion of career education, transition services, vocational training options, employment options, and sources of career information. The chapter begins with a brief discussion of professional staffings, report writing, and the development of Individual Education Plans.

INTEGRATING ASSESSMENT DATA: THE STAFFING

The transdisciplinary school-based vocational assessment process is one in which various school professionals, using different assessment tools and techniques, are responsible for gathering information about a student. Although the data-gathering responsibilities of these professionals will vary from one school setting to another, the assessment process will be one in which *different* professionals gather *overlapping* information about a student using *different* assessment techniques. This "triangulation" of data-gathering techniques, discussed in chapter 4, is designed to minimize instrumentation and assessor variables in data gathering, and to increase the reliability and validity of the overall assessment process.

The staffing provides an opportunity for involved professionals to share with one another the information they have gathered about the student. Based upon such information sharing, the transdisciplinary team can synthesize and integrate this information, draw conclusions about the student's functioning in the assessed areas, and develop educational and vocational recommendations. The goal of the staffing is to develop an integrated and holistic picture of the student's current functioning and educational/vocational needs.

Although it is beyond the scope of this chapter to discuss issues related to the effectiveness of team functioning, it should be noted that competent team functioning is likely to result in productive planning. However, group decision making is not automatically effective, nor is it necessarily more effective than individual decision making (Huebner & Hahn, 1990). Team members must possess certain skills in order for the team to function effectively. Thus, transdisciplinary teams should be trained prior to their functioning. According to Dyer (1987), the team should develop procedures for (a) facilitating effective communication, (b) clarifying roles, (c) setting goals, (d) solving problems, (e) developing collaboration of effort, (f) ensuring follow-through and completion of tasks, and (g) conducting product and process evaluations. Team members should be trained in group process, problem-solving, and communication skills. Clear roles should be established for team members, and a team leader should be identified. A systematic approach that draws upon the resources of all team members for communicating, organizing, and utilizing assessment data should be established. In most cases, team building and training should take place prior to the implementation of assessment services. However, this process should be conceptualized as both an initial and *ongoing* process, in that it will often be necessary to integrate new team members and retrain existing team members over time. For more information on effective team functioning, readers are referred to Huebner and Hahn (1990), Dyer (1987), and Maher and Yoshida (1985).

Based upon the transdisciplinary staffing, a vocational assessment report should be developed that clearly summarizes the findings of the assessment and the recommendations of the team. These findings and recommendations should be integrated into the Individual Education Plans of all students with disabilities who are assessed.

THE VOCATIONAL ASSESSMENT REPORT

The vocational assessment report is designed to be a permanent record of the assessment and should clearly communicate the transdisciplinary team's findings and recommendations. According to McCray (1982), the VEWAA-CARF Vocational Evaluation and Work Adjustment Standards with Interpretive Guidelines and VEWAA Glossary (1978) define the vocational evaluation report as:

A well planned, carefully written means of communicating vital vocational information about a client. It is a studied, permanent record of significant vocational data observed as a client and an evaluator interact in various types of work or work-like situations. It puts the plan, action, findings, logic, and interpretation of the evaluation in writing. It usually includes a picture of the client's worker traits and how they compare to minimal requirements of selected jobs or work areas, physical capacities, learning ability, personal characteristics, social competence, other vocational factors, and recommendations for future services. It may also provide a prescriptive-descriptive sequence of experiences which are aimed at maximizing an individual's vocational potential. (p. 16)

The transdisciplinary vocational assessment report should integrate the findings of all team members and should minimally include the following information: identifying information, reason for referral/purpose of assessment, background information, assessment techniques/methods/strategies used, behavioral observations, assessment results, summary, and recommendations. A more detailed outline of this recommended format is provided in Figure 8-1.

Although the professional who is responsible for writing the transdisciplinary vocational assessment report will vary from one setting to the next, this person should be chosen carefully. Because the report is designed to communicate to others what must be done in order for the student to progress, the evaluation itself may be of limited value if the report is poorly written. That is, if the report does not adequately communicate to other professionals what services must be initiated and what these professionals must do to accommodate and meet the needs of the individual student, the value of the assessment may be lost.

Although other members of the team may be responsible for producing their own reports (i.e., a school psychologist may produce a report on the psychological evaluation completed), the vocational assessment report should be a holistic report that integrates and summarizes all assessment results. Thus, major findings of the school psychologist (already discussed in detail in the psychological report) should be summarized and reproduced in the vocational assessment report as well. The same is true of other professionals (e.g., guidance counselor, social worker) who might be involved in the assessment and who might produce their own individual reports.

In order to assist professionals in producing effective reports, the following guidelines and suggestions, adapted from Sattler (1988), are offered:

— Write the report as soon as possible after the staffing.

— Write clearly and coherently and explain findings in sufficient detail but as simply as possible.

Figure 8-1.
Suggested Vocational Assessment Report Format

Student Name: _____   Birth Date: _____

Address:_____   Age: _____

_____   Parent's Name: _____

Phone: _____   Teacher: _____

School:_____

Purpose of Assessment:

Assessment Techniques Utilized:

Background Information:

Assessment Results:

—Psychological Functioning

—Educational/Academic Functioning

—Social Functioning

—Vocational Functioning

—Physical Functioning

Summary and Recommendations:

Transdisciplinary Team Conducting Assessment:

_____   _____
Vocational Evaluator   Teacher

_____   _____
Psychologist   Teacher

_____   _____
Guidance Counselor   Community Agency Representative

_____   _____
Teacher   Community Agency Representative

— Include only assessment results that are believed to be both reliable and valid. Generalizations should only be made from reliable findings that form a consistent and clear pattern.

— Interpretations of the student's performance should take into account *all* sources of available information.

— If scores are reported, provide a precision range or confidence interval for the scores so as to reduce potential misinterpretation. (See chapter 3 for a discussion of confidence intervals and precision ranges.)

— Organize assessment results by detecting common themes through and across procedures and use these themes for summarizing major findings.

— Emphasize strengths rather than weaknesses, abilities rather than disabilities, and omit information that has little relevance or importance or may be potentially damaging to the student.

— Be definitive in writing when the findings are clear; be cautious in writing when the findings are questionable.

— Use behavioral examples (i.e., behaviors in which the student engaged during the assessment) to support whatever inferences or interpretations are drawn.

— Deemphasize a listing of test scores and instead interpret what the scores mean. Focus on describing the student, not the test or the student's test scores.

— Use percentile ranks whenever possible to describe a student's performance (because they are easily understood by parents and other professionals).

— Reduce or eliminate the use of technical terms and jargon that might be misunderstood by others.

— Ensure that the report is written in a grammatically correct fashion.

Recommendations that emanate from the transdisciplinary vocational assessment should be included in the report and should address the following issues:

1. designing appropriate instructional adaptations or curriculum modifications, so as to increase the likelihood of student success in vocational and academic classes;

2. developing specific vocational objectives, including recommendations for vocational exploration, vocational or postsecondary training, job placement, and residential living/community functioning, which can be incorporated into the student's IEP and ITP;

3. identifying prevocational training needs;

4. identifying any adaptive equipment that the student might need in order to achieve success in vocational or postsecondary training and community functioning;

5. designing any behavioral treatment strategies that may need to be implemented;

6. identifying any community agencies with which the student should become involved, or support services (psychological counseling, for example) that the student should receive.

INDIVIDUAL EDUCATION PLAN DEVELOPMENT

Results of the transdisciplinary vocational assessment should be used to develop a vocational component to a student's IEP, which should be included even at the elementary school level. P.L. 94-142 requires that the IEP include several components such as:

—A statement of the student's current level of educational performance. This should include a statement about functioning in the following areas: academic achievement, social functioning, prevocational and vocational skills, psychomotor skills, and self-help/independent living skills.

—A statement of the annual goals that describe the educational performance expected by the end of the academic year.

—A statement of short-term instructional objectives in each area.

—A statement of the specific educational and support services needed by the student. This includes all related special education support services and any special instructional or curricula modifications necessary so as to increase the student's chance of achieving success in a given program.

—The date when all of the above-listed services will commence, and the length of time for which they will be provided.

—A description of the extent to which the student will participate in the regular educational program.

—A justification for the educational placement being enacted.

—A listing of the professionals responsible for delivering the needed services (implementation of the IEP).

—Objective criteria for evaluating the extent to which educational objectives have been met.

Additionally, for students who are 16 years of age or older (or for younger students when considered appropriate), the IEP must include a statement of services the student needs in order to make a successful transition from school to work and community living.

Wehman, Moon, Everson, Wood, and Barcus (1988) have offered some guidelines regarding the vocational issues that should be addressed within the IEP at various educational levels. These objectives are largely drawn from career education, which will be discussed shortly. Because career awareness is a major developmental objective during the elementary school years, Wehman et al. (1988) recommend that objectives designed to teach students about the importance and value of work, the rewards that exist in different jobs, and the role of different workers should be included in the IEPs of elementary school students. Additionally, they recommend that the IEP address the self-care and independent living skills, functional academic skills, and social skills necessary for employment and community adjustment.

In that career exploration is a major developmental objective during the middle school years, Wehman et al. (1988) recommend that the IEP continue to include activities designed to expose students to various jobs at this level. Also at this level, they recommend that the IEP continue to address communication, self-care, and independent living skills and begin to address work habits and the specific vocational training necessary to secure eventual employment in the local area. At the middle school level, the IEP should also address the community services a student may need in order to make a successful transition from school to the workplace and community. As such, the IEP might be expanded to include the development of an Individual Transition Plan (ITP), and the team responsible for developing the IEP might be expanded to include community agency personnel.

Career preparation and job placement should be emphasized at the high school level. As such, Wehman et al. (1988) recommend that the IEP/ITP at the high school level emphasize activities necessary to facilitate successful transition from school to work and community living. Objectives related to specific vocational training, residential living, and placement should be included in the IEP/ITP at the high school level.

PROFESSIONAL ATTITUDES/VALUES IN THE PLANNING AND PLACEMENT PROCESS

As Levinson, Peterson, and Elston (in press) have suggested, the extent to which assessment data are successfully used to plan an appropriate vocational program for a student may depend upon the attitudes and values possessed by the professionals involved in the planning. Professionals must believe that, with proper vocational training and support services, all individuals with disabilities can be fully employed. Professionals should be familiar with best practices in providing vocational training and support services, preferably have direct experience with individuals with disabilities who have been successfully employed, and understand the increasing range of jobs in which these individuals have been successfully placed. Professionals working with individuals with disabilities should also have a commitment to the community integration of these individuals. This includes a belief that mentally retarded persons, both mildly and severely disabled, should have opportunities for interactions with nondisabled persons in integrated settings. Relatedly, professionals should encourage individuals with disabilities to be involved in the vocational planning process to the maximum extent possible. This means that students with disabilities should be invited to IEP and ITP meetings, should be fully informed of assessment results, and should be actively involved in establishing vocational goals. Vocational assessment, planning, and placement are not to be done "to" an individual. Rather, vocational services are designed to assist an individual in meeting his or her own goals.

Too often, individuals with disabilities have been considered incapable of making their own decisions. As a result, professionals and family members have assumed this decision-making role for them. Certainly, many individuals with disabilities may have difficulty processing the information neccessary in making decisions and may need assistance from others in simplifying and clarifying decisions and options. Two very real dangers exist in this process. On the one hand, parents and professionals sometimes encourage an individual with disabilities to accept options in which he or she is not interested. On the other hand, without assistance, individuals with disabilities may flounder and select options that are clearly unrealistic in light of local resources and opportunities. Professionals must walk a tightrope between these two extremes when involving individuals with disabilities in vocational planning.

CAREER EDUCATION

In order to make realistic and informed vocational choices, students need to possess adequate self-awareness (i.e., be knowledgeable about their interests, abilities, values, or limitations), occupational awareness (i.e., be knowledgeable about the various vocational options and jobs available, and the requirements, demands, and rewards associated with these jobs), and decision-making skills. In order to make a successful adjustment to work and community living, students need to possess strong social/interpersonal skills and positive work habits and attitudes. Career education programs that operate in schools are designed to provide students with such knowledge and skills. These programs usually follow a model similar to that depicted in Figure 8-2. The activities and experiences that make up career education programs are usually integrated into the regular education curriculum and are implemented by a variety of school personnel including teachers, school psychologists, and guidance counselors. As Figure 8-2 suggests, the career education process can be broken down into four stages: awareness, orientation, exploration, and preparation. The grades/ages encompassed by each of these stages and the specific objectives recommended at each stage are based upon career development theory. The specific objectives that are established for a particular student, however, should be based upon both career development theory *and* the results of the vocational assessment conducted with the student.

Consistent with the notion that career development is a lifelong process, career education is initiated in kindergarten and continues throughout the course of a student's education. In that normal progression through career development stages is somewhat variable, the four stages of career education are overlapping.

Figure 8-2.
Phases of Career Education Programs

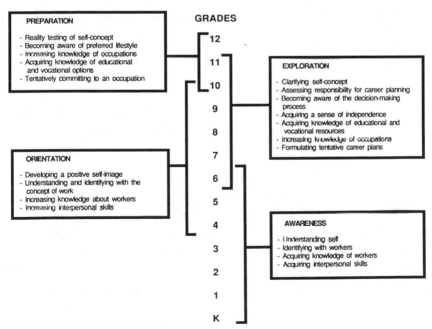

Awareness—The awareness stage encompasses grades kindergarten through 6, and is concerned with increasing self- and occupational awareness. Activities designed to teach children (a) about themselves, (b) about community jobs, and (c) how to get along with others are frequently a part of this stage of career education.

Orientation—The orientation stage encompasses grades 4 through 10 and is concerned with the development of attitudes and skills necessary for successful vocational adjustment. Activities designed to encourage the development of (a) a healthy and positive self-concept and (b) positive attitudes about work are frequently conducted during this stage. Continuing to encourage the development of positive interpersonal relationships and self- and occupational awareness is also a focus during the orientation stage.

Exploration—The exploration stage encompasses grades 6 through 11 and is concerned with providing students with the information and skills they need to begin exploring realistic vocational alternatives. Activities designed to encourage students to (a) improve decision-making skills; (b) assume responsibility for career planning; (c) acquire information about educational, vocational, and occupational options; and (d) establish tentative career plans are conducted during this stage.

Preparation—The preparation stage encompasses grades 10 through 12 and focuses upon vocational preparation. Activities designed to encourage students to establish tentative career goals, and to begin pursuing the education and training necessary to reach these goals, are conducted during this stage.

In contrast to the K–12 career education model just discussed, Lynch, Kiernan, and Stark (1982) have defined a three-phase approach to providing career/vocational education, which commences in grade 7:

Phase I (Grades 7–8)—Activities conducted during this phase are prevocational in nature and are designed to facilitate self- and occupational awareness. During this phase, the following activities are recommended:

Structured site visits—Students participate in field trips to specific work settings, gather information about jobs during these visits, and share information with one another in posttrip discussions.

Shadowing—Students follow an individual worker around for a period of time and acquire information about jobs via observation and limited hands-on experience.

Simulated site visits—Students are exposed to slide/tape presentations that simulate actual work settings.

Simulated work samples—Students are exposed to work tasks which are representative of the various vocational course options available to them, and the local jobs that emanate from training in these courses.

Vocationally related classroom experiences—Students are involved in industrial arts, home economics, and other vocationally related classes.

Academic classroom experiences—Guest speakers, media resources, and role-playing activities are incorporated into regular academic instruction in order to expose students to various vocational options.

Phase II (Grades 9–10)—Many of the same activities conducted during Phase I are repeated during Phase II. However, by this time, students, via exposure to vocational options in Phase I, should have narrowed their interests to a handful of careers. Thus, Phase II is narrower in focus than Phase I and allows students to explore high-interest occupational areas in more depth. In addition to the activities noted in Phase I, the following activities could be included in Phase II:

Visits to vocational settings—Students visit work settings where jobs consistent with their interests are performed.

Skill exploration in vocational courses—Students rotate through various shop classes consistent with their interests and are provided with some basic instruction consistent with entry-level jobs in the vocational area.

Classroom activities—Students are exposed to career information in high-interest occupational areas and are introduced to such job-seeking skills as finding jobs, writing resumes, filling out applications, and interviewing.

Phase III (Grades 10–12)—During this phase, students are provided with vocational instruction in one or two selected areas. Emphasis is placed upon acquisition of specific job skills and development of specific work behaviors. Some of the activities that could be included in this phase are:

Job-seeking skills training—Students are actively involved in finding jobs, filling out applications, and interviewing.

Classroom activities—Students are provided with instruction specific to transition from high school to work, or to further training.

Work experiences—Students are provided with work experience via real jobs in the community, both volunteer and paid.

Job training—Training programs that provide students with the skills needed for entry-level employment in a specific job are conducted more intensely than in Phase II.

The remainder of this section will discuss actions designed to facilitate career planning that are often a part of career education programs. As is clear from the prior discussion, attempts to facilitate realistic career decision making need to focus upon increasing self-awareness, increasing occupational/vocational exploration and awareness, improving decision-making skills, and facilitating job readiness and placement. The following sections describe some actions that can be taken to accomplish these objectives.

Increasing Self-Awareness

A variety of commercial materials exist that can be used to promote self-awareness. Job Lab 1 (Houghton-Mifflin, Boston), Toward Affective Development (American Guidance Service), SRA Self-Awareness Kits (Science Research Associates, Chicago), and Learning About Me: Developing Self-Concept (Q-ED Productions, Coram, NY) are a few of these materials. Self-understanding can also be promoted by assigning students classroom jobs, evaluating their performance, and providing the students with feedback. Discussions following job performance can focus upon how much each student liked the job, how well the student performed the job, and so on. Students can be asked to keep a diary or book in which to compile information they learn about themselves as a result of these experiences. Classroom discussions designed to identify student strengths and weaknesses can also be helpful in improving self-awareness.

Increasing Occupational Awareness

A number of commercial materials, including filmstrips, books, and activity kits, are available and can be used to promote occupational awareness. *The Dictionary of Occupational Titles* (U.S. Employment Service, 1981) and the *Occupational Outlook Handbook* (U.S. Department of Labor, 1982) are particularly valuable publications for use with junior high and senior high school students. These publications will be discussed in more detail later in this chapter. Local business and labor organizations are also a good source of printed occupational information. At the elementary school level, units on "community helpers," field trips to local work establishments or vocational training facilities, or Career days that include guest lecturers in various occupational areas will also aid in increasing occupational awareness. Weisgerber, Dahl, and Appleby (1981) have suggested initiating class discussions of a Job of the Week and playing a game of "What's My Job" in quiz show format. Students can also involve themselves in role playing of various workers, and can join job clubs and organizations (such as Future Farmers of America or Distributive Education Clubs of America), which operate in many schools. When selecting materials or techniques to increase occupational awareness, professionals should use their knowledge of the student (gleaned from vocational assessment) to select materials that provide information about realistic and appropriate occupational areas.

Improving Decision-Making Skills

Because high school students frequently make decisions based upon limited information and knowledge, it is important to ensure that they have adequate understanding of themselves and of the world of work before entering into the decision-making process. Even with adequate information, however, inadequate decision making may still occur. Because decision making is often an anxiety-producing task, adolescents (and even adults) often procrastinate and put it off for so long that options become limited or decisions occur by default. Group discussions designed to encourage the acceptance of anxiety yet also stimulate an understanding of the necessity and importance of making timely decisions can be helpful. If significant emotional or personal problems appear to be inhibiting effective decision making, individual counseling can be recommended. Such problems should be addressed prior to encouraging decision making. Adolescents are often overly influenced by peers and parents when making decisions. Individual and group counseling are appropriate interventions to consider when student decisions are being overly influenced by peers or parents. In some cases, family counseling may be indicated when parents inadvertently sabotage or inhibit effective decision-making practices. Professionals can encourage adequate decision making in students by establishing classes specifically to teach and model these skills. Activities can be initiated that require students to role-play actual decision-making situations, thereby allowing students to improve these skills via practice, feedback, and reinforcement. A variety of commercial materials exist that can be used to promote acquisition of effective decision-making skills, including Grow Power (Educational Activities, Coram, NY), and The Coping With Series (American Guidance Service, Circle Pines, MN).

Facilitating Job Readiness and Placement

Job readiness involves the development of positive job attitudes and behaviors. Such attitudes and behaviors include punctuality, concern for quality workmanship, responding to criticism, relationships with co-workers, and so forth, and are best encouraged by modeling. In public schools, transforming a classroom into a simulated work environment (in which the teacher functions as a supervisor or employer and the students function as employees) can help teach students positive job attitudes and behaviors. Such a program, developed for emotionally disturbed students, has been described by Levinson (1984). Vocational rehabilitation facilities frequently offer work adjustment training programs that are designed to facilitate proper work habits and attitudes. Weisgerber, Dahl, and Appleby (1981) have suggested including such things as sign in sheets, "tool licenses," competency checks, job evaluations, and "Worker of the Week" awards in classes to facilitate positive job attitudes and behaviors.

Kimeldorf and Tornow (1984) have described job clubs that can be established to facilitate both job readiness and placement. Job clubs utilize a curriculum based upon "job search education" (Kimeldorf, 1984), peer support, and behavioral principles and encourage the development of job-seeking skills and job acquisition. Azrin and Bezalel (1980) developed the job club model as a behaviorally based adaptation of job-seeking skills training. In this approach, individuals are provided both job-seeking skills training and active support in the job-seeking process. A counselor or teacher works with a small group of individuals who commit to a full-time job search. Students are taught to write application letters, complete applications, develop resumes, read employment ads, prepare for inter-views, and make employer contacts. Students are also involved in half-day sessions in which they make contacts over the telephone to develop job leads, improve other job-seeking skills, and develop resumes. During the other half of the day, they go on job interviews. Assistance and sup-port are provided by the counselor or teacher, and clerical services are provided for the development of resumes. The program involves use of a buddy system and encourages active family support. Particular focus is placed on developing and using personal and professional networks of contacts to develop job leads. Research has shown this approach to be effective with a wide variety of individuals with special needs including mildly mentally retarded individuals (Azrin, Flores, & Kaplan, 1977).

ACCESSING CAREER INFORMATION

In order for students to gain the occupational awareness necessary for realistic and informed vocational decision making, and in order for pro-fessionals to identify potentially realistic vocational options for students with whom they work, both must have an understanding of how to access information about careers. This section discusses the various classification systems used to organize career information and discusses some materials that can be used to access career information.

Dictionary of Occupational Titles (DOT)

Of all the methods for organizing and classifying information about occupations, the *Dictionary of Occupational Titles* (DOT) is the most widely used. Occupations are classified according to nine categories. Within each of these categories, occupations are further subdivided by occupational divisions and groups. Table 8-1 provides a listing of the nine occupational groups and provides a sampling of some occupational divisions and groups.

Each occupation is assigned a nine-digit code. The first three digits indicate how the occupation has been classified: The first digit represents the occupational category; the first and second digits combined represent the occupational division; and the first, second, and third digits combined represent the occupational group. For example, the first three digits assigned to the occupation "dentist" are 072. The "0" indicates that the occupation falls within the "Professional, technical, and managerial" group (first digit 0/1). The "07" indicates that the occupation falls within the "medicine and health" occupational group (07). The "072" is specifically assigned for "dentist." Related occupations have similar codes. For example, veterinarian is "073," dietician is "077," and physician and surgeon is "070."

The second set of three digits (the fourth, fifth, and sixth digits) in the DOT code provides information on tasks performed in the occupation. The DOT assumes that all occupations require some involvement with data, people, and/or things. The fourth digit represents the kind of involvement the occupation requires with data; the fifth digit represents the kind of involvement the occupation requires with people; and the sixth digit represents the kind of involvement the occupation requires with things. Table 8-2 lists the numbers and associated functions in each of these three areas. More complex functions are assigned lower numbers; less complex functions are assigned higher numbers. Definitions for each of the functions can be found in the appendix to the DOT.

The last three digits in the nine-digit DOT code are used to differentiate occupations that have the same first six digits. The DOT provides a reasonably comprehensive but brief description of each job as it is usually performed. Any technical terms associated with the work that are included in the job description are defined in the glossary included in the DOT.

Guide for Occupational Exploration (GOE)

The Guide for Occupational Exploration (GOE) was published by the U.S. Department of Labor (1979) to be used as a companion volume to

Table 8-1.
Summary Listing of Occupational Categories, Divisions, and Groups

Occupational Categories

0/1	Professional, technical, and managerial occupations
2	Clerical and sales occupations
3	Service occupations
4	Agricultural, fishery, forestry, and related occupations
5	Processing occupations
6	Machine trades occupations
7	Benchwork occupations
8	Structural work occupations
9	Miscellaneous occupations

Two-Digit Occupational Divisions

Professional, Technical, and Managerial Occupations

00/01	Occupations in architecture, engineering, and surveying
02	Occupations in mathematics and physical sciences
04	Occupations in life sciences
05	Occupations in social sciences
07	Occupations in medicine and health
09	Occupations in education
10	Occupations in museum, library and archival sciences
11	Occupations in law and jurisprudence
12	Occupations in religion and theology
13	Occupations in writing
14	Occupations in art
15	Occupations in entertainment and recreation
16	Occupations in administrative specializations
18	Managers and officials, n.e.c.
19	Miscellaneous professional, technical, and managerial occupations

Clerical and Sales Occupations

20	Stenography, typing, filing, and related occupations
21	Computing and account-recording occupations
22	Production and stock clerks and related occupations
23	Information and message distribution occupations
24	Miscellaneous clerical occupations
25	Sales occupations, services
26	Sales occupations, consumable commodities
27	Sales occupations, commodities, n.e.c.
29	Miscellaneous sales occupations

Service Occupations

30	Domestic service occupations
31	Food and beverage preparation and service occupations
32	Lodging and related service occupations
33	Barbering, cosmetology, and related service occupations
34	Amusement and recreation service occupations
35	Miscellaneous personal service occupations
36	Apparel and furnishings service occupations
37	Protective service occupations
38	Building and related service occupations

(continued)

Table 8-1.
(Continued)

Three-Digit Occupational Groups

Professional, Technical, and Managerial Occupations

00/01	*Occupations in architecture, engineering, and surveying*
001	Architectural occupations
002	Aeronautical engineering occupations
003	Electrical/electronics engineering occupations
005	Civil engineering occupations
006	Ceramic engineering occupations
007	Mechancial engineering occupations
008	Chemical engineering occupations
010	Mining and petroleum engineering occupations
011	Metallurgy and metallurgical engineering occupations
012	Industrial engineering occupations
013	Agricultural engineering occupations
014	Marine engineering occupations
015	Nuclear engineering occupations
017	Drafters, n.e.c.
018	Surveying/cartographic occupations
019	Occupations in architecture, engineering, and surveying, n.e.c.
02	*Occupations in mathematics and physical sciences*
020	Occupations in mathematics
021	Occupations in astronomy
022	Occupations in chemistry
023	Occupations in physics
024	Occupations in geology
025	Occupations in meteorology
029	Occupations in mathematics and physical sciences, n.e.c.
04	*Occupations in life sciences*
040	Occupations in agricultural sciences
041	Occupations in biological sciences
045	Occupations in psychology
049	Occupations in life sciences, n.e.c.
05	*Occupations in social sciences*
050	Occupations in economics
051	Occupations in political science
052	Occupations in history
054	Occupations in sociology
055	Occupations in anthropology
059	Occupations in social sciences, n.e.c.
07	*Occupations in medicine and health*
070	Physicians and surgeons
071	Osteopaths
072	Dentists
073	Veterinarians
074	Pharmacists
075	Registered nurses
076	Therapists
077	Dietitians
078	Occupations in medical and dental technology
079	Occupations in medicine and health, n.e.c.

(continued)

Table 8-1.
(Continued)

09	*Occupations in education*
090	Occupations in college and university education
091	Occupations in secondary school education
092	Occupations in preschool, primary school, and kindergarten education
094	Occupations in education of the handicapped
096	Home economists and farm advisers
097	Occupations in vocational education, n.e.c.
099	Occupations in education, n.e.c.
10	*Occupations in museum, library, and archival sciences*
100	Librarians
101	Archivists
102	Museum curators and related occupations
109	Occupations in museum, library, and archival sciences, n.e.c.
11	*Occupations in law and jurisprudence*
110	Lawyers
111	Judges
119	Occupations in law and jurisprudence, n.e.c.
12	*Occupations in religion and theology*
120	Clergy
129	Occupations in religion and theology, n.e.c.
13	*Occupations in writing*
131	Writers
132	Editors: publication, broadcast, and script
137	Interpreters and translators
139	Occupations in writing, n.e.c.
14	*Occupations in art*
141	Commercial artists: designers and illustrators, graphic arts
142	Environmental, product, and related designers
143	Occupations in photography
144	Fine artists: painters, sculptors, and related occupations
149	Occupations in art, n.e.c.
15	*Occupations in entertainment and recreation*
150	Occupations in dramatics
151	Occupations in dancing
152	Occupations in music
153	Occupations in athletics and sports
159	Occupations in entertainment and recreation, n.e.c.
16	*Occupations in administrative specializations*
160	Accountants and auditors
161	Budget and management systems analysis occupations
162	Purchasing management occupations
163	Sales and distribution management occupations
164	Advertising management occupations
165	Public relations management occupations
166	Personnel administration occupations
168	Inspectors and investigators, managerial and public service
169	Occupations in administrative specializations, n.e.c.

(continued)

Table 8-1.
(Continued)

18	*Managers and officials, n.e.c.*
180	Agriculture, forestry, and fishing industry managers and officials
181	Mining industry managers and officials
182	Construction industry managers and officials
183	Manufacturing industry managers and officials
184	Transportation, communication, and utilities industry managers and officials
185	Wholesale and retail trade managers and officials
186	Finance, insurance, and real estate managers and officials
187	Service industry managers and officials
188	Public administration managers and officials
189	Miscellaneous managers and officials, n.e.c.
19	*Miscellaneous professional, technical, and managerial occupations*
191	Agents and appraisers, n.e.c.
193	Radio operators
194	Sound, film, and videotape recording, and reproduction occupations
195	Occupations in social and welfare work
196	Airplane pilots and navigators
197	Ship captains, mates, pilots, and engineers
198	Railroad conductors
199	Miscellaneous professional, technical, and managerial occupations, n.e.c.

the DOT. It utilizes an occupational grouping system similar to that used by many interest inventories. As such, the GOE provides a means by which students can easily access career information on occupations identified as "high interest" via interest assessment. Each GOE occupational listing includes a series of DOT occupational titles and code numbers that allows

Table 8-2.
Data, People, Things Coding

Data (4th digit)	People (5th digit)	Things (6th digit)
0 Synthesizing	0 Mentoring	0 Setting up
1 Coordinating	1 Negotiating	1 Precision working
2 Analyzing	2 Instructing	2 Operating—controlling
3 Compiling	3 Supervising	3 Driving—operating
4 Computing	4 Diverting	4 Manipulating
5 Copying	5 Persuading	5 Tending
6 Comparing	6 Speaking—signaling	6 Feeding—offbearing
	7 Serving	7 Handling
	8 Taking instructions—helping	

students to refer to the DOT for more specific information about jobs associated with a particular interest area.

The GOE grouping is based on 12 interest factors: artistic, scientific, plants and animals, protective, mechanical, industrial, business detail, selling, accommodating, humanitarian, leading-influencing, and physical performing. Brief definitions of each of these areas are provided in Table 8-3. The 12 interest areas are divided into 66 work groups that are further subdivided into 348 subgroups. A six-digit coding system is used in which the first two digits represent the interest area in which the occupation is classified, the first four digits represent the work group in which the occupation is classified, and all six digits represent the subgroup. For example, the humanitarian interest area is coded "10." The work group "social services" (within the humanitarian interest area) is coded 10.01. Religious occupations and counseling/social work occupations (both within the social services work group) are coded 10.01.01 and 10.01.02, respectively.

Table 8-3.
Definition of GOE Interest Factors

1. *Artistic:* Interest in creative expression of feelings or ideas.

2. *Scientific:* Interest in discovering, collecting, and analyzing information about the natural world and in applying scientific research findings to problems in medicine, life sciences, and natural sciences.

3. *Plants and Animals:* Interest in activities involving plants and animals, usually in an outdoor setting.

4. *Protective:* Interest in the use of authority to protect people and property.

5. *Mechanical:* Interest in applying mechanical principles to practical situations, using machines, hand tools, or techniques.

6. *Industrial:* Interest in repetitive, concrete, organized activities in a factory setting.

7. *Business Detail:* Interest in organized, clearly defined activities requiring accuracy and attention to detail, primarily in an office setting.

8. *Selling:* Interest in bringing others to a point of view through personal persuasion, using sales and promotion techniques.

9. *Accommodating:* Interest in catering to the wishes of others, usually on a one-to-one basis.

10. *Humanitarian:* Interest in helping others with their mental, spiritual, social, physical, or vocational needs.

11. *Leading-Influencing:* Interest in leading and influencing others through activities involving high-level verbal or numerical abilities.

12. *Physical Performing:* Interest in physical activities performed before an audience.

Each work group area provides a description of what workers in the work group do, and the kinds of settings where jobs of that type are typically found. Additionally, information designed to answer the following five questions is provided:

—What kind of work would you do?

—What skills and abilities do you need for this kind of work?

—How do you know if you would like or could learn to do this kind of work?

—How can you prepare for and enter this kind of work?

—What else should you consider about these jobs?

Standard Occupational Classification System (SOC)

As summarized by Isaacson (1986), the SOC was designed to describe all occupations where work is performed for pay or profit. The SOC uses a four-level classification system. Twenty-two divisions are separated into 60 major groups. The major groups are divided into minor groups (there are 212 minor groups) and are further divided into unit groups (there are 538 unit groups). Table 8-4 lists the divisions and major groups.

Table 8-4.
Standard Occupational Classification (SOC) — Divisions and Major Groups

Executive, Administrative, or Managerial Occupations
11	Officials and Administrators, Public Administration
12-13	Officials and Administrators, Other
14	Management-Related Occupations

Engineers, Surveyors, and Architects
16	Engineers, Surveyors, and Architects

Natural Scientists and Mathematicians
17	Computer, Mathematical, and Operational Research Occupations
18	Natural Scientists

Social Scientists, Social Workers, Religious Workers, and Lawyers
19	Social Scientists and Urban Planners
20	Social, Recreational, and Religious Workers
21	Lawyers and Judges

Teachers, Librarians, and Counselors
22	Teachers, College, University, and other Postsecondary Institutions
23	Teachers, except Postsecondary Institutions
24	Vocational and Educational Counselors
25	Librarians, Archivists, and Curators

Health Diagnosing and Treating Practitioners
26	Physicians and Dentists
27	Veterinarians
28	Other Health Diagnosing and Treating Practitioners

(continued)

Table 8-4.

(Continued)

Registered Nurses, Pharmacists, Dieticians, Therapists, Physicians' Assistants
29 Registered Nurses
30 Pharmacists, Dieticians, Therapists, Physicians' Assistants

Writers, Artists, Entertainers, and Athletes
32 Writers, Artists, Performers, and Related Workers
33 Editors, Reporters, Public Relation Specialists, and Announcers
34 Athletes and Related Workers

Health Technologists and Technicians
36 Health Technologists and Technicians

Technologists and Technicians, Except Health
37 Engineering and Related Technologists and Technicians
38 Science Technologists and Technicians
39 Technicians, Except Health, Engineering, and Science

Marketing and Sales Occupations
40 Supervisors, Marketing, and Sales Occupations
41 Insurance, Securities, Real Estate, or Business Service Sales Occupations
42 Sales Occupations, Commercial, Except Retail
43 Sales Occupations, Retail
44 Sales-Related Occupations

Administrative Support Occupations, including Clerical
45 Supervisors: Administrative Support Occupations, Including Clerical
46-47 Administrative Support Occupations, Including Clerical Service Occupations

Service Occupations
50 Private Household Occupations
51 Protective Service Occupations
52 Service Occupations, Except Private Household and Protective

Agricultural, Forestry, and Fishing Occupations
55 Farm Operators and Managers
56 Other Agricultural and Related Occupations
57 Forestry and Logging Occupations
58 Fishers, Hunters, and Trappers

Mechanics and Repairers
60 Supervisors: Mechanics and Repairers
61 Mechanics and Repairers

Construction and Extractive Occupations
63 Supervisors: Construction and Extractive Occupations
64 Construction Occupations
65 Extractive Occupations

Precision Production Occupations
67 Supervisors: Precision Production Occupations
68 Precision Production Occupations
69 Plant and System Operators

Production Working Occupations
71 Supervisors: Production Occupations
73-74 Machine Set-Up Operators
75-76 Machine Operators and Tenders
77 Fabricators, Assemblers, Hand Working Occupations
78 Production Inspectors, Tutors, Samplers, and Weighers

(continued)

Table 8-4.
(Continued)

Transportation and Material Moving Occupations
   81   Supervisors: Transportation and Material Moving Occupations
   82   Transportation Occupations
   83   Material Moving Occupations, Except Transportation

Handlers, Equipment Cleaners, Helpers, and Laborers
   85   Supervisors: Handlers, Equipment Cleaners, Helpers, Laborers
   86   Helpers
   87   Handlers, Equipment Cleaners, and Laborers

Military Occupations
   91   Military Occupations

Miscellaneous Occupations
   99   Miscellaneous Occupations

Occupational Outlook Handbook (OOH)

The Occupational Outlook Handbook (OOH) is one of the most comprehensive, accurate, and up-to-date single sources of nationwide information on occupations and career options (Otto, 1984). It is also one of the most frequently used sources of career information by high school students. The OOH is published by the U.S. Department of Labor and a new edition comes out once every 2 years. It provides information on about 200 occupations, organized according to the major occupational groupings of the Standard Occupational Classification System. Each entry provides information on the nature of the work performed by people in a particular occupation, working conditions associated with the occupation, employment trends, training and other qualifications required to enter the occupation, advancement opportunities, job outlook, and earnings. Entries also identify related occupations and sources of additional information on the occupation. An index provides a cross-reference of SOC codes and DOT numbers for all occupations described in the OOH. Hence, moving between the OOH and DOT is relatively easy.

Holland Classification/Coding System

Holland (1973) has developed an occupational classification/coding system based upon his "Theory of Vocational Personalities and Work Environments." Six types of work environments are proposed: realistic, investigative, artistic, social, enterprising, and conventional. Although an occupation usually resembles one type of work environment more than it does another, most occupations present demands that are characteristic of several work environments. Based upon the requirements and demands inherent in a particular occupation, occupations are assigned a three-letter code. Each letter of the code represents one of the work environments. Hence, an occupation that is coded as SIA places on workers the demands most closely resembling those characteristic of the social work environment, but also those characteristic of investigative and artistic work environments as well. The code types assigned to various occupations can be accessed using the *Dictionary of Holland Occupational Codes* (Gottfredson, Holland, & Ogawa, 1982). For a more detailed description of Holland's work environments, readers are referred to the discussion of his theory in chapter 2.

VOCATIONAL TRAINING OPTIONS

There are numerous methods by which students may be provided with specific vocational training. In addition to school district–operated vocational education classes, there are work experience programs, apprenticeship programs, the military, trade and technical schools, community colleges/junior colleges, and colleges and universities, all offering programs that may be suitable vocational training options for students. These options should be given consideration when establishing students' vocational goals.

Vocational Education

Almost all students have access to school-based vocational education programs. Most programs are approximately 2 years in duration and prepare students for entry-level employment in a given occupational area. Unfortunately, not all school districts offer all of the programs their students need or desire. To do so would be nearly impossible. Thus, many school districts have developed cooperative arrangements with other districts to broaden the number of vocational training options available to their students. That is, districts will try not to duplicate the vocational offerings of their neighboring districts, and will allow students from other districts to enroll in their programs. Vocational education courses offered in a given district should adequately represent the employment options available in the local area.

Work Experience Programs

Many districts have established work experience programs at the secondary school level. These programs allow students to attend school for part of the day and work for another part of the day. The purpose of these programs is to prepare students for employment while completing the educational requirements necessary for graduation. These programs are frequently offered to students in their junior and senior years of high school and usually require students to attend school in the morning and work in the afternoon. On-the-job training is provided by the employer, and the student is supervised while at work by someone in the job setting. The student is paid for his or her work, and all aspects of the job experience are totally realistic. The student also usually receives academic credit for the experience. A school staff member acts as a liaison between the school and the employer and maintains close contact with both. The student is often enrolled in a class at school that is designed to provide instruction in such areas as money management, employee–employer relationships, or taxes.

Apprenticeship Programs

Apprenticeship programs have existed as far back as the Middle Ages (Issacson, 1986). Federal regulations define an apprenticeable occupation as one that is customarily learned in a practical way through a structured, systematic program of supervised on-the-job training; is clearly identified and commonly recognized throughout the industry; involves manual, mechanical, or technical skills and knowledge that require a minimum of 2,000 hours of on-the-job work experience; and requires related instruction to supplement the on-the-job training. An agency now known as the Bureau of Apprenticeship and Training (BAT) has established standards for apprenticeships, and there are currently apprenticeship programs in over 425 occupational areas including carpentry, electronics, plumbing, pipe fitting, and toolmaking.

Because apprenticeships exist in a variety of trades, the standards set by BAT are necessarily broad. BAT recommends that both employers and employees jointly develop programs that are mutually satisfactory. BAT has also encouraged the development of 6- to 8-week prejob programs that introduce potential apprentices to skilled trades and determine their suitability before a formalized apprenticeship contract is awarded. Students who successfully complete the prejob program are eligible to enter a regular apprenticeship program.

Apprentices must be at least 16 years of age (some programs require that apprentices be at least 18 years of age). Qualifications for apprenticeships vary; however, many require a high school diploma or its equivalent (although some have minimum standards as low as the 6th-grade level). Regardless, most programs require that apprentices have a solid background in reading, writing, and mathematics, all of which are basic to the skilled trades (Otto, 1984). Apprenticeships last anywhere from 1 to 6 years, and employment is organized in a way that allows the apprentice to gain experience in all aspects of the occupation. Typically, apprentices work under the supervision of a journeyman (a worker at the next highest level of certification who has learned the trade and is experienced). A progressively increasing wage scale is established for the apprentice (which usually begins at about 50% of the journeyman rate), and at least 144 hours of related classroom instruction must be completed. Periodic evaluation of the apprentice's progress in both job performance and classroom instruction is made, and recognition of successful completion of the apprenticeship is provided by the employer.

Military Training

There are many military occupations that have civilian counterparts and for which military training and experience are directly transferable. High school graduation is preferred and in some cases required for all military inductees. Relatedly, the jobs from which a student may choose are largely determined by the student's scores on the Armed Services Vocational Aptitude Battery (U.S. Department of Defense, 1984). All services guarantee job training, provided that enlistees qualify. High school students can sometimes guarantee training in a specific occupational area by enrolling in the military's delayed entry program. In this program, students enlist in a specific occupational training program, and reporting for active duty is delayed until after high school graduation. Typically, enlistees complete a basic military training program that lasts between 6 and 10 weeks. Training in the enlistee's selected occupational area follows this basic program. The military provides enlistees with several educational benefits in addition to job-oriented training, including college tuition assistance. For students who are considering the military as their career, enrolling in one of the service academies, the Reserve Officers Training Corps (ROTC, present on many college campuses), or Officer Candidates School may be a viable option.

Trade and Technical Schools

There are well over 10,000 trade and technical schools in the United States offering training in a wide variety of occupational areas. Most of these schools are private schools operated by their owners as businesses. Training programs generally last from 6 months to 2 years. Some trade and technical schools offer training in degree programs that are approved by state departments of education and are similar to those offered by community colleges. Trade and technical schools are accredited by the National Association of Trade and Technical Schools.

Community Colleges and Junior Colleges

Community colleges and junior colleges are generally synonymous terms applied to the same type of institution. These are generally 2-year institutions that have a dual purpose: They provide the first 2 years of the educational program typically required of students enrolled in a baccalaureate program at a 4-year college or university (and, hence, students can transfer from a community college to a 4-year college or university for the last 2 years) or they provide 2-year (or shorter) vocational training necessary for entry-level employment in a specific occupational area. In some cases, community colleges provide vocational programs similar to those offered by vocational-technical high schools. In places where both institutions offer similar programs, the public school and community college sometimes work out cooperative arrangements that allow students who receive credit in high school for partial completion of a vocational program to transfer that credit to the community college when continuing on for additional training in the same area. The admission requirements of community colleges vary, and some are open admission. In most cases, the admission requirements of community colleges are less stringent than are those of 4-year institutions. Increasingly, community colleges are employing support personnel to provide individuals with disabilities and high-risk students with the services they need in order to complete their programs successfully. This is especially true of community colleges that have an open admission policy.

Colleges and Universities

Traditional colleges and universities provide training in largely professional occupations, and program completion usually requires 4 years. Although admission requirements differ from one institution to another, most require that high school transcripts and standardized college admission test scores (like the SAT or ACT) be submitted. Some also require that standardized achievement test scores be submitted. Still fewer require that applicants complete a personal interview. As do community colleges, 4-year colleges and universities provide student support services designed to assist individuals with disabilities and at-risk students. As a result, these institutions have seen an influx of individuals with disabilities (particularly students with learning disabilities) in recent years.

EMPLOYMENT OPTIONS

As Levinson, Peterson, and Elston (in press) have noted, the vocational options for individuals with disabilities are many and are expanding as vocational services improve—particularly for moderately and severely retarded persons. Options include competitive employment, supported competitive employment, supported employment, and sheltered employment.

Competitive Employment

Competitive employment refers to situations in which individuals with disabilities are placed in competitively salaried jobs in which they receive the same wages and benefits as do nondisabled individuals in the same job. Individuals with disabilities may be provided with "time-limited" support services (services that may be intensive, but are provided for only a given amount of time).

Supportive Competitive Employment

This model provides individuals with special assistance in locating an appropriate job and with intensive job-site training and support. Training and support are provided on a one-to-one basis. Once the individual is employed, he or she is immediately paid full wages and benefits by the employer. Supportive competitive employment contrasts with supported employment (discussed in the next section) in that the support service that is provided in the former is on a time-limited basis only and is then withdrawn. That is, as the client acquires the skills necessary to perform a job independently and at a level consistent with industrial standards, support service is terminated. Support service is generally ongoing in the supported employment model.

Supported Employment

Supported employment was included in Title VII(c) of the Rehabilitation Act Amendments of 1986 for the first time as a vocational rehabilitative objective. The amendments define supported employment as:

> . . . competitive work in integrated settings—(a) for individuals for whom competitive employment has not traditionally occurred . . . [with] services available (but not limited to) provision of skilled job training, on-the-job training, systematic training, job development, [and] follow-up services. . . . (p. 8911, October, 2, 1986)

Supported employment is a new approach to job placement and follow-up for persons with more severe disabilities. In supported employment, individuals are placed on jobs with special assistance from "job coaches" and are provided with ongoing follow-up support. This may include supportive follow-up contacts, availability of a professional to assist in solving problems that may develop on the job, or assistance in retraining. Characteristics of the supported employment model include integration with nondisabled co-workers; permanent, ongoing, or intermittent support through the duration of employment; and real pay for real work (Wehman et al., 1988).

Six phases of service delivery are common to most supported employment options: (1) initial assessment, (2) plan development, (3) job placement, (4) training, (5) ongoing support, and (6) periodic assessment (Szymanski, Buckley, Parent, Parker, & Westbrook, 1988).

Initial Assessment—Two types of activities are conducted during this phase: an assessment of the individual's specific work characteristics and an assessment of the supported empoyment options available in the local community. In regard to the latter, the specific skills necessary for completion of identified jobs are determined.

Plan Development—Rehabilitation counselors, who are frequently involved in the implementation of supported employment services, assume responsibility for developing an Individualized Written Rehabilitation Plan (IWRP). This plan is similar to an IEP and includes short-term and long-term objectives, justification for the services to be provided and a description of who is responsible for service delivery, and a description of how performance will be measured. In contrast to the IEP, which is educational in nature, the IWRP is employment related.

Job Placement—A job site is identified by attempting to match the client's characteristics with the demands and requirements of various jobs.

Training—Following placement, training is initiated by a job coach or employment training specialist and focuses on (a) initial job skill acquisition and development of a production rate and level of performance consistent with industrial standards, and (b) non–work-related skills like transportation, residential living, and social skills.

Ongoing Support—Services are continually provided to the client to ensure satisfactory job performance.

Periodic Assessment—In addition to ongoing support, a systematic follow-up program is initiated to assess any need for retraining, additional support service, and identification of any problems that could risk job maintenance.

As Levinson, Peterson, and Elston (in press) have noted, numerous demonstration projects have led to the development of the supported employment model. Over the years, progressive rehabilitation facilities have used variations of this approach via enclaves in industry, work crews, and other arrangements where work training was provided in the community and some degree of ongoing support service was made available. With the passage of the 1986 amendments to the Rehabilitation Act, however, supported employment has been added as a new component of the vocational rehabilitation service delivery system, and a variety of "systems change" projects have recently been funded throughout the country to focus on changes from providing sheltered employment to persons who have more severe work disabilities to providing supported employment in integrated work settings. A number of variations of the supported employment model exist that vary in the degree of social integration provided. These include: individual supported jobs, enclave in industry, work crews, unpaid work, and clustered part-time employment (Levinson, Peterson, & Elston, in press).

In the *individual supported jobs approach*, intensive on-the-job training is typically provided one-on-one by a special trainer who gradually fades intervention efforts and assists existing supervisors and co-workers in taking over training and supervision (Moon, Goodall, Barcus, & Brooke, 1986). Ongoing support is provided to assist the individual in maintaining employment.

In an *enclave in industry*, a small group of special workers functions as a unit within a regular industry or business. Continuous, long-term, on-site supervision and training may be provided by the industry in which the clients are placed but is more typically provided by supervisors hired by a rehabilitation facility, public school, or other service agency sponsoring the workers. Workers may be hired into the regular industry setting as they meet production, quality, and behavioral standards, or may remain employed by the business or agency that originally placed them. Opportunities are provided in this approach for interaction with nondisabled persons.

Work crews are similar to enclaves. However, work crews are most often mobile and move from place to place performing work. Examples include lawn maintenance and janitorial work crews. The sponsoring agency contracts with community businesses or individuals to have the work completed, and the workers are paid by the sponsoring agency. The work crew is supervised by a single manager who is responsible for all facets of the operation including the supervision and training of workers, and ensuring that the work is completed according to pre-established standards.

Fredericks (1986) has developed a variation of the supported jobs model, identified as *clustered part-time employment*, in which single skill tasks are identified in a number of businesses and a series of part-time jobs negotiated for a specific individual. For instance, a variety of machine shops may have periodic needs to sort metal screws and other materials.

Pooling the needs of several such shops may result in somewhat stable part-time employment. Brown, Shiraga, York, and Kessler (1985) have advocated *unpaid, extended training* and, in some cases, unpaid employment as an option for individuals whose work and behavioral skills are not sufficient for them to meet the requirements of paid employment. He indicates that the intrinsic value and self-esteem generated by work and the opportunity for social interaction with individuals without disabilities is, in and of itself, of considerable value to individuals with disabilities.

Sheltered Employment

Sheltered employment refers to businesses or industries run by human service agencies that primarily employ disabled persons to perform service or small contract work. Rehabilitation facilities that use sheltered work as a transitional tool for work adjustment and vocational skills training may be divided into three categories — sheltered industries, sheltered workshops, and work activity centers. These differ primarily in the production and behavioral skills required and the level of wages paid. Sheltered workshops provide participants with bench work under sheltered conditions, working among other individuals with disabilities. Sheltered workshop employees typically earn an average of $1 to $4 per day (Wehman et al., 1988).

Increasingly, employment of individuals with disabilities in settings in which they are segregated from nondisabled persons has been questioned by professionals and parents alike (Brown et al., 1985; Wehman et al., 1988). Although some feel that sheltered employment must be maintained as an option (Bellamy, 1984), others indicate that such segregation is inappropriate. Numerous problems have been cited with sheltered workshops including: clients earn insignificant wages; sheltered workshops are underfunded; sheltered workshops have failed to incorporate current business and industrial technology; sheltered workshop staff are insufficiently prepared to perform the marketing and management functions necessary to maximize profits and client wages; and few clients "graduate" into competitively salaried jobs in the workforce (Wehman et al., 1988). As such, supported and competitive employment options are preferred over sheltered employment options under most circumstances for individuals with disabilities.

TRANSITION PLANNING

In an effort to facilitate successful transition from school to work and community living, federal and state governments are making the issue of school-to-work transition a priority for all individuals with disabilities.

Although the professional literature has generally treated transition planning separately from vocational assessment, the two are intimately linked. That is, successful transition planning can not occur without the information gleaned from a comprehensive vocational assessment. Relatedly, vocational assessment data are virtually worthless if not used to recommend services designed to facilitate successful transition from school to work and community living. Given the clear relationship between vocational assessment and transition planning, it makes little sense to discuss each separately. In this author's opinion, transition planning should be embedded within an overall vocational assessment and planning model. The transdisciplinary vocational assessment model advocated by this author essentially integrates the two processes. The data gathered via the TVA are used to recommend the services a student needs to make a successful adjustment to work and community living. Based upon the results of the TVA, an Individual Transition Plan summarizing these services is developed or a similar plan is developed and included in a student's Individual Education Plan.

Because the professional literature generally treats transition services separately from vocational assessment, and because entire books have been written on this topic alone, the following section provides an overview of the transition literature. Definitions of transition, basic considerations in transition planning, transition models, transition program development, and individual transition planning are discussed. However, the reader should note that much of what is recommended and discussed here is discussed in relation to vocational assessment throughout this book and is embedded within the vocational planning stage of the TVA model.

Definitions

Wehman, Kregel, and Barcus (1985, as cited in Wehman, Moon, Emerson, Wood, & Barcus, 1988) offer the following definition of vocational transition:

> Vocational transition is a carefully planned process, which may be initiated either by school personnel or by adult service providers, to establish and implement a plan for either employment or additional vocational training of a handicapped student who will graduate or leave school in three to five years; such a process must involve special educators, parents and/or the student, an adult service system representative, and possibly an employer. (p. 3)

This definition clearly suggests that transitioning efforts must involve a variety of school and community personnel (thus being transdisciplinary in nature), must include the parent of the student or the student him- or herself, is a planned and systematic process, and is a process that occurs well before the student is eligible to leave school. Although the definition provided by Wehman et al. (1985) emphasizes school-to-work transition, many transition specialists argue that transition programs must focus upon community adjustment as well. Madeline Will, of the Office of Special Education and Rehabilitative Services, in the landmark document "OSERS Programming for the Transition of Youth with Disabilities: Bridges from School to Working Life" (1986) defined transition as follows:

> The transition from school to working life is an outcome oriented process encompassing a broad array of services and experiences that lead to employment. Transition is a period that includes high school, the point of graduation, additional postsecondary education or adult services, and the initial years of employment. Transition is a bridge between the security and structure offered by the school and the opportunities and risks of adult life. Any bridge requires both a solid span and a secure foundation at either end. The transition from school to work and adult life requires sound preparation in the secondary school, adequate support at the point of school leaving, and secure opportunities and services, if needed, in adult situations. (Will, 1986; p. 10)

Will's document has essentially become the generic roots from which transitional programs have developed. A comprehensive transition program will provide individuals with the services they need in order to develop interpersonal and social skills, independent and home living skills, and skills necessary for employment.

In October, 1990, Congress enacted the *Education of the Handicapped Act Amendments of 1990* (P.L. 101-476), an amendment of P.L. 94-142, the Education of the Handicapped Act (EHA). Under this new law, the name EHA has been changed to the Individuals With Disabilities Education Act (IDEA). IDEA requires that transition plans be developed for all handicapped students and be included in the student's IEP by the time the student reaches age 16. Section 602(a) of IDEA defines transition services as

> a coordinated set of activities for a student, designed within an outcome-oriented process, which promotes movement from school to post-school activities, including post-secondary education, vocational training, integrated employment (including supported employment), continuing and adult education, adult services, independent living, or community participation. The coordinated set of activities shall be based upon the individual student's needs, taking into account the student's preferences and interests, and shall include

instruction, community experiences, the development of employment and other post-school adult living objectives, and, when appropriate, acquisition of daily living skills and functional vocational evaluation. (Education of the Handicapped Act Amendments of 1990, P.L. 101-476, Section 602(a) [20 U.S.C. 1401(a)]

Basic Considerations in Transition Planning

As Levinson and McKee (1990b) have noted, when one considers the knowledge and information needed by school-based professionals when facilitating successful transitioning of students, one must first take into account the skills students need to adjust to community living and to obtain and maintain employment. These skills can be broken down into three major areas: daily living skills, personal-social skills, and occupational/vocational skills (Wehman et al., 1988). Daily living skills necessary for independent living include managing finances, maintaining a home, caring for personal needs, buying and preparing food, buying and caring for clothing, engaging in recreation and leisure pursuits, and being mobile within the community. Personal/social skills include maintaining hygiene and appearance, accepting praise and criticism, exhibiting situationally appropriate behavior, exhibiting appropriate interpersonal skills, exhibiting adequate problem-solving skills, and exhibiting adequate communication skills. Occupational/vocational skills include understanding and exploring occupational and vocational alternatives, exhibiting appropriate work habits and behaviors, possessing marketable vocational skills, and exhibiting appropriate job-seeking skills. The degree to which students already possess these skills, or the extent to which students possess needs in each of these areas, can be determined via TVA.

Having identified the individual needs of a particular student and having determined the particular skills this student needs to learn, school personnel must then structure the educational curriculum accordingly. Generally, this will involve the development of a *functional curriculum*. A functional curriculum is one in which the goals and objectives are based upon the demands of adult life across a variety of settings (Wehman et al., 1988). In such a program, the particular skills a student lacks across the domains cited previously (daily living, personal/social, occupational/vocational) are taught in a way that enables the student to use the skills in the workplace, leisure and residential settings, and community facilities. Given the difficulty that many individuals with severe cognitive disabilities have in generalizing skills taught in one setting to another, it is sometimes necessary to conduct instruction in the setting itself. Consequently, professionals involved in transitional services must be familiar with residential and community-based educational programs.

Knowledge of local vocational employment options available for individuals with disabilities is also necessary for those developing transition plans for students. Generally, options include competitive employment, supported employment, and sheltered employment. The appropriateness of each of these employment options for a particular student depends upon that student's individual skills. As previously discussed, competitive employment options are those in which individuals are placed in competitively salaried community jobs without the provision of ongoing support services. Supported employment options are those in which individuals are placed in jobs with special assistance from "job coaches" who provide continual, ongoing support (including training, retraining, and problem resolution). Sheltered employment options are those in which individuals are placed in businesses operated by human service agencies (typically termed sheltered workshops or work activity centers). The various residential options available in the community for individuals with disabilities must also be considered by transition personnel when planning for students. Residential options may include independent living in single-family or shared group homes and apartments, living with family or friends, foster homes, nursing homes, and other private and public residential facilities. Again, the appropriateness of each of these alternatives will be determined by the unique needs and circumstances of each student.

Transition Models

As mentioned in a previous chapter, P.L. 98-199 is designed to improve the quality of the transition experience for individuals with disabilities. As such, the bill authorized the Office of Special Education and Rehabilitative Services (OSERS) to spend $6.6 million in grants and contracts for the purpose of enhancing education and related services to improve the transition of individuals with disabilities into postsecondary education, employment, or other adult services. The major objectives of this section of the legislation are to stimulate the development of secondary special education programs and to coordinate the services that are involved in the transition process (Rusch & Phelps, 1987).

As noted previously, "OSERS Programming for the Transition of Youth with Disabilities: Bridges from School to Working Life" was published in 1984 and became the base from which many other transition models grew (Will, 1986). According to Levinson and McKee (1990a), there are three underlying assumptions inherent in the OSERS model: that the individual who is leaving the school system is leaving a somewhat organized system and entering a more complex and confusing system that is not well understood by professionals, let alone by parents and consumers; that transition plans should address all persons with disabilities and it is the responsibility of professionals to identify the services needed to assist in the transition of each individual; and that paid employment is the goal of the transition plan. This model calls for a firm high school foundation in which the curricula in both special and vocational education are adequate in terms of allowing students to leave school with job skills appropriate for the local community.

The "bridges" from high school to employment, as defined in this model, are: (1) transition without special services — individuals use their own resources to find gainful employment or to continue their education at the postsecondary level; (2) transition with time-limited services — individuals use such services as vocational rehabilitation and job training programs to assist in gaining employment; once employment is secured the individual functions independently; and (3) transition with ongoing services — individuals use ongoing adult services to obtain and maintain employment as an alternative to custodial or sheltered employment.

Paul Wehman (1986) of Virginia Commonwealth University has developed a plan that expands and enhances many of the concepts outlined in the OSERS model. His model emphasizes a three-stage transition process. These stages are (1) input and foundation — school instruction, (2) process — planning for the transition process, and (3) employment outcome — placement into meaningful employment.

The school instruction portion of this plan emphasizes the importance of a functional curriculum within which activities are specifically designed to prepare students for vocational placement. This is in marked contrast to traditional use of a developmental curriculum, which generally emphasizes remedial academic skills. Wehman's model calls for integrated school services, exposure to natural work settings, and community-based training. The model emphasizes community-based instruction in which students over the age of 12 spend decreasing amounts of time in the classroom and increasing amounts of time at job sites learning job, interpersonal, and other skills that will directly benefit them when they leave the school environment.

The process of planning for vocational transition includes the development of an individualized transition plan that specifies the competencies to be achieved and the transition services to be provided to the student both during and after the completion of school. This plan should emphasize functional skills required on the job, at home, and in the community. Participation of the parent/guardian is viewed as critical, and this model calls for parent education activities to improve the background information and the skill effectiveness of parents as they participate in transition planning. Interagency cooperation is also an aspect of the planning phase. Finally, this plan presents several outcomes that provide alternative employment approaches to individuals with disabilities, including competitive employment, supported competitive employment, enclaves, and specialized industrial training.

Other transition models have been developed in various states, including Missouri, Minnesota, Pennsylvania, Washington, and Oregon. Some, like the OSERS and Virginia Commonwealth models described above, focus upon employment. Others view employment as one component of the overall transition process.

Halpern (1985) has developed a model that emphasizes the nonvocational aspects of transition. He views living successfully in the community as the goal of successful transition, and sees quality of life and the adequacy of one's social and interpersonal network as being equal to employment in importance. Based upon research conducted in several states, Halpern has concluded that success in employment does not necessarily correlate with success in other areas of life. As such, he advocates programs that look at all quality-of-life dimensions when determining the need for services.

The use of a functional curriculum, with emphasis placed on vocational and career issues as well as life skills issues, is inherent in most transition models. Brolin (1984b) has developed a "Life-Centered Career Education (LCCE) Model for the Transition from School to Work," which emphasizes the inclusion of career-oriented education even at the preschool level. Brolin presents 12 propositions that were developed based on research on the career development/education/training of individuals with disabilities. Included in his model are the following characteristics: the integration of career education in all areas of instruction; "hands-on" learning experiences wherever possible; active partnership among schools, parents/guardians, business and industry, and community agencies; and the creation of a position for a Training Resource Coordinator who would assume responsibility for transition services. Brolin describes this as a total-person approach, which emphasizes all aspects of the individual's development—not just the vocational aspect.

Development of Transition Programs

As was suggested earlier, transitional programming involves a variety of school and community-based professionals. The steps involved in developing transition services parallel the steps involved in establishing school-based vocational assessment services discussed in chapter 6.

The initial step in developing a transition program at the local level is to identify, organize, and mobilize the various professionals and agencies who will be involved in providing the services necessary to ensure a smooth transition from school to work and community living. Wehman et al. (1988) advocate the establishment of a local core transition team to include such professionals as a special education administrator, a vocational education administrator, a vocational rehabilitation administrator, the director of mental health/mental retardation, a developmental disabilities planning council member, and a parent and/or client advocate. Other professionals who could serve on this team might be a university representative, a private industry council representative, and a Social Security Administration representative. According to Wehman et al. (1988), this local core team has the following responsibilities:

1. Conducting a needs assessment or gathering existing needs assessment information.

The purpose of the needs assessment is to determine the adequacy of existing school, employment, and adult service programs. School programs should be evaluated to determine the relationship between educational/vocational programs and employment opportunities available in the local community, the number of students who have successfully been placed in jobs and residential facilities following graduation, the functional nature of the educational program, and the extent to which students have access to community-based vocational training. Employment programs should be evaluated to determine the number of individuals placed in employment, the retention rate of placed clients, wages earned by employees, and the nature and type of follow-along services provided. Adult service programs should be evaluated to determine the type of vocational assessment and postsecondary training services provided and the availability of supported and sheltered employment opportunities. The quality of community living arrangements, transportation, recreational and leisure programs, and medical and psychological services available in the local area should also be evaluated.

2. Establishing guidelines for interagency programming.

Based upon the needs assessment data gathered, the team recommends improvements in school and community services and begins developing transition planning procedures. Decisions such as the age at which to begin formal transitional planning, the types of students to receive transitional services, the format and components of the individual transition plans to be developed for students, the professionals to be involved in developing individual transition plans, and the roles of these professionals, and so on, are made by this local core team.

3. Developing a local interagency agreement and action plan.

The team verifies the procedural decisions made with formal written agreements, which have the purpose of further defining the various school and community agency roles and responsibilities in transition programming. Because many states have developed similar interagency agreements at the state level, these should be reviewed and considered when developing local agreements. According to Wehman et al. (1988), the core team identifies and verifies participation of key agencies and organizations, establishes flow patterns of students with disabilities across local agencies and organizations (i.e., when a particular student is likely to be serviced by a particular agency and the nature of the services likely to be provided), and identifies the means by which services will be evaluated.

Individual Transitional Programming

Having established interagency agreements that specify the kinds of transitional services to be provided by the various agencies (school and community) involved and the population to whom these services are to be provided, individual transitional programming can be initiated. According to Wehman et al. (1988), the first step in implementing this programming is the establishment of Individual Transition Planning Teams (ITPTs) for all students for whom plans are to be developed. Both school and community agency personnel participate on these teams. Appropriate school personnel include teachers (regular, special education, and vocational education), counselors, psychologists, and administrators. Representatives from community agencies such as Mental Health/Mental Retardation, Vocational Rehabilitation, and Social Services also participate on the ITPT. Parents should also to be involved in these meetings because research has indicated that parental participation increases the effectiveness of transitional services (Hasazi, Gordon, & Roe, 1985; Schalock & Lilley, 1986).

As Levinson and McKee (1990b) have noted, an overlap obviously exists between those school-based professionals who are involved in development of the student's Individual Education Plan (IEP) and those who should be involved in the development of the student's Individual Transition Plan (ITP). Thus, it makes sense to hold initial ITP meetings as part of annual IEP meetings for students with disabilities, and to incorporate the individual transition plan within the student's IEP. That is, at a certain designated point during a student's educational career (the point at which transition planning is to be initiated), the IEP team should be expanded to include relevant community agency personnel. Although the age at which this transition planning should begin is debatable, Levinson and McKee (1990b) have suggested that planning should be initiated at least 4 years prior to the student leaving school. With individuals who have more severe disabilities, transition planning should probably be initiated earlier in the student's educational career.

P.L. 101-476 requires that a student's IEP address the issue of transition and that transition planning be initiated by at least age 16. Specifically, IDEA lists the following additional requirements for the IEP:

(D) a statement of needed transition services for students beginning no later than age 16 and annually thereafter (and, when determined appropriate for the individual, beginning at age 14 or younger), including when appropriate, a statement of the interagency responsibilities or linkages (or both) before the student leaves the school setting,

and

(F) in the case where a participating agency, other than the educational agency, fails to provide the agreed upon services, the educational agency shall reconvene the IEP team to identify alternative strategies to meet the transition objectives. (As cited in Ysseldyke, Algozzine, & Thurlow, 1992, p. 54)

Thus, although separate transition plans may be developed for students, new regulations now require that IEPs address the issue of transition as well.

The purpose of transition planning is to identify realistic and desirable employment and community living outcomes for the student and the school and community agency services that will be needed to generate these outcomes. Clearly, these outcomes emanate from assessment of the student's skills in the various areas identified earlier. Much like an IEP, the transition plan developed for a student should list these outcomes as long-term goals and, for each long-term goal, should cite sequential actions to be taken to accomplish these goals. Transition plans should be reviewed, revised, and updated annually. A sample transition plan is included in Appendix B.

SUMMARY

Vocational assessment data are designed to be used by school-based professionals to assist in vocational planning. As such, professionals who are involved in the vocational assessment process must have an understanding of both the process by which assessment data can be integrated and used to generate vocational recommendations and the types of programs and services that may be recommended and enacted based upon the results of the completed assessment. In that transdisciplinary vocational assessment involves a team of professionals who must integrate assessment data, communicate the results of the assessment to other professionals, and use this assessment data to develop a written educational, vocational, and/or transition plan for a student, this chapter has included a discussion of professional staffings, report writing, and the development of Individual Education Plans. Additionally, this chapter has included a discussion of how assessment data may be used to recommend career education activities, transition services, vocational training opportunities, and employment options. The means by which career information can be accessed based upon the use of assessment data are also discussed.

REFERENCES

Azrin, N., & Bezalel, V. (1980). *Job club counselor manual.* Baltimore, MD: University Park Press.

Azrin, N., Flores, T., & Kaplan, S. (1977). Job finding club: A group assisted program for finding employment. *Rehabilitation Counseling Bulletin, 21*(2), 130-139.

Bellamy, G., et al. (1984). Quality and equality in employment services for adults with severe disabilities. *Journal of the Association for Persons with Severe Handicaps, 9*(4), 270-277.

Brolin, D. E. (1986). *Life centered career education: A competency based approach.* Reston, VA: The Council for Exceptional Children.

Brown, L., Shiraga, B., York, J., & Kessler, K. (1985). *Integrated work opportunities for adults with severe handicaps: The extended training option.* Madison, WI: University of Wisconsin & Madison Metropolitan School District.

Dyer, W. G. (1987). *Team building: Issues and alternatives* (2nd ed.). Reading, MA: Addison-Wesley.

Fredericks, B. (1986). Part time work for high school students. *Teaching Research, 15*(1), 1-7.

Gottfredson, G. D., Holland, J. L., & Ogawa, D. K. (1982). *Dictionary of Holland occupational codes.* Palo Alto, CA: Consulting Psychologists Press.

Halpern, A. (1985). Transition: A look at the foundations. *Exceptional Children, 51*(6), 479-486.

Hasazi, S. B., Gordon, L. R., & Roe, C. A. (1985). Factors associated with the employment status of handicapped youth exiting high school from 1979 to 1983. *Exceptional Children, 51*(6), 455-469.

Holland, J. (1973). *A theory of vocational personalities and work environments.* Englewood Cliffs, NJ: Prentice-Hall.

Huebner, E. S., & Hahn, B. M. (1990). Best practices in coordinating multidisciplinary teams. In A. Thomas & J. Grimes (Eds.), *Best practices in school psychology — II.* Washington, DC: National Association of School Psychologists.

Isaacson, L. E. (1986). *Career information in counseling and career development* (4th cd.). Boston, MA: Allyn and Bacon.

Kimeldorf, M. (1984). *Job search education.* New York: Education Design.

Kimeldorf, M., & Tornow, J. A. (1984). Job clubs: Getting into the hidden labor market. *Pointer, 28,* 29-32.

Levinson, E. M. (1984). A vocationally oriented secondary school program for the emotionally disturbed. *Vocational Guidance Quarterly, 33*(1), 76-81.

Levinson, E. M., & McKee, L. M. (1990). Best practices in transitional services. In A. Thomas & J. Grimes (Eds.), *Best practices in school psychology—II*. Washington, DC: National Association of School Psychologists.

Levinson, E. M., & McKee, L. M. (1991). The exceptional child grows up: Transitions. In M. Fine (Ed.), *Collaboration with parents of exceptional children*. Brandon, VT: Clinical Psychology Publishing.

Levinson, E. M., Peterson, M., & Elston, R. (in press). Vocational counseling with the mentally retarded. In D. C. Strohmer & H. T. Prout (Eds.), *Counseling and psychotherapy with mentally retarded persons*. Brandon, VT: Clinical Psychology Publishing.

Lynch, K. P., Kiernan, W. E., & Stark, J. T. (1982). A systems approach to career and vocational education programs for special needs students, grades 7-12. In K. P. Lynch, W. E. Kiernan, & J. T. Stark (Eds.), *Prevocational and vocational education for special needs youth: A blueprint for the 1980s*. Baltimore, MD: Paul H. Brookes.

Maher, C. A., & Yoshida, R. K. (1985). Multidisciplinary teams in the schools: Current status and future possibilities. In T. R. Kratochwill (Ed.), *Advances in school psychology* (Vol. 4, pp. 13-44). Hillsdale, NJ: Lawrence Erlbaum.

McCray, P. (1982). *Vocational evaluation and assessment in school settings*. Menomonie, WI: Research-Training Center, Stout Vocational Rehabilitation Institute, University of Wisconsin - Stout.

Moon, S., Goodall, P., Barcus, M., & Brooke, V. (1986). *The supported work model of competitive employment for citizens with severe handicaps: A guide for job trainers*. Richmond, VA: Rehabilitation Research and Training Center, Virginia Commonwealth University.

Otto, L. B. (1984). *How to help your child choose a career*. New York: M. Evans.

Rusch, F. R., & Phelps, L. A. (1987). Secondary special education and transition from school to work: A national priority. *Exceptional Children, 53*(6), 487-492.

Sattler, J. (1988). *Assessment of children* (3rd ed.). San Diego, CA: Author.

Schalock, R. L., & Lilley, M. A. (1986). Placement from community-based mental retardation programs: How well do clients do after 8 to 10 years? *American Journal of Mental Deficiency, 90*(6), 669-676.

Szymanski, E. M., Buckley, J., Parent, W. S., Parker, R. M., & Westbrook, J. D. (1988). Rehabilitation counseling in supported employment: A conceptual model for service delivery and personnel preparation. In S. E. Rubin & N. M. Rubin (Eds.), *Contemporary challenges to the rehabilitation counseling profession*. Baltimore, MD: Paul H. Brookes.

United States Department of Defense. (1984). *Test manual for the Armed Services Vocational Aptitude Battery*. North Chicago, IL: United States Military Entrance Processing Command.

United States Department of Labor. (1979). *Guide for Occupational Exploration*. Washington, DC: Government Printing Office.

United States Department of Labor. (1982). *Occupational Outlook Handbook*. Washington, DC: U.S. Department of Labor.

United States Employment Service. (1981). *Dictionary of occupational titles.* Washington, DC: U.S. Employment Service.

Vocational Evaluation and Work Adjustment Association. (1975). Vocational evaluation project final report [Special Edition]. *Vocational Evaluation and Work Adjustment Bulletin, 8.*

Wehman, P., Moon, M. S., Everson, J. M., Wood, W., & Barcus, J. M. (1988). *Transition from school to work: New challenges for youth with severe disabilities.* Baltimore, MD: Paul H. Brookes.

Wehman, P. (1986). Transition for handicapped youth from school to work. In J. Chadsey-Rusch & C. Hanley-Maxwell (Eds.), *Enhancing transition from school to the workplace for handicapped youth: Personnel preparation implications* (pp. 26-43). Champaign, IL: National Network for Professional Development in Vocational Special Education.

Wehman, P., Kregel, J., & Barcus, J. M. (1985). From school to work: A vocational transition model for handicapped students. *Exceptional Children, 52*(1), 25-37.

Weisgerber, R. A., Dahl, P. R., & Appleby, J. A. (1981). *Training the handicapped for productive employment.* Rockville, MD: Aspen Systems.

Will, M. (1986). OSERS programming for the transition of youth with disabilities: Bridges from school to working life. In J. Chadsey-Rusch & C. Hanley-Maxwell (Eds.), *Enhancing transition from school to the workplace for handicapped youth: Personnel preparation implications.* Champaign, IL: National Network for Professional Development in Vocational Special Education.

Ysseldyke, J. E., Algozzine, B., & Thurlow, M. L. (1992). *Critical issues in special education* (2nd ed.). Princeton, NJ: Houghton Mifflin.

APPENDIX A
SAMPLE FORMS

This appendix contains several forms that may be adapted for use by those professionals involved in the development and implementation of transdisciplinary school-based vocational assessment programs. Although the forms can be used "as is," it is more likely that professionals will want to use them as an initial draft or "jumping off" point in the development of forms to be used in their assessment programs. Just as vocational assessment programs must be tailored to the unique characteristics of a specific locality, so too must forms be developed with local needs in mind. Hence, professionals are encouraged to modify the forms provided in the current chapter for use in their programs.

The following forms are provided:

1. Data Collection/Summation Form
2. Teacher Information Form
3. Parent Interview Form — I
4. Parent Interview Form — II
5. Student Interview Form — I
6. Student Interview Form — II
7. Living Skills Checklist
8. Vocational Education Course Information Form
9. Individual Transition Plan Form

VOCATIONAL ASSESSMENT PROGRAM
DATA COLLECTION/SUMMATION FORM

Referring Person:

Grade Level _____ Age _____

Student Name[1] _____ DOB _____ Sex _____
                Last   First   Middle

Address[1] _____ City _____ Zip _____

Home Telephone Number[1] _____ Parents/Guardian _____

Person to Contact in Case of Emergency[1] _____ Emergency Phone No. _____

Does the student get free or reduced lunch?* Yes____ No____
(If so, please include a copy of the approval form from your principal)

Reason for Referral: *(Indicate vocational options/IEP request)* _____

_____

Is the student enrolled in a vocational training program?* Yes____ No____

Name of Program _____ School _____

Describe any difficulties the student may be experiencing in school:* *(Attendance, Behavior)*

_____

Is the student working for a regular diploma?* _____ Number of credits to date _____

Primary Diagnosis:* _____ Special Considerations: (wheelchair, etc.) _____

Medical Problems and/or Medication:* _____

Will staffing be necessary? _____ If yes, person to be notified _____

Please include an up-to-date copy of the student's transcript and a list of courses scheduled for this school year.

Phase I Vocational Evaluation Report will be sent to the Special Education Administrator.

(continued)

ACADEMIC

Test _____ Date of Test _____ CA _____

Reading: Grade Level _____

Strengths _____

Weaknesses_____

Math: Grade Level[1] _____

Strengths _____

Weaknesses_____

Spelling: Grade Level[1] _____

Written Expression
Strengths* _____

Weaknesses* _____

WISC/WAIS:[1] *(circle one)*   Date of Test _____ CA _____

Verbal IQ[1] _____   Performance IQ _____   Full Scale IQ _____

Subtests:[1]
Block Design _____ Object Assembly _____ Coding _____

LEARNING STYLES*
(circle one)

Does this student learn language better from hearing words spoken or from seeing words written on a blackboard?

Auditory Language   Visual Language

Does the student learn math better from hearing numbers and oral explanations or from seeing numbers written down?

Auditory Numerical   Visual Numerical

Does this student learn best by experience, doing, self-involvement—a combination of stimuli? Does this student seek to handle, touch, and work with what he/she is learning?

Yes   No

(continued)

Does this student express him/herself better orally or in writing?

>   Oral Expression   Written Expression

Does the student learn better individually or in a group?

>   Individual Learner   Group Learner

Does this student exhibit an ability to learn skills from repetition?

>   Little repetition   Moderate repetition   Much repetition

MOTIVATIONAL CUES*

List effective reinforcers for this student (e.g., verbal approval, verbal disapproval, teacher reinforcement, parent reinforcement, peer reinforcement, concrete rewards—money, grades, tokens, free time, etc.)

_____

_____

List ineffective reinforcers: _____

_____

COMMUNICATION*
(circle one)

A. Speech - (volume)   soft   moderate   loud
   (understandability)   good   poor: covers mouth with hand____ low volume____
   speech impediment _____

B. Eye Contact -   generally present   occasionally   hardly ever   none

C. General Reaction to one-to-one situation - relaxed   somewhat nervous   quiet tense

D. Relevance of Responses -
          pertinent to questions   unrelated to questions   initially pertinent, then rambles

E. Initiative -
     initiates conversational topics   responds to leader   answers briefly after direct question

F. General Attitude -   polite   sullen   outgoing   shy   cooperative   uncooperative
          apparently motivated   apathetic

G. Other (Transcript of Previous Grades, etc.)

Special Education Administrator completes[1]
*Special Education Teacher completes**

TEACHER INFORMATION FORM

TO: Special Education Teacher

Before a student is placed in a vocational program it is necessary to establish a better understanding of the student. By completing the form, you can assist us by providing pertinent information the vocational teacher can utilize in planning and delivery of appropriate instruction.

Name _____ Date _____

School _____ Telephone _____

Program Name (courses) _____

Goal of Program _____

_____

_____

STUDENT INFORMATION

1. ACADEMIC
   Reading level vocabulary _____
   Reading comprehension _____
   Mathematics _____
   Spelling _____
2. LEARNING STYLE
   Type of learning (visual, auditory, kinesthetic, or combined) _____
   Structure _____
   Reinforcements _____
3. SOCIAL _____
   _____
4. PHYSICAL
   Vision _____
   Hearing _____
   Health considerations _____
   Limitations _____
5. VOCATIONAL
   Work behavior _____
   Skill _____
   Interests _____
   Physical abilities and limitations _____
6. APTITUDE
   Please describe why you feel this particular vocational program would benefit the student.
   _____
   _____
   _____

7. What specific goals do you propose the student accomplish in the vocational program?
   _____
   _____
   _____

VOCATIONAL ASSESSMENT PROGRAM
PARENT INTERVIEW FORM—I

Student's Name _____ Date _____

Parent/Guardian Name_____

Address _____ Phone Number _____

1. What kinds of high school program would you like your child to take?
   (check one or more of the following)

   a. Classes preparing for college _____

   b. Classes in which basic reading, math, writing, and world of work skills

      are taught _____

   c. One-half day classes and one-half day work for school credit

      (work study/on-the-job training) _____

   d. Vo-Tech training _____

2. What kinds of skills would you like your child to learn in school? (e.g., math, reading, writing, spelling, job-seeking skills, job-keeping skills, etc.)

   Please list _____

   _____

3. If a one-half day class/one-half day work program was recommended for your child during high school, would you consider such a program?

   Yes _____   No _____

4. What do you see your child doing after high school? *(circle one)*

   College   Military
   Jr. College   Trade School
   Skilled Employment (mechanic,   Semiskilled employment (grocery store,
      welder, carpenter, etc.)   restaurant, factory, construction, labor, etc.)
   Other

5. List two jobs you think your child could enjoy and successfully perform.

   _____

6. Based on discussions with your child, what are his/her vocational interests?

   _____

Parent Signature _____ Date _____

Interviewed by _____ Date _____

Visiting Teacher completes

PARENT INTERVIEW FORM—II

Name of Student _____ Date _____

Address _____

_____

Phone _____ SS# _____ DOB _____

Father's Name _____

Mother's Name _____

Mother's Occupation _____

EXPECTATIONS

1. What do you see your child doing after high school?

   College   Employment—Type of Job? _____

   Military Service   Other _____

   Trade School

2. What kind of job or work does your child seem interested in at this time?

   _____

3. Has your child had any previous work training? (Training under parent, relative, friend)

   _____

4. What job skills would you like your child to learn in school?

   _____

5. What does your child like to do most when he/she is not working or going to school?

   _____

6. Are there vocational education courses you want your child to take while he/she
   is in school?_____

7. Are you aware of any behavior that might interfere with your child's getting and holding
   a job? _____

(continued)

STUDENT'S ATTITUDE *(check the ones that describe your child best)*

	Most of the time	Sometimes	Never
Dependable	_____	_____	_____
On time for appointments	_____	_____	_____
Patient	_____	_____	_____
Even-tempered	_____	_____	_____
Completes tasks	_____	_____	_____
Well-groomed	_____	_____	_____
Likes to work with others	_____	_____	_____
Likes to work alone	_____	_____	_____
Likes to learn something new	_____	_____	_____
Does daily chores/handles responsibilities at home	_____	_____	_____

PARENT ESTIMATION *(please give your own estimation rather than ask student)*

1. Does he/she have any chores at home?

   _____ yard work   _____ take out trash

   _____ clean room   _____ make home repairs

   _____ help with cooking/dishes   Other _____

2. Does he/she accept responsibility at home?

   _____ job assignments   _____ getting up in the morning

   _____ dressing for school on time   _____ getting to school on time

   _____ prepares homework   Other _____
   assignments

3. Has he/she ever had or does he/she presently have a job outside the home? If so, list:

   _____

4. Does he/she seem to prefer working

   _____ by him-/herself?   _____ with small group (3–5 people)?

   _____ with one person?   _____ with large group (4–6 people)?

5. Would he/she rather work   _____ inside?   _____ outside?

6. Would he/she rather work

   _____ sitting in one place most of the time?   _____ moving around most of the time?

7. Is he/she able to stay with an assigned job long enough to complete it?

   _____ yes   _____ no   If yes, approximate length of time _____

(continued)

8. What types of work interest him/her most?

_____ machine operated   _____ working with hands

_____ scientific/technical   _____ contact with people

_____ routine   _____ helping people

_____ assembly line   Other _____

_____ organized   _____

9. Is he/she punctual and does he/she keep appointments?

_____ yes   _____ no

10. Does he/she attend school regularly?

_____ yes   _____ no

11. What are his/her favorite subjects?_____

_____

12. What are his/her least favorite subjects? _____

_____

13. What extracurricular activities does he/she like?

_____ indoor games   _____ sewing

_____ contact sports   _____ child care

_____ individualized sports   _____ personal shopping for clothes, records, etc.

_____ building models   _____ auto/motorcycle repair

_____ hunting/fishing   _____ hiking/camping

_____ gardening   _____ bicycling

_____ dancing   _____ boating

_____ watching TV   _____ small construction projects (do-it-yourself repairs, etc.)

_____ cooking

Other _____

14. Does the student have experience in money management?

_____ receives allowance   _____ goes shopping alone:

_____ has checking account   _____ clothes/records, etc.

_____ earns personal money   _____ small items (candy, drink, lunch, etc.)

_____ uses charge accounts

15. If he/she could choose a job/career today, what do you think he/she would select?

_____

Parent Signature _____

VOCATIONAL ASSESSMENT PROGRAM
STUDENT INTERVIEW FORM—I

Name _____ Date _____

Address _____ Age _____ Grade _____

ATTITUDES TOWARD DISABILITY

1. Do you have any sort of disability? _____

2. Are you in a special education program? _____
   Which one? _____ Why? _____

3. How do you feel about being in this program? _____

4. How do your family and friends feel about it? _____

INTERESTS AND ACTIVITIES

5. What do you do in your leisure time? (sports, hobbies, church, etc.) _____
   _____

6. Do you have any jobs at home? _____ What? _____

7. What job do you think you would like to do and be good at? _____
   _____

8. Name three other jobs you are interested in. _____

9. What jobs do you really think you would not like? _____
   Why? _____

10. Have you ever had a job before? _____ Where? _____

OCCUPATIONAL AND CAREER AWARENESS

11. Name as many jobs as you can (up to 15). _____
    _____
    _____

12. Name three jobs available in a supermarket. _____

13. What are ways to find out about job openings? _____
    _____

14. What do employers look for when they hire someone?_____
    _____

15. What are some reasons people get fired from jobs? _____

16. What would an employer like about you? _____
    Not like?_____

17. What should you do if you are going to be late or absent from work?
    _____

18. Have you ever filled out a job application? _____ Where? _____

(continued)

WORK AND CLASSROOM PREFERENCES

19. What classes do you like the best? _____

    Why? _____

    Which least? _____

    Why? _____

20. Do you like to work by yourself or with a group? _____

21. On a job, would you rather sit most of the time or move around a lot? _____

22. Would you rather work outside or inside, or both? _____

23. How do you feel about working where it is cold? _____

    Hot? _____ Wet? _____

    Where there are dangerous things? _____

24. What kinds of people do you not like to work with?_____

EDUCATIONAL INTERESTS

25. What courses would you like to take? _____

    What do you not want to take? _____

26. Would you like to enroll in a vocational training program? _____

    If yes, list programs in which you are interested: _____

    _____

FUNCTIONAL SKILLS

27. If you lived by yourself and had a job, what are some of the things you would have

    to spend your money on each month?_____

    _____

28. How much does it cost for groceries for two people each week if you cook at home?

    _____

29. Can you use a telephone? _____ How do you dial emergency?_____

30. If you had a job, how would you get to work? _____

    Can you drive? _____

31. Do you go shopping by yourself? _____

    What do you buy? _____

FAMILY

32. How do your folks feel about your working? _____

33. What job would they like you to do? _____

Student Signature _____ Date _____

Interviewed by _____ Date _____

STUDENT INTERVIEW FORM—II

Name _____ Date _____

School _____ Grade _____ DOB _____

INTERESTS AND ACTIVITIES

1. What do you like to do most when you are not working or going to school?

   _____

   Sports? _____

   Clubs, Organizations?_____

   Hobbies? _____

2. Do you watch much television? _____

   What is your favorite show? _____

3. Do you have any jobs at home? _____ What? _____

4. How do you feel about doing these chores? _____

5. Do you usually do the chores without your parents reminding you to do them? ____

6. What job(s) do you think you would like to do and be good at doing? _____

   _____

7. Are there any jobs that you know you would not like? _____

EDUCATIONAL INTERESTS

1. What are your favorite classes in school, either now or in the past?_____

   _____

2. What are your least favorite classes? _____

3. Are there any courses you have not had, but would like to take? _____

4. Do you take part in any school activities? (For example, clubs, sports, office worker)?

   _____ Which ones? _____

5. Would you like to take vocational courses? _____ Which ones? _____

   _____

6. Do you have a job outside your home now? _____What is it?_____

7. Of any outside jobs or work you have done, what are your favorites? _____

_____

8. What do you plan to do after high school?

    College   Employment—Type of Job? _____

    Military Service   Other _____

    Trade School   _____

9. What job/career would you choose for yourself?

    a. now _____

    b. in the future _____

OCCUPATIONAL AND CAREER AWARENESS

1. What do employers look for when they hire someone?

    _____

    _____

2. What are some reasons people get fired from jobs?

    _____

3. What would an employer like about you?

    _____

    Not like? _____

Student Signature _____ Date _____

LIVING SKILLS CHECKLIST

Student _____

Date _____ Completed by _____

A—Asset   U—Unknown   L—Limitation

	A	L	U

PERSONAL HYGIENE/GROOMING

1. Washes hands ___ ___ ___
2. Washes hair ___ ___ ___
3. Washes body ___ ___ ___
4. Uses deodorant ___ ___ ___
5. Combs/brushes hair ___ ___ ___
6. Brushes teeth ___ ___ ___
7. Shaves using razor (electric or straight edge) ___ ___ ___
8. Cleans/clips fingernails and toenails ___ ___ ___
9. (Female) Handles feminine hygiene ___ ___ ___
10. Uses kleenex/handkerchief ___ ___ ___
11. Wears clean clothes ___ ___ ___
12. Wears clothes that fit and are in good repair ___ ___ ___

HOUSEKEEPING

1. Dry mops/sweeps floor ___ ___ ___
2. Wet mops floor ___ ___ ___
3. Cleans bathroom ___ ___ ___
4. Washes dishes ___ ___ ___
   a. Uses sink ___ ___ ___
   b. Uses dishwasher ___ ___ ___
5. Dries dishes ___ ___ ___
6. Stores dishes/pans/utensils in proper place ___ ___ ___
7. Cleans counter/table ___ ___ ___
8. Disposes of garbage in garbage disposal or garbage container ___ ___ ___

LAUNDRY/CLOTHING CARE

1. Sorts clothes (light/white, dark/colored) ___ ___ ___
2. Uses regular washer ___ ___ ___
3. Uses regular dryer ___ ___ ___
4. Folds/hangs clothes ___ ___ ___
5. Mends clothes (buttons, hems, seams) ___ ___ ___

(continued)

	A	L	U

TIME

1. Distinguishes units of time ___ ___ ___
   a. day/night ___ ___ ___
   b. morning/evening/afternoon ___ ___ ___
2. Distinguishes a.m./p.m. ___ ___ ___
3. Distinguishes workdays/non-workdays ___ ___ ___
4. Tells time by hour and ½ hour ___ ___ ___
5. Sets/uses alarm clock ___ ___ ___
6. Arrives on time: meals, work, appointments ___ ___ ___
7. Identifies date: day, month, year ___ ___ ___
8. Identifies numbers of days in week ___ ___ ___
9. Uses calendar ___ ___ ___
10. Estimates amount of time to do task ___ ___ ___
    a. cleaning ___ ___ ___
    b. shopping ___ ___ ___
    c. cooking ___ ___ ___
    d. leisure activity ___ ___ ___
    e. shower/bath ___ ___ ___
    f. walk to mall ___ ___ ___

NUMBERS

1. Recognizes numerals:
   a. 0 to 12 ___ ___ ___
   b. above 12 ___ ___ ___
2. Copies numerals:
   a. 0 to 12 ___ ___ ___
   b. above 12 ___ ___ ___
3. Counts objects:
   a. 0 to 12 ___ ___ ___
   b. above 12 ___ ___ ___
4. Uses calculator to add, subtract, multiply, divide ___ ___ ___
5. Uses measuring cups and spoons ___ ___ ___
6. Uses a ruler and tape measure ___ ___ ___

WRITING

1. Writes/copies full name in manuscript or cursive ___ ___ ___
2. Writes/copies:
   a. Address ___ ___ ___
   b. Social Security number ___ ___ ___
   c. Telephone number ___ ___ ___
   d. Date of birth ___ ___ ___

(continued)

	A	L	U

WRITING (continued)

3. Writes/copies sentences/letters ___ ___ ___

4. Addresses envelope ___ ___ ___

5. Mails letters ___ ___ ___

6. Fills out job application ___ ___ ___

MONEY

1. Gives correct coin amounts for:

   a. five cents ___ ___ ___

   b. ten cents ___ ___ ___

   c. fifteen cents ___ ___ ___

   d. twenty-five cents ___ ___ ___

   e. fifty cents ___ ___ ___

2. Uses coins/coin combinations for:

   a. food at lunch time ___ ___ ___

   b. pop machine ___ ___ ___

   c. snack machine ___ ___ ___

   d. pay telephone ___ ___ ___

3. Identifies/gives correct bill(s) for:

   a. one dollar ___ ___ ___

   b. five dollars ___ ___ ___

   c. ten dollars ___ ___ ___

4. Uses concept of "more than"/"less than" ___ ___ ___

5. Estimates cost of purchase ___ ___ ___

6. Uses checkbook ___ ___ ___

7. Carries own money/Performs cash transactions/Waits for
   change if necessary ___ ___ ___

READING

1. Reads own name ___ ___ ___

2. Reads important signs/functional words ___ ___ ___

3. Reads newspaper: ___ ___ ___

   a. locates want ads ___ ___ ___

   b. uses want ads to find job ___ ___ ___

PERSONAL/SOCIAL SKILLS

1. Carries identification (I.D.) ___ ___ ___

2. Responds when spoken to ___ ___ ___

3. Communicates basic needs: verbally, nonverbally ___ ___ ___

4. Communicates full name: verbally, using I.D., written ___ ___ ___

5. Communicates address, phone number: verbally, using I.D.,
   written ___ ___ ___

(continued)

	A	L	U
PERSONAL/SOCIAL SKILLS (continued)			
6. Communicates school or place of work: verbally, using I.D., written	—	—	—
7. Uses others' names when interacting	—	—	—
8. Uses "please," "thank you," etc.	—	—	—
9. Expresses anger in acceptable manner	—	—	—
10. Expresses fear in acceptable manner	—	—	—
11. Expresses affection in acceptable manner: same sex, opposite sex	—	—	—
12. Expresses dislike in acceptable manner	—	—	—
13. Apologizes	—	—	—
14. Initiates interactions with:			
a. staff	—	—	—
b. peers	—	—	—
c. visitors	—	—	—
d. sales persons/waitresses	—	—	—
15. Converses with:			
a. staff	—	—	—
b. peers	—	—	—
c. visitors	—	—	—
16. Refrains from talking to strangers unless necessary	—	—	—
17. Uses telephone	—	—	—
18. Answers door in acceptable manner	—	—	—
19. Practices acceptable manners in/at:			
a. restaurant	—	—	—
b. theater/spectator event	—	—	—
c. party/dance	—	—	—
d. church	—	—	—
e. doctor	—	—	—
f. dentist	—	—	—
20. Practices acceptable manners as:			
a. customer	—	—	—
b. guest	—	—	—
c. host	—	—	—
21. Demonstrates a complying attitude:	—	—	—
a. follows directions from staff	—	—	—
b. follows activity schedule			—
c. performs duties	—	—	—
d. works on training objectives	—	—	—

(continued)

	A	L	U

PERSONAL/SOCIAL SKILLS (continued)

22. Demonstrates trustworthiness:
    a. conduct can be trusted in unsupervised situations
    b. tells the truth
    c. takes responsibility for personal actions and decisions
    d. asks permission to use others' possessions/things
23. Accepts/adjusts to situations that are contrary to own will or desire
24. Abides by group decisions
25. Accepts/adjusts to staff changes
26. Accepts/adjusts to novel situations: visitors, schedule changes
27. Uses acceptable table manners
28. Engages in a passive activity: TV, radio, stereo, movie
29. Engages in solitary games
30. Engages in games with others
31. Engages in hobby/craft activity
32. Engages in active socialization with friends, family, groups, parties, members of opposite sex, social clubs

FOOD PREPARATION/COOKING

1. Identifies kitchen utensils/cookware:
   table knife, spoon, fork, can opener, turner/spatula, sharp knife, measuring cup/spoons, scraper, soup ladle, pot holder/mitt, hot pad, napkin, cheese slicer, fry pan, saucepan, broiler pan, cake pan, pizza pan, cookie sheet, toaster
2. Identifies dishes:
   plate, cup, cereal bowl, soup bowl, mixing bowl, glass, cup, saucer, salt/pepper shaker, sugar bowl, platter
3. Identifies appliances, etc..
   stove, oven, refrigerator, dishwasher, cupboard, table, chair, sink, freezer

MOBILITY

1. Walks
2. Rides bicycle
3. Rides city bus
4. Rides bus to another city
5. Gets to nearest:
   a. grocery store
   b. laundromat
   c. bus stop
   d. shopping mall
   e. church
   f. doctor/dentist office

(continued)

	A	L	U

MOBILITY (continued)

5. Gets to nearest: (continued)

    g. parental home   ___ ___ ___

    h. friend's home   ___ ___ ___

6. Identifies/reads street signs   ___ ___ ___

7. Identifies/reads house numbers   ___ ___ ___

8. Identifies appropriate places to go if lost: gas station, business place, home of another   ___ ___ ___

HEALTH/SAFETY

1. Treats simple health problems:

    a. cuts/scrapes   ___ ___ ___

    b. slivers/splinters   ___ ___ ___

    c. upset stomach   ___ ___ ___

    d. cold   ___ ___ ___

2. Contacts another for health problems more difficult to handle:

    a. fever   ___ ___ ___

    b. diarrhea   ___ ___ ___

    c. burn   ___ ___ ___

    d. fainting spell   ___ ___ ___

    e. seizure   ___ ___ ___

    f. eye problems   ___ ___ ___

    g. poisoning/overdose   ___ ___ ___

    h. animal bite   ___ ___ ___

3. Takes medication   ___ ___ ___

4. Refills prescription   ___ ___ ___

5. Reports/handles seizures   ___ ___ ___

6. Uses telephone to call in sick   ___ ___ ___

7. Recognizes importance of not combining alcohol and medication   ___ ___ ___

8. Has basic understanding of human sexuality/sex education   ___ ___ ___

9. Follows fire drill instructions   ___ ___ ___

10. Follows other disaster instructions   ___ ___ ___

11. Wears safety goggles when operating power tools   ___ ___ ___

VOCATIONAL EDUCATION COURSE INFORMATION FORM

In order to ensure the appropriateness of a student's placement in a vocational education program, we need to establish an understanding of each program. By completing the form below, you can assist us in obtaining a better understanding of your program's goals, objectives, and requirements. We have also provided a section at the end of the form for your comments and any special considerations that you may have regarding your program. Thanks for your cooperation!!!

Date _____

Instructor's Name _____ Title _____

School _____Telephone Number _____

Program Name (Courses taught)_____

Goal of Program (briefly describe)_____

_____

_____

ACADEMIC REQUIREMENTS

1. Do you use a textbook in your course? _____Yes _____No

   Textbook name _____ Required reading level _____

2. Could a student who can read only a few words succeed in your class?

   _____ Yes   _____ No

3. What type of written instructions do you use in your classroom?

   a. None _____   b. One or two words _____

   c. Simple sentences _____   d. Complex written _____

4. Is a student required to write in your classroom?

   a. No _____   b. One or two words _____

   c. Simple sentences _____   d. Complex sentences _____

   e. Other (please describe) _____

5. What type of verbal instructions must the student follow in your classroom?

   a. One or two words _____   b. Simple sentences _____

   c. Complex sentences _____   d. Other (please describe) _____

   _____

6. Is the student required to follow diagrammatical instructions? _____ Yes _____ No

7. Do you use demonstrated instructions in your classroom? _____ Yes _____ No

8. What percentage of time do you use the following types of instruction in your classroom? *(please approximate)*

   a. Verbal _____%   b. Written _____%

   c. Demonstration _____%   d. Diagrammatical _____%

   e. Other _____%

(continued)

9. What percentage of time would someone working in your profession use the following types of instructions?

   a. Verbal _____%   b. Written _____%

   c. Demonstration _____%   d. Diagrammatical _____%

   e. Other _____%

10. What type of, if any, mathematical abilities are required in your classroom?

    a. Addition ____yes ____no   b. Subtraction ____yes ____no

    c. Multiplication ____yes ____no   d. Division ____yes ____no

    e. Measurement ____yes ____no   f. Other _____

    If checked *yes* to *measurement*, describe what type of measurement (example: metric ruler, standard ruler, read to nearest fractional unit: 1/8", 1/4", cups, pints, etc.)

    _____

    _____

11. Grading—Please express in percentages the weight given in grading to each of the following: *(Total should equal 100)*

    a. Exams: Essay_____%   Short Answers_____%   Multiple Choice_____%

    b. Homework: Reading-Writing_____%   Project_____%

    c. Classwork: Reading-Writing_____%   Project_____%

    d. Other: _____%   _____%

PHYSICAL REQUIREMENTS

In order to succeed in your classroom (career), a student must (be able to) (have): *(Please check yes or no for each)*

a. Full use of arms   _____Yes   _____No

b. Full use of legs   _____Yes   _____No

c. Full use of hands   _____Yes   _____No

d. Full use of fingers _____Yes   _____No

e. Stand   _____Yes   _____No

f. Stoop   _____Yes   _____No

g. Kneel   _____Yes   _____No

h. Crouch   _____Yes   _____No

i. Crawl   _____Yes   _____No

j. Push and pull   _____Yes   _____No

k. Lift and carry _____Yes   _____No

   (If required to lift, specify how many pounds) _____

l. Sight   _____Yes   _____No

m. Hearing _____Yes   _____No

(continued)

n. Speech   _____Yes   _____No

o. Color discrimination   _____Yes   _____No

p. Work in dust, lint, related materials   _____Yes   _____No

q. Work inside   _____Yes   _____No

r. Work outside   _____Yes   _____No

s. Work both inside and outside   _____Yes   _____No

t. Climb and/or balance   _____Yes   _____No

u. Reaching, handling, fingering, and/or feeling   _____Yes   _____No

v. Temperature changes (extreme heat or cold)   _____Yes   _____No

w. Wet and humid conditions   _____Yes   _____No

x. Noise and vibrations   _____Yes   _____No

y. Spatial perception   _____Yes   _____No

z. Form perception   _____Yes   _____No
    (Observing detail in objects or drawings. Noticing differences in shapes or shadings)

SPECIFIC APTITUDE—REQUIREMENTS FOR YOUR PROGRAM

1. Please list what qualities or skills you would like to have in a student who is just
   beginning your program. (This is very important for successful placement of students
   into your program, so please be as specific and complete as possible).

   _____

   _____

   _____

   _____

   _____

   _____

   _____

   _____

2. Please list the specific skills that you hope your students will achieve in your program.
   (Please be as specific as possible) (Example: Will be able to use power saw, will be able
   to use adding machine, will be able to thread pipe, will be able to repair small engines, etc.)

   _____

   _____

   _____

   _____

   _____

   _____

   _____

   _____

(continued)

3. Please list any course(s) that would be helpful to a student before entering your program.

_____

4. How long does it usually take a student to complete your program? _____

EMPLOYMENT POSSIBILITIES

1. After a student successfully completes your program, what type of entry-level positions are available to him or her? (Please list as many as you can)

_____   _____

_____   _____

_____   _____

2. Please list advanced-level positions that your students move into.

_____   _____

_____   _____

3. At this time, how available are these positions in:

	many	some	few	none	don't know
a. County/City	____	____	____	____	____
b. State	____	____	____	____	____
c. Country	____	____	____	____	____

4. Have you ever had students with disabilities (special education) in your program?

_____ Yes   _____ No

If yes, type of disability:_____

How have these students generally performed in your program:

very well ____   well ____   fair ____   barely passed ____   failed ____

5. How can a student with a disability be successful in your program?

_____

_____

_____

_____

6. In which grade, or at what age, can a student begin your program?_____

Comments or special considerations (Please add any information regarding your program that would be valuable for us to know):

_____

_____

_____

_____

_____

_____

THANK YOU FOR TAKING THE TIME TO COMPLETE THIS FORM

INDIVIDUAL TRANSITION PLAN FORM

Student's Name _____   Home School _____

      Last   First   Middle

Address _____   Date of Birth _____ Age _____

Parents' Names _____   Telephone _____

Date of Meeting _____   Proposed Graduation Date _____

PARTICIPANTS   AGENCY   POSITION   TELEPHONE

_____ _____ _____ _____

_____ _____ _____ _____

_____ _____ _____ _____

_____ _____ _____ _____

MAJOR GOAL

Employment _____

Residential Living _____

Community Functioning _____

(continued)

ACTION PLAN:

		EMPLOYMENT				RESIDENTIAL LIVING				COMMUNITY FUNCTIONING		
		Action	Timeline	Person	Position	Action	Timeline	Person	Position	Action	Timeline	Person	Position
SCHOOL	1.					1.				1.			
	2.					2.				2.			
	3.					3.				3.			
VOCATIONAL REHABILITATION	1.					1.				1.			
	2					2.				2.			
	3.					3.				3.			
MENTAL HEALTH/ MENTAL RETARDATION	1.					1.				1.			
	2.					2.				2.			
	3.					3.				3.			
OTHER _____	1.					1.				1.			
	2.					2.				2.			
	3.					3.				3.			
OTHER _____	1.					1.				1.			
	2.					2.				2.			
	3.					3.				3.			

APPENDIX B
VOCATIONAL ASSESSMENT PROGRAMMING, AND TRANSITIONING: A BIBLIOGRAPHY FOR THE PROFESSIONAL

This appendix contains an alphabetical listing of books and articles that can be consulted by the reader to gain additional information on the topics discussed in this book.

Abeson, A. (1978). The logic and law for parent participation in the education of handicapped students. *Journal of Career Education, 5*(1), 35-43.

Adelman, F. A., & Phelps, L. A. (1978). Learning to teach handicapped learners. *American Vocational Journal, 53*(4), 27-29.

Albright, L. (1977). Resources for special needs personnel development. *Journal of Industrial Teacher Education, 14*(4), 46-55.

Albright, L., & Cobb, R. B. (1988). Curriculum based vocational assessment. A concept whose time has come. *Journal for Vocational Special Needs Education, 10*(2), 13-16.

Alcorn, C., & Nicholson, C. (1975). A vocational assessment battery for the educable mentally retarded and low literate. *Education and Training of the Mentally Retarded, 10*(2), 78-83.

American Vocational Association. (1973). Manpower, human assessment, and the disadvantaged: A consumer report on the use and misuse of standardized testing. *American Vocational Journal, 48*(1), 85-100.

Anderson, W. T. (1982a). Assessment roles for vocational school psychologists. *The Journal for Vocational Special Needs Education, 4*(3), 14-17.

Anderson, W. T. (1982b). Vocational interest assessment procedures. In T. H. Hohenshil, W. T. Anderson, & J. F. Salwan (Eds.), *Secondary school psychological services: Focus on vocational assessment procedures for handicapped students*. Blacksburg, VA: Virginia Tech. (ERIC Reproduction Service No. 229704)

Anderson, W. T. (1985). Prevocational and vocational assessment of handicapped students. In P. J. Lazarus & S. S. Strichart (Eds.), *Psychoeducational evaluation of school age children with low incidence handicaps*. New York: Grune and Stratton.

Anderson, W. T., Hohenshil, T. H., Capps, C. F., & Levinson, E. M. (1986). Proactive reevaluation through vocational assessment of adolescents. In *Proceedings of the Eighteenth Annual Convention of the National Association of School Psychologists*, 113-114.

Anderson, W. T., Hohenshil, T. H., Heer, K., & Levinson, E. M. (1990). Best practices in vocational assessment of handicapped students. In A. Thomas & J. Grimes (Eds.), *Best practices in school psychology-II*. Washington, DC: National Association of School Psychologists.

Appell, M. J. (1977). Some policies and practices in the federal sector concerning career education for the handicapped. *Journal of Career Education, 3*(3), 75-91.

Appell, M. J. (1978). A study of career education proposals, Fiscal Year 1978. *Career Development for Exceptional Individuals, 2*, 3-11.

Appleby, J. A. (1978). *Training programs and placement services*. Salt Lake City, UT: Olympus.

Ayers, G. (Ed.). (1968, April). Assessing the vocational potential of the socially handicapped. In *Proceedings of the Vocational Evaluation and Work Adjustment Association Sectional Meeting*, NRA, St. Louis, MO.

Ayers, G. (1971). Making vocational evaluation relevant to our clients: The challenge of the disadvantaged. *Rehabilitation Literature, 32*(9), 258-262.

Azrin, N., & Bezalel, V. (1980). *Job club counselor manual*. Baltimore, MD: University Park Press.

Azrin, N., Flores, T., & Kaplan, S. (1977). Job finding club: A group assisted program for finding employment. *Rehabilitation Counseling Bulletin, 21*(2), 130-139.

Baker, B. C., Geiger, W. L., & deFur, S. (1988). *Competencies for transition personnel*. Paper presented at the Mid-East Regional Conference of the Career Development Division of the Council for Exceptional Children, White Sulphur Springs, WVA, November, 1988.

Ballamy, G. T., Wilson, D. J., Adler, E., & Clarke, J. Y. (1980). A strategy for programming vocational skills for severely handicapped youth. *Exceptional Education Quarterly, 1*, 85-97.

Bame, E., & Gatewood, T. (1983). Brain functioning: Implications for curriculum and instruction in industrial arts. *Journal of Industrial Teacher Education, 20*(20), 36-44.

Barber, R. M. (1981). Vocational assessment procedures for handicapped students: A generic approach. In T. H. Hohenshil & W. T. Anderson (Eds.), *School* psychological services in secondary vocational education: Roles in programs for handicapped students. Blacksburg, VA: Virginia Tech. (ERIC Document Reproduction Service No. 215245)

Barber, R. M. (1982). U.S. Employment Service aptitude testing batteries and the handicapped student. In T. H. Hohenshil, W. T. Anderson, & J. F. Salwan (Eds.), *Secondary school psychological services: Focus on vocational assessment procedures for handicapped students.* Blacksburg, VA: Virginia Tech. (ERIC Document Reproduction Service No. 229704)

Barrett, S. P. (1987). The legal implications of testing. In P. LeConte (Ed.), *Using vocational assessment results for effective planning.* Stevens Point, WI: The Department of Public Instruction.

Batsche, C. (1982a). *Handbook for vocational school psychology.* Des Moines, IA: Iowa Department of Education.

Batsche, C. (1982b). Vocational education of handicapped youth: State of the art. In T. H. Hohenshil & W. T. Anderson (Eds.), *School psychological services in secondary vocational education: Roles in programs for handicapped students.* Blacksburg, VA: Virginia Tech. (ERIC Document Reproduction Service No. 215245)

Batsche, C. (1984). Providing vocational education for special needs populations. In C. H. Mayer, R. J. Illback, & J. E. Zins (Eds.), *Organizational psychology in the schools.* Springfield, IL: Charles C. Thomas.

Beane, A., & Zachmanoglow, M. A. (1979). Career education for the handicapped: A psychosocial impact. *Vocational Guidance Quarterly, 28*(1), 44-47.

Becker, R. L. et al. (1979). Career education for trainable mentally retarded youth. *Education and Training of the Mentally Retarded, 14*(2), 101-105.

Beley, W., & Felker, S. (1981). Comprehensive vocational evaluation for clients with psychiatric impairments. *Rehabilitation Literature, 42*(7), 194-201.

Benz, M. R., & Halpern, A. S. (1987). Transition services for secondary students with mild disabilities: A statewide perspective. *Exceptional Children, 53*(6), 507-514.

Bergman, M., & Hanson, D. (1975). T and I for the handicapped? You've got to be kidding. *American Vocational Journal, 50*(2), 78-83.

Biller, E. F. (1987). *Career decision making for adolescents and young adults with learning disabilities.* Springfield, IL: Charles C. Thomas.

Biller, E. F., & White, W. J. (1989). Comparing special education and vocational rehabilitation in serving persons with specific learning disabilities. *Rehabilitation Counseling Bulletin, 33*(1), 4-17.

Bingham, G. (1975). Career attitudes and self-esteem among boys with and without specific learning disabilities. *Dissertation Abstracts International, 36,* 02A-75347. (University Microfilms No. 75-17, 340)

Bingham, G. (1978). Career attitudes among boys with and without specific learning disabilities. *Exceptional Children, 44,* 341-342.

Bingham, G. (1980). Career maturity of learning disabled adolescents. *Psychology in the Schools, 17,* 135-139.

Bingham, G. (1981). Exploratory process in career development: Implications for learning disabled students. *Career Development for Exceptional Individuals, 4,* 77-80.

Blevins, B. A. (1982). Vocational assessment procedures for the deaf and hard of hearing. In T. H. Hohenshil, W. T. Anderson, & J. F. Salwan (Eds.), *Secondary school psychological services: Focus on vocational assessment procedures for handicapped students.* Blacksburg, VA: Virginia Tech. (ERIC Document Reproduction Service No. 229704)

Bodien, J. (1975). Vocational evaluation: A functional analysis. *Rehabilitation Review, 1*(1).

Bolton, B. (1976). *Handbook of measurement and evaluation in rehabilitation.* Baltimore, MD: University Park Press.

Bolton, B. (1982). *Vocational adjustment of disabled persons.* Austin, TX: Pro-Ed.

Booton, W. (1978). Motivating and managing behavior. *Industrial Education, 64*(4), 24-25.

Borba, C. E., & Guizicki, J. A. (1980). Project Invest: Instructional network for vocational education and specialized training. *Career Education for Exceptional Individuals, 2,* 83-86.

Botterbusch, K. (1974). Test use in vocational evaluation. *Vocational Evaluation and Work Adjustment Bulletin, 7*(2), 6-9.

Botterbusch, K. (1976a). *A comparison of seven vocational evaluation systems.* Menomonie, WI: Stout Vocational Rehabilitation Institute, University of Wisconsin – Stout.

Botterbusch, K. (1976b). *The use of psychological tests with individuals who are severely disabled.* Menomonie, WI: University of Wisconsin – Stout, Materials Development Center.

Botterbusch, K. (1977). *A comparison of four vocational evaluation systems.* Menomonie, WI: University of Wisconsin – Stout, Materials Development Center.

Botterbusch, K. (1978). *Psychological testing in vocational evaluation.* Menomonie, WI: University of Wisconsin – Stout, Materials Development Center.

Botterbusch, K. F., & Michael, N. C. (1985). *Testing and test modification in vocational evaluation.* Menomonie, WI: University of Wisconsin – Stout, Materials Development Center.

Bottoms, G., & O'Kelley, G. L. (1974). Vocational education as a differential process. *The School Psychology Digest, 3,* 33-40.

Bowe, F. (1980). *Rehabilitating America toward independence for disabled and elderly people.* New York: Harper & Row.

Bowe, F., & Razeghi, J. A. (1979). Enabling the disabled through career counseling. *Voc Ed, 54*(7), 44-47.

Bowers, J. G. (1978). Cooperative work-education. *Industrial Education, 67*(3), 16-23.

Bregman, M. (1968). The use and misuse of vocational evaluation in the counseling process. *Vocational Evaluation and Work Adjustment Bulletin, 1*(2), 6-8.

Brickey, M., & Campbell, K. (1981). Fast food employment for moderately and mildly retarded adults: The McDonalds Project. *Mental Retardation, 19*(3), 113-116.

Brolin, D. (1973). Vocational evaluation: Special education's responsibility. *Education and Training of the Mentally Retarded, 8*(1), 12-17.

Brolin, D. E. (1976). *Vocational preparation of retarded citizens*. Columbus, OH: Charles E. Merrill.

Brolin, D. E. (1986a). *Life centered career education: A competency based approach*. Reston, VA: The Council for Exceptional Children.

Brolin, D. E. (1986b). A model for providing comprehensive transitional services: The role of special education. In J. Chadsey-Rusch & C. Hanley-Maxwell (Eds.), *Enhancing transition from school to the workplace for handicapped youth: Personnel preparation implications*. Champaign, IL: National Network for Professional Development in Vocational Special Education.

Brolin, D. E., & D'Alonzo, B. J. (1979). Critical issues in career education for handicapped students. *Exceptional Children, 45*, 246-253.

Brolin, D. E., & Elliot, T. R. (1984). Meeting the lifelong career development needs of students with handicaps. *Career Development for Exceptional Individuals, 7*(1), 12-21.

Brolin, D. E., & Gysbers, N. C. (1979). Career education for persons with handicaps. *The Personnel and Guidance Journal, 58*, 258-262.

Brolin, D. E., & Kokaska, C. J. (1979). *Career education for handicapped children and youth*. Columbus, OH: Charles E. Merrill.

Brolin, D. E., McLay, D. J., & West, L. L. (1977). Personnel preparation for career education for handicapped students. *Journal of Career Education, 3*(3), 54-74.

Brolin, D. T. (1982). University training in vocational school psychology. In T. H. Hohenshil & W. T. Anderson (Eds.), *School psychological services in secondary vocational education: Roles in programs for handicapped students*. Blacksburg, VA: Virginia Tech. (ERIC Document Reproduction Service No. 215245)

Brown, D. T. (1990). Computerized techniques in career assessment. *Career Planning and Adult Development Journal, 6*(4), 27-36.

Brown, D. T., & Cobb, H. (1982a). The school psychologist's role in vocational assessment of the mentally retarded. *The Journal for Vocational Special Needs Education, 4*(3),18-20.

Brown, D. T., & Cobb, H. (1982b). Vocational assessment procedures for the mentally retarded. In T. H. Hohenshil, W. T. Anderson, & J. F. Salwan (Eds.), *Secondary school psychological services: Focus on vocational assessment procedures for handicapped students*. Blacksburg, VA: Virginia Tech. (ERIC Document Reproduction Service No. 229704)

Brown, L. (1982). Vocational assessment for learning disabled students. In T. H. Hohenshil, W. T. Anderson, & J. F. Salwan (Eds.), *Secondary school psychological services: Focus on vocational assessment procedures for handicapped students*. Blacksburg, VA: Virginia Tech. (ERIC Document Reproduction Service No. 229704)

Brown, L., Shiraga, B., York, J., & Kessler, K. (1985). *Integrated work opportunities for adults with severe handicaps: The extended training option*. Madison, WI: University of Wisconsin & Madison Metropolitan School District.

Browning, P., & Irvin, L. K. (1981). Vocational evaluation, training, and placement of mentally retarded persons. *Rehabilitation Counselor Bulletin, 24*, 374-408.

Buck, J. N. (1981). Influence of identity, and decision-making style on the career decision-making process (Doctoral dissertation, Southern Illinois University at Carbondale, 1981). *Dissertation Abstracts International, 42,* 2027A. (University Microfilms No. 81-22, 622).

Burdett, A. (1963). An examination of selected prevocational techniques utilized in programs for the mentally retarded. *Mental Retardation, 1,* 230-237.

Bursch, C. A. (1983). Vocational psychology: What part should we play in the schools? In *Proceedings of the Fifteenth Annual Convention of the National Association of School Psychologists,* Detroit, MI.

Calhoun, C., & Finch, A. (1976). *Vocational and career education: Concepts and operation.* Belmont, CA: Wadsworth.

Canonico, A., & Lombardi, T. P. (1984). Effects of career adaptive behavior activities and its assessment in mentally handicapped students. *Exceptional Children, 50*(6), 545-547.

Capps, C. F. (1981). Reflections of a school psychologist's involvement with CETA funded alternative secondary schools. In T. H. Hohenshil & W. T. Anderson (Eds.), *School psychological services in secondary vocational education: Roles in programs for handicapped students.* Blacksburg, VA: Virginia Tech. (ERIC Document Reproduction Service No. 215245)

Capps, C. F. (1982). The measurement of adaptive behavior in public secondary schools: The school psychologist's role. In T. H. Hohenshil, W. T. Anderson, & J. F. Salwan (Eds.), *School psychological services in secondary vocational education: Roles in programs for handicapped students.* Blacksburg, VA: Virginia Tech. (ERIC Document Reproduction Service No. 215245)

Capps, C. F., Houff, K., & Blevins, B. (1982). The school psychologist as a career counselor for handicapped students. In *Proceedings of the Fourteenth Annual Convention of the National Association of School Psychologists,* Toronto.

Capps, C. F., Levinson, E. M., & Hohenshil, T. H. (1985). Vocational aspects of psychological assessment: Part 3. *The Communique, 13*(5), 5-6.

Carmel, L., & Renyulbo, R. (Eds.). (1977). *Barriers and bridges.* Sacramento, CA: California Advisory Council on Vocational Education.

Carpenter, R. L., & Robson, D. L. (1978). The potential effect of the new special education legislation on the field of vocational education. *Journal of Industrial Teacher Education, 15*(2), 50-54.

Carsrud, A. L., Carsrud, K. B., Dodd, B. C., Thompson, M., & Gray, W. K. (1981). Predicting vocational aptitude of mentally retarded persons: A comparison of assessment systems. *American Journal of Mental Deficiency, 86,* 275-280.

Cartledge, G. (1989). Social skills and vocational success for workers with learning disabilities. *Rehabilitation Counseling Bulletin, 33*(1), 74-79.

Cawley, J. F. et al. (1989). Vocational education and students with learning disabilities. *Journal of Learning Disabilities, 22*(10), 630-634.

Clark, D. (1969). Evaluation: A psychologist's view. *Vocational Evaluation and Work Adjustment Bulletin, 2*(2), 3-6.

Clark, G. M. (1977). Guidelines and strategies for coordination of special needs teacher education. *Journal of Industrial Teacher Education, 14*(4), 28-35.

Clark, G. M. (1979). *Career education for the handicapped child in the elementary classroom.* Denver: Love.

Clark, G. M. (1980). Career preparation for handicapped adolescents: A matter of appropriate education. *Exceptional Education Quarterly, 1*(2), 11-17.

Clayton, I. (1983). Career preparation and the visually handicapped student. *Education of the Visually Handicapped, 14*(4), 115-120.

Cobb, R. B. (1981). Vocational assessment of special needs learners: The utility of commercial work sampling systems. *The Journal for Vocational Special Needs Education, 3*(3), 30-32.

Cobb, R. B., & Phelps, L. A. (1983). Analyzing individual education programs for vocational components: An exploratory study. *Exceptional Children, 50*(1), 62-64.

Cook, P. F., Dahl, P. R., & Fale, M. A. (1978). *Vocational opportunities, vocational training and placement of the severely handicapped.* Salt Lake City, UT: Olympus.

Cooper, B. S. (1977). Occupational help for the severely disabled: A public school model. *Rehabilitation Literature, 3*(3), 66-74.

Coughran, L., & Daniels, J. (1983). Early vocational intervention for the severely handicapped. *Journal of Rehabilitation, 49*(1), 24-28.

Crawford, G. B. (1979). Perceived inservice needs of North Dakota vocational teachers concerning disadvantaged/ handicapped students. *The Journal of Vocational Education Research, 4*(3), 15-26.

Cromwell, F. (1959). A procedure for pre-vocational evaluation. *The American Journal of Occupational Therapy, 13*(1), 1-4.

Dahl, P. (1982). Maximizing vocational opportunities for handicapped clients. *Vocational Guidance Quarterly, 31*(1), 43-52.

Dahl, P. et al. (1980). Mainstreaming guidebook for vocational educators teaching the handicapped. In Occupational Curriculum Laboratory, *An implementation manual for vocational assessment of students with special needs.* Denton, TX: East Texas State University.

Dahl, P. R., Appleby, J. A., & Lipe, D. (1978). *Mainstreaming guidebook for vocational educators.* Salt Lake City, UT: Olympus.

D'Alonzo, B. J. (1978). Career education for handicapped youth and adults in the 70's. *Career Development for Exceptional Individuals, 1,* 4-12.

Daughtrey, W. (1972). Vocational evaluation: Some fundamental propositions. *Vocational Evaluation and Work Adjustment Bulletin, 5*(1), 12-17.

Davis, S., & Ward, M. (1978). *Vocational education of handicapped students: A guide for policy development.* Reston, VA: Council for Exceptional Children.

Dawis, R. V., England, G. W., & Lofquist, L. H. (1964). A theory of work adjustment. *Minnesota Studies in Vocational Rehabilitation,* No. XV. Minneapolis: Industrial Relations Center, University of Minnesota.

Dawis, R. V., Lofquist, L. H., & Weiss, D. J. (1968). A theory of work adjustment. A revision. *Minnesota Studies in Vocational Rehabilitation,* No. XXIII. Minneapolis: Industrial Relations Center, University of Minnesota.

Devries, D. (1981). Vocational education programs for handicapped students in Virginia. In T. H. Hohenshil & W. T. Anderson (Eds.), *School psychological services in secondary vocational education: Roles in programs for handicapped students*. Blacksburg, VA: Virginia Tech. (ERIC Document Reproduction Service No. 215245)

Dickson, M. B. (1979). Job-seeking skills program for the blind. *Journal of Visual Impairment and Blindness, 73*, 20-25.

Dietrich, D. (1980). Vocational mainstreaming for educable mentally retarded students. *Career Development for Exceptional Individuals, 2*, 101-108.

Ditty, J. A., & Reynolds, K. (1980). Traditional vocational evaluation: Help or hindrance? *Journal of Rehabilitation, 46*(4), 22-25.

Dodson, E., & Turrentine-Jenkins, M. (1982). School psychologists in a community college vocational assessment center. In T. H. Hohenshil, W. T. Anderson, & J. F. Salwan (Eds.), *Secondary school psychological services: Focus on vocational assessment procedures for handicapped students*. Blacksburg, VA: Virginia Tech. (ERIC Document Reproduction Service No. 229704)

Donohue, K. (1977). The vocational school psychologist as a teacher consultant. In *Proceedings of the Ninth Annual Convention of the National Association of School Psychologists*.

Donohue, K. (1978). Career education for the handicapped: The vocational school psychologist as a consultant. *School Psychology Digest, 7*(1), 55-59.

Doty, C. R. (1979). Priorities for research for career education for the handicapped. *Journal of Industrial Teacher Education, 16*(4), 46-55.

Dunn, D., Korn, T., & Andrew, J. (Eds.). (1976). *Critical issues in vocational evaluation*. Menomonie, WI: University of Wisconsin—Stout, Materials Development Center.

Eads, F. D., & Gill, D. H. (1975). Prescriptive teaching for handicapped students. *American Vocational Journal, 50*(8), 52-57.

Edgar, E. (1987). Secondary programs in special education: Are they justifiable? *Exceptional Children, 53*(6), 555-561.

Edgar, E. (1988). Transition from school to community: Promising programs. *Teaching Exceptional Children, 20*(2), 73-75.

Ehrle, R. et al. (1975). Glossary of terms used in vocational evaluation. *Vocational Evaluation and Work Adjustment Bulletin, 8*, 85-93.

Elksnin, L., & Elksnin, N. (1990). Using collaborative consultation with parents to promote effective vocational programming. *Career Development for Exceptional Individuals, 13*(2), 135-142.

Ellsworth, S., & Noll, A. (1978). *Vocational evaluators in school settings: Task analyses, certification, qualification, and status data*. Menomonie, WI: University of Wisconsin - Stout, Materials Development Center.

Elrod, G. F. et al. (1989). Assessing transition-related variables from kindergarten through grade 12: Practical applications. *Diagnostique, 14*(4), 247-261.

Elrod, G. F., & Sorgenfrei, T. B. (1988). Toward an appropriate assessment model for adolescents who are mildly handicapped. Let's not forget transition! *Career Development for Exceptional Individuals, 11*(2), 92-98.

Epstein, M. H. (1982). Special education programs for the handicapped adolescent. *School Psychology Review*, *11*(4), 384-390.

Esser, T. (1975). *Client rating instruments for use in vocational rehabilitation agencies*. Menomonie, WI: University of Wisconsin — Stout, Materials Development Center.

Esser, T. (1977). Client orientation: Introducing you to vocational evaluation. In A. Sax (Ed.), Innovations in vocational evaluation and work adjustment. *Vocational Evaluation and Work Adjustment Bulletin*, *10*(3), 42-44.

Fafard, M., & Hubrick, P. (1981). Vocational and social adjustment of learning disabled young adults: A follow-up study. *Learning Disability Quarterly*, *4*(2), 122-129.

Fagan, T. (1976). Career education concepts in school psychology training programs. In *Proceedings of the Eighth Annual Convention of the National Association of School Psychologists*, Kansas City.

Fagan, T. (1978). [Review of *Vocational education for special groups: Sixth yearbook of the American Vocational Association*]. *The School Psychology Digest*, *7*, 68-71.

Fagan, T. (1981). Role expansion in the eighties: Counseling and vocational school psychology. *The Communique*, *9*(6),1-2.

Fagan, T. (1982a). An interview with Dr. Thomas Hohenshil. *The Communique*, *11*(3), 4-5.

Fagan, T. (1982b). Vocational school psychology: Determining what lies ahead. *The Journal for Vocational Special Needs Education*, *4*(3), 33-37.

Fagan, T., & Hohenshil, T. (1976). The integration of career education into the training of school psychologists. *Psychology in the Schools*, *13*, 334-350.

Fair, G. W., & Sullivan, A. R. (1980). Career opportunities for culturally diverse handicapped youth. *Exceptional Children*, *46*, 626-631.

Fardig, D. B., Algozzine, R. F., Schwartz, S. E., Hensel, J. E., & Westling, D. L. (1985). Postsecondary vocational adjustment of rural, mildly handicapped students. *Exceptional Children*, *52*(2), 115-121.

Finley, J. R. (1979). The psychologist's consultant role in the state vocational rehabilitation agency. *Journal of Rehabilitation*, *45*(1), 46-47.

Flanagan, W. M., & Schoepki, J. M. (1978). *Lifelong learning and career development needs of the severely handicapped*. Columbia, MO: University of Missouri.

Fredericks, B. (1986). Part time work for high school students. *Teaching Research*, *15*(1), 1-7.

Gadla, L. (1978). Program changes to accommodate students. *American Vocational Journal*, *53*(3), 29-33.

Gannaway, T. W., Sink, J. M., & Becket, W. C. (1980). A predictive validity study of a job sample program with handicapped and disadvantaged individuals. *The Vocational Guidance Quarterly*, *29*, 4-11.

Garcia, G., Jr., & Plansker, C. M. (1990). A reaction to an analysis of nine computer-assisted career guidance systems. *Journal of Career Development*, *17*(2), 113-117.

Gardner, D. C., & Warren, S. A. (1978). *Careers and disabilities: A career education approach.* Stanford: Greylock.

Gellman, W. (1957). Vocational evaluation of the emotionally handicapped. *Journal of Rehabilitation, 23*(4), 9-10.

Gellman, W. (1971). Principles guiding vocational evaluation. In R. Pacinelli (Ed.), *Research in utilization in rehabilitation facilities.* Washington, DC: International Association of Rehabilitation Facilities.

Gellman, W., & Soloff, A. (1976). Vocational evaluation. In B. Bolton (Ed.), *Handbook of measurement and evaluation in rehabilitation.* Baltimore, MD: University Park Press.

Gibson, J., & Lazar, A. L. (1977). Orange Unified School District's special education career and vocational program. *Career Education Quarterly, 2*(4), 21-28.

Gilberg, J. A. (1983). Career opportunities and function of school psychologists in correctional institutions. In *Proceedings of the Fifteenth Annual Convention of the National Association of School Psychologists,* Detroit, MI.

Gillett, P. (1980). Career education and the learning disabled student. *Career Development for Exceptional Individuals, 2,* 67-73.

Gills, W. S. (1972). The psychologist and rehabilitation. In J. G. Cull & R. E. Hardy (Eds.), *Vocational rehabilitation: Profession and process.* Springfield, IL: Charles C. Thomas.

Ginzberg, E., Ginsburg, S. W., Axelrad, S., & Herma, J. L. (1951). *Occupational choice: An approach to a general theory.* New York: Columbia University Press.

Goldberg, R. T. (1981). Toward an understanding of the rehabilitation of the disabled adolescent. *Rehabilitation Literature, 42*(3), 66-74.

Goodwill of Wyoming. (1977). *Vocational goal development.* Cheyenne, WY: Human Services Center, Rehabilitation Department.

Gorelick, M. C. (1968). Assessment of vocational realism of educable mentally retarded adolescents. *American Journal of Mental Deficiency, 73,* 154-157.

Gottfredson, G. D. (1977). Career stability and redirection in adulthood. *Journal of Applied Psychology, 62,* 436-445.

Gottfredson, G. D. (1981, August). *Why don't interests predict job satisfaction better than they do?* Paper presented at American Psychological Association Convention, Los Angeles, CA.

Graff, R. W., & Beggs, D. L. (1984). Personal and vocational development in high school students. *Journal of School Psychology, 12*(1), 17-23.

Grisafe, J. P. (n.d.). *Occupational assessment handbook.* Riverside, CA: Riverside County System of Schools. (ERIC Document Reproduction Service No. 187879)

Growlick, B. S. (1981). Facilitating career education for the handicapped. *Educational Perspectives, 18*(2), 24-28.

Gugerty, J. (1978). Discovering what works best in educating handicapped students. *American Vocational Journal, 53*(4), 34-36.

Gust, T. (1967). The psychological-vocational evaluation report: Reciprocal referral responsibility. *Rehabilitation Counselor Bulletin, 10*(3), 108-111.

Halpern, A. S. (1978). Principles and practices of measurement in career education for handicapped students. *Career Development for Exceptional Individuals, 1,* 13-24.

Halpern, A. (1985). Transition: A look at the foundations. *Exceptional Children, 51*(6), 479-486.

Halpern, A. S., Raffeld, P., Irvin, L. K., & Link, R. (1975). Measuring social and prevocational awareness in mildly mentally retarded adolescents. *American Journal of Mental Deficiency, 80,* 81-89.

Harren, V. A. (1979). A model of career decision making for college students. *Journal of Vocational Behavior, 14,* 119-133.

Hasazi, S. B., Gordon, L. R., & Roe, C. A. (1985). Factors associated with the employment status of handicapped youth exiting high school from 1979 to 1983. *Exceptional Children, 51*(6), 455-469.

Hastings, L. O., Hill, J. T., & DeLuca, J. (1982). Clarification of occupational direction: A consultation model for handicapped adolescents. In *Proceedings of the Fourteenth Annual Convention of the National Association of School Psychologists,* Toronto.

Hastings, L. O., Hill, J. T., & Klindinger, R. M. (1983). Vocational preparation: Training students to be workers. *The Journal for Vocational Special Needs Education, 6,* 12-14.

Heinlein, W. E. (1987). *Clinical utility of the Wechsler scales in psychological evaluations to estimate vocational aptitude.* Unpublished doctoral dissertation, Virginia Polytechnic Institute and State University, Blacksburg, VA.

Heinlein, W. E., Nelson, M. D., & Hohenshil, T. H. (1985). Vocational aspects of psychological assessment, Part 2. *The Communique, 13*(4).

Heller, H. W., & Schilit, J. (1979). Career education for the handicapped: Directions for the future. *Career Development for Exceptional Individuals, 2,* 91-96.

Hereshenson, D. B. (1984). Vocational counseling with learning disabled adults. *Journal of Rehabilitation, 50*(2), 40-44.

Hoffman, P. (1970). An overview of work evaluation. *Journal of Rehabilitation, 36*(1), 16-18.

Hoffman, P. R. (1973). Work evaluation: An overview. In R. E. Hardy & J. G. Cull (Eds.), *Vocational evaluation for rehabilitation services.* Springfield, IL: Charles C. Thomas.

Hohenshil, T. H. (1974a). Career education and school psychology. *School Psychology Digest, 3*(3), 2-3.

Hohenshil, T. H. (1974b). The vocational school psychologist: A specialty in quest of a training program. *Psychology in the Schools, 11*(1), 16-18. Reprinted in *School Psychology Digest, 3*(3), 51-54.

Hohenshil, T. H. (1975). Call for redirection: A vocational evaluator views school psychology. *Journal of School Psychology, 13,* 58-69.

Hohenshil, T. H. (1978). Vocational education for youth with special learning needs: Roles for the vocational school psychologist. *School Psychology Digest, 7*(1), 3-4.

Hohenshil, T. H. (1979a). Adulthood: New frontier for vocational school psychology. *School Psychology Digest, 8*(2), 193-198.

Hohenshil, T. H. (1979b). Renewal in career guidance and counseling: Rationale and programs. *Counselor Education and Supervision, 18*(3), 199-208.

Hohenshil, T. H. (1981). Roles for school psychology in vocational education programs for handicapped students. In T. H. Hohenshil & W. T. Anderson (Eds.), *School psychological services in secondary vocational education: Roles in programs for handicapped students*. Blacksburg, VA: Virginia Tech. (ERIC Document Reproduction Service No. 215245)

Hohenshil, T. H. (1982a). School psychology + vocational counseling = vocational school psychology. *The Personnel and Guidance Journal, 61*(1), 11-14.

Hohenshil, T. H. (1982b). Secondary school psychological services: Vocational assessment procedures for handicapped students. In T. H. Hohenshil, W. T. Anderson, & J. F. Salwan (Eds.), *Secondary school psychological services: Focus on assessment procedures for handicapped students*. Blacksburg, VA: Virginia Tech. (ERIC Document Reproduction Service No. 229704)

Hohenshil, T. H. (1983). Vocational school psychology. In T. Kratochwill (Ed.), *Advances in school psychology* (Vol. 3). Hillsdale, NJ: Lawrence Erlbaum.

Hohenshil, T. H. (1984a). Vocational aspects of psychological assessment, Part 1. *The Communique, 13*(3).

Hohenshil, T. H. (1984b). The vocational aspects of school psychology: 1974-1984. *School Psychology Review, 13*(4), 503-509.

Hohenshil, T. H. (1986). Vocational assessment for adolescents. In R. Harrington (Ed.), *Testing adolescents*. Kansas City: Test Corporation of America.

Hohenshil, T. H., Anderson, W. T., Fagan, T., Brown, D., & Prout, T. (1982). Vocational school psychology—Current status and future promise. In *Proceedings of the Fourteenth Annual Convention of the National Association of School Psychologists*, Toronto.

Hohenshil, T. H., Anderson, W. T., & Salwan, J. F. (1982). *Secondary school psychological services: Focus on vocational assessment procedures for handicapped students*. Blacksburg, VA: Virginia Polytechnic Institute and State University.

Hohenshil, T. H., Brown, D., & Fagan, T. (1980). Vocational school psychology: Past, present, and future. In *Proceedings of the Tenth Annual Convention of the National Association of School Psychologists*, Washington, DC.

Hohenshil, T. H., Dunn, N., & Kravitz, S. (1973). The comprehensive career education model and the school psychologist: A new role? In *Proceedings of the Fifth Annual Convention of the National Association of School Psychologists*, New York.

Hohenshil, T. H., Humes, C. W., & Anderson, W. T. (1984). School psychologists facilitating career development programs in secondary education. *Career Development for Exceptional Individuals, 7*(2), 51-58.

Hohenshil, T. H., Hummel, D. L., & Maddy-Bernstein, C. (1980). The impact of work patterns upon family development. *School Psychology Review, 9* 312-318.

Hohenshil, T. H., Levinson, E. M., & Buckland-Heer, K. (1985). Best practices in vocational assessment for handicapped students. In J. Grimes & A. Thomas (Eds.), *Best practices in school psychology*. Washington, DC: National Association of School Psychologists.

Hohenshil, T. H., & Warden, P. (1978). The emerging vocational school psychologist: Implications for special needs students. *The School Psychology Digest, 1,* 5-17.

Holland, J. L. (1966). *The psychology of vocational choice*. Waltham, MA: Blaisdell.

Holland, J. L. (1973). Some practical remedies for providing vocational guidance for everyone. *Center for the Study of Social Organization of Schools, 163.*

Holland, J. (1985). *A theory of vocational personalities and work enviroments*. Englewood Cliffs, NJ: Prentice-Hall.

Holmes, D., Wanner, C., & Biskel, M. A. (1983). Career education in an educational program for visually impaired. *Education of the Visually Handicapped, 14*(4), 121-125.

Hooper, P. G. (1980). Guidance and counseling: Potential impact on youth unemployment. *Journal of Career Education, 6,* 270-287.

Houff, J. K. (1982). Occupational social competence/skills: A necessary component of vocational assessment for school psychologists. In T. H. Hohenshil, W. T. Anderson, & J. F. Salwan (Eds.), *Secondary school psychological services: Focus on vocational assessment procedures for handicapped students*. Blacksburg, VA: Virginia Tech. (ERIC Document Reproduction Service No. 229704)

Hoyt, K. (1976). *Career education for special populations: Monographs on career education*. Washington, DC: Government Printing Office. (Stock No. 017-080-01612-5)

Huber, C. H. (1979). Career planning with mildly retarded students: A model for school counselors. *Vocational Guidance Quarterly, 27,* 223-228.

Humes, C., & Hohenshil, T. H. (1985). Career development and career education for handicapped students: A re-examination. *Vocational Guidance Quarterly, 34*(1), 31-40.

Humes, C., & Hummel, D. (1981). Vocational counseling (career planning) processes for handicapped students. In T. H. Hohenshil & W. T. Anderson (Eds.), *School psychological services in secondary vocational education: Roles in programs for handicapped students*. Blacksburg, VA: Virginia Tech. (ERIC Document Reproduction Service No. 215245).

Hummel, D. C., & Hohenshil, T. H. (1974). The psychological foundations of career education: Potential roles for the school psychologist. *School Psychology Digest, 3*(3), 4-11.

Hursh, N. (1984). Vocational evaluation of learning disabled adults and older adolescents. *Journal of Rehabilitation, 50*(2), 45-52.

Hursh, N. C. (1989). Vocational evaluation with learning disabled students: Utilization guidelines for teachers. *Academic Therapy, 25*(2), 201-215.

Ianocone, R. N., & Sigmond, M. V. (1977). Experience based career education: Innovative application for the handicapped. *Career Education Quarterly*, *2*(4), 29-36.

Irvin, L. K. et al. (1981). Vocational skill assessment of severely mentally retarded adults. *American Journal of Mental Deficiency*, *85*(6), 631-638.

Irvin, L. K. et al. (1984). Validating vocational assessment of severely mentally retarded persons: Issues and application. *American Journal of Mental Deficiency*, *88*(4), 411-417.

Irvin, L. K., & Halpern, A. S. (1975). A process model of diagnostic assessment. In G. T. Bellamy, G. O'Connor, & O. C. Karan (Eds.), *Vocational rehabilitation of severely handicapped persons*. Baltimore, MD: University Park Press.

Irvin, L. K., & Halpern, A. S. (1977). Reliability and validity of the Social and Prevocational Information Battery for mildly retarded individuals. *American Journal of Mental Deficiency*, *81*(6), 603-605.

Irvin, L. K., Halpern, A. S., & Reynolds, W. (1972). Assessing social and prevocational awareness in mildly and moderately retarded individuals. *American Journal of Mental Deficiency*, *82*, 266-272.

Jewett, R. J., & Dardig, J. C. (1978). Towards community employment: A comprehensive data based training system for mentally retarded adults. *Career Development for Exceptional Individuals*, *2*, 31-39.

Johnson, C. M. (1978). Career education for exceptional individuals. *Career Development for Exceptional Individuals*, *2*, 12-29.

Johnson, D. R. (1979). Project Explore—a vocational assessment model for youth with special needs. *Career Development for Exceptional Individuals*, *2*, 40-47.

Johnson, D. R., Bruininks, R. H., & Thurlow, M. L. (1987). Meeting the challenge of transition service planning through improved interagency cooperation. *Exceptional Children*, *53*(6), 522-530.

Johnson, N., Flowers, A., Campbell-Johnson, S., & Johnson, J. (1980). A career awareness program for educable mentally retarded students. *The Vocational Guidance Quarterly*, *28*, 328-334.

Jones, J. W. (1983). An established, successful program integrating handicapped students into vocational schools. In *Proceedings of the Fifteenth Annual Convention of the National Association of School Psychologists*, Detroit.

Jones, R. (1979). Work evaluation in the public schools. *Florida Vocational Journal*, 27-29.

Jordan, J. B. (1978). *Exceptional students in secondary schools*. Reston, VA: Council for Exceptional Children.

Kanchier, C. (1990). Career education for mentally handicapped adolescents. *Journal of Career Development*, *16*(4), 269-281.

Kelly, K. R., & Colangelo, N. (1990). Effects of academic ability and gender on career development. *Journal for the Education of the Gifted*, *13*(2), 168-175.

Kelsey, E. F. (1982). Vocational assessment procedures for handicapped blacks. In T. H. Hohenshil, W. T. Anderson, & J. F. Salwan (Eds.), *Secondary school psychological services: Focus on vocational assessment procedures for handicapped students*. Blacksburg, VA: Virginia Tech. (ERIC Document Reproduction Service No. 229704)

Kendall, W. S. (1981). Affective and career education for the learning disabled adolescent. *Learning Disability Quarterly, 4*, 69-75.

Kent, C. N. (1977). Mainstreaming in the shop class. *Industrial Education, 4*, 24-26.

Kiernan, W. E., & Dybwad, R. (Eds.) *Prevocational and vocational education for special needs youth: A blueprint for the 1980s.* Baltimore, MD: Paul H. Brookes.

Kimeldorf, M. (1984). *Job search education.* New York: Education Design.

Kimeldorf, M., & Tornow, J. A. (1984). Job clubs: Getting into the hidden labor market. *Pointer, 28*, 29-32.

Kirchner, C., & Peterson, R. (1979). Employment: Selected characteristics. *Journal of Visual Impairment and Blindness, 73*, 239-242.

Kirk, D. (1982). Vocational assessment of visually impaired secondary students. In T. H. Hohenshil, W. T. Anderson, & J. F. Salwan (Eds.), *Secondary school psychological services: Focus on vocational assessment procedures for handicapped students.* Blacksburg, VA: Virginia Tech. (ERIC Document Reproduction Service No. 215245)

Kirkman, R. (1983). Career awareness and the visually impaired student. *Education of the Visually Handicapped, 14*(4), 105-114.

Kleinschmidt, G. (1971). A comparison of psychological and psychomotor tests to determine the best predictor of vocational success. *Vocational Evaluation and Work Adjustment Bulletin, 4*(1), 16-20.

Kohring, C., & Tracht, V. (1978). A new approach to a vocational program for severely handicapped high school students. *Rehabilitation Literature, 39*(5), 138-146.

Kokaska, C. (1978). Career awareness for handicapped students in the elementary schools. *Career Development for Exceptional Individuals, 1*, 25-35.

Kokaska, C., & Kolstoe, O. P. (1977). Special education's role in career education. *Journal of Career Education, 3*(3), 4-18.

Kolstoe, O. (1981). Career education for the handicapped: Opportunities for the '80's. *Career Development for Exceptional Individuals, 4*(1), 3-11.

Krantz, G. D. (1970). Vocational evaluation in the public schools. In W. A. Pruitt (Ed.), *Readings in work evaluation I.* Menomonie, WI: University of Wisconsin.

Krumboltz, J. D. (1979). A social learning theory of career decision making. In A. M. Mitchell, G. B. Jones, & J. D. Krumboltz (Eds.), *Social learning and career decision making.* Cranston, RI: Carroll Press.

Krumboltz, J. D., & Baker, R. (1973). Behavioral counseling for vocational decisions. In H. Borow (Ed.), *Career guidance for a new age.* Boston: Houghton Mifflin.

Krumboltz, J. D., & Hamel, D. A. (1977). *Guide to career decision making skills.* New York: The College Entrance Examination Board.

Krumboltz, J. D., Mitchell, A. M., & Jones, G. B. (1976). A social learning theory of career selection. *The Counseling Psychologist, 6*, 71-80.

Lane, T. (1972). The initial interview in vocational evaluation: Some practical considerations. *Vocational Evaluation and Work Adjustment Bulletin, 5*(4), 14-19.

Laskin, S., & Palmo, A. (1983). The effect of decisions and outcomes on career maturity of high school students. *Journal of Vocational Behavior, 23*(1), 22-34.

Leach, J. A. (1979). A comparative study between CETA, special needs, and office occupations students on attainment of the occupational survival skills and career attitude maturity. *Journal of Industrial Teacher Education, 16*(3), 21-28.

Lemons, S. L., & Sweeney, P. (1979). Veterans' vocational rehabilitation: A program in transition. *The Personnel and Guidance Journal, 58*, 295-297.

Levinson, E. M. (1983). Secondary/vocational school psychology: Differentiating psychologist and counselor roles. *Virginia Association of School Psychologist Newsletter, 14* (3), 6, 11, 12. Reprinted in *The Alberta School Psychologist* (Canada), *3*(1), 15, 18 and *Oregon School Psychologists Association Bulletin*, June, 1983, 4-5.

Levinson, E. M. (1984a). Vocational/career assessment in secondary school psychological evaluations: Rationale, definition, and purpose. *Psychology in the Schools, 21*(1), 112-117.

Levinson, E. M. (1984b). A vocationally oriented secondary school program for the emotionally disturbed. *Vocational Guidance Quarterly, 33*(1), 76-81.

Levinson, E. M. (1985). Vocational and career-oriented secondary school programs for the emotionally disturbed. *The School Counselor, 33*(2), 100-106.

Levinson, E. M. (1986a). School psychology and programs for college learning disabled students: Training and service possibilities. *Psychology in the Schools, 23*(3), 295-302.

Levinson, E. M. (1986b). A vocational evaluation program for handicapped students: Focus on the counselor's role. *Journal of Counseling and Development, 65*(2), 105-106.

Levinson, E. M. (1987a). Children and career development. In A. Thomas & J. Grimes (Eds.), *Children's needs: Psychological perspectives*. Washington, DC: National Association of School Psychologists.

Levinson, E. M. (1987b). Incorporating a vocational component into a school psychological evaluation: A case example. *Psychology in the Schools, 24*(3), 254-264.

Levinson, E. M. (1988). Correlates of vocational practice among school psychologists. *Psychology in the Schools, 25*(3), 297-305.

Levinson, E. M. (1990). Vocational assessment involvement and use of the Self-Directed Search by school psychologists. *Psychology in the Schools, 27*(3), 217-227.

Levinson, E. M. (1987a). Incorporating a vocational component into a school psychological evaluation: A case example. *Psychology in the Schools, 24*(3), 254-264.

Levinson, E. M. (1987b). Vocational assessment and programming of the handicapped: A need for school counselor involvement. *The School Counselor, 35*(1), 6-8.

Levinson, E. M., & Capps, C. F. (1984). Issues in the establishment of school based vocational assessment services for the handicapped. In *Proceedings of the Sixteenth Annual Convention of the National Association of School Psychologists*, 86-87. Philadelphia, PA.

Levinson, E. M., & Capps, C. F. (1985). Vocational assessment and special education triennial reevaluations at the secondary school level. *Psychology in the Schools*, *22*(3), 283-292.

Levinson, E. M., & Hohenshil, T. H. (1983). The practice of vocational school psychology in business and industry: Possibility or pipe dream? *Psychology in the Schools*, *20*(3), 321-327.

Levinson, E. M., & McKee, L. M. (1990). Best practices in transitional services. In A. Thomas & J. Grimes (Eds.), *Best practices in school psychology-II*. Washington, DC: National Association of School Psychologists.

Levinson, E. M., & McKee, L. M. (1991). The exceptional child grows up: Transitions. In M. Fine (Ed.), *Collaboration with parents of exceptional children*. Brandon, VT: Clinical Psychology Publishing.

Levinson, E. M., Peterson, M., & Elston, R. (in press). Vocational counseling with the mentally retarded. In D. C. Strohmer & H. T. Prout (Eds.), *Counseling and psychotherapy with mentally retarded persons*. Brandon, VT: Clinical Psychology Publishing.

Levinson, E. M., & Shepard, J. W. (1982). Integrating vocational assessment data into school psychological evaluations. In T. H. Hohenshil, W. T. Anderson, & J. F. Salwan (Eds.), *Secondary school psychological services: Focus on vocational assessment services for handicapped students*. Blacksburg, VA: Virginia Polytechnic Institute and State University. (ERIC Document Reproduction Service No. 229704)

Levinson, E. M., & Shepard, J. W. (1986). School psychology in business and industry: A possibility becomes reality. *Psychology in the Schools*, *23*, 152-157.

Levitan, S. A., & Taggart, R. (1977). *Jobs for the disabled*. Washington, DC: George Washington University Center for Manpower Policy Studies.

Lofquist, L. H., & Dawis, R. V. (1984). *A psychological theory of work adjustment*. Minneapolis: Industrial Relations Center, University of Minnesota.

Lombana, J. H. (1979). Facilitating career guidance for deaf students: Challenge and opportunities for counselors. *Vocational Guidance Quarterly*, *27*, 350-358.

Lombardi, T. P., & Hotsinpiller, P. (1979). Strengthening career foundations skills for the developmentally disabled. *Career Development for Exceptional Individuals*, *2*, 74-79.

Lunneborg, P. W. (1978). Sex and career decision-making styles. *Journal of Counseling Psychology*, *25*, 299-305.

Lynch, K. P. (1979). Toward a skill-oriented prevocational program for trainably and severely mentally impaired students. In G. T. Bellamy, G. O'Connor, & O. C. Karan (Eds.), *Vocational rehabilitation of severely handicapped persons*. Baltimore, MD: University Park Press.

Maddy-Bernstein, C. (1990). Special considerations regarding career assessment for special groups. *Career Planning and Adult Development Journal*, *6*(4), 37-40.

Maki, D., McCrackin, N., Pape, D. A., & Scofield, M. E. (1979). A systems approach to vocational assessment. *Journal of Rehabilitation*, *40*(2), 48-51.

Malmberg, P., & Morely, R. (1972). *Vocational evaluation and curriculum modification*. Des Moines, IA: Iowa Department of Public Instruction.

Malters, C. H. (1974). Serving the handicapped and disadvantaged in special programs. *American Vocational Journal, 49*(2), 34-35.

Management Analysis Center. (1976). *Improving occupational programs for the handicapped.* Washington, DC: Author.

Marinelli, R. P., Tunic, R. H., & Leconte, P. (1988, November). *Vocational evaluation education: Regional programs.* Paper presented at the Mid-East Regional Conference of the Career Development Division of the Council for Exceptional Children, White Sulphur Springs, WVA.

Marinoble, R. M. (1980). Community jobs for handicapped students: A career technique. *Vocational Guidance Quarterly, 29*, 172-177.

Marshall, B. (1981). Career decision making patterns of gifted and talented adolescents: Implications for career education. *Journal of Career Education, 7*(4), 305-310.

Maryland State Department of Education. (1977). *Vocational evaluation in Maryland public schools: A model guide for student assessment.* Baltimore, MD: Division of Vocational-Technical Education.

Mason, V., & Graham, C. (1976). Vocational evaluation services help clients assess work skills. *Research Review, 2*(6), 5-8.

McCray, P. (1982). *Vocational evaluation and assessment in school settings.* Menomonie, WI: Research and Training Center, Stout Vocational Rehabilitation Institute, University of Wisconsin—Stout.

McCray, P. (1979). *Learning assessment in vocational evaluation.* Menomonie, WI: University of Wisconsin—Stout. (ERIC Document Reproduction Service No. 187881)

McGough, R. (1981). CETA programs for the handicapped and the role of school psychology: Working with CETA. In T. H. Hohenshil & W. T. Anderson (Eds.), *School psychological services in secondary vocational education: Roles in programs for handicapped students.* Blacksburg, VA: Virginia Tech. (ERIC Document Reproduction Service No. 215245)

McKinney, L. A. (1976). Special needs education: The message is more. *American Vocational Journal, 51*(9), 26.

Medway, F. J. (1978). An approach to training school psychologists in career education. *Psychology in the Schools, 15*, 243-245.

Meers, G. D. (1977). Inservice programs for preparing special needs personnel. *Journal of Industrial Teacher Education, 14*(4), 41-45.

Meers, G. D. (1980). *Handbook of special vocational needs education.* Rockville, MD: Aspen Systems.

Meister, R. K. (1976). Diagnostic assessment in rehabilitation. In B. Bolton (Ed.), *Handbook of measurement and evaluation in rehabilitation.* Baltimore, MD: University Park Press.

Menchel, J. (1958). Pre-vocational evaluation in the workshop. *American Journal of Physical Science, 37*, 28-34.

Menchel, J. (1960). Pre-vocational evaluation of the mentally retarded. *Vocational Guidance Quarterly, 8*, 209-211.

Merachnik, D. (1970). Assessing work potential of the handicapped in public schools. *Vocational Guidance Quarterly, 18*, 225-229.

Miller, A. L., & Tiedeman, D. V. (1972). Decision making for the '70s: The cubing of the Tiedeman paradigm and its application in career education. *Focus on Guidance, 5*, 1-16.

Miller, J. (1981). Overview of career education for gifted and talented. *Journal of Career Education, 7*(4), 266-270.

Miller, S. R., & Schloss, P. J. (1982). *Career/vocational education for handicapped youth.* Rockville, MD: Aspen Systems.

Mills, J., & Rushing, T. (1982). The vocational disciplines and support services take stock. *Journal of the American Vocational Association, 57*(6), 44-45.

Minner, S. (1982). Expectations of vocational teachers for handicapped. *Exceptional Children, 48*, 451-453.

Minner, S., & Knutson, R. (1980). Improving vocational educators' attitudes toward mainstreaming. *Career Development for Exceptional Individuals, 2*, 93-100.

Mithaug, D. E., Horiuchi, C. N., & Fanning, P. N. (1985). A report on the Colorado statewide follow-up survey of special education students. *Exceptional Children, 51*(5), 397-404.

Moed, M. (1959). Pre-vocational and vocational evaluation of individuals with cerebral palsy. *Cerebral Palsy Review, 20*, 3-5.

Moon, S., Goodall, P., Barcus, M., & Brooke, V. (1986). *The supported work model of competitive employment for citizens with severe handicaps: A guide for job trainers.* Richmond, VA: Rehabilitation Research and Training Center, Virginia Commonwealth University.

Mori, A. A. (1979a). Career exploration for handicapped pupils in the middle schools. *Career Development for Exceptional Individuals, 2*, 67-73.

Mori, A. A. (1979b). Vocational education and special education: A new partnership in career education. *Journal of Career Education, 6*(1), 55-69.

Mori, A. (1982). Career attitudes and job knowledge among junior high school regular, special, and academically talented students. *Career Development for Exceptional Individuals, 5*(1), 62-69.

Morris, J. (1974). For the retarded: Career counseling plus. *The School Guidance Worker, 30*(2), 13-17.

Morris, T., & Levinson, E. (in press). Intelligence and occupational/vocational adjustment: A literature review. *Journal of Counseling and Development.*

Murphey, L. C., & Banta, T. W. (1981). Career education for handicapped: A model for cooperative programming for effective mainstreaming. *Journal of Career Education, 7*, 236-242.

Murray, P. (1975). *An analysis of the role of the school psychologist in the Commonwealth of Virginia.* Unpublished doctoral dissertation, Virginia Polytechnic Institute and State University.

Mutter, D., & McClung, R. (1981). Vocational assessment procedures for handicapped students: An assessment center approach. In T. H. Hohenshil & W. T. Anderson (Eds.), *School psychological services in secondary vocational education: Role in programs for handicapped students.* Blacksburg, VA: Virginia Tech. (ERIC Document Reproduction Service No. 215245)

Nadolsky, J. (1971a). *Development of a model for vocational evaluation of the disadvantaged* (interim report). Auburn, AL: Auburn University, Department of Vocational and Adult Education.

Nadolsky, J. (1971b). Review of vocational evaluation theory. In C. Smolkin & B. Cohen (Eds.), *New directions in vocational rehabilitation: The stroke patient*. Baltimore: Sinai Hospital of Baltimore.

Nadolsky, J. (1973a). A client-centered rationale for vocational evaluation. *Vocational Evaluation and Work Adjustment Bulletin, 6*(2), 7-11.

Nadolsky, J. (1973b). The role of ancillary personnel in the vocational evaluation process. *Vocational Evaluation and Work Adjustment Bulletin, 6*(4), 2-5.

Nadolsky, J. (1973c). Vocational evaluation as a preventive service. *Vocational Evaluation and Work Adjustment Bulletin, 6*(1), 8-10.

Nadolsky, J. (1976). The counseling function in vocational evaluation. *Vocational Evaluation and Work Adjustment Bulletin, 9*(4), 34-38.

Nadolsky, J. M. (1981). Vocational evaluation in the public schools: Implications for future practice. *Journal for Vocational Special Needs Education, 3*, 5-9.

National Assessment of Vocational Education, United States Department of Education. (1989). *Final Report, Volume 1: Summary of findings and recommendations*. Washington, DC: Author.

National Association of State Boards of Education. (1979). *Vocational education of handicapped youth: State of the art*. Washington, DC: Author.

National Association of Vocational Education Special Needs Personnel. (1981). Working paper on vocational assessment: Feedback wanted. *Newsnotes, 6*(1).

Neely, M. A., & Kosier, M. W. (1977). Physically impaired students and the vocational exploration group. *Vocational Guidance Quarterly, 26*(1), 37-44.

Neff, W. S. (1970). Vocational assessment: Theories and models. *Journal of Rehabilitation, 36*, 27-29.

New Jersey State Department of Education. (1978). *Guidelines for establishing a vocational assessment system for the special needs student*. New Brunswick, NJ: Division of Vocational Education, Bureau of Special Programs.

Niles, S. G., & Tiffany, S. A. (1990). Strategies for an effective vocational assessment program. *Academic Therapy, 25*(5), 547-559.

Noll, A. (1978). Certification of vocational evaluators in public school settings: A survey. *Vocational Evaluation and Work Adjustment Bulletin, 11*(2), 18-21.

O'Brien, T. (1980). Vocational training and placement of the handicapped. *Industrial Education, 69*(3), 29 & 31.

Okolo, C. M., & Sitlington, P. (1988). The role of special education in LD adolescents' transition from school to work. *Learning Disability Quarterly, 11*(3), 292-306.

Osipow, S. H. (1976). Vocational development problems of disabled. In H. Rusalem & D. Malikan (Eds.), *Contemporary vocational rehabilitation*. New York: New York University Press.

O'Toole, J. (Ed.). (1973). *Work in America: Report of a special task force to the Secretary of Health, Education, and Welfare*. Cambridge, MA: MIT Press.

Otto, L. B. (1984). *How to help your child choose a career*. New York: M. Evans.

Overs, R. (1970). Vocational evaluation: Research and implications. *Journal of Rehabilitation, 36*(1), 18-21.

Palmer, J. T. (1984). Career development and special needs students. *Career Development for Exceptional Individuals*, 7(1), 3-11.

Palmer, J., Stieglitz, M., Lambardi, C., & Henfield, P. (1982). A career education program for students with physical disabilities. *Career Development for Exceptional Individuals*, 5(1), 13-23.

Parker, S. (1974). *Programs for the handicapped.* Washington, DC: Government Printing Office.

Parnicky, J. R., & Presnall, D. M. (1978). Interest inventories and the retarded. *Rehabilitation Counseling Bulletin*, 20, 118-128.

Parrish, L. H. (1979). Entry level competencies for handicapped students in vocational agriculture. *Career Development for Exceptional Individuals*, 2, 97-104.

Parsons, F. (1909). *Choosing a vocation.* Boston: Houghton Mifflin.

Patten, M. (1981). Components of the prevocational/vocational evaluation. *Career Development for Exceptional Individuals*, 4, 81-87.

Patterson, C. (1964). Methods of assessing the vocational adjustment potential of the mentally handicapped. *Training School Bulletin*, 61, 129-152.

Peterson, M. (1981). Vocational special needs and vocational evaluation: The needed marriage of two fields. *Journal for Vocational Special Needs Education,* 3(3), 15-32.

Peterson, M. (1986). *Vocational assessment of special students: A procedural manual.* Starkville, MS: VOC-AIM.

Peterson, M. (1989). Models of vocational assessment of handicapped students. *American Annals of the Deaf*, 134(4), 273-276.

Petzy, L. A. (1979). A model for employer commitments to job development. *Career Development for Exceptional Individuals*, 2, 80-90.

Pfeffer, R. (1978). *Proposed functions for school psychologists in career education.* Unpublished doctoral dissertation, Virginia Polytechnic Institute and State University.

Phelps, L. A. (1978a). Key legislative provisions and research priorities for special needs populations in vocational education. *Journal of Vocational Education Research*, 3(4), 1-12.

Phelps, L. A. (1978b). Vocational education for special needs learners: Past, present, and future. *The School Psychology Digest*, 7(1), 18-34.

Phelps, L. A., & Clark, G. M. (1977). Personnel preparation for vocational programming of special needs students. *Journal of Career Education*, 3(3), 35-51.

Phelps, L. A., & Halloran, W. D. (1976). Assurance for handicapped learners. *American Vocational Journal*, 51(8), 36-39.

Phelps, L. A., & Halloran, W. D. (1977). Legislation and special needs teacher education: The Education for all Handicapped Children Act of 1975 (PL 94-142) and the Rehabilitation Act of 1973 (PL 93-516). *Journal of Industrial Teacher Education*, 14(4), 23-27.

Phelps, L. A., & Lutz, R. J. (1977). *Career exploration and preparation for the special needs learner.* Boston: Allyn and Bacon.

Phelps, L. A., & McCarty, T. (1984). Student vocational assessment practices. *Career Development for Exceptional Individuals*, *7*(1), 30-38.

Phelps, L. A., & Wentling, T. L. (1977). A proposed system for identification, assessment and evaluation of special needs learners. *Journal of Industrial Teacher Education*, *14*(3), 19-35.

Phillips, L. (1977). Career development services for the handicapped: The California Plan. *The School Psychology Digest*, *7*, 49-50.

Pittman, R. L., & Stadt, R. W. (1979). Attitudes of vocational teachers, counselors, and administrators toward mentally retarded students in area vocational schools. *Journal of Industrial Teacher Education*, *16*(3), 50-59.

Plata, M. (1981). Occupational aspirations of normal and emotionally disturbed adolescents: A comparative study. *Vocational Guidance Quarterly*, *30*, 130-138.

Poplin, P. (1982). The development and execution of the IEP: Who does what, when, to whom. In T. H. Hohenshil & W. T. Anderson (Eds.), *School psychological services in secondary vocational education: Roles in programs for handicapped students*. Blacksburg, VA: Virginia Tech. (ERIC Document Reproduction Service No. 215245)

Portigal, A. H. (1976). *Towards the measurement of work satisfaction*. Paris: Organization for Economic Cooperation and Development.

Post, J. O., & Petzy, V. (1977). A career accessibility model for special needs individuals. *Career Education Quarterly*, *2*(4), 6-14.

Power, P. W. (1984). *A guide to vocational assessment*. Baltimore, MD: University Park Press.

Prediger, D., Roth, J., & Noeth, R. (1973). A nationwide study of student career development: Summary of results. *ACT Research Reports*, p. 61.

Prout, H. T., & Sheldon, K. (1981). The school psychologist's role in the comprehensive rehabilitation center. In T. H. Hohenshil & W. T. Anderson (Eds.), *School psychological services in secondary vocational education: Roles in programs for handicapped students*. Blacksburg, VA: Virginia Tech. (ERIC Document Reproduction Service No. 215245)

Pruitt, W. (1976). Vocational evaluation: Yesterday, today, and tomorrow. *Vocational Evaluation and Work Adjustment Bulletin*, *9*(4), 846.

Pruitt, W. A., & Longfellow, R. (Eds.). (1970a). A colloquy on work evaluation. *Journal of Rehabilitation*, *36*(1).

Pruitt, W. A., & Longfellow, R. E. (1970b). Work evaluation: The medium and the message. *Journal of Rehabilitation*, *36*, 8-9.

Quinones, W. (1978). A test battery for assessing the vocational competency of moderately mentally retarded persons. *Mental Retardation*, *16*(6), 412-415.

Razeghi, J. A., & Davis, S. (1979). Federal mandates for the handicapped: Vocational education, opportunity and employment. *Exceptional Children*, *45*, 353-359.

Revell, W., & Wehman, P. (1978). Vocational evaluation of profoundly mentally retarded clients. *Rehabilitation Literature*, *39*(8), 226-231.

Roberts, C. L. (1970). Definition, objectives, and goals in work evaluation. *Journal of Rehabilitation*, *36*, 13-15.

Rodd, J. E. (1977). A philosophy and paradigm for a career education program for deaf learners. *Journal of Career Education, 3*(4), 34-40.

Roe, A. (1956). *The psychology of occupations.* New York: Wiley.

Rosenthal, I. (1989). Model transition programs for learning disabled high school and college students. *Rehabilitation Counseling Bulletin, 33*(1), 54-66.

Rosher, J. H., & Howell, F. M. (1978). Physically disabled students and achievement orientation: Self-concept curriculum track, and career aspirations. *Journal of Vocational Behavior, 13*(1), 35-44.

Rubinton, N. (1980). Instruction in career decision making and decision-making styles. *Journal of Counseling Psychology, 26,* 581-588.

Rudrud, E. (1981). Job openings and client placements: Over and undermet needs. *Vocational Evaluation and Work Adjustment Bulletin, 14,* 80-82.

Rudrud, E., Ziarnik, J., Bernstein, G., & Ferrara, J. (1984). *Proactive vocational habilitation.* Baltimore, MD: Paul H. Brookes.

Rusch, F. R., & Phelps, L. A. (1987). Secondary special education and transition from school to work: A national priority. *Exceptional Children, 53*(6), 487-492.

Salwan, J. F., & Nelson, M. D. (1984). Alternate settings for vocationally trained school psychologists. In *Proceedings of the Sixteenth Annual Convention of the National Association of School Psychologists*, 244-245.

Sankovsky, R. (1970). Toward a common understanding of vocational evaluation. *Journal of Rehabilitation, 36,* 10-12.

Saradovlias, L. (1975). Getting handicapped students into the mainstream. *American Vocational Journal, 50*(5), 22-25.

Sarkees, M. D., & Gill, D. H. (1981). Vocational educator's role in the comprehensive delivery of services to handicapped individuals. *Career Development for Exceptional Individuals, 4,* 88-95.

Schalock, R. L., & Karan, O. C. (1979). Relevant assessment: The interaction between education and training. In G. T. Bellamy, G. O'Connor, & O. C. Karan (Eds.), *Vocational rehabilitation of severely handicapped persons.* Baltimore, MD: University Park Press.

Schalock, R. L., & Lilley, M. A. (1986). Placement from community-based mental retardation programs: How well do clients do after 8 to 10 years? *American Journal of Mental Deficiency, 90*(6), 669-676.

Scheiber, B. (1981). Toward equal opportunity handicapped students: No substitute for Voc. Ed. *Voc Ed, 56*(1), 46-47.

Schloss, C., & Schloss, P. (1982). The influence of exceptional labels on employer expectations for the training and success of special needs adolescents. *The Journal for Vocational Special Needs Education, 4*(2), 5-8.

Scholl, G., & Schnur, R. (1976). *Measures of personal, vocational, and educational functioning in the blind and visually handicapped.* New York: American Foundation for the Blind.

Schutz, R. P., & Rusch, F. R. (1982). Competitive employment: Toward employment for mentally retarded persons. In K. P. Lynch, W. E. Kiernan, & J. A. Stark (Eds.), *Prevocational and vocational education for special needs: A blueprint for the 1980s.* Baltimore, MD: Paul H. Brookes.

Scorzelli, J., & Scorzelli, M. R. (1982). Deafness. In T. F. Harrington (Ed.), *Handbook of career planning for special needs students*. Rockville, MD: Aspen.

Scott, R. (1982). The visually impaired. In T. F. Harrington (Ed.), *Handbook of career planning for special needs students*. Rockville, MD: Aspen.

Seligman, L. (1980). *Assessment in developmental career counseling*. Cranston, RI: The Carroll Press.

Sheldon, K. L., & DuBose, L. (1982). Vocational assessment of the orthopedically handicapped. In T. H. Hohenshil, W. T. Anderson, & J. F. Salwan (Eds.), *Secondary school psychological services: Focus on vocational assessment procedures for handicapped students*. Blacksburg, VA: Virginia Tech. (ERIC Document Reproduction Service No. 229704)

Sheldon, K. L., & Prout, H. T. (1982a). Comprehensive vocational rehabilitation and the school psychologist. *The Journal for Vocational Special Needs Education, 4*(3), 21-22.

Sheldon, K. L., & Prout, H. T. (1982b). Vocational resources for the learning disabled adult. In *Proceedings of the Fourteenth Annual Convention of the National Association of School Psychologists*, Toronto.

Shelton, J. (1975). Vocational appraisal of the EMR adolescent: An exploratory study of a public school class. *The Journal of the Association of Pupil Personnel Workers, 19*, 156-158 and 205-207.

Shepard, J. W. (1981). A school psychologist's participation in CETA programs. In T. H. Hohenshil & W. T. Anderson (Eds.), *School psychological services in secondary vocational education: Roles in programs for handicapped students*. Blacksburg, VA: Virginia Tech. (ERIC Document Reproduction Service No. 215245)

Shepard, J. W. (1985). The school psychologist's role in career education for secondary aged handicapped students. *Journal of Career Development, 11*(4), 273-280.

Shepard, J. W., Drelman, M., & Ellenwood, A. (1984). School psychologists and vocational education programs: Participation in career development for the handicapped. *The Journal for Vocational Special Needs Education, 6*(2), 13-15.

Shepard, J. W., & Hohenshil, T. H. (1983). Career development functions of practicing school psychologists: A national study. *Psychology in the Schools, 20*, 445-449.

Shepard, J. W., & Levinson, E. M. (1985). Vocational assessment for school psychologists at the secondary level. *Journal of Psychoeducational Assessment, 3*(3), 257-266.

Shroka, J., & Schwartz, S. (1982). Job placement of handicapped persons: A positive approach. *Career Development for Exceptional Individuals, 5*(2), 117-121.

Siefferman, L. D. (1983). Vocational education: The secondary connection for learning disabled students. *The Journal for Vocational Special Needs Education, 5*(2), 28-29.

Sinick, D. (1979). Career counseling with handicapped persons. *The Personnel and Guidance Journal, 58*, 252-257.

Sink, J. M., Field, T. F., & Raulerson, M. H. (1978). Vocational evaluation services for the deaf and hearing impaired: State of the art. *American Annals of the Deaf, 123*, 937-944.

Sitlington, P. L. (1981). Vocational assessment and the individualized vocational plan. *Journal for Vocational Special Needs Education, 3*(3), 27-32.

Sitlington, P. L., & Wimmer, D. (1978). Vocational assessment techniques for the handicapped adolescent. *Career Development for Exceptional Individuals, 1*, 74-87.

Smith, B. B., Brown, J. M., & Kayser, T. F. (1983). A psychological model for special needs instruction and research. *The Journal for Vocational Special Needs Education, 4*(3), 29-32.

Smith, J. (1978). A school psychologist as a coordinator of a learning center in an Oklahoma vocational/technical school. *The School Psychology Digest, 7*(1), 51-55.

Smith, R. L. (1983). *The vocational counselor and guidance team* (5th ed.). Commerce, TX: Occupational Curriculum Laboratory, East Texas State University.

Snider, R. C. (1978). Can we go back to the basics in the mainstream with career education for the handicapped? *Journal of Career Education, 5*(1) 16-23.

Solly, D. C. (1982). Prevocational assessment: Applications for elementary, middle, and junior high school students. In T. H. Hohenshil, W. T. Anderson, & J. F. Salwan (Eds.), *Secondary school psychological services: Focus on vocational assessment procedures for handicapped students.* Blacksburg, VA: Virginia Tech. (ERIC Document Reproduction Service No. 229704)

Solly, D. C., Kelsey, E., & Salwan, J. (1983). A practical guide to vocational assessment. In *Proceedings of the Fifteenth Annual Convention of the National Association of School Psychologists*, Detroit, MI.

Special Task Force to the Secretary of Health, Education, and Welfare. (1973). *Work in America.* Cambridge, MA: The MIT Press.

Spergel, P. (1970a). Assessment of the disadvantaged. *Vocational Evaluation and Work Adjustment Bulletin, 3*(1), 8-10.

Spergel, P. (1970b). Vocational evaluation: Research and implications for maximizing human potential. *Journal of Rehabilitation, 36*(1), 21-24.

Stark, J. A., Baker, D. H., Menousek, P. E., & McGee, J. J. (1982). Behavioral programming for severely mentally retarded/behaviorally impaired youth. In K. P. Lynch, W. E. Kiernan, & J. A. Stark (Eds.), *Prevocational and vocational education for special needs youth: A blueprint for the 1980s.* Baltimore, MD: Paul H. Brookes.

Steinmiller, G., & Retish, P. (1980). The employer's role in the transition from school to work. *Career Development for Exceptional Individuals, 2*, 87-91.

Stodden, R. A., & Iancone, R. N. (1981). Career/vocational assessment of the special needs individual: A conceptual model. *Exceptional Children, 47*, 600-608.

Stodden, R. A., Meecham, K. A., Bisconer, S. W., & Hodell, S. L. (1989). The impact of vocational assessment information on the individualized education planning process: Supporting curriculum-based assessment. *Journal for Vocational Special Needs Education, 12*(1), 31-36.

Stout State University. (1965). *Vocational evaluation curriculum development workshop.* Menomonie, WI: Author.

Sullivan, J. A. (1978). Who are the special needs students and how can special education and industrial teacher education work together and help them. *Journal of Industrial Teacher Education, 15*(2), 42-50.

Super, D. (1957). *The psychology of careers.* New York: Harper & Row.

Super, D. E. (1942). *The dynamics of vocational adjustment.* New York: Harper & Row.

Szymanski, E. M., Buckley, J., Parent, W. S., Parker, R. M., & Westbrook, J. D. (1988). Rehabilitation counseling in supported employment: A conceptual model for service delivery and personnel preparation. In S. E. Rubin & N. M. Rubin (Eds.), *Contemporary challenges to the rehabilitation counseling profession.* Baltimore, MD: Paul H. Brookes.

Taymans, J., & Frith, G. (1983). Involving parents in the IEP process: A priority for secondary vocational programs. *The Journal for Vocational Special Needs Education, 5*(2), 9-12.

Tellefsen, D. J. (1982). Comprehensive vocational/career assessment of emotionally disturbed adolescents and adults. In T. H. Hohenshil, W. T. Anderson, & J. F. Salwan (Eds.), *Secondary school psychological services: Focus on vocational assessment procedures for handicapped students.* Blacksburg, VA: Virginia Tech. (ERIC Document Reproduction Service No. 229704)

Telzrow, C. F. (1975). The school psychologist as a director of career education. *Psychology in the Schools, 12,* 197-199.

Tennessee Department of Education. (1987). *Vocational assessment information.* Nashville: Author.

Tesolowski, D. G., & Halpin, G. (1978). Effects of training program on the job readiness of physically handicapped sheltered workshop employees. *The Journal of Vocational Education Research, 3*(1), 1-8.

Tesolowski, D. G., & Halpin, G. (1979). Modifying work personalities of the handicapped. *Vocational Guidance Quarterly, 27,* 334-340.

Texas Education Agency. (1985). *Serving special needs students in vocational education.* Austin, TX: Texas Education Agency.

Texas Rehabilitation Commission. (1974a). *Prevocational training instructor's guide.* Austin, TX: Author.

Texas Rehabilitation Commission. (1974b). *Prevocational training workbook.* Austin, TX: Author.

Thomas, S. W., & Coleman, N. (1988). *Vocational assessment training manual.* Raleigh, NC: Division of Vocational Education, North Carolina Department of Public Instruction.

Tiedeman, D. (1974). Introducing school psychology into career education through ERIC. *The School Psychology Digest, 3*(3), 11-19.

Tiedeman, D. V., & O'Hara, R. P. (1963). *Career development: Choice and adjustment.* New York: College Entrance Examination Board.

Timm, F. H., Myrick, J., & Rosenburg, R. (1982). School psychologists in corrections: A new frontier. *The Journal for Vocational Special Needs Education, 4*(3), 25-28.

Tindall, L. W. (1970). Education for all handicapped persons: A mandate for the new year. *American Vocational Journal, 53*(1), 26-29.

Tindall, L. W. (1975). Breaking down barriers for disabled students. *American Vocational Journal, 50*(8), 47-51.

Turner, K. G., & Bayne, G. K. (1979). Kentucky assesses the vocational education needs of the disadvantaged and handicapped. *Journal of Industrial Teacher Education, 16*(4), 35-45.

Vandergoot, D. (1987). Placement and career development in rehabilitation. In R. M. Parker (Ed.), *Rehabilitation counseling.* Austin, TX: Pro-Ed.

Vasa, S. F., & Steckelburg, A. L. (1980). Parent programs in career education for the handicapped. *Career Development for Exceptional Individuals, 2,* 74-82.

Villemarette, J. (1968). The many dimensions of voc eval. *Vocational Evaluation and Work Adjustment Bulletin, 1*(4), 11-13.

Virginia Commonwealth University. (1966). *Proceedings of a training institute in work evaluation.* Richmond, VA: Author.

Vocational Evaluation and Work Adjustment Association. (1975). Vocational evaluation project final report [Special Edition]. *Vocational Evaluation and Work Adjustment Bulletin, 8.*

Wagner, E., & Hawver, D. (1965). Correlations between psychological tests and sheltered workshop performance for severely retarded adults. *American Journal of Mental Deficiency, 69*(5), 685-691.

Walker, R. (1970a). A future for vocational evaluation. *Journal of Rehabilitation, 36*(1), 38-39.

Walker, R. (1970b). Special problems in vocational evaluation of the deaf. In W. Pruitt (Ed.), *Readings in work evaluation,* I. Menonomie, WI: University of Wisconsin—Stout.

Wall, J. E. (Ed.). (1976). *Vocational education for special groups.* Washington, DC: American Vocational Association.

Wallbrown, J. D. (1979). The occupational implications of learning patterns: A case study for secondary learning disabled students. *The School Psychology Digest, 8*(2), 240-244.

Walls, R. T., Tseng, M. S., & Zarin, H. N. (1976). Time and money for vocational rehabilitation of clients with mild, moderate, and severe mental retardation. *American Journal of Mental Deficiency, 80,* 595-601.

Walls, R., & Werner, T. (1977). Vocational behavior checklists. *Mental Retardation, 15*(4), 30-35.

Walther, R. (1975). *The measurement of work-relevant attitudes.* Washington, DC: The George Washington University, Manpower Research Projects.

Warden, P. G., Kinnison, L. R., & Accord, J. (1982). A team approach for providing programs for handicapped learners in vocational and technical education. *The Journal for Vocational Special Needs Education, 4*(3), 9-13.

Wargo, W. D. (1978). Prevocational industrial arts for handicapped boys and girls. *American Vocational Journal, 53*(3), 29-33.

Webster, R. E. (1981). Vocational-technical training for emotionally disturbed adolescents. *Teaching Exceptional Children, 14,* 75-79.

Wehman, P. (1986). Transition for handicapped youth from school to work. In J. Chadsey-Rusch & C. Hanley-Maxwell (Eds.), *Enhancing transition from school to the workplace for handicapped youth: Personnel preparation implications* (pp. 26-43). Champaign, IL: National Network for Professional Development in Vocational Special Education.

Wehman, P., Kregel, J., & Barcus, J. M. (1985). From school to work: A vocational transition model for handicapped students. *Exceptional Children, 52*(1), 25-37.

Wehman, P., & McLaughlin, D. (1980). *Vocational curriculum for developmentally disabled persons.* Baltimore, MD: University Park Press.

Wehman, P., Moon, M. S., Everson, J. M., Wood, W., & Barcus, J. M. (1988). *Transition from school to work: New challenges for youth with severe disabilities.* Baltimore, MD: Paul H. Brookes.

Weisgerber, R. A. (1978). *Vocational education: Teaching the handicapped in regular classrooms.* Reston, VA: Council for Exceptional Children.

Weisgerber, R. A., Dahl, P. R., & Appleby, J. A. (1981). *Training the handicapped for productive employment.* Rockville, MD: Aspen Systems.

Wentling, T. L., Butterwick, T. C., & Zook, G. A. (1976). Career education and evaluation for hearing impaired adolescents: An example program. *Volta Review, 78*(3), 144-151.

Westbrook, B. W. et al. (1988). Career maturity in grade 9: Can students who make appropriate career choices for others also make appropriate career choices for themselves? *Measurement and Evaluation in Counseling and Development, 21*(2), 64-71.

Whieford, E. B., & Anderson, D. H. (1977). The mainstreaming of special needs students: Home economics teachers are copying. *American Vocational Journal, 52*(5), 42-44.

Whitaker, J. V. (1982). The school psychologist: Serving the special needs students in the vocational school setting. *Journal for Vocational Special Needs Education, 4*(3), 23-24.

White, F. (1982). Career guidance for special needs learners. *Journal of Career Education, 9*(2), 141-146.

White, P., Reardon, R., Barker, S., & Carlson, A. (1979). Increasing career center accessibility for the blind. *The Personnel and Guidance Journal, 58*, 292-295.

Wickman, J. R. (1983). Vocational/career awareness for institutionalized and delinquent youth. *Journal for Vocational Special Needs Education, 5*(3), 35-36.

Will, M. (1986). OSERS programming for the transition of youth with disabilities: Bridges from school to working life. In J. Chadsey-Rusch & C. Hanley-Maxwell (Eds.), *Enhancing transition from school to the workplace for handicapped youth: Personnel preparation implications.* Champaign, IL: National Network for Professional Development in Vocational Special Education.

Wilson, E. (1971). The use of psychological tests in diagnosing the vocational potential of visually handicapped persons who enter supportive and unskilled occupations. *The New Outlook for the Blind*, 79-87.

Winer, J. L. et al. (1988). Vocational assessment of learning disabled students using the SDS-E. *Research in Rural Education*, *5*(2), 27-30.

Woodbury, R., & Pate, D. H. (1977). Vocational and personality dimensions of adjudicated delinquents. *Measurement and Evaluation for Guidance*, *10*, 106-112.

Wurster, M. (1983). Career education for visually impaired students. Where we've been and where we are. *Education of the Visually Handicapped*, *14*(4), 99-104.

SUBJECT INDEX

A

I

J

K

L

W